Democracy in Eastern Asia

With the 'Asian Century' now upon us, bringing with it many profound economic and political changes to the world order, it is very timely to assess the state of democracy in the Asian region. Focusing on Eastern Asia, this book provides such a review, highlighting lines of connections between the states and peoples of this complex and dynamic region.

Featuring chapters on China, Japan, Taiwan, South Korea, Hong Kong, Indonesia, Malaysia, Singapore, Thailand, the Philippines, Cambodia and Myanmar, this book provides a detailed analysis of the state of democracy in each country or territory, and shows how each is different and distinctive, whilst simultaneously drawing out important similarities. Further, it provides up-to-date analysis of political changes in the region relating to the processes of democratization, and, in some cases, to the ongoing quest for democracy. Critically examining the current state of political development in the region, the chapters explore the issues and problems that challenge the region's governments in terms of democratic transition, democratic consolidation, democratic improvement and good governance.

With contributions from leading international scholars, this book will be of great interest to students and scholars interested in Asian politics, and politics and democratization studies more broadly.

Edmund S.K. Fung is Professor of Asian Studies at the University of Western Sydney, Australia and a Fellow of the Australian Academy of the Humanities.

Steven Drakeley is Senior Lecturer in Asian and Islamic Studies and a member of the Religion and Society Research Centre at the University of Western Sydney, Australia.

Politics in Asia series

ASEAN and the Security of South-East Asia
Michael Leifer

China's Policy towards Territorial Disputes
The case of the South China Sea islands
Chi-kin Lo

India and Southeast Asia
Indian perceptions and policies
Mohammed Ayoob

Gorbachev and Southeast Asia
Leszek Buszynski

Indonesian Politics under Suharto
Order, development and pressure for change
Michael R.J. Vatikiotis

The State and Ethnic Politics in Southeast Asia
David Brown

The Politics of Nation Building and Citizenship in Singapore
Michael Hill and Lian Kwen Fee

Politics in Indonesia
Democracy, Islam and the ideology of tolerance
Douglas E. Ramage

Communitarian Ideology and Democracy in Singapore
Beng-Huat Chua

The Challenge of Democracy in Nepal
Louise Brown

Japan's Asia Policy
Wolf Mendl

The International Politics of the Asia-Pacific, 1945–1995
Michael Yahuda

Political Change in Southeast Asia
Trimming the banyan tree
Michael R.J. Vatikiotis

Hong Kong
China's challenge
Michael Yahuda

Korea versus Korea
A case of contested legitimacy
B. K. Gills

Taiwan and Chinese Nationalism
National identity and status in international society
Christopher Hughes

Democracy in Eastern Asia

Issues, problems and challenges in a region of diversity

Edited by Edmund S.K. Fung and Steven Drakeley

Routledge
Taylor & Francis Group

LONDON AND NEW YORK

First published 2014
by Routledge
2 Park Square, Milton Park, Abingdon, Oxfordshire OX14 4RN

and by Routledge
711 Third Avenue, New York, NY 10017

First issued in paperback 2015

Routledge is an imprint of the Taylor & Francis Group, an informa business

British Library Cataloguing in Publication Data
A catalogue record for this book is available from the British Library

Library of Congress Cataloging in Publication Data
Democracy in Eastern Asia: issues, problems and challenges in a region of
diversity/edited by Edmund S.K. Fung and Steven Drakeley.
  pages cm. – (Politics in Asia series)
  Includes bibliographical references and index.
  1. Democracy–Asia. 2. Democratization–Asia. 3. Asia–Politics and
  government–21st century. I. Fung, Edmund S.K., editor of compilation.
  II. Drakeley, Steven, editor of compilation. III. Jain, Purnendra.
  Democracy in Japan
  JQ36.D48 2013
  320.95–dc23
                                                                    2013019386

ISBN13: 978-1-138-12048-8 (pbk)
ISBN13: 978-0-415-70300-0 (hbk)

Typeset in Times New Roman
by Wearset Ltd, Boldon, Tyne and Wear

Contents

Figures

Tables

Contributors

William Case is Professor in the Department of Asian and International Studies and former Director of the Southeast Asia Research Centre (SEARC) at City University of Hong Kong. His research interests include comparative politics and the politics of Southeast Asia. He is the author of *Politics in Southeast Asia: Democracy or Less* (Curzon 2002) and numerous articles on Malaysian politics published in international journals.

Pavin Chachavalpongpun is Associate Professor at Kyoto University's Centre of Southeast Asian Studies. He is the author of *A Plastic Nation: The Curse of Thainess in Thai-Burmese Relations* (University Press of America 2005) and *Reinventing Thailand: Thaksin and His Foreign Policy* (Institute of Southeast Studies 2010). He is also the editor of *Good Coup Gone Bad: Thailand's Political Developments since Thaksin's Downfall* (Institute of Southeast Studies forthcoming) and co-editor of *Bangkok, May 2010: Perspectives on a Divided Thailand* (Institute of Southeast Studies 2010).

Joseph Y.S. Cheng is Chair Professor of Political Science and Coordinator of the Contemporary China Research Project, City University of Hong Kong. He has published widely on political development in China and Hong Kong, Chinese foreign policy and local government in southern China. His recent works include two edited volumes, *Whither China's Democracy? Democratization in China since the Tiananmen Incident* (City University of Hong Kong Press 2011) and *Guangdong: Challenges in Development and Crisis Management* (City University of Hong Kong Press 2010).

Melissa Curley is Lecturer in International Relations in the Department of Political Science and International Studies at the University of Queensland, Australia. Her research and teaching interests include: non-traditional security issues including human trafficking and migrant smuggling, and infectious and pandemic disease, East Asian regional security, and civil society and democratization in Southeast Asia. Her most recent book is *Security and Migration in Asia: The Dynamics of Securitisation*, co-edited with Wong Siu-lun (Routledge 2008).

Shih-chan Dai is PhD candidate in the Department of Political Science, University of New Orleans.

Steven Drakeley is Senior Lecturer in Asian and Islamic Studies and a member of the Religion and Society Research Centre at the University of Western Sydney, Australia. His principal area of research is the role of Islam in Indonesia's post-independence political history. He is the author of *The History of Indonesia* (Greenwood Press 2005).

Chongyi Feng is Associate Professor of China Studies at the University of Technology, Sydney. His research explores intellectual and political changes, the growth of rights consciousness and democratic forces in particular, leading to constitutional democracy in China. He is the author of 11 books (in Chinese) on various aspects of modern and contemporary China, the latest being *Liberalism within the CCP: From Chen Duxiu to Lishenzhi* (Mirror Books 2009).

Edmund S.K. Fung is Professor of Asian Studies at the University of Western Sydney and a Fellow of the Australian Academy of the Humanities. He is the author of *In Search of Chinese Democracy: Civil Opposition in Nationalist China, 1929–1949* (Cambridge University Press 2000) and *The Intellectual Foundations of Chinese Modernity: Cultural and Political Thought in the Republican Era* (Cambridge University Press 2010), among others.

Purnendra Jain is Professor of Japanese Studies at the University of Adelaide, Australia and currently President of the Asian Studies Association of Australia. Author and editor of 14 books and numerous scholarly articles, his most recent co-edited books are *Japan's Strategic Challenges in a Changing Regional Environment* (with Lam Peng Er) (Word Scientific 2012); *Japanese Politics Today: From Karaoke to Kabuki Democracy* (with Takashi Inoguchi) (Palgrave Macmillan 2011) and *Japan in Decline: Fact or Fiction?* (with Brad Williams) (Global Oriental 2011).

Helen James is Associate Professor (Adjunct) at the Australian Demographic and Social Research Institute, CASS, Australian National University. She researches and lectures politics, history and international studies of Southeast Asia, Thailand and Myanmar (Burma). She has published eight books and over 50 articles and chapters in books, including *Security and Sustainable Development in Myanmar* (RoutledgeCurzon 2006) and the edited volume *Civil Society, Religion and Global Governance: Paradigms of Power and Persuasion* (Routledge 2007).

Chong-Min Park is Dean of the College of Political Science and Economics and professor of public administration at Korea University in Seoul, South Korea. His main research focuses on the quality of democratic governance and comparative political behaviour. His articles appear in *Asian Survey*, *Japanese Journal of Political Science*, *Social Indicators Research*, *International Review of Sociology* and several other journals and books. He directs the Asian Barometer Survey in South Korea.

Nathan Gilbert Quimpo is Associate Professor of Political Science and International Relations at the University of Tsukuba, Japan. He is the author of

Contested Democracy and the Left in the Philippines after Marcos (Yale University Southeast Asia Studies 2008), *The Politics of China in the Philippines* (Anvil 2010). He is also co-editor of *Subversive Lives: A Family Memoir of the Marcos Years* (Anvil 2012).

Netina Tan is Assistant Professor of Political Science Department at McMaster University, Canada. Her PhD dissertation from the University of British Columbia, *Access to Power: Hegemonic Party Rule in Singapore and Taiwan,* was awarded the 2011 Vincent Lemieux Prize for the best PhD thesis submitted at a Canadian Institution in 2009 or 2010 by the Canadian Political Science Association. It is being revised for publication as a book.

Chung-li Wu is Research Fellow at the Institute of Political Science, Academia Sinica. He is the author of numerous articles on American politics (political institutions), urban and minority politics, comparative politics, and international relations, published in *Party Politics, The China Quarterly, Parliamentary Affairs, Journal of Black Studies, Asian Survey, Issues & Studies, International Relations of the Asia-Pacific, Japanese Journal of Political Science, Southeastern Political Review* and *American Review of Politics*.

Acknowledgements

This book had its genesis in Edmund Fung's undergraduate unit: Democracy in Asia. Over the years of teaching it, we have been obliged to consider (and repeatedly reconsider) our thoughts on democracy in the Asian region generally and in the particular countries of our interest and expertise. Accordingly we must begin by thanking the generations of students who have selected the unit, thereby (albeit unwittingly) providing the forum in which our ideas have gestated. We are extremely grateful to them for their interest, for their many stimulating questions, and for their capacity to constantly challenge our basic assumptions. Other colleagues, who have also contributed regularly to the teaching of the unit, in particular our good friend and colleague Dr David Walton, also warrant our heartfelt thanks.

We must also thank Professor Gary Smith, who in his then capacity as Dean of the College of Arts at the University of Western Sydney generously committed to providing funding support for the project. In the same vein we express our gratitude to Professor Peter Hutchings, who as Dean of the School of Humanities and Communication Arts unhesitatingly honoured Gary's commitment after a restructure. This support funded our travel to the March 2012 Association for Asian Studies Conference in Toronto where we convened a panel composed of several contributors to this volume. We thank the panel participants for their comments on the papers presented. Likewise we wish to express our gratitude to the Religion and Society Research Centre and the School of Social Sciences and Psychology at UWS for providing the funds to cover the indexing costs. Thanks must also go to our publishers for their support and professionalism, in particular the Asian Studies commissioning editor, Stephanie Rogers, the project manager at Wearset, Amy Ekins, and the copy-editor, Cathryn Primrose-Mathisen. Last but certainly not least we must thank the contributors without whom of course the volume would not have been possible. We greatly appreciate their professionalism in delivering high quality manuscripts on time (and within word limits!) and for their cooperation in compliance with all other editorial requirements. We count ourselves fortunate indeed to have had the opportunity to work with so many excellent scholars in the field.

Introduction

Edmund S.K. Fung and Steven Drakeley

Following the West's triumph in the Cold War, faith in the universality of democracy became fashionable again. Brave predictions were made of democracy's inevitable eventual global triumph as the final form of government, as Francis Fukuyama (1989) put it. Prominently exemplifying this belief was the decision by the George W Bush administration to attempt a democratic regime change as part of its invasion of Saddam Hussein's Iraq in 2001. That it proved rather more difficult in practice to transform Iraq into a beacon of democracy in the Middle East dampened optimism for democracy's future, as did similarly disappointing results from the ambitious democratization efforts in Afghanistan. The trend of global politics over much of the next decade reinforced the renewed pessimism, not only because of the convulsions and gloomy atmospherics associated with the 'war on terror', but also because the so-called 'third wave' of global democratization ebbed. According to Larry Diamond (2010: 24), no fewer than 18 countries experienced a reversal of democracy between 1999 and 2009.

And then suddenly an unexpected series of revolts and campaigns for democracy occurred beginning in Tunisia in December 2010. The examples of the so-called 'Jasmine Revolution' and the 'Arab Spring' proved highly contagious, not only convulsing the Middle East but sending a chill down the spines of authoritarian regimes everywhere. Protests and upheavals in some Middle Eastern countries led to the beginnings of democratic institution building, with elections considered competitive and credible being held before the end of 2011 in Tunisia and Egypt. But it now appears that the initial rush of enthusiasm and idealism has waned and that the 'Arab Spring' is unlikely to deliver the significant advances towards democracy in the Arab world that many had hoped it would, at least in the short term, as most recent events in the Middle East and North Africa demonstrate. These events have nevertheless proven that significant numbers of people in the Middle East and North Africa want democracy and indeed are prepared to risk their lives to attain it. Olivier Roy (2012: 6) suggests that at the very least the Arab Spring signalled the early stages of a democratization of Arab societies. Arguments for the cultural incompatibility of democracy beyond the West, which were often applied with respect to Asia in the 1980s and 1990s, lost much of their force as democracy gained considerable ground there, notably with respect to the Philippines and Thailand, and a little more recently to

Indonesia. The recent events in the Middle East must further undermine the notion of democracy as culturally West-specific.

In Asia, it appears that the 'third wave' has not yet run its course, or perhaps a new wave is coming, as Larry Diamond (2012) suggests. To see history in terms of 'waves' or trends and movements towards imagined 'end' points is of course seductively tempting for the pattern-loving human brain. By the same token, sorting history into cycles exerts the same attraction. Lately, and perhaps borrowing from both these historiographical heritages, there has been much talk of the looming 'Asian Century'. The notion is predicated on current economic growth trends, which indicate that Asian economies collectively will soon dwarf the economies of the West. China is predicted to assume the mantle of the largest economy in the world shortly, to be joined at the top some time later by India. Thus by the middle of the twenty-first century, the prediction goes, China and India will resume the places they inhabited for most of recorded history until around 1800 as the two largest economies on the planet. Not far behind will be several other Asian economies, including Japan, South Korea and Indonesia. According to Credit Suisse's *Global Wealth Report 2012*, Asia has recently surpassed Europe in terms of household wealth, an unprecedented development. There can be little doubt that this economic sea change will have some equally profound implications for the world political order. Quite what they will be evokes far less consensus. But amongst the Asian Century's many possible effects clearly there are profound implications for democracy, particularly in Asia itself. As the spectre of the Asian Century begins to assume a tangible form, it seems particularly pertinent therefore to apply renewed scrutiny to the current state of democracy in Asia and to identify any apparent trends.

This book represents such an effort focusing on Eastern Asia, a convenient term used by Australian scholars for referring to both East and Southeast Asia, suggesting lines of connections between the states and peoples of the region. Eleven key countries and one territory have been selected for this study. (Unavoidably, for reasons of space, several other countries of the region could not be included, namely Mongolia, North Korea, Vietnam, Brunei and Laos.) Each of those selected is different and distinctive in some ways, despite some similarities among them. Freedom House's 2013 annual report on political rights and civil liberties designates Japan, Taiwan, South Korea and Indonesia 'free'; Malaysia, Singapore, Thailand, the Philippines and Hong Kong 'partly free'; China, Cambodia and Myanmar as 'not free'. Myanmar (previously known as Burma), a 'second wave' democracy until Ne Win's coup d'état in 1962, has been a stubborn bastion of uncompromising authoritarianism over the past five decades, and was, until 2012, deemed 'the worst of the worst' along with North Korea. Now Myanmar is showing signs of democratic change, having registered significant gains over the previous year and continuing to push ahead with a process of democratic reform with plenty of international goodwill.[1]

Freedom House also underlines a continued pattern of global backsliding, with countries showing decline in levels of freedom outnumbering those with improvements over the past seven years. Likewise, the Economist Intelligence Unit's

(EIU) *Democracy Index 2011* reports that democracy has been under stress in many parts of the world, including the developed countries of North America and Western Europe. While democracy may still be 'the only game in town' (Linz and Stepan 1996a: 15), there could be reverses over the coming years in some of the electoral democracies. Building a sturdy democracy is no easy task. Even in long-established ones, democracy can corrode if not nurtured and protected. Those in Eastern Asia, like many elsewhere, face a range of issues and problems that fuel popular discontent, aided by the impact of a continued global economic crisis. Even Japan and South Korea, two stable liberal democracies, are confronted by challenges. Apparently, all democratic and not so democratic governments are under pressure to make changes to meet popular demands.

Building on previous scholarship on Asian democracy (Schmiegelow 1997; Laothamatas 1997; Diamond and Plattner 1998; Wood 2004; Chu *et al.* 2008; Dalton *et al.* 2008; Lye and Hofmeister 2011; Croissant and Bünte 2011), this book provides an up-to-date analysis of political changes in Eastern Asia that relate to the democratization processes and, in some cases, to the ongoing quest for democracy. Falling under the theme issues, problems and challenges, the chapters are organized in four groups based on the different stages of development and on some similarities among the countries in each group. The first group (Part I) consists of Japan, South Korea and Taiwan. According to *Democracy Index 2011*, Japan and South Korea are the only two 'full democracies' in Asia. Japan, a 'second wave' democracy that experienced significant political change in the post-Second World War period, is the oldest and most stable democracy in the region. South Korea, a 'third-wave' democracy, achieved a democratic breakthrough in the late 1980s, followed by a period of consolidation over the next decade. Yet as mature as they may be, both face strong societal pressures to make changes to strengthen their democratic institutions. And Taiwan's new democracy, 'flawed' until quite recently, is wrestling with some similar problems as it consolidates in liberal fashion. The second group (Part II) consists of Indonesia, Thailand, the Philippines and Cambodia, a mix of 'free, partly free and not free' countries, all of which face some similar problems and are in need of further democratic consolidation, despite recent gains. The third group (Part III) comprises Malaysia and Singapore, electoral soft authoritarian regimes now facing rigorous competition from opposition parties that compels them to make some changes in order to maintain their hold on power. The last group (Part IV) consists of Myanmar, Hong Kong and China, three very different societies. Myanmar has long been a repressive state controlled by the military, while post-1990s China has become what Linz and Stepan term a 'mature post-totalitarianism' (1996a: 42) and, in 2011, the world's second largest economy. The Hong Kong Special Administrative Region of the PRC is a 'hybrid regime' with a limited democratic political system, but it has retained wide-ranging civil and individual liberties since 1997, making it China's freest city by far. Common to all three is the uncertainty about transitions to democracy.

Four sets of empirical questions are posed reflecting the theme of the book. The first set includes: What is the current state of political development in the region? How may each of the selected countries and territory in the region be characterized politically? The second set concerns the issues and problems that pose challenges to the government of the day in terms of democratic transition, democratic consolidation, democratic improvement and good governance. How is each democracy performing? How are governments or ruling parties respond-ing to the challenges? Are there dangers of a democratic reversal? The third set concerns the way in which society (or civil society) is responding to the current state of democracy. Are the people satisfied or disaffected? Are they pro-government, anti-government or apathetic? Finally, what does the future hold for democracy and democratization in the region?

Not every contributor responds to all these questions in the same sequence or in the same manner. We appreciate that Eastern Asia is a region of great cultural and religious diversity that harbours a variety of political systems and modes of governance. It is home to countries that are predominantly Muslim, Buddhist, Confucian and Daoist, and Christian, and which have had markedly different historical experiences. Thus, while there is a large body of literature on the theory of democracy, none alone can fully explain the many nuances and com-plexity of the Eastern Asian experience with it. Accordingly, instead of con-straining contributors by mandating employment of a common theoretical framework and a common structure for all the chapters, contributors were invited to adopt an approach that best serves his or her purposes. Interestingly, as it turns out, all the contributors, without disregarding international factors and influ-ences, have focused on the respective domestic issues and challenges that have evidently had considerable impact in shaping democracy and democratization in the countries concerned. Together, the chapters provide a wide picture of Eastern Asian democracies, illustrating the different threads that we will seek to weave here into a coherent pattern and the parallels that we will try to stress where appropriate.

Democracy is not a perfect form of government. It is, as Winston Churchill said, 'the worst form of government except all those other forms that have been tried from time to time.' As a goal, democracy is to be attained incrementally over time in a trial and error fashion rather than overnight. And even where it can be said to exist it needs adjustment constantly and amelioration from time to time. Democratic values may well be universal, but how democracy is practised effectively varies from society to society according to local conditions, religious, cultural and philosophical traditions, and the stage of economic development, among other things. This is not to engage in cultural relativism, less to revive the 1990s debates on 'Asian values', and least of all to invoke the provocative notion of 'Asian exceptionalism'. Rather, we need to remind ourselves of the need to reconcile the claims of cultural diversity with those of universalism in political thought (Parekh 1993) and to acknowledge that Asian leadership styles and the people's expectations of their national leaders could be in some ways quite dif-ferent from those of their Western counterparts, which are themselves far from uniform.

Improving liberal democracies

Liberal democracy, in its various forms, is widely regarded as the best form of government and enjoys the accolade of 'full democracy'. Yet liberal democracy is not perfect; political participation can still be limited. Nor does liberal democracy guarantee peaceful conflict resolution, government for the 'common good', or good governance, let alone social justice and a fair society. The eminent political theorist, Robert A. Dahl, has argued that no modern state has reached the ideal of democracy. To reach it requires meeting five criteria: effective participation; voting equality at the decisive stage; (citizens') enlightened understanding (of their choices); control of the political agenda; and inclusiveness. These criteria, Dahl contends, 'fully specify the democratic process', giving meaning to political equality (Dahl 1989: 130). Liberal democracies are 'polyarchies', which distinguish themselves by the presence of seven institutions: elected officials, free and fair elections, inclusive suffrage, rights to run for public offices, freedom of expression, access to alternative sources of information and associational autonomy (Dahl 1989: 233). These institutions are necessary for the achievement of a 'full democracy'. However, in themselves they are not sufficient to advance democracy across the key terrains of society. Moreover, as David Held (1993: 13–14) has argued, liberal democracy betrays tensions between its variable liberal and democratic components, and it may have serious flaws in the protection of personal and associational freedoms. It is not something 'simply fixed or given; rather, its nature and form are both contestable and malleable' (Held 1991: 877). Even established democracies need to be adjusted and improved as circumstances require.

At the outset, Asian democracies invariably appeared somewhat different from democracies in the West and hence to be in greater need of improvement. Japanese democracy is often regarded as somewhat 'inauthentic' on account of its conflict-free, harmony-oriented political culture, which has enabled the postwar conservative Liberal Democratic Party (LDP) to maintain a strong hold on power (unbroken for nearly four decades until 1993) and the bureaucracy to dominate in policymaking. Writing in 2005, Takashi Inoguchi (2005: 112) noted that 'the Japanese political system has not yet fully developed into a system of representative democracy'. Others have asserted that the LDP has undergone a profound transformation since the 1994 electoral reform of the House of Representatives and other reforms thereafter. Once a highly decentralized political party led by a comparatively weak leader, the LDP was more centralized under Prime Minister Junichiro Koizumi (2001–2006), who presided over policymaking while citizens were more broadly represented (Krauss and Pekkanen 2008). At the same time, the bureaucracy, too, became a subject of reform (Kawabata 2008). Japan today is certainly a liberal, hence a 'full democracy'. The Japanese public undoubtedly regard their government as democratic, despite the fact that their understanding of democracy remains 'primarily static and system-oriented rather than dynamic and process-oriented' (Ikeda and Kohno 2008: 185). Yet this has not stopped one recent Japanese scholar from criticizing it as a 'malfunctioning democracy' (Kobayashi 2012).

Writing in Chapter 1, Purnendra Jain takes a different view, lauding Japan as 'a fully functioning mature democracy, notwithstanding some remaining weaknesses in the system'. He acknowledges, though, that the Japanese state 'remains under constant societal pressure for change'. The challenge for Japan's democracy is to become more strongly institutionalized at all levels of government and in the wider community. Not contenting himself with democracy at the national level alone, Jain is interested in the societal pressure that comes from the subnational government level and from civil society through civic groups, citizen movements and social media. These demands for change represent the voices from the periphery and from below, which are channelled into the national institutions and practices. Jain argues that 'improvement in the quality of [Japanese] democracy can be better understood and appreciated through opening our viewing lens to the grassroots and civil society'. Subnational government dynamism and ideas and actions from the bottom up have produced a 'more strongly institutionalized' democracy. Although Japanese democracy is by no means perfect, Jain's conclusion that '[a]s civil society matures and a more competitive political environment emerges, democracy in Japan will strengthen' resonates in many other parts of the world.

If the people of Japan are generally satisfied with the state of Japanese democracy, South Korea, another 'full democracy' in the region, is a different case. South Korea has been remarkably successful in consolidating democracy since the early 1990s. Chong-Min Park in Chapter 2 describes it today as 'one of the most consolidated third-wave democracies in East Asia', which has lost none of its 'resilience and vibrancy' during the recent global 'democratic recession'. However, utilizing recent opinion polls data, Park discovered that to ordinary Koreans, South Korea has recently become a 'disaffected democracy', if not a 'flawed democracy', as they have become increasingly cynical of representative political institutions, 'sceptical of democracy as a universal value, and disengaged themselves from conventional politics.' They are concerned about political inequalities, flaws in the rule of law, and limited scope of citizen participation. Particularly noteworthy is Park's finding that 'ordinary Koreans have higher standards for democracy than most [Western] experts of democratic assessment', such as *Democracy Index 2011*. (A similar point is made by Chung-li Wu and Shih-chan Dai about the Taiwanese in Chapter 3.) They have very high expectations of their national leaders when it comes to political institutions, the rule of law and good governance. To be sure, political discontent does not translate into a desire to return to political authoritarianism. But it poses a challenge to the government to alleviate the political malaise by making political institutions 'more responsive to and representative of diverging interests and expectations.' Park concludes that South Korea has yet to become a high-quality liberal democracy in contrast to the optimistic assessments of Western experts, including Larry Diamond (2012).

These two chapters underscore the importance of citizen participation and expectations, suggesting a real problem with theorists concerned primarily with electoral politics. As Helen James has demonstrated (2006; 2007), citizen demands and expectations for higher quality of services, higher morality in public life and the like are more meaningful, deliberative participation than merely minimalist politics.

Taiwan, officially known as the Republic of China (ROC), is the most vibrant democracy in the Chinese-speaking world, regarded by many as being among the ranks of Asia's 'consolidated liberal democracies' (Diamond 2012: 6). Likewise, Freedom House and such indicators as Polity IV suggest that Taiwan, alongside Japan and South Korea, is a full democracy in East Asia. Yet *Democracy Index 2011* has some reservations and designates Taiwan a 'flawed democracy'. Certainly, Taiwan has come a long way. The past four decades have seen a gradual transformation of the Nationalist Party, or the KMT, from a hard authoritarian regime through soft authoritarianism to a liberal democracy in response to the China factor as well as to domestic challenges from native Taiwanese.

Chung-li Wu and Shih-chan Dai in Chapter 3 provide an account of this transformation and its underpinning ideology since the mid-1980s. Until 2000, when the opposition Democratic Progressive Party (DPP) composed of local Taiwanese as distinct from the mainlanders who arrived after 1949 won the presidential election for the first time, the KMT had enjoyed five decades of single-party hegemony. Chiang Ching-kuo, who succeeded his father Chiang Kai-shek as President of the ROC and leader of the KMT, recognized the need to democratize Taiwan in order to build the island nation into a separate political entity and to counter communism on the mainland. His successor, Lee Teng-hui, maintained the democratizing momentum during the 1990s. As the DPP grew in strength, the KMT rose to the challenge by evolving into a competitive authoritarian regime, thereby maintaining political dominance until the 2000 presidential election. The DPP's electoral victory in 2000 led by Chen Shui-bian marked the end of the hegemonic party system and the dawn of liberal democracy in Taiwan. But it was a flawed democracy, marked by corruption, electoral manipulation, vote buying and some violence, as evidenced by the assassination attempt on President Chen Shui-bian during the 2004 election campaign.

Not until 2008 did the KMT led by Ma Ying-jeou return to power, and four years later Ma was re-elected as President of the ROC. The results of the 2012 elections were encouraging, with minimal reports of vote buying, leading the American law professor, Jerome A. Cohen (Ma's former mentor at Harvard University), to comment that Taiwan now has the ability to conduct a clean and peaceful poll and that the DPP is back on its feet, with the country moving towards party politics and Taiwan's democracy having an influence on mainland China (Cohen 2012).[2] The political scientist, Yun-han Chu, adds that over the past ten years Taiwanese trust and confidence in dictatorship, strong-man politics, party politics and the media has dropped significantly, and that the voters not only cast their ballots at elections as high as 70 per cent on average but also sustain their concerns about political issues (Chu 2012b).

Wu and Dai credit the KMT leadership with some positive political reforms as the Party transforms itself. Yet they fault Ma Ying-jeou for failing to implement real institutional or structural change that will make the Party more democratic and more competitive in the elections ahead. Their conclusion is that 'Taiwan is institutionally close to a "stable liberal democracy" as defined by Larry Diamond (1994)'. Close but not good enough, which is why Taiwanese give their government a lower rating than most Western analysts would. The challenge for Ma, whose approval rating has been consistently low, is to be more responsive to citizen demands and societal pressures.

Flawed democracies, developing democracies and democratic consolidation

Many of the electoral democracies in Eastern Asia, old and new, are flawed. Despite improvements since 2011, those states remain in a process of democratic consolidation. They are constantly put to tests that they might not pass as they face problems of political instability, ethnic, sectarian and religious strife, socio-economic inequality, official corruption, rising unemployment, failing education and public health, soaring crime rates and external challenges. As Diamond has long maintained, successful democratization requires a firm commitment by the country's elites, political parties, legal institutions, social organizations, interest groups and the mass public to make it work (Diamond 1999: 69). Furthermore, it requires a vibrant and independent civil society; an autonomous political society with a consensus about procedures of governance; a rule of law based on constitutionalism; a usable bureaucracy by democratic leaders; and an institutionalized economic society (Linz and Stepan 1996b).

Democracy in Indonesia, surprisingly reborn in 1998 after more than four decades of authoritarian rule, now appears to be both stable and vibrant despite a rocky start; indeed, Indonesia has enjoyed the Freedom House designation 'free' since 2005. It is now clearly the most liberally democratic nation in Southeast Asia, not hesitating to promote democracy in the region (Sukma 2011). This is some turnaround given that liberal democratic ideals and practices were systematically derided as fundamentally alien to Indonesian (and other Asian) values and traditions during both the Sukarno and Soeharto regimes. Emerging quite against the grain of a global democratic regression, one could even argue that Indonesian democracy is the real father of the Arab Spring (not the US intervention in Iraq), since it demonstrated that a Muslim country (indeed the world's largest by population) could implement democracy and do so under its own impetus. The international implications of Indonesia's stunning transformation may yet prove to be far more profound than has been appreciated to date. Yet Steven Drakeley writing in Chapter 4 judges that, while Indonesian democracy can now be regarded as consolidated, it has several serious flaws that ensure that it remains stuck at a low-quality level. The principal problems are severe deficiencies in the practices of parliament, endemic corruption and vote buying, and the system's almost complete capture by an entrenched elite (the reinvention or reconstitution of the old oligarchy as Robison and Hadiz (2004) put it). Combined, not only do these defects grossly distort the democratic process, but they obstruct the delivery of good governance, which as Emmerson (2012) reminds us undermines the legitimacy of democracy and so jeopardizes it. Notwithstanding some positives, including a vibrant civil society and broad commitment to liberal democratic principles, Drakeley concludes that unless addressed, the flaws are of sufficient magnitude to risk Indonesia's rapid slide down the Freedom House 'league table' to the positions occupied by Thailand and the Philippines, or even to risk a return to authoritarian rule. Now, as the 2014 elections approach, Indonesia's democracy will face a stern test. Disappointment levels are already high due to the underwhelming performance of President Susilo Bambang Yudhoyono during his second term and to the persistence of corruption. Adding to a growing sense of frustration is the lacklustre field of presidential aspirants manoeuvring for support ahead of the 2014 elections and the inability of the lowly regarded political parties to reform themselves or to pay any attention to policy development.

Thailand, after an extended period of democracy was the democratic role model for Southeast Asia until the military staged its eighteenth coup in 2006. Not for the first time was Thailand's apparent success in putting military interventions in politics behind it shown to be illusory. Despite Thailand's many changes, a core problem has remained unresolved: the need for an effective reconciliation of democracy with a revered and powerful monarchy. Unfortunately, becoming increasingly entangled with this delicate question since the late 1990s is another contradiction at the heart of modern Thailand. On the one hand, dramatic economic development has ushered in equally profound social changes, along with new and/or increased discontents and aspirations, especially amongst the rural poor. On the other hand, an entrenched elite has remained reluctant to embrace the new Thailand and all too willing to turn to the familiar military solution. Thus, as Pavin Chachavalpongpun explains in Chapter 5, the 2006 coup was due largely to the intransigence of these establishment forces, centred on the monarchy and the military, unwilling to accept an unpalatable democratic outcome in the form of the populist Thaksin Shinawatra government. Thaksin had swept to power in 2001, and swept back in again in 2005, largely by appealing to the large rural poor constituency, previously taken for granted. Albeit, now reinstated, democracy remains fragile in Thailand and surely cannot consolidate without fundamental reforms, including the depoliticization of the monarchy, judiciary and the military. But for this to happen a profound cultural shift is needed whereby the establishment finally and fully accept the democratic 'rules of the game', including that the people are the sole and final arbiter, even if their choice happens to fall upon a man with a reputation for abuses of power, including corruption and human rights violations. Chachavalpongpun suggests therefore that Thailand has reached a dangerous crossroads as the latest elections have once again delivered an outcome contrary to the interests of the establishment with the election of Thaksin's sister, Yingluck Shinawatra.

The Philippines has also recently returned to a more democratic condition since the victory in the 2010 presidential election of Benigno Aquino III. Since the Marcos era the Philippines has experienced an extended period of democracy, but one periodically threatened by military intervention and marred by political violence, corruption and large-scale electoral irregularities. Political institutions, perennially weak, were undermined further under the presidency of Gloria Macapagal-Arroyo (Hutchcroft 2008). The 2010 elections offer the tantalizing glimpse of genuine improvement, not just because of the election of the reformist Benigno Simeon ('Noynoy') Aquino III, but because of the legitimacy supplied by his commanding victory in a surprisingly clean and orderly poll (Thompson 2010). Yet Nathan Gilbert Quimpo in Chapter 6 asserts that while a positive development, the improvement merely represents a shift from a predatory to a clientelist electoral regime, essentially a modestly progressive shift in the way the oligarchic elite wields power. In the World Bank's annual governance ratings, the Philippines ranked in the bottom quartile of all countries in corruption control, and not much better (the bottom third) in rule of law (Kaugmann *et al.* 2010). It is this dismal record that Aquino has promised to tackle, along with poverty reduction. Quimpo credits Aquino with real progress in his fight against corruption and for good governance. But he is sceptical of how far the reforms can be taken since real progress depends upon implementing far more fundamental reform, which would necessitate confronting and defeating the firmly ensconced oligarchic elite, the very class to which Aquino himself belongs.

Cambodia, after its dark 'killings fields' history of the Khmer Rouge period and Vietnamese occupation/supervision (1978–1991), underwent an abrupt transition to democracy under UN supervision in 1993. From second place in the 1993 elections, the Cambodian People's Party (CPP) led by former Khmer Rouge cadre and Vietnamese client Hun Sen, has steadily expanded and tightened its grip on power, winning 90 out of 123 seats in the 2008 elections (Gainsborough 2012: 38). As Melissa Curley in Chapter 7 shows, the increasing fusion between the party and state, with the increasingly dominant CPP using its business and societal networks to maintain and extend its grip on power, combined with the ongoing weakness of opposition parties, means that such lopsided electoral outcomes are likely to become a fixture. Cambodia therefore could be described as a deeply flawed electoral democracy, but might also be characterized as a 'competitive authoritarian' regime (Levitsky and Way 2010).

Much of the problem of Cambodian democracy lies in the judicial system, which, writes Curley, the ruling political elite, mobilizes 'to intimidate political opponents and stifle political speech and activities which run counter to the government's political and economic agenda'. Cambodia is sliding from the rule of law to rule *by* law, putting the survival of its democracy under severe pressure. Nevertheless, while Cambodian civil society matures and levels of prosperity increase, the government continues to face opposition to its attempts to wind back the democratic gains of 1993.

These four Southeast Asian countries are dissimilar in many respects with markedly differing historical experiences, including during the colonial era to give just one example. Thus drawing comparisons here is challenging. Yet all four began their post-colonial era journeys as democracies, only for those democracies to founder on the rocks of various problems linked closely to under-development and Cold War circumstances. Authoritarian regimes of various kinds followed, only to be supplanted by democracies again, but these democracies all struggle, albeit with greater or lesser success, to consolidate in the teeth of their respective domestic problems. Not least of these obstacles in all four is the resistance to democratization of their respective elites who have thoroughly availed themselves of the benefits of the market economy but have not truly embraced the liberal democracy that is supposed to accompany it. And while they may have somewhat grudgingly accepted democracy they have certainly not accepted the 'rules of the game'. Moreover, none of these countries have attained the levels of development and prosperity that would make proponents of the modernization thesis expect a democratic form of government. Arguably, however, with the probable exception of Cambodia, they are all more democratic than two of their much wealthier neighbours in Southeast Asia, Malaysia and Singapore.

Democratization under hegemonic party regimes

According to *Democracy Index 2011*, Malaysia is a 'flawed democracy', and Singapore a 'hybrid regime'. Yet they are grouped together in the third part of the book because the two countries share some distinctiveness and some interesting parallels. Both of them inherited the British parliamentary system but both have been ruled by dominant parties from the outset, the United Malays National Organisation (UMNO) in the former and the People's Action Party (PAP) in the latter. Both UMNO and PAP have delivered relatively good government, but they have also limited civil liberties in the interest, supposedly, of civil order. Largely this is because the major political fault lines are determined by ethnic divisions that, in addition to posing many vexing policy issues, are held to contain an inherent danger of catastrophic inter-communal conflict. Government policies in both countries privilege the dominant ethnic community (the Malays in Malaysia, the Chinese in Singapore). Resentment to date from the minority communities has been relatively muted. In the case of Malaysia in particular they have acquiesced to their situation as the price of inter-communal peace. Today, however, both ruling parties face mounting pressure for change as their decades-old single-party hegemony seems no longer sustainable. These pressures for change and the concomitant opposition gains have reached the point whereby both countries may be considered to have joined the ranks of 'competitive authoritarianisms'.

In Malaysia and Singapore, a change of government is a realistic proposition for the first time in their histories as opposition forces grow stronger. The ruling parties in both countries face a dilemma. Dan Slater (2012) suggests that they would be well advised to follow the examples of Japan, South Korea and Taiwan, which underwent successful strong state democratizations, marrying democracy with prosperity and stability. By oversighting and shepherding the process before the pressures from below became irresistible and destructive, the ruling parties in Taiwan and to a lesser extent South Korea gained additional credit to add to their good governance credentials. The upshot is that they remain the dominant parties in their new democratic contexts. Moreover, because of the strength of the state in both these cases the transitions, despite some pain and ruction along the way, did not jeopardize these nations' prosperity or lead to civil strife. Feasibly Singapore and Malaysia could make the same relatively painless transition. It remains to be seen whether UMNO and PAP will take this road. As Slater points out, the same key factor, the strong state, which makes such a transition viable, also means these regimes probably have the capacity to postpone it indefinitely. At present, in neither case does the ruling party seem prepared to countenance defeat at the polls, but their respective strategies for preventing such an outcome are subtly but significantly different. Obduracy rules in Malaysia, whereas in Singapore the ruling party is undergoing a minimalist process of strategic dominant-party transformations in order to cope with the new challenges posed by opposition politics and socio-economic changes.

For William Case in Chapter 8, the decades long success of 'an adjustable mix of authoritarian controls and democratic procedures', which have underpinned Malaysia's 'electoral authoritarianism', seems to have run its course. The government suffered a major setback in the 2008 elections and the now credible opposition, although still an unstable alliance of unlikely bedfellows pushed the government to the brink of defeat in the 2013 elections. Non-Malays have become more assertive, partly in response to a 'creeping Islamization', and many Malays, especially from the growing middle class, have become reluctant to continue tolerating the patronage and corruption arising from the UMNO-government intimacy. And many from both groups seem no longer prepared to accept the electoral manipulations and restrictions on civil liberties that have for so long kept oppositions from attaining government. Recognising these growing pressures, Prime Minister Najib Razak has implemented only superficial reforms, such as repealing the infamous Internal Security Act that allowed for indefinite detention without trial. But the deck remains heavily stacked against the opposition; hence, the reforms have done nothing to placate the government's critics.

No doubt it is the transformation of Malaysian society at root that has made Malaysia a candidate for the 'competitive authoritarianism' category. But the more competitive position of the opposition is also due to more narrowly political factors. Partly due to the charismatic leadership of former UNMO Deputy Prime Minister Anwar Ibrahim, the opposition parties have adopted a disciplined pragmatism driven by their collective desire to defeat the government. Beyond that goal, however, they remain divided on fundamental issues related to their representation of quite different communally-based constituencies. Thus, for all the change, apparently Malaysian society has not yet transformed to the point where identity politics has ceased to be the principal mode of political organization. While that remains the case, democratic prospects in Malaysia remain low.

Many Singaporeans are increasingly fed up with the arrogance of the PAP. They want greater checks and balances on the PAP and to rein in its heavy-handed technocratic style of government. Elements within the PAP acknowledge the need to move with the times, as evidenced by Lee Kuan Yew's retirement from the Cabinet after the PAP's lacklustre showing in May 2011. They desire more political pluralism, a more liberal society and transparent governance. One-party hegemony is clearly under pressure.

Netina Tan in Chapter 9 shows how although the Singaporean political landscape has indeed shifted, the 'new normal' is unlikely to result in an imminent change of government. Tan notes that the majority of Singaporeans are not yet ready to abandon their support for the PAP, and the opposition does not yet appear to be a credible alternative. Moreover, while the ever pragmatic PAP seems willing to make some astute but modest concessions, notably in the field of freedom of speech, it is highly unlikely to embrace any reforms that will endanger let alone dismantle the hegemonic party system. Rather, it will continue to explore ways to diffuse opposition and dissent with 'calibrated reforms' that will not alter the nature of the system.

Uncertain transitions to democracy

Transitions from authoritarian to democratic governance are often perceived to be uncertain. This is because they are emerging phenomena and because we lack an historical basis for their respective contexts that would allow us to judge their prospects with any confidence. Helen James in Chapter 10 investigates Myanmar's uncertain yet stunning transition from a military state to one that is undergoing rapid reforms pursuant to the 2010 elections based on a formal constitution, and following the seating in Parliament in 2012 of the country's prominent dissident, leader of the National League for Democracy, Aung San Suu Kyi. James examines the underlying dynamics that precipitated this transition, arguing that Myanmar faces numerous domestic problems including ongoing ethnic violence, a fragile socio-economic fabric, a populace unaccustomed to democratic politics, and an education sector in dire need of a thoroughgoing overhaul. She notes that the peacemaker, President Thein Sein, has recently been welcomed in the USA, and publicly extended the hand of reconciliation to Aung San Suu Kyi. On the face of it, this apparent rapprochement augurs well for future cooperation on the extensive reform programme required to bring Myanmar up to the socio-economic level of its Southeast Asian neighbours.

Many signs are positive. President Thein Sein has acknowledged the need to bring peace and inclusive policies for socio-economic development to the ethnic minority peoples. He has recently set in train an extensive cabinet reshuffle designed to provide increased capacity for economic reform among his top advisors and cabinet colleagues. Yet this sudden *volte-face* could be subject to a number of threats. These include the possibility of the Myanmar opposition provoking a reversal of political fortune through mismanagement of the internal political dynamics, the possibility of the USA and its allies overplaying their hand and provoking a military coup that could see a return to the former pro-China policy, and the conflicts between Buddhists and minority Muslim communities. James concludes that Myanmar's democratic transition will continue with the backing of the international community. Yet the challenge is an enormous one for both the government and the opposition party whose unity and capacity to compete for power will be severely tested.

In the case of Hong Kong, the uncertainly about its transition to democracy is due to the China factor. Following its return to China in 1997 as a Special Administrative Region of the PRC, a pro-democracy movement began to develop, which could be understood as a reaction to communist rule on the mainland. From the start, it was 'truly a mass movement' that was 'in no way confined to a small, Western-educated elite or any other small group' (Ng 1998: 13). Ten years on, a survey showed that the people of Hong Kong were passionate about democracy (both electoral and substantive), making strong demands on the HKSAR government to perform and to govern in a democratic manner (Lam and Kuan 2008). Every year large crowds of pro-democracy elements mark the anniversary of the 4 June Tiananmen Square Incident by holding a candlelight vigil for the victims, in Victoria Park. According to a recent poll, the people of Hong Kong now have less trust in the central government in Beijing than at any time since the 1997 handover (Hong Kong University POP, 19 June 2012, cited in *Mingpao News*, 20 June 2012). Many fear that the current Chief Executive, C.Y. Leung, perceived as too close to Beijing, would roll back some of the territory's cherished civil liberties.

To date, Hong Kong's transition to democracy has been one of immense frustrations. Yet Joseph Cheng in Chapter 11 argues that Hong Kong is a 'theoretical exception', a case study that poses challenges to modernization theory. He notes that in contrast to the former British administration, which secured its legitimacy by performance, the HKSAR government suffers from a legitimacy deficit due to unsatisfactory performance, which explains the rising popular discontent. Yet he contends that the response of most people in the territory has been a sense of helplessness, not anger, because of a reluctance to confront the Beijing government. The major question is whether political participation is part of a meaningful life for them. According to Cheng, they have tended to derive their satisfaction from family life and career development, they had been politically alienated in a previous colonial setting, and historically they had a refugee mentality. Cheng, who has been a long-time democracy advocate in the territory, insists that most Hongkongers would not fight hard for democracy because the costs are too high and that for many of them there is the option of emigration to the West.

Finally, we come to China, which is a peculiar case in two respects. First, it belies the conventional wisdom that as the country grows richer it will become more liberal and democratic following essentially the same path as Japan, South Korea and Taiwan. Quite the contrary, spectacular economic growth has improved living standards so substantially that the population on the whole is likely to support the status quo, despite the existing socio-economic gap and inequalities. More importantly, it has emboldened China's leaders to maintain their resolve to reject liberal democracy, multiparty competitive systems and unrestrained personal freedoms. Second, China is a fierce competitor to democracy that could have a significant influence on the developing countries in the region, notably its near neighbours Cambodia, Vietnam, Myanmar and North Korea. Not only did the Chinese Communist Party's (CCP) durability, adaptability and resilience save China from disintegrating like the former Soviet Union, it has had the vision and strategies to transform the country into an economic and military power.

Today's China exhibits the characteristics of a mature post-totalitarian regime. Post-totalitarianism is understood as a political rather than an historical category after the Cold War. Using Linz and Stepan's defining characteristics of it (1996a: 44–45), we may describe today's China as follows: There is no political pluralism, as the CCP retains a monopoly of power and plays the leading role that is still sacrosanct. Socially and culturally, although the space is widening, pluralism is still limited. While there is a thriving private sector, state domination of the economy through the powerful state-owned enterprises remains overwhelming. There are dissident groups formed consciously in opposition to the CCP regime as well as liberal elements within the Party. Some of those groups are tolerated, others repressed. There is a more liberal press, but censorship remains strict. Marxism, or socialism with Chinese characteristics, still exists officially as the guiding ideology and part of the social reality, but faith in Marxism has been significantly eroded. There has been a shift of emphasis from ideology to pragmatic consensus that is presumably based on rational decision-making without too much reference to Marxism. The top leaders, collective in style, are not charismatic like Mao Zedong. Checks on their powers are provided routinely through party structures, procedures and/or intra-party democracy. The CCP remains hierarchically organized, superior to and intertwined with the state bureaucracy. It has lost much interest in mobilizing the population within state-sponsored organizations to achieve conformity and compliance.

In order to maintain their hold on power, post-totalitarian regimes implement limited and cautious political change. Accordingly, there has been much talk of moderate political reform in China in order to sustain economic growth, to curb official corruption and to strengthen the rule of law. The trouble, though, is that factions within the Party cannot agree on what the political reform would be, much less on how to achieve it without endangering stability and even CCP control. Also, the nation's professional elite and growing middle class are so closely linked to the party-state (Goodman 2008) and benefiting so much from government policies that they would not want to challenge the regime. Meanwhile, the majority of Chinese accept CCP rule because of the achievements of 'late industrialization', state-led development combined with 'socialist legacies' (Wright 2010) and rising national prestige on the world stage. There is no display of a popular desire for a regime change, despite growing social unrest and the rise of middle-class restlessness over environmental issues.

Writing in Chapter 12, Chongyi Feng, a liberal and long-time democracy advocate, takes a cue from Linz and Stepan to characterize today's China as a post-totalitarian party-state but argues that the conditions are ripe for a transition to democracy. His argument rests on two assumptions: first, the CCP faces a crisis of legitimacy and governance, and second, the 'moderates' within the leadership have come to realize that without political reforms economic growth cannot be sustained and the problems of social injustice and economic inequality will remain unresolved. Feng draws attention to the ongoing rights defence movement begun at the turn of the twenty-first century and links it with the movement for constitutional democracy. He points out that while the rights advocates, many of them lawyers, seek to defend citizens' rights that are guaranteed by the Constitution of the PRC, their ultimate goal is liberal constitutional government. Feng concludes on an optimistic note: 'There is now a possibility that bold political reforms may be initiated by the moderates within the Party to accommodate the "rights defence movement" and to bring about a breakthrough towards constitutional democracy.'

Many, both inside and outside China, may not share Feng's optimism, but there can be no doubt that the greatest challenge for the regime is to demonstrate a political will and implement the much-needed reforms. Optimists may have high expectations of the new CCP General Secretary and Head of State, Xi Jinping, who has exhibited a different leadership style – more people-friendly and more open than his predecessor – and won popular support for his anti-corruption, anti-waste, anti-formalism and anti-bureaucratic drive. But it remains to be seen whether the new leadership will usher in an era of political liberalization.

In an 'Asian Century', the direction of China in this regard will likely have a great bearing on whether a fourth wave of democracy is indeed imminent, at least in the Eastern Asian region, where China's weight and influence are most profound. Yet if the contributors to this volume are correct then we must be careful not to lay too much emphasis on the broader international context. Each in their own way in the chapters that follow shows that domestic circumstances are the prime determinant of the prospects for democracy in a country.

Notes

1 With the exception of Myanmar, Freedom House's designations of these countries are the same as in its 2012 annual report, suggesting no changes in their freedom status from the previous year.
2 For an analysis of the Taiwan factor in China's future democratization, see Yun-han Chu (2012a).

References

Chu Yun-han (2012a) 'The Taiwan factor', *Journal of Democracy*, 23(1), 4–56.
Chu Yun-han (2012b) 'How the Public Views Democracy and its Competitors in East Asia: Taiwan in Comparative Perspective'; www.worldjournal.com/view/full_news/18734268/article accessed 8 August 2012.
Chu Yun-han, Diamond, Larry, Nathan, Andrew J. and Doh Chull Shin (eds) (2008) *How East Asians View Democracy*, New York: Columbia University Press, pp. 161–186.

Cohen, Jerome A. (2012) 'On Taiwan Election Results', New York: U.S.–Asia Law Institute, New York University Law School; http://archive.feedblitz.com/611992/~4131951#0 accessed 1 October 2012.

Croissant, Aurel and Bünte, Marco (eds) (2011) *The Crisis of Democratic Governance in Southeast Asia*. Hounmills: Palgrave Macmillan.

Dahl, Robert A. (1989) *Democracy and Its Critics*, New Haven: Yale University Press.

Dalton, Russell J., Shin, Doh Chull and Chu Yun-han (eds) (2008) *Party Politics in East Asia: Citizens, Elections, and Democratic Development*, Boulder: Lynne Reinner.

Diamond, Larry (1994) 'Rethinking civil society: toward democratic consolidation', *Journal of Democracy*, 5(3), 3–17.

Diamond, Larry (1999) *Developing Democracy: Toward Consolidation*, Baltimore: Johns Hopkins University.

Diamond, Larry (2010) 'Indonesia's Place in Global Democracy', in Aspinall, Edward and Marcus Mietzner (eds) *Problems of Democratisation in Indonesia*, Singapore: Institute of Southeast Asian Studies, pp. 21–49.

Diamond, Larry (2012) 'The coming wave', *Journal of Democracy*, 23(1), 5–13.

Diamond, Larry and Plattner, Marc F. (eds) (1998) *Democracy in East Asia*, Baltimore: The Johns Hopkins University Press.

Economist Intelligence Unit (2011) *Democracy Index 2011*, London.

Emmerson, Donald K. (2012) 'Minding the gap between democracy and governance', *Journal of Democracy*, 23(2), 62–73.

Fukuyama, Francis (1989) 'The end of history?' *National Interest*, 16(Summer), 3–18.

Freedom House (2012) 'Freedom in the World 2012', London; www.freedomhouse.org accessed 10 April 2012.

Freedom House (2013) 'Freedom in the World 2013: Democratic Breakthroughs in the Balance', London; www.freedomhouse.org accessed 10 March 2013.

Gainsborough, Martin (2012) 'Elites vs. reform in Laos, Cambodia, and Vietnam', *Journal of Democracy*, 23(2), 34–46.

Global Wealth Report 2012 Zurich: Credit Suisse Research Institute; www.thewealthreport.net accessed 10 April 2012.

Goodman David (ed.) (2008). *The New Rich in China: Future Rulers, Present Lives*, London: Routledge.

Held, David (1991) 'The possibilities of democracy', *Theory and Society*, 20(6), 875–889.

Held, David (1993) 'Democracy: From City-States to a Cosmopolitan Order?' in David Held (ed.) *Prospects for Democracy: North, South, East, West*, Cambridge, UK: Polity Press, pp. 13–54.

Hutchroft, Paul D. (2008) 'The Arroyo imbroglio in the Philippines', *Journal of Democracy*, 19(1), 141–155.

Ikeda, Ken'ichi and Masaru Kohno (2008) 'Japanese attitudes and values toward democracy', in Chu Yun-han, Larry Diamond, Andrew J. Nathan and Doh Chull Shin (eds) *How East Asians View Democracy*, New York: Columbia University Press, pp. 161–186.

Inoguchi Takashi (2005) *Japanese Politics*, Melbourne: Trans Pacific Press.

James, Helen (2006) *Security and Sustainable Development in Myanmar*, London and New York: RoutledgeCurzon.

James, Helen (ed.) (2007) *Civil Society, Religion and Global Governance: Paradigms of Power and Persuasion*, London and New York: Routledge.

Kaugmann, Daniel, Kraay Aart, and Mastruzzi, Massimo (2010) *The Worldwide Governance Indicators: Methodology and Analytical Issues*, World Bank Policy Research Working Paper No. 5430.

Kawabata E. (2008) 'Reforming the Bureaucracy', in Sherry L. Martin and Gill Steel (eds) *Democratic Reform in Japan: Assessing the Impact*, Boulder: Lynne Rienner.

Kobayashi, Yoshiaki (2012) *Malfunctioning Democracy in Japan*, Lanham: Lexington Books.

Krauss, Ellis S. and Pekkanen, Robert (2008) 'Reforming the Liberal Democratic Party', in Sherry L. Martin and Gill Steel (eds) *Democratic Reform in Japan: Assessing the Impact*, Boulder: Lynne Rienner, pp. 11–38.

Lam Wai-man and Hsin-chi Kuan (2008) 'Democratic transition frustrated: the case of Hong Kong', in Chu Yun-han, Larry Diamond, Andrew J. Nathan and Doh Chull Shin (eds) *How East Asians View Democracy*, New York: Columbia University Press, pp. 187–208.

Laothamatas, Anek (ed.) (1997) *Democratization in Southeast and East Asia*, Singapore: Institute of Southeast Asian Studies.

Levitsky, Steven and Way, Lucan (2010) *Competitive Authoritarianism: Hybrid Regimes after the Cold War*, New York: Cambridge University Press.

Linz, Juan and Stepan, Alfred (1996a) *Problems of Democratic Transition and Consolidation: Southern European, South America, and Post-Communist Europe*, Baltimore: The Johns Hopkins University Press.

Linz, Juan and Stepan, Alfred (1996b) 'Toward Consolidated Democracies', *Journal of Democracy*, 7(2), 124–133.

Lye Liang Fook and Hofmeister, Wilhelm (eds) (2011) *Political Parties, Party Systems and Democratization in East Asia*, Singapore: World Scientific Publishing.

Mingpao News (online edition), 20 June 2012; www.mingpaonews.com accessed 20 June 2012.

Ng, Margaret (1998) 'Why Asia needs democracy: a view from Hong Kong', in Larry Diamond and Marc F. Platter (eds) *Democracy in East Asia*, Baltimore: The Johns Hopkins University, pp. 3–16.

Parekh, Bhikhu (1993) 'The cultural particularity of liberal democracy', in David Held (ed.) *Prospects for Democracy: North, South, East, West*, Cambridge, UK: Polity Press, pp. 156–175.

Robison, Richard and Hadiz, Vedi R. (2004) *Reorganising Power in Indonesia: The Politics of Oligarchy in an Age of Markets*, London and New York: RoutledgeCurzon.

Roy, Olivier (2012) 'The transformation of the Arab world', *Journal of Democracy*, 23(3), 5–18.

Schmiegelow, Michèle (eds) (1997) *Democracy in Asia*, New York: St. Martin's Press.

Slater, Dan (2012) 'Strong-state democratization in Malaysia and Singapore', *Journal of Democracy*, 23(2), 19–33.

Sukma, Rizal (2011) 'Indonesia finds a voice', *Journal of Democracy*, 22(4), 110–123.

Thompson, Mark R. (2010) 'Reformism vs. Populism in the Philippines', *Journal of Democracy*, 21(4), 154–168.

Wood Alan T. (2004) *Asian Democracy in World History*, New York and London: Routledge.

Wright, Teresa (2010) *Accepting Authoritarianism: State-Society Relations in China's Reform Era*, Stanford: Stanford University Press.

Part I

Improving liberal democracies

1 Democracy in Japan

National, subnational and grassroots perspectives

Purnendra Jain

> *We may approach democracy as we would a horizon, and do so in ways that may be better or worse, but it can never be fully attained.*
>
> Czech revolutionary and President, Vaclav Havel

Introduction

Vaclav Havel's prescient observation, learned through a lifetime actively seeking and practising democracy, provides a useful place to anchor this survey of democracy in Japan. Democracy is, after all, a slippery term, perhaps an ideal state, and no nation in the world that is popularly recognized as democratic is or can be the ideal type that presents the features we generally associate with democracy in perfect form. Each democratic country has inherent weaknesses and pitfalls. Japan is no different.

Japan is the only non-Western and Asian country that has functioned as a democratic state without interruption since the end of the Second World War and it demonstrated some institutional and societal elements of democracy even in the pre-war era (Scalapino 1953). In post-war Japan, through universal suffrage regulated by a strict code of election laws, elections from village to national level have been held regularly, producing directly elected heads of all levels of government and a large number of legislators nationwide. As I make clear in this study through international comparisons and cross-country survey results, democratic political institutions in Japan are generally robust and on almost all macro indicators Japan scores highly. This is why I believe the nation can rightly be regarded as a fully functioning mature democracy, notwithstanding some remaining weaknesses in the system.

Nevertheless, some of Japan's political processes and practices have attracted scathing criticisms from scholars and analysts both within Japan and beyond. As Martin observes, 'the problems do not lie with the institutions of democracy [in Japan] but with the practices that elected officials have evolved over time to reproduce the status quo' (Martin 2011: 47). Many political practices and procedural weaknesses of the past have been addressed through reform processes over the years. The reform process has forced through demands made within Japanese society and through global pressures. The Japanese state remains under constant societal pressure for change, as has recently been witnessed in the wake of the March 2011 nuclear crisis in Japan through mass demonstrations on Tokyo streets and elsewhere. Political and societal change in post-war Japan is slow and evolutionary, achieved through democratic processes and civic means rather than violent or disruptive interventions.

In this chapter I first set the context by considering some of the most discussed weaknesses in institutions, processes and practices at the national level and map out how reforms and new processes put in place in recent years have made a difference to Japanese democracy. I then turn to two specific areas that have attracted scant attention in the democracy literature but that have made significant contribution to improving the quality of Japanese democracy. These are: (1) developments at subnational government level, and (2) the continued rise of civil society represented through civic groups both organized (non-governmental organizations [NGOs], non-profit organizations [NPOs]) and less formally organized (citizen movements, social networks, and so forth) including the emergence of social and alternative media. It is important to examine the role of both areas in some detail to develop a rounded picture of Japanese democracy. On the basis of these new developments, I conclude that while democracy in Japan is maturing through reforms and changes introduced at the national level, improvement in the quality of democracy can be better understood and appreciated through opening our viewing lens to grassroots and civil society, which channels ideas and demands into the national institutions and practices to energize and strengthen democracy in Japan.

Democracy at the national level

Despite Japan's strong democratic institutional frameworks, Japanese democracy has been characterized as an 'uncommon democracy' (Pempel 1990), a 'pseudo democracy' (Herzog 1993), a dysfunctional (Bowen 2003) and a 'malfunctioning democracy' (Kobayashi 2012). These characterizations are based on systemic features that have included single-party domination and a weak opposition (Kataoka 1992; Scheiner 2006), money politics and corruption (Woodall 1996), special dispensation for some interest groups (the farm sector, for example) (George Mulgan 2011) while others are kept on the periphery, a patron–client relationship (Ike 1972) and close alliance between business, bureaucracy and the Liberal Democratic Party (LDP), popularly known as Japan's iron triangle of governance.

Many of these characteristics of Japanese politics emerged from the late 1950s with the high rate of economic growth that continued through to the bubble economy period of the late 1980s. Although traces remain ingrained in the political culture, they are now fading rapidly from the system. The single most important change affecting democracy in almost six decades is the end of the LDP's monopoly on political power with the landslide victory by the Democratic Party of Japan (DPJ) in the 2009 general election. Even though the LDP was defeated once before at the general election in 1993 after 38 years of uninterrupted rule since its formation in 1955, the party bounced back quickly; the very short-lived coalition government formed from its opposition parties in 1993 crumbled fast through lack of internal cohesion. The LDP's domination, although in a somewhat weakened form, continued virtually until the August 2009 election. In the December 2012 general election, however, the DPJ suffered a crushing defeat while the LDP sprang back with a thumping majority in the lower house and formed government under the leadership of Shinzo Abe, who had previously served as Japan's Prime Minister from 2006 to 2007. Abe's position has further strengthened with the July 2013 upper house elections delivering a stable majority to his LDP and coalition partner Komeito. The LDP is once again back in a dominant position as it now controls both houses of parliament.

One-party domination may have made Japan's democracy uncommon as Pempel (1990) argued, but the LDP's tenacious rule was by no means undemocratic. Elections were held regularly and multiple political parties contested parliamentary seats. The main opposition party – the Japan Socialist Party until the late 1980s and later the Social Democratic Party of Japan – seemed to offer a sizeable challenge to the LDP, but never came close to replacing the LDP. While weak opposition certainly gave the LDP an advantage, the ruling party ably utilized the electoral system to its advantage, and in times of crisis when it realized its electoral advantage was eroding it very cleverly compensated those who mattered most for the party (Calder 1991). The party did not hesitate to co-opt the opposition agenda or adopt popular policy developed at the local level and thus continued governing Japan through what Pempel (1982) described as 'creative conservatism'. The LDP was branded a 'catch all party'.

Any polity that is run by a single political party for a long time inevitably breeds political malpractices, cronyism, patronage and corruption. While the LDP remained in office, scholars and commentators continued to argue that Japan needed an occasional change in government 'to invigorate and cleanse the system' (Tani 1992: 99). But this change was many years in coming. When the end of the one-party dominant regime finally came in 2009, it was seen to be of seismic proportion, 'an electoral super earthquake', as the eminent Japan scholar Arthur Stockwin termed it (Stockwin 2011: 18). This 'political earthquake' has seemingly changed Japan from an 'uncommon' to a 'common' democracy through an emerging two-party competitive system. With the LDP back in power, one might interpret that an era of truly competitive party politics has dawned in Japan. However, it is still early days and may take some time for a real competitive culture to take deeper roots in the body polity.

Associated with the LDP rule was 'money politics' and corruption. 'Money politics' came to play a major role in Japanese political life after 1960 (Kataoka 1992: 15), followed by 'machine politics' that took centre stage with Kakuei Tanaka's political style in the 1970s. Johnson observed that under Tanaka, 'money was indeed the mother's milk of politics and whoever controlled the largest amounts of it in the political system, controlled the system' (Johnson 1995: 193). The average money required to win a parliamentary seat ran into millions of yen. Political scandals involving huge sums of money made headline news nationally and internationally. Best known were the Lockheed scandal involving Prime Minister Tanaka (1972–1974) himself and later the Recruit and Sagawa Kyubin scandals in the 1980s and early 1990s involving key LDP political figures such as Shin Kanemaru. Such large-scale political scandals have not surfaced in Japanese politics in recent years, although traces of them still linger through the alleged money-related scandal involving former LDP heavyweight Ichiro Ozawa, who left the party in 1993 and since then has been responsible for creating alternative political parties including the Democratic Party of Japan, which he abandoned in July 2012 to form yet another new party called People's Life First (*Kokumin seikatsu ga dai'ichi*). Ozawa's political career is nearing the end as his newly-formed Japan Future Party (*Nippon Mirai no To*) suffered an embarrassing setback by winning only nine of the 480 lower house seats in the 2012 election and none at the 2013 upper house elections.

The patron–client relationship reflected in the LDP's special dispensation to the interest groups and their affiliates that mattered most for the party's electoral successes is also on the decline. Politically the most protected and heavily compensated interest group, the agriculture sector, has been hit hard over the last two decades, but most notably with the DPJ coming to power. Special interest representation in both politics and bureaucracy has shown some signs of decline, as George Mulgan (2011) explains in her study of the agriculture group.

The other aspect that made Japan appear to be a less democratic state was the close nexus between the LDP and the bureaucracy. Debate has raged for years about which of these two holds greater power and influence on policymaking in Japan. Strong arguments have been made that bureaucrats have enjoyed disproportionate influence over politicians. Some observers even claimed that in Japan bureaucrats rule while politicians reign (Johnson 1982, 1995). Muramatsu and Krauss (1984) argued that politicians play a key role despite influential bureaucrats. For Ramseyer and Rosenbluth (1993) and Muramatsu (2004), on the other hand, bureaucrats are essentially subservient to their political masters; these scholars argue that politicians are principals while bureaucrats are agents. While opinion is divided on the precise nature and degree of bureaucrats' power, Japanese bureaucrats are known to play a dominant role in national political decision-making, even after government attempts in recent years to reform this situation.

It is broadly accepted that in a democratic system the role of the public service is to implement laws and policies while politicians as the elected representatives make laws and policies. However, Japan's pre-war legacy of bureaucratic dominance continued into the post-war period, mainly because the public service remained untouched when sweeping political reforms were carried out by the Occupation authorities following Japan's defeat in the Second World War. Perhaps not surprisingly then, the view that the bureaucratic system needed to be reformed became prevalent. The short-lived political interim when the LDP was out of office after the 1993 general elections raised the prospect of some change in this direction.

The political strategist who masterminded the long-ruling LDP's defeat in 1993 was Ichiro Ozawa. One of his reform platforms was to weaken the influence of bureaucrats to make them more responsive politically through a number of changes, such as restricting their role of answering questions in the Diet, upgrading parliamentary vice ministers, adding politicians to key ministries as political counsellors and so forth (Johnson 1995: 228). But this reform and others were stalled when the LDP sprang back quickly to elected office and some of the reforms supported by the non-LDP Hosokawa government (1993–1994) did not mature. More recently, cases of inefficiency and corruption in the bureaucracy have tarnished its image of infallibility. In the twenty-first century in particular, reforms have been introduced to make bureaucracy less powerful (Jain 2002: 20–21). The DPJ especially has pledged to make bureaucracy responsible, accountable and efficient. But redistribution of power back to elected politicians is slow in the face of bureaucratic resistance and a culture of bureaucratic dominance that has existed for more than a century.

The relationship between politicians and bureaucrats is just one area of evolving change. Another is the system of hierarchical, time-bound promotion that has long defined Japan's bureaucratic structure, with its separate promotional paths for career and non-career bureaucrats. Changes now being considered will likely revolutionize the national government and the bureaucratic system, as Inatsugu has argued (2011: 47). In light of the 2011 Fukushima nuclear disaster, the role of the Ministry of Economy, Trade and Industry (METI, formerly MITI that won accolades for its industrial policy that drove Japan's spectacular post-war economic growth) has come under the spotlight. Public scrutiny has been much more serious than ever following the 1996 revelation that Ministry of Health and Welfare officials had concealed evidence that HIV-tainted blood was being given to patients (Inoguchi 1997: 104–105).

More recent assessments present a rather positive picture of Japanese democracy, especially since Junichiro Koizumi became prime minister (2001–2006). Kabashima and Steel, for example, describe Japan as a 'dynamic democracy' and call the prevalent view of Japanese politics as stagnant and essentially undemocratic a myth. They argue that now government increasingly acts in the 'interests of citizens', that is, serving 'the average voter's preferences' (Kabashima and Steel 2010: 1). Their assessment indicates that the old practices and processes that gave special dispensation to a select group through a clientelist system are weakening. They argue for an 'increasing accountability in a society in which citizens have more tools to judge government performance and punish or reward accordingly and the government shows increasing sensitivity to these judgements' (Kabashima and Steel 2010: 2).

Assessing Japanese democracy in the light of recent developments, especially during the prime ministership of Koizumi and the subsequent defeat of the LDP and formation of a DPJ government, Inoguchi and Jain have argued that the old karaoke style of democracy where 'bureaucrats provided political leaders with scripts on policy statements' (Inoguchi and Jain 2011) has changed to kabuki-style democracy of direct communication, engagement and responsiveness. They explained how Japan is moving away from a classical form of representative democracy to what Keane has called 'monitory democracy': 'Whereas representative democracy has intermediary institutions between government and people, monitory democracy makes it critical for government and people to interact directly and intermittently with limited interference by intermediate-level societal groups' (Inoguchi and Jain 2011: 6).

Japan's democratic credentials are also reinforced through some key indicators based on international comparisons. First, I looked at the 2011 report prepared by the Economic Intelligence Unit *The Democracy Index 2011*, which categorizes the world's democracies into two types: full democracies and flawed democracies. The Index takes into account a combination of indicators: electoral processes and pluralism, functioning of government, political participation, political culture and civil liberties. Only 25 countries in the world were assessed as full democracies, with only two of these in Asia: Japan and South Korea. Japan's overall score was 8.08 out of 10 and it ranked 21 out of the 25 full democracies (Economic Intelligence Unit 2011). This ranking suggests shortcomings by the *Democracy Index* measures, but in general these results reinforce my argument that Japan is a robust and fully functioning democracy.

Second, I examined the Freedom House 2013 annual report, which ranks countries on their civil liberties and political rights conditions. Ranking of 1 represents the most free and 7 the least free. The freedom status has three categories: free, partly free and not free. Japan ranks as a 'free' nation with a score of 1 for political rights and 2 for civil liberties (Freedom House 2013). Japan is in the same league as South Korea. These rankings suggest the relative strength of the nation's political institutions and electoral system, and the lesser strength of the exercise and protection of civil liberties – a comment on the nature as well as the solidity of democracy in Japan.

The third survey I consulted was the corruption index developed by Transparency International (2011). Here a score of 0 indicates highly corrupt and 10 corruption free. Japan and Germany share number 14 position with an overall score of 8, much higher than the UK, France and the USA. This scorecard suggests the relative inaccuracy of the popular image that Japanese politics is highly corrupt. Indeed, the only country in Asia ranked higher than Japan was Singapore and the next in Asia after Japan was Taiwan, ranked at 32, while South Korea was ranked at 43.

On the internationally recognized standards of *Democracy Index*, Freedom House and Transparency International, Japan performs reasonably well. The indicators they use position Japan very well internationally and as an Asian leader in terms of national democratic health. Nevertheless, there is room for improvement, as I discuss later in this chapter.

Democracy in action at subnational level

Japan's local or subnational governments (SNGs) at all levels – prefecture, city, town and village – tell a story rather different from that at the national level portrayed briefly above. At the SNG level we clearly see democracy in action from and by the grassroots of society – manifest particularly in political dynamism, change in elected leaders drawn from different political persuasions, greater public participation in civic life and better representation of the citizens and their expressed interests. All of these features enrich the democratic experience of the people of Japan and their political behaviour.

Typical of democracy in action, at this level of governance the people are physically closer to their governing bodies and so have better opportunity for direct participation in democratic processes. But they are also closer to their SNG representatives because of the structure of the political system. Whereas the national level operates under the Westminster system, the structure at the SNG level resembles that of the presidential system where the people elect both the chief political executive and local assembly members by direct vote.

In the immediate post-war period when Japan's national mantra was 'economic growth', most political heads of SNGs were elected from the ranks of the conservative party, which also ruled at the national level, making it easier for local leaders to bring home the political bacon through their direct pipelines to the national politicians. This system worked for some years, until the practical consequences of economic resurgence and the intensive industrialization and urbanization that enabled it began to register in the daily lives of large swathes of the population, particularly in urban areas. As people on the ground in their growing urban communities faced difficult issues such as shortages of urban housing, of medical facilities and of childcare centres, and ultimately serious consequences for their quality of life from industrial pollution, they turned to their local leaders to address these problems. From here on, the local political landscape began to change swiftly. The SNGs responded creatively and with some flexibility to meet the needs of the people who were closer to their SNGs on the ground in their own locality than to the national government perhaps miles away in the national capital. This was true even among those who lived in Tokyo but nonetheless turned to their SNGs. With their SNGs the people could generally make their voices heard – putting human flesh and blood on the institutional bones of democracy through political activity in the streets and local community groups.

Since conservative local leadership ignored the rising mountain of social and welfare issues faced especially by urban communities, local elections swept into office a large number of left-leaning political chief executives. Most progressive (*kakushin*) leaders were backed by leftist parties, mainly comprising the socialists and communists that had languished politically at the national level where the conservatives dominated. During this period from the late 1960s until the early 1980s, democratic processes at the SNG level matured. The people created their own citizen movements against industrial pollution and unresponsive leaders across Japan, forcing many local conservative leaders from power and installing progressives who were responsive to their needs and voices (Steiner *et al.* 1980).

Although Japan has a centralized governance system and SNGs depend largely on the national government for their finances and other needs, this has not stopped local leaders from challenging the national government and initiating innovative policies way ahead of their national counterparts. Many progressive local leaders initiated policies that set higher standards in social welfare benefits and pollution control than those of the national government. The national government, after initially offering some resistance, ultimately co-opted those policy initiatives in the national policy agenda. Tani observed that political parties and their leaders at the local level had 'plenty of chances to try their policies, despite the centralization of administrative power and the weak financial basis of most local governments', circumstances that enabled them to present 'an alternative to [existing] Japanese politics' (Tani 1992: 90, 92).

The new political behaviour of citizen participation and local government openness and responsiveness injected by progressive local administrations did not disappear with the end of the progressive administrations in the mid-1980s. It had created a new political culture. A new breed of independent reformist leaders (*kaikakuha*) and other SNG heads who inherited this culture continued seeking to best satisfy the interests of their local communities (Jain 2004). Even now, although a quarter of a century later and with many of the prefectural governors and other local leaders in fact retired bureaucrats from the central ministries, they, too, often work to serve local interests as elected leaders rather than blatantly representing central government interests. Citizens' responses at grassroots level to community needs and political inertia in the 1970s effectively embedded lasting democratic practices and ethos into the nation's political culture.

In the post-progressive era, greater access to government information has been one particular area where SNGs have played a pioneering role that enhances the democratic climate. Many established freedom of information ordinances, after the first in 1982 by the small SNG of Kaneyama in Yamagata prefecture. In 1994, the mayor of Niseko town in Hokkaido prefecture, with a population of about 4,500, set a precedent by making many kinds of information publicly available, including public access to all meetings held at the level of section chiefs. SNGs nationwide dispatched teams to observe Niseko's initiatives (*Asahi Shinbun* 1999). By 2005, almost all SNGs in Japan had passed ordinances to broaden information disclosure to the public. Similarly, SNGs moved to recognize the importance of personal privacy and after the first ordinances to protect personal information were established in the mid-1980s, two decades later more than 98 per cent of SNGs had adopted these ordinances (Takao 2007: 76–78). Importantly, in all of these issues and in many others towards more democratic practice since the late 1960s, SNGs took the lead role. The national government then followed SNGs' initiatives.

In more recent years, municipal charters (*jichi kihon jorei*) or local constitutions (*jichitai no kenpo*) are becoming a norm of local governance in Japan (Tsujiyama 2003; Kisa and Osaka 2003). Their purpose is to build trust between citizens and administrative bodies of SNGs and clarify the role that both sides are to play in local governance. Takanobu Tsujiyama of Jichi Soken, a leading local government research institute in Tokyo, has established a database of Japanese municipal governments that have established a municipal charter. By the end of April 2008, 126 of about 1,700 municipal governments had done so since 2001 when the first was established by Niseko town, which was at the forefront of freedom of information action in the early 1990s.[1] Many municipalities now use the term 'citizens' (*shimin*) rather than 'residents' (*jumin*). The charter of the city of Tama in Tokyo (Article 3 [2]), for example, includes under the category of 'citizens' all those who live, work, study or are engaged in business and other forms of activity within the city's municipal areas irrespective of their actual place of residence (Ohsugi 2007). Through these charters, municipalities are establishing new by-laws leading to greater participation of local residents in administration and decision-making processes.

Local heads and elected representatives whose policy preferences do not resonate with the community are often subject to referenda and recalls. Elected local representatives who promoted unwanted public works facilities, such as dams, nuclear power plants and so forth, have faced such referenda and recalls (Jain 2000; Lam 2005), which have served as important instruments for grassroots democracy. Very often such unpopular leaders are replaced by those who are willing to listen to the people's voice. Yasuo Tanaka, who served as governor of Nagano Prefecture from 2000 to 2006, was an extreme example of reformist leaders. When the prefecture's people elected him as governor he halted the construction of dams and a number of other public works projects and made new policies to tighten environment laws (Nathan 2004). His actions were so non-traditional and anti-business (mainly construction industry) but pro-people and transparent that the local assembly (conservative members) revolted and passed a no-confidence motion forcing him to resign two years after he was first elected. But Tanaka was so popular among voters that he won the election again and served as governor for another term of four years.

The recent rise of Toru Hashimoto on the political scene of Osaka – first as governor and then from December 2011 as mayor of Osaka – clearly demonstrates rising dissatisfaction with the national government's status quo, go-slow policy, even under a DPJ government that promised through its electoral manifesto to fast track political decentralization and give more power to localities through devolution (Jain 2011). The messy politics at the national level that is failing to respond satisfactorily to popular needs is again creating conditions that prompt people to push at local level for greater participation and local democratic processes.

Toru Hashimoto is gradually emerging as a national figure and steering Japanese politics in a new direction, away from the nationally-based party system. It was for the first time at the 2012 general election that a regional political party – Japan Restoration Party (*Nippon Ishin no Kai*) – was launched nationally as a third force in Japanese politics and gained 54 seats, only slightly behind the DPJ, which won just 57 seats. Former Tokyo Governor Shintaro Ishihara and some other high-profile local political figures have also supported Hashimoto (Jain 2012).

New research is producing mounting evidence that developments at local levels – referenda and recall, transparency through information disclosure, and emergence of new political leaders – are embedding democracy more deeply in Japan. The message is clear that the national government cannot simply sit on its hands and do nothing to respond to requests for policy change that meets the needs of the people at large. Martin has observed that grassroots political action 'has slowly forced the national elite political establishment to respond to demands to deepen democracy' (Martin 2011: 24). Public distrust in both politics and national level politicians coexists with voters satisfied with democracy 'because grassroots citizenship practices sustain the belief that voters can exercise greater control over political elites, starting from the ground up' (Martin 2011: 46). For roughly the past four decades SNGs have been the political conduit for the people and fuller democratic process is the national outcome.

Grassroots: civil society

Beyond the subnational government level, the increasing role of civil society has helped to further mature Japanese democracy. Grassroots activities and civil society have long been part of the Japanese polity but, according to Chan (2011: 130), have come to occupy a critical role in Japan since the 1980s. Civil society is developed through the activities of societal agents such as NGOs, NPOs, social media, the Internet, volunteer groups, and any other types of social networks. All of these strengthen democratic institutions and practices by enhancing participation and representation, enabling public input to government decision-making, popularizing public contributions to political life in communities and other political processes. The rising importance of civil society can be seen clearly in the wake of the 3/11 triple disaster, when citizens from most walks of life rallied together to support suffering communities after the March 2011 earthquake, tsunami and nuclear crisis.

Civic groups have played a role in civic life since the pre-war period when they were influenced and socialized by state guidance and worked broadly as agents for the state (Garon 1998). Their efficacy as independent actors has become more prominent only recently, especially since a new NPO law was passed in 1988. Kawato and Pekkanen (2008: 193–195) have observed that despite its positive impact on democracy through improving participation, representation, and accountability, this legislation has not fundamentally changed Japanese civil society or state–civil society relations; improvement to the quality of Japanese democracy is less dramatic than many proponents had hoped for.

Others have a different view. Schwartz and Pharr (2003), for example, argue that the literature presents clear evidence that civil society is taking deeper roots in Japan. Ikeda and Richey observe of Japan that 'activity in voluntary associations and daily social networks follows the same logic and provides the same benefits as proposed by social capitalists in the West' (2012: 1) and that because so, in Japan 'democracy is basically as deliberative and participatory as in such countries as the United States' (2012: 123). Haddad has concluded similarly from her case study research of two citizen groups that through groups like these, Japanese citizens have democratized their political culture at the grassroots. She argues that non-Western democracies like Japan require 'not only the modification of a traditional political culture but also the development of new, indigenous, democratic ideas and practices' and Japan has clearly achieved these (Haddad 2010: 997). Elsewhere she states emphatically that 'Japan's volunteer organizations have helped Japan continually develop its democracy by revitalizing and renewing its political culture in ways that make its government more transparent and accountable and its civic organizations more open and diverse' (Haddad 2011: 141).

While opinions and overall assessment vary, the response of civil society to the 3/11 triple disaster attests firmly that civil society in Japan is now deep-rooted. The government's slow and unsatisfactory response has heightened public frustration and distrust towards political leaders and public officials, forcing large numbers of residents to turn to civil society groups to contribute or to receive desperately needed effective action. Aldrich writes, 'A civil society that for decades has appeared weak and non-participatory has awakened and citizens are carrying out bottom-up responses to the accident, effecting change with grassroots science and activism' (2012: 1).

Government and some corporate responses to the Fukushima nuclear disaster resemble those of the Minamata pollution case from 1956 when government–big-business collusion used lies, cover up and deceit to deny responsibility to protect citizens poisoned by chemical flow-on from Chisso corporation into Minamata Bay. But in the second decade of the twenty-first century, Japan's political economy and its people have changed considerably from the 1950s when the country was still on a narrowly conceived path to high economic growth and the people generally believed in and supported the authorities, recognizing that they had little option. More than half a century later, Japanese civil society today is positioned like much of civil society worldwide – much more active, better informed and networked through social media. And no longer so dependent on mainstream media, the people recognize that they need not – indeed, should not – trust government and business until they are informed widely by various sources that are now easily accessible.

Civil society in Japan, as elsewhere, actively uses the Internet as a social medium to connect volunteer and citizen groups for advocacy and activism in the public sphere. They also use this medium in their attempts to influence public policy on domestic and international issues (e.g. the controversial dispatch of Japan's Self Defence Force to Iraq (Ducke 2007: 124–137). On nuclear radiation, most people do not trust the government or the energy producer TEPCO that owned the Fukushima plant and for the sake of cost saving failed to maintain it effectively until the government socialized the plant after the disaster for the public purse to absorb the enormous losses. Many people understand they must instead look for alternative sources of more reliable information that they can access easily through social media. And they do. Many have posted on Internet sites their disbelief in reassurances by government authorities and TEPCO about nuclear safety issues; one popular site reported 600,000 such comments during the six months following the Fukushima explosion (Gliona 2012).

Mothers of young children, for example, have established a parents' group and stay connected through Twitter and Facebook. Social groups conduct their own radiation measurements, rejecting government readings that they suspect are in league with big business and underplay the true levels. The Fukushima Network for Saving Children from Radiation (Kodomo Fukushima), for example, is at the forefront of efforts pushing the Japanese government to abandon the 20 milli-sievert limit of radiation exposure for children. This is part of their strategy to force the authorities into swifter and much more rigorous clean-up of schools to reduce radiation exposure of local children and provide them with space where they can play outdoors at school without harmful exposure to radiation. A leading Japanese newspaper observed, 'While still fledgling, it's the kind of grass-roots activism that some say Japan needs to shake up a political system that has allowed the country's problems to fester for years'.[2] The Radiation Defense Project (RDP) also arose from a Facebook social media group and is now an information source for many in Japan who are concerned about radiation levels. The RDP is conducting soil tests independently to find out more about radioactive particles from the Fukushima Daiichi nuclear accident.[3] More than 150,000 follow Tweets sent by nuclear physicist Ryugo Hayano, sharing his view that mainstream media's stories are neither complete nor accurate (Gliona 2012). The same rationale applies to television. OurPlanet TV, launched originally as an alternative medium after the 9/11 terrorist attacks in the USA, became a reliable source on nuclear issues following the Fukushima nuclear disaster, and people flocked to it while rejecting the mainstream media. In the wake of this disaster, OurPlanet TV viewership shot up from 1,000 to more than 100,000 as people sought alternative sources presenting more trustworthy information (Gliona 2012).

Popular frustration at the government's inept response, still clearly bound up in the long-standing government–business alliance, has again sparked a wave of large public protests, much like the government ineptitude on severe industrial pollution in the 1960s. Today, as distrust grows in government and business (central government in particular and TEPCO in the case of the Fukushima nuclear meltdown) through their reported lies, deceit and cover up, more and more people are attracted to direct appeal and direct action through their own networks rather than waiting for government and bureaucrats to take serious remedial action. Many have abandoned their long-held trust in the mainstream media. Aldrich observes, 'protests are significant not only because they are relatively rare and indicate new levels of activism, but also because the very act of participation in public protest deepens Japan's democracy and enhances the presence of often unrepresented demographics, such as urban workers and youth, in the public sphere' (Aldrich 2012: 9).

Direct action has returned to common place in Japan. These actions are less about income inequality than those of Occupy Wall Street and the larger Occupy movement in the USA and incipiently in other locations. They oppose nuclear power plants and government failure, now expressed as 'Occupy Kasum-igaseki' – where government ministry buildings are concentrated in central

Tokyo. Anti-nuclear activists have occupied public space in front of the building housing METI (the ministry that oversees administration of nuclear energy and is responsible for Japan's overall energy policy), including two semi-permanent tents with banners declaring 'we oppose nuclear power plants' and 'no more Fukushima'. Ryota Sono, the anti-nuclear activist leading Occupy METI, has captured the details of these movements in his book (Sono 2011).[4] Rikkyo University politics professor Ikuo Gonoi identifies these movements and direct actions as significant examples of direct democracy in Japan.[5] They exemplify how direct democracy is alive and well – on the street, if not literally kicking – in Japan today.

These are still early days for the rise of direct democracy. We are yet to see both what it will bring the government to do and what the movement itself will do to achieve its aims for the well-being of Japanese society and with international counterparts for global society, particularly through reducing dependence on nuclear energy. Research will continue to cast light on changing relations between the national government and local government on the one hand and the state and society on the other, as social media further enable civil society to reach its members and its representatives directly and indirectly (Kingston 2012).

Conclusion

This chapter has argued that Japan is not a perfect democracy, which no democracy can be in practice. Assessment of Japan's democracy has long been divided; even in the 1970s, eminent Japan observer Ezra Vogel lauded Japan as 'now a more effective democracy than America' (Vogel 1979: 97), while others criticized serious institutional and procedural deficiencies. But many of these weaknesses have been addressed over the past two decades, especially since 1993 when the LDP lost its long-held grip on national government for the first time. The LDP's quick return to the national helm slowed this process, but the forces of reform unleashed in 1993 could not be stopped. Defeat of the LDP at the 2009 general election ushered in a new era in Japanese politics beyond 'uncommon democracy' with the possibility of truly competitive party politics. Party disunity, leadership changes and even split have damaged the DPJ government's policy performance. Party politics in Japan is set to change again with Ichiro Ozawa's fading influence as seen in the poor performance of his Japan Future Party, created just prior to the 2012 election and the flamboyant leader Toru Hashimoto launching his party (Japan Restoration Party) nationally with great electoral success. Yet by comparison with Japan's economic boom years up to the early 1990s, political representatives now better understand their responsibility, are inclined towards greater transparency and accountability, and have continued to introduce reforms that strengthen democratic life (Haddad 2010). As Rosenbluth observes, Japan's democracy is doubtlessly healthier today than ever, despite political mess at the national level (Rosenbluth 2011). In light of the Fukushima nuclear disaster and poor national government response, concerns have been naturally expressed about the quality and nature of Japanese democracy (Asano 2012; Rafferty 2012). But as I have explained above, Japanese democracy has never been perfect and there is ample room for improvement. As civil society matures and a more competitive political environment emerges, democracy in Japan will strengthen.

Subnational government dynamism, including greater transparency of government operations and freedom of information, and creation of local constitutions, indicates how bottom-up action from grassroots has produced a fully institutionalized democracy, which has produced a more democratic nation. So it is among the people themselves, through greater direct democracy and stronger civil society. Democracy may remain forever on the horizon, as Vaclav Havel presciently observed. But so long as its distant presence serves as a beacon to the people and their governments to aspire to life where well-informed citizens are governed fairly by fairly elected representatives, democracy has a palpable presence within communities large and small. That is true of Japan today, as this chapter has tried to convey.

Notes

1 Professor Takanobu Tsujiyama of the Jichi Soken (Japan Research Institute for Local Government) made a copy of the database available to this author in November 2008.
2 Can Web-savvy activist moms change Japan? *Mainichi* (2011).
3 www.radiationdefense.jp/investigation/?lang=en.
4 In December 2011, I interviewed Mr Sono in one of the tents outside METI.
5 Professor Gonoi of Tokyo's Rikkyo University made this point during my discussion with him in December 2011.

References

Aldrich, Daniel P. (2012) *Post-Crisis Japanese Nuclear Policy: From Top-Down Directives to Bottom-Up Activism*, Asia Pacific Issues, East–West Center, No. 103, January.
Asahi Shinbun, 11 July 1999
Asano, Shiro (2012) 'Minshushugi no kiki' (Crisis of democracy), *Governance* (Japanese), June.
Bowen, Roger W. (2003) *Japan's Dysfunctional Democracy*, New York: M. E. Sharp.
Calder, Kent E. (1991) *Crisis and Compensation: Public Policy and Political Stability in Japan 1949–1986*, Princeton: Princeton University Press.
Chan, Jennifer (2011) 'Civil society and global citizenship in Japan', in Takashi Inoguchi and Purnendra Jain (eds), *Japanese Politics Today: From Karaoke to Kabuki Democracy*, New York: Palgrave Macmillan.
Ducke, Isa (2007) *Civil Society and the Internet in Japan*, London: Routledge.
Economic Intelligence Unit (2011) 'The Democracy Index 2011'; www.eiu.com/public/thankyou_download.aspx?activity=reg&campaignid=DemocracyIndex2011 accessed 29 February 2012.
Freedom House (2013) 'Freedom in the World 2012'; http://freedomhouse.org/report/freedom-world/freedom-world-2012 accessed 1 March 2013.
Garon, Sheldon (1998) *Moulding Japanese Minds: The State in Everyday Life*, Princeton: Princeton University Press.

George Mulgan, Aurelia (2011) 'The farm lobby', in Takashi Inoguchi and Purnendra Jain (eds) *Japanese Politics Today: From Karaoke to Kabuki Democracy*, New York: Palgrave Macmillan.

Gliona, John M. (2012) 'Post-disaster, Japanese are less trusting of authority', *Los Angeles Times*, reprinted in *Daily Yomiuri*, 9 January.

Haddad, Mary Alice (2010) 'The State-in-society Approach to the study of democratization with examples from Japan', *Democratization*, 17(5), October, 997–1023.

Haddad, Mary Alice (2011) 'Volunteer organizations (re)making democracy in Japan', in Alisa Gaunder (ed.) *Routledge Handbook of Japanese Politics*, London and New York: Routledge, pp. 140–151.

Herzog, Peter J. (1993) *Japan's Pseudo Democracy*, Kent: Japan Library.

Ike, Nobutaka (1972) *Japanese Politics: Patron–Client Democracy, New York: Knopf.*

Ikeda, Ken'ichi and Sean Richey (2012) *Social Networks and Japanese Democracy: The Beneficial Impact of Interpersonal Communication in East Asia*, London, New York: Routledge.

Inatsugu, Hiroaki (2011) 'The system of bureaucrats in Japan', in Takashi Inoguchi and Purnendra Jain (eds) *Japanese Politics Today: From Karaoke to Kabuki Democracy*, New York: Palgrave Macmillan.

Inoguchi, Takashi (1997) 'Japanese bureaucracy: coping with new challenges', in Purnendra Jain and Takashi Inoguchi (eds) *Japanese Politics Today: Beyond Karaoke Democracy?* Melbourne: Macmillan.

Inoguchi, Takashi and Purnendra Jain (2011) 'Introduction: from Karaoke to Kabuki democracy: Japanese politics today', in Takashi Inoguchi and Purnendra Jain (eds) *Japanese Politics Today: From Karaoke to Kabuki Democracy*, New York: Palgrave Macmillan.

Jain, Purnendra (2000) '*Jumin Tohyo* and the Tokushima Anti-Dam Movement in Japan: the people have spoken', *Asian Survey*, 40(4), 551–570.

Jain, Purnendra (2002) 'Much ado about nothing? The limited scope of political reform in Japan', in Javed Maswood (ed.) *Japan: Change and Continuity*, London: Routledge-Curzon.

Jain, Purnendra (2004) 'Local political leadership in Japan: a harbinger of systematic change in Japanese politics', *Policy and Society*, 23(1), 58–87.

Jain, Purnendra (2011) 'Osaka Voters Revolt against the Status Quo', *Asia Times Online*, 1 December; www.atimes.com/atimes/Japan/ML01Dh01.html accessed 24 July 2013.

Jain, Purnendra (2012) 'Third Force' Parties Crowd Japan's Political Scene; *East Asia Forum*, 6 December; www.eastasiaforum.org/2012/12/06/third-force-parties-crowd-japans-national-political-scene/ accessed 25 July 2013.

Johnson, Chalmers (1982) *MITI and the Japanese Miracle: The Growth of Industrial Policy, 1925–1975*, Stanford: Stanford University Press.

Johnson, Chalmers (1995) *Japan: Who Governs? The Rise of the Developmental State*, New York: W. W. Norton.

Kabashima, Ikuo and Gill Steel (2010) *Changing Politics in Japan*, Ithaca: Cornell University Press.

Kataoka, Tetsuya (ed.) (1992) *Creating Single-Party Democracy: Japan's Postwar Political System*, Stanford, California: Hoover Institution Press.

Kawato, Yuko and Robert Pekkanen (2008) 'Civil society and democracy; reforming non-profit organization law', in Sherry L. Martin and Gill Steel (eds) *Democratic Reform in Japan: Assessing the Impact*, Boulder: Lynne Rienner.

Kingston, Jeff (ed.) (2012) *Natural Disaster and Nuclear Crisis in Japan: Response and Recovery after Japan's 3/11*, London, New York: Routledge.

Kisa, Shigeo and Osaka Seiji (2003) *Watashitachi no machi no kempō* (Our town constitution), Tokyo: Nihon Keizai Hyōronsha.

Kobayashi, Yoshiaki (2012) *Malfunctioning Democracy in Japan*, Lanham: Lexington Books.

Lam, Peng Er (2005) 'Local governance: The role of referenda and the rise of independent governors', in Glenn Hook (ed.) *Contested Governance in Japan: Sites and Issues*, New York: RoutledgeCurzon.

Mainichi (2011) Can Web-savvy activist moms change Japan? 30 December; previously available at http://mdn.mainichi.jp/features/news/20111230p2g00m0fe009000c.html accessed 31 December 2011.

Martin, Sherry L. (2011) *Popular Democracy in Japan: How Gender and Community are Changing Modern Electoral Politics*, Ithaca: Cornell University Press.

Muramatsu, Michio (2004) 'An Arthritic Japan? The Relationship between Politicians and Bureaucrats', *Asia Program Special Report*, 117, Woodrow Wilson International Center for Scholars, 26–33.

Muramatsu, Michio and Ellis S. Krauss (1984) 'Bureaucrats and politicians in policymaking: the case of Japan', *American Political Science Review*, 78(1), 126–146.

Nathan, John (2004) *Japan Unbound: A Volatile Nation's Quest for Pride and Purpose*, Boston: Houghton Mifflin.

Ohsugi, Satoru (2007) 'People and Local Government: Residential Participation in the Management of Local Governments', *Papers on the Local Governance System and its Implementation in Selected Fields in Japan*, No. 1, Tokyo, CLAIR/COSLOG/GRIPS.

Pempel, T. J. (1982) *Policy and Politics in Japan: Creative Conservatism*, Philadelphia: Temple University Press.

Pempel, T. J. (ed.) (1990) *Uncommon Democracies: The One-Party Dominant Regimes*, Ithaca: Cornell University Press.

Rafferty, Kevin (2012) 'The Eerie Silence of Japan's Dying Democracy', *Japan Times Online*, 25 July; previously available at www.japantimes.co.jp/text/eo20120725a3.html accessed 25 July 2012.

Ramseyer, J. Mark and Frances McCall Rosenbluth (1993) *Japan's Political Marketplace*, Cambridge, MA: Harvard University Press.

Rosenbluth, Frances McCall (2011) 'Japan in 2010: messy politics but healthier democracy', *Asian Survey*, January February, 51(1), 41–53.

Scalapino, Robert A. (1953) *Democracy and the Party Movement in Prewar Japan: The Failure of the First Attempt*, Berkeley: University of California Press.

Scheiner, Ethan (2006) *Democracy without Competition: Opposition Failure in a One-Party Dominant State*, Cambridge: Cambridge University Press.

Schwartz, Frank J. and Susan Pharr (eds) (2003) *The State of Civil Society in Japan*, Cambridge: Cambridge University Press.

Sono, Ryota 2011 *Boku ga Toden mae ni tatta wake* (Why I stood in front of the TEPCO Building), Tokyo: Sanichi Shobo.

Steiner, Kurt, E. S. Krauss and S. C. Flanagan (eds) (1980) *Political Opposition and Local Politics in Japan*, Princeton: Princeton University Press.

Stockwin, J. A. A. (2011) 'Political earthquake in Japan: how much of a difference will it make?', in Purnendra Jain and Brad Williams (eds) *Japan in Decline: Fact or Fiction?* Folkestone: Global Oriental.

Takao, Yasuo (2007) *Reinventing Japan: From Merchant Nation to Civic Nation*, New York: Palgrave Macmillan.

Tani, Satomi (1992) 'The Japan Socialist Party before the mid-1960s: an analysis of its stagnation', in Kataoka Tetsuya (ed.) *Creating Single-Party Democracy*, Stanford, California: Hoover Institution Press.

Transparency International (2011) 'Corruption Perceptions Index'; http://cpi.transparency.org/cpi2011/results/ accessed 29 February 2012.

Tsujiyama, Takanobu (2003) *Jichikihonjoreiwa naze hitsuyoka* (Why are local charters essential?) Tajimi City Booklet No. 5, Tokyo: Kojin no yusha.

Vogel, Ezra (1979) *Japan as Number One*, Tokyo: Tuttle.

Woodall, Brian (1996) *Japan under Construction: Corruption, Politics, and Public Works*, Berkeley, California: University of California Press.

2   South Korea's disaffected democracy

Chong-Min Park

Introduction

Over the past quarter of a century South Korea (Korea hereafter) has maintained an electoral democracy and made great strides towards democratic consolidation (Diamond and Shin 2000; Kim 2003). Since the dramatic democratic transition in 1987, Korea has regularly held free and fair elections at all levels of government. The right to vote has been fully guaranteed to all adults and potential access to public office has been open to all citizens. The limits of civil liberties and political rights have been greatly expanded. If democracy is characterized by universal suffrage, free and fair elections, and multiparty competition (Dahl 1971), Korea's current political regime meets these minimal standards of 'thin' democracy. More importantly, achieving two peaceful transfers of political power, Korea became the first third-wave democracy in East Asia to pass 'the two-turnover test' of democratic consolidation (Huntington 1991). What is more remarkable is that steady democratic progress was made despite in 1997 the worst economic crisis since the Korean War. In the midst of a recent global 'democratic recession', Korean democracy never lost its resilience and vibrancy (Diamond 2008). There is no doubt that Korea is one of the most consolidated third-wave democracies in East Asia (Chu *et al.* 2008).

Yet, various public opinion surveys indicate growing political disaffection among ordinary Koreans, especially since the second decade of democracy (Park 2011). For instance, citizen preference for democracy declined from 65 per cent in 1996 to 43 per cent in 2006. Satisfaction with the working of democracy dropped from 61 per cent in 2003 to 48 per cent in 2006. More ominous is the erosion of confidence in political institutions. Trust in the National Assembly plummeted from 49 per cent in 1996 to 7 per cent in 2006. Likewise, trust in political parties plunged from 39 per cent in 1996 to 9 per cent in 2006. Rising popular disaffection with democratic institutions was accompanied by growing public disengagement from conventional politics. For instance, voter turnout for presidential elections dropped from 89 per cent in 1987 to 63 per cent in 2007, while that for parliamentary elections fell from 76 per cent in 1988 to 46 per cent in 2008.

For the last two decades ordinary Koreans have lost their confidence in political institutions of representation, remained dissatisfied with democratic performance, become sceptical of democracy as a universal value, and disengaged themselves from conventional politics. As in trilateral advanced democracies (Pharr and Putnam 2000), symptoms of political disaffection constitute an increasingly salient feature of the Korean political landscape. While it is widely known as an East Asian model of democracy and prosperity, Korea appears to have become a nation of political discontent.

This chapter primarily focuses on a recent phenomenon of political disaffection in Korea. By using public opinion data drawn from a series of nationwide sample surveys, we examine how ordinary Koreans evaluate their democratic institutions and practices and how their evaluations have changed especially since the second decade of democracy. In doing so, we shed some light on the nature and sources of the political malaise in one of the most successful third-wave democracies in East Asia.

Institutional democratization

Before exploring how ordinary Koreans evaluate current political institutions and practices, we briefly present the institutional democratization over the last quarter of a century. The democratic transition in Korea resulted in the adoption of a democratic constitution and the holding of a founding election in 1987. Since the transition, a series of democratic institutional reforms have been carried out (Diamond and Shin 2000). Prior to the transition, political institutions and practices had been characterized with limited public contestation for power, executive domination over the legislature and the judiciary, government control of mass media, and curtailment of civil liberties and political rights. The new constitution restored the basic principles and institutions of liberal democracy.

The constitution provides for direct popular election of the president. As in the past, the president represents the state and heads the executive branch of government. Yet, the chief executive's powers are now reduced considerably, while those of the legislative and judicial branches have been expanded greatly. The president's powers regarding emergency decrees and dissolution of the National Assembly have been abolished. In contrast, legislative oversight over the executive has been strengthened and the legislature is no longer a rubber stamp of the executive as in the authoritarian past. The courts have become independent in their rulings and in the appointment of judges, and furthermore a Constitutional Court has been established for strengthening judicial reviews. The limits of political rights and civil liberties are now greatly expanded, although the National Security Law, a potential encroachment on freedom, remains effective. The constitution protects political parties against arbitrary decisions to disband while it requires them to promote internal democracy. The constitution also declares the political neutrality of the military.

Since the transition to democracy, no political parties or politicians have been excluded from the political process. By establishing a level playing field, public contestation for power has become more competitive. Elections have been freely and fairly conducted and their outcomes have honestly reflected voters' choices.

The scope of public offices subject to public contestation has been extended to subnational levels of government. By lowering voting age, the extent of political participation has become more inclusive. The reach and inclusiveness of popular control has been steadily expanded since the transition. Equally significant is that civilian control of the military has become firmly entrenched.

These institutional reforms and practices are reflected in various expert-based assessments of democracy. One of the best-known measures of democracy is Freedom House's ratings of political rights and civil liberties. The scores of each scale range from 1 (most free) to 7 (least free). Korea received an average score of 2.5 in each of the first five years after the transition in 1987, 2.0 in each of the 12 years from 1993 through 2004, and 1.5 in every year since 2005. Thus one of the most widely used indicators of liberal democracy confirms that Korea ranks with the world's most advanced democracies in the West.

Another commonly used indicator of democracy is the Polity IV score, which emphasizes the presence of constraints on the chief executive (Marshall 2013). A single democracy-autocracy score is constructed by subtracting scores on a 10-point autocracy scale from those on a 10-point democracy scale. In each year of the first decade after the transition, Korea received a Polity score of 6, with 7 on the democracy scale and 1 on the autocracy scale. In every year since 1998, it received a Polity score of 8, with 8 on the democracy scale and 0 on the autocracy scale. Although it remains short of a perfect constitutional democracy, Korea has made huge progress in institutionalizing constraints on the executive.

The World Bank's Worldwide Governance Indicators are widely used to monitor good governance. They measure the quality of six dimensions of governance: voice and accountability, political stability and absence of violence or terrorism, government effectiveness, regulatory quality, rule of law, and control of corruption. In each of the years covered since 1996, Korea received positive ratings in all the dimensions. According to its latest report, in 2011 Korea received higher percentile ranking on every dimension except for political stability on which it was a middling performer. Although the indicators lack comparability over time, the pattern of ratings suggests that Korea has improved democratic strength and constitutionalism.

Lastly, according to the Economist Intelligence Unit's *Democracy Index* (Economist Intelligence Unit 2011), whose scores run from 0 to 10, in 2006 Korea was rated a flawed democracy, with a total score of 7.88. In 2008, 2010 and 2011 Korea was rated a full democracy with a total score of 8.01, 8.11 and 8.06, respectively. Among the five general categories (electoral process and pluralism, civil liberties, the functioning of government, political participation, and political culture), in each of the last three years covered, Korea had the highest mark on electoral process and pluralism, while having the lowest mark on political participation. After more than two decades of democratization, Korea emerges as one of the two full democracies in Asia, with the other being Japan.

These expert-based assessments of democracy clearly demonstrate that Korea has made great strides toward institutional democratization over the last quarter of a century. Now the question is whether ordinary Koreans feel the same way about the scope and depth of democratization. In the following sections we examine the state of democracy in Korea from the perspective of ordinary citizens, the final, if not the best, judges. To do this, we utilize public opinion data from the Asian Barometer Survey series (2003, 2006 and 2011) as well as the Korea Democracy Barometer series (1996, 1997, 1998, 1999 and 2001) (Shin and Lee 2006).

Perceived democratic quality

General quality

What is evident is that most ordinary Koreans do not deny that their country is a democracy. When asked about the extent of democracy, those who replied 'a full democracy' constituted only a tiny minority (5 per cent in 2006 and 4 per cent in 2011). However, those who replied 'a democracy with minor problems' accounted for 56 per cent in 2006 and 63 per cent in 2011 whereas those who replied 'a democracy with major problems', 34 per cent in 2006 and 28 per cent in 2011. In contrast, those who replied 'not a democracy' constituted the smallest group (2 per cent in 2006 and 3 per cent in 2011). After more than two decades of democracy nearly everyone admits that they live in a democracy. Yet, perceived levels of democracy varied from one person to another. Only a few considered it a full democracy while most, a flawed democracy. Noteworthy is that among those who found their democracy flawed, those indicating minor problems far outnumbered those indicating major ones. On average, two in three viewed the current regime as either a full or slightly flawed democracy, which suggests that ordinary Koreans have higher standards for democracy than most experts of democratic assessment.

For the last decade, public satisfaction with democratic performance has not improved much. When asked how satisfied or dissatisfied they were with the way democracy worked, those who replied either 'very satisfied' or 'fairly satisfied' accounted for 61 per cent in 2003, 48 per cent in 2006 and 59 per cent in 2011. The level of satisfaction with democracy plunged during the Roh Moo Hyun government and bounced back during the Lee Myung Bak government. The recent rise occurred in the wake of the global economic crisis in 2008–2009, which suggests that economic performance alone may not determine satisfaction with democracy. Whatever the reasons for the drop or rise, citizen satisfaction with democracy apparently was not robust across time. On average, fewer than three in five expressed some degree of satisfaction with democracy, indicating that the supply of democracy remained short of citizen expectations.

Procedural qualities

Both perceived extent of democracy and satisfaction with democracy capture only a general evaluation of democratic performance. Since democracy is a multidimensional phenomenon, both measures are not adequate in ascertaining the extent to which different elements of democracy are supplied. Hence, research on democratic performance seeks to identify dimensions of democratic quality (Lijphart 1999; Altman and Perez-Linan 2002; Morlino *et al.* 2011). Following this line of research, we examine how Koreans evaluate democratic performance in eight dimensions – rule of law, control of corruption, participation, electoral competition, vertical accountability, horizontal accountability, freedom, and equality (Diamond and Morlino 2004). The first six dimensions pertain to procedures of democracy whereas the last two its contents.

First, the rule of law dimension of democratic quality concerns the effectiveness of legal institutions constraining the exercise of government power. For the last five years public assessment of the rule of law remained largely negative. In 2006 when asked how often national government officials abide by the rules, only less than one-fifth (17 per cent) replied either 'always' or 'most of the time.' In the same survey when asked whether they agreed or disagreed with the statement 'Our current courts always punish the guilty even if they are high-ranking officials', only as few as 13 per cent replied either 'strongly agree' or 'agree'. By contrast, in 2011 when asked how often government leaders break the law or abuse their powers, more than a quarter (29 per cent) chose either 'rarely' or 'sometimes'. In the same survey when asked how often officials who commit crimes go unpunished, two-fifths (40 per cent) answered either 'rarely' or 'sometimes'. Although the rule of law apparently had improved over the past five years, it remained far short of citizen expectations. On average, only one in three considered the rule of law working.

Second, control of corruption is an important indicator of the rule of law. According to Transparency International's *Corruption Perception Index*, Korea ranked 50th out of 130 countries surveyed in 2003, 41st out of 163 countries surveyed in 2006, and 43rd out of 182 countries surveyed in 2011. Yet, public perceptions of corruption diverged from the expert assessment. When asked about the extent of corruption in the national government, those who replied either 'hardly anyone' or 'not a lot of officials' accounted for 53 per cent in 2003, 50 per cent in 2006 and 45 per cent in 2011. When asked about the extent of corruption in local governments, those who replied either 'hardly anyone' or 'not a lot of officials' accounted for 56 per cent in 2003, 55 per cent in 2006 and 52 per cent in 2011. Despite various reforms on campaign financing, government transparency, and public service ethics, perceptions of government corruption have deteriorated, albeit slightly. In each of the years covered, only about half considered government corruption controlled.

Third, the participation dimension of democratic quality refers to the condition that practically all adults have the right to vote in the elections of government leaders. Since the democratic transition, there has been no restriction on voting rights, the key political right of democratic citizenship. In fact, even under authoritarian rule no voting right was denied to any segment of the population based on gender or illiteracy, although voters were not free to express their preferences and not all politicians were allowed to run for elective public offices. One of the notable reforms for enhancing participation included lowering voting age limits from age 20 to age 19 in 2005, rendering the political space more inclusive. Nonetheless, ordinary Koreans have disengaged themselves from voting which is non-compulsory. For instance, voter turnout for presidential elections declined from 89 per cent in 1987 (so-called a founding election) to 82 per cent in 1992, 81 per cent in 1997, 71 per cent in 2002 and 63 per cent in 2007, before it turned around with 76 per cent in the most recent election in 2012. Similarly, voter turnout for parliamentary elections fell from 76 per cent in 1988 to 72 per cent in 1992, 64 per cent in 1996, 57 per cent in 2000, 61 per cent in 2004 and 46 per cent in 2008. Although a polling day is set as a legal holiday, the importance ordinary Koreans attach to voting has rapidly declined especially over the last decade.

Consistent with declining voter turnout, citizen political activism appears to be weak. In 2011 when asked whether they agreed or disagreed with the statement 'Most citizens don't make much effort to influence government decisions', only two-fifths (39 per cent) replied either 'strongly disagree' or 'disagree'. In the same survey when asked 'How many people in your neighborhood or community voice their interests and concerns in local affairs', only three-tenths (30 per cent) replied either 'most people' or 'quite a lot of people.' On average, only one in three considered their fellow citizens to be active in the political process. Lower political activism may reflect citizen apathy to or disaffection with the ongoing political order which could undermine the vibrancy of democracy.

Fourth, the electoral competition dimension of democratic quality concerns the extent to which political parties or candidates compete freely and fairly in elections. It presupposes that practically all adults have the right to run for elective offices of government. Since the democratic transition, no politicians or political parties have been denied their rights to compete for power. The fact that there have been two alternations of power since the democratic transition illustrates the competitiveness of presidential elections. The fact that political parties with majority legislative seats frequently changed over the past two decades demonstrates the competitiveness of parliamentary elections as well.

Reflecting such developments, in 2006 when asked about the 2004 parliamentary elections, just more than one-tenth (13 per cent) replied 'completely free and fair' while more than two-fifths (44 per cent), 'free and fair but with minor problems'. In contrast, almost one-fifth (18 per cent) answered 'free and fair with major problems' while only close to one-tenth (9 per cent), 'not free or fair'. Overall, about three in five voters viewed the 2004 parliamentary elections as more or less free and fair. In 2011 when asked about the 2007 presidential elections, a quarter (25 per cent) replied 'completely free and fair' while half (50 per cent), 'free and fair with minor problems'. In contrast, about a tenth (9 per cent) replied 'free and fair with major problems' while only a few (5 per cent), 'not free or fair'. Overall, three in four voters considered the 2007 presidential elections more or less free and fair.

Yet, Korean voters had mixed attitudes toward the quality of electoral contests. When asked whether they agreed or disagreed with the statement 'Political parties or candidates have equal access to the mass media during the elections', two-thirds (66 per cent in 2006 and 65 per cent in 2011) chose either 'strongly agree' or 'agree'. In contrast, when asked 'how often the elections offer the voters a real choice between different parties or candidates', only about a half (47 per cent in 2006 and 51 per cent in 2011) replied either 'always' or 'most of the time'. Although a large majority viewed elections as fair and competitive, only a bare majority considered electoral contests meaningful. Such evaluation may have to do with the nature of political parties in Korea whose electoral support is largely based on regional identity and personal loyalties (Kim 2000). Since they hardly distinguish themselves from one another with distinctive programmes or platforms, elections are mere contests between political parties that looked more or less the same in the eyes of informed voters.

Fifth, the vertical accountability dimension of democratic quality concerns the extent to which voters hold government leaders accountable to their decisions. This type of accountability runs from citizens to government leaders. The fact that there have been two alternations of power since the democratic transition proves the working of vertical accountability. However, vertical accountability requires more than electoral accountability. It means that people are able to monitor the government and demand justification for its decisions even between elections.

When asked whether they agreed or disagreed with the statement 'Between elections the people have no way of holding the government responsible for its actions', 36 per cent in 2006 and 35 per cent in 2011 respectively disagreed. Despite periodic elections at all levels of government, on average, only one in three Koreans considered non-electoral accountability working in off-years between elections. When asked whether they agreed or disagreed with the statement 'People have the power to change a government they don't like', 44 per cent in 2006 and 51 per cent in 2011 respectively agreed. Despite two alternations of power for the past two decades, on average, less than one in two considered popular control effective. Such evaluation may have to do with regional politics in which regional loyalty crucially determines electoral choices, thereby greatly constraining electoral accountability (Kang 2003).

Lastly, the horizontal accountability dimension of democratic quality concerns the effectiveness of institutional checks and balances (Schedler *et al.* 1999). One of the notable institutional reforms in Korea is the establishment and strengthening of horizontal accountability institutions. As noted earlier, institutional reforms restored the principle of limited government, especially separation of power and checks and balances. The power of the executive over other branches of government has been reduced substantially. The National Assembly becomes assertive and the judiciary independent. Especially, the newly created Constitutional Court plays an active role in judicial reviews. Although the executive still has more effective centralized authority than other branches of government, institutional checks and balance of power has been largely reconstituted. Yet, public evaluation of the provision of horizontal accountability institutions remained mixed.

When asked to evaluate the efficacy of legislative oversight, barely half (53 per cent in 2006 and 50 per cent in 2011) said that the National Assembly is either 'very capable' or 'capable' of keeping government in check. Although the National Assembly possesses an array of weapons to influence the executive branch, there existed considerable popular scepticism of the efficacy of legislative control. When asked whether they agreed or disagreed with the statement 'When government leaders break the laws, there is nothing the court can do', only less than half (43 per cent in 2006 and 40 per cent in 2011) chose either 'strongly disagree' or 'disagree'. Despite growing judicial intervention in the decisions of executive agencies, the power of the independent judiciary remained limited in the eyes of the public. Despite institutionalizing constraints on the executive, only less than one in two considered institutional checks and balances working. Perhaps it may have to do with the persistence of political practices and governing styles associated with 'an imperial' or 'delegative' presidency (Im 2004; Lee 2007).

Substantive qualities

If any assessment of democratic quality is to be made in terms of its content, it should include the provision of freedom and equality because they constitute the ultimate goals of democracy. First, the freedom dimension of democratic quality concerns the extent to which political rights and civil liberties are guaranteed. As presented earlier, there has been steady progress in extending the limits of civil liberties and political rights since the democratic transition. Perhaps the last serious obstacle to further extending freedom is the National Security Law, which human rights activists have regarded as a potential encroachment on civil liberties. Roughly consistent with expert-based assessments, ordinary Koreans' evaluation of freedom is largely positive. When asked whether they agreed or disagreed with the statement 'People are free to speak what they think without fear', more than half (57 per cent in 2006 and 52 per cent in 2011) answered either 'strongly agree' or 'agree'. When asked whether they agreed or disagreed with the statement 'People can join any organization they like without fear', nearly two-thirds (64 per cent in 2006 and 66 per cent in 2011) answered either 'strongly agree' or 'agree'. On average, three in five believed that they enjoyed freedoms of speech and association.

The equality dimension of democratic quality here primarily concerns equal treatment by government. The constitution provides for equal treatment of all citizens. Yet, public evaluation of equal treatment in the hands of government remained overwhelmingly unfavourable. In 2006 when asked whether they agreed or disagreed with the statement 'Everyone is treated equally by the government', only a tiny minority (13 per cent) replied either 'strongly agree' or 'agree'. Although the left-leaning government of Roh Moo Hyun pursued policies for more economic and social equality, only one in ten considered treatment by government equal.

In 2011 when asked whether they agreed or disagreed with the statement 'Rich and poor people are treated equally by the government', only a small minority (19 per cent) replied either 'strongly agree' or 'agree'. In view of growing economic inequality and polarization of wealth, it is hardly surprising that only one in five found little discrimination based on economic status. Although Korea still remains ethnically homogenous, the number of mixed marriages and multicultural families has been on the rise in recent years. In 2011 when asked whether they agreed or disagreed with the statement 'All citizens from different ethnic communities are treated equally by the government', only one-third (33 per cent) found little discrimination based on ethnic status by replying either 'strongly agree' or 'agree'. After more than two decades of democratic rule, equal worth and dignity is not guaranteed to all citizens in the eyes of ordinary Koreans.

Summary

Figure 2.1 summarizes how ordinary Koreans evaluate each dimension of democratic quality. The percentage of each dimension was constructed by averaging the percentage of those giving favourable responses to a pair of its constituent questions. The figure reveals the extent to which each democratic quality is perceived as present. In the eyes of ordinary citizens Korean democracy suffered most from the inadequacy of political equality. In contrast, it suffered least from deficiencies in freedom and electoral competition. Korean democracy was found more lacking in the rule of law and political participation than in accountability and control of corruption. From the perspective of ordinary citizens, Korea has yet to become a high-quality liberal democracy or a full democracy, in contrast with the optimistic assessments of experts.

Confidence in political institutions

Trust in public institutions has been widely used as one of the key indicators of support for democracy-in-practice (Dalton 2004). Public institutions surveyed often include the parliament, courts, political parties, the armed forces, the

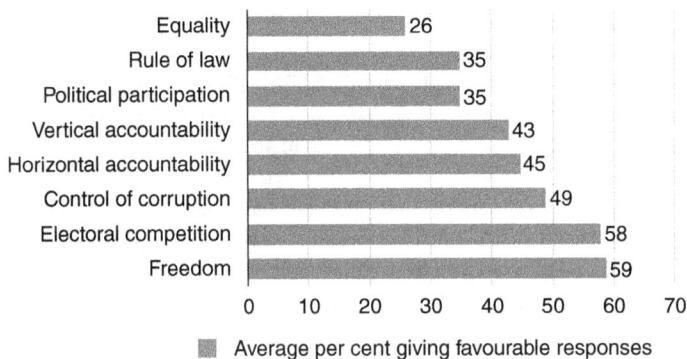

Figure 2.1 Evaluation of democratic quality: Summary (source: Asian Barometer Survey in Korea (2011)).

police, and the civil service. Of them the parliament and political parties constitute core political institutions of democracy. A lack of confidence in these institutions reflects political disaffection or discontent distinguishable from citizen
beliefs in democratic legitimacy (Torcal and Montero 2006).

Figure 2.2 shows the percentage expressing some degree of trust in the
National Assembly and political parties. For each institution, citizen confidence
had declined dramatically for the second decade of democracy, before it turned
around in 2011. Those who had either 'a great deal of trust' or 'quite a lot of
trust' in the National Assembly plummeted from 49 per cent in 1996 to 21 per
cent in 1997 and further declined to 15 per cent in 2003 and 7 per cent in 2006,
and then rose slightly to 11 per cent in 2011. Similarly, those who had either 'a
great deal of trust' or 'quite a lot of trust' in political parties plunged from 39 per
cent in 1996 to 19 per cent in 1997 and further declined to 15 per cent in 2003,
and 9 per cent in 2006 and then rose slightly to 12 per cent in 2011. The trend in
citizen trust in the representative institutions is the most telling testimony to
widespread political disaffection in Korea today.

Citizen confidence in other public institutions also declined for the same
period but the drop was not that steep. For instance, as shown in the same figure,
those who exhibited some degree of trust in the military fell from 74 per cent in
1996 to 66 per cent in 1997, 59 per cent in 2003, and 48 per cent in 2006 and
then rose to 58 per cent in 2011. Likewise, those who expressed some degree of
trust in the police fell from 57 per cent in 1996 to 41 per cent in 1997, 50 per
cent in 2003, and 43 per cent in 2006 and then rose to 49 per cent in 2011.

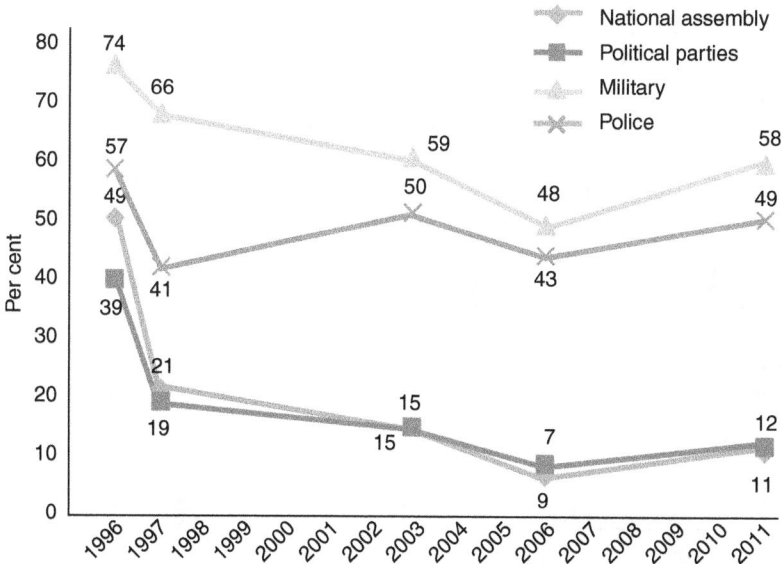

Figure 2.2 Trends in institutional trust (source: Korea Democracy Barometer (1996 and
1997) and Asian Barometer Survey in Korea (2003, 2006 and 2011)).

In each of the years surveyed trust in the representative institutions has never been higher than trust in the security institutions which had served the needs of autocratic rulers. More importantly, the trust gap between both types of institutions has even widened. For instance, the trust gap between the police and the National Assembly was 8 percentage points in 1996 whereas it was 38 percentage points in 2011. The trust gap between the military and the National Assembly was 25 percentage points in 1996 rising to 47 percentage points in 2011. A prolonged lack of confidence in the parliament and political parties may indicate a crisis of representative institutions, if not democracy itself, in Korea.

A further analysis suggests that the decline in institutional trust reflects largely period effects. Figure 2.3 shows the percentage of those who had trust in the National Assembly within birth cohorts. Between 1996 and 2006 it fell sharply within every birth cohort. Between 2006 and 2011 it rose within every birth cohort except for the newly entering one (born between 1977 and 1986). Notably, the size of the decline varied little across birth cohorts. Similarly, the size of the increase varied not much across birth cohorts. Both downward and upward shifts occurred simultaneously within all birth cohorts, indicating period effects. Yet, the downward shift was huge whereas the upward shift small, indicating differential effects of both periods.

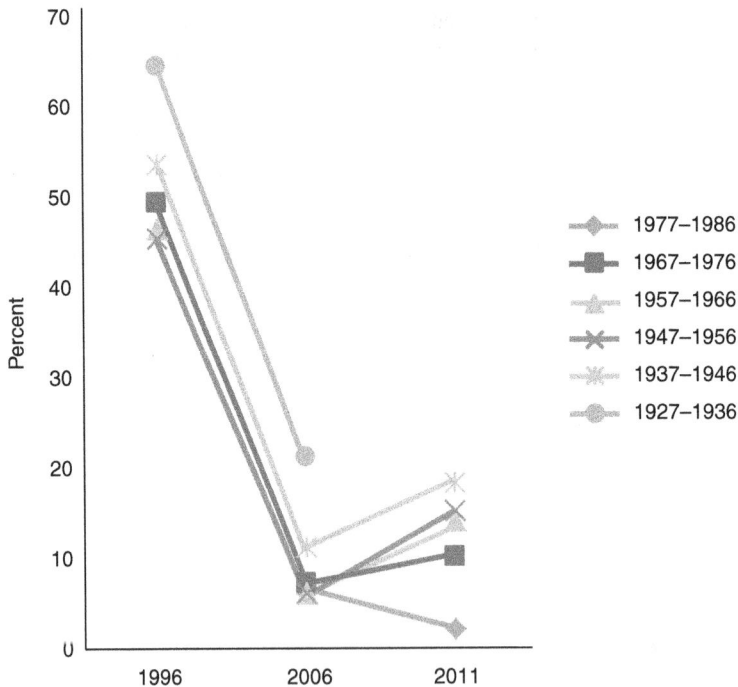

Figure 2.3 Trust in National Assembly by birth cohort (source: Korea Democracy Barometer (1996) and Asian Barometer Survey in Korea (2006 and 2011)).

The gaps between lines reveal that in 1996 there was a notable difference between the oldest birth cohort and the other birth cohorts. Even after the simultaneous downward shift, the difference remained stable, which suggests some generational effects. In 2006 the percentage of those cynical of the parliament in each birth cohort except for the oldest one converged while in 2011 it diverged somewhat. Significantly, the percentage declined within the newly entering birth cohort while increasing within the other cohorts, suggesting some generational difference.

As shown in Figure 2.4, the percentage of those who had trust in political parties displayed a similar trend. Between 1996 and 2006 it fell sharply within every birth cohort. Between 2006 and 2011 it slightly increased within all birth cohorts except for the newly entering one. The size of the decline varied somewhat across birth cohorts, suggesting some generational effects. In contrast, the size of the increase varied not much across birth cohorts. Both downward and upward shifts occurred simultaneously within all birth cohorts, indicating period effects. As with trust in the parliament, the downward shift was huge whereas the upward shift small, suggesting that both periods had differential effects.

The gaps between lines show that in 1996 there was not much difference between birth cohorts. After the downward shift, there was a notable difference

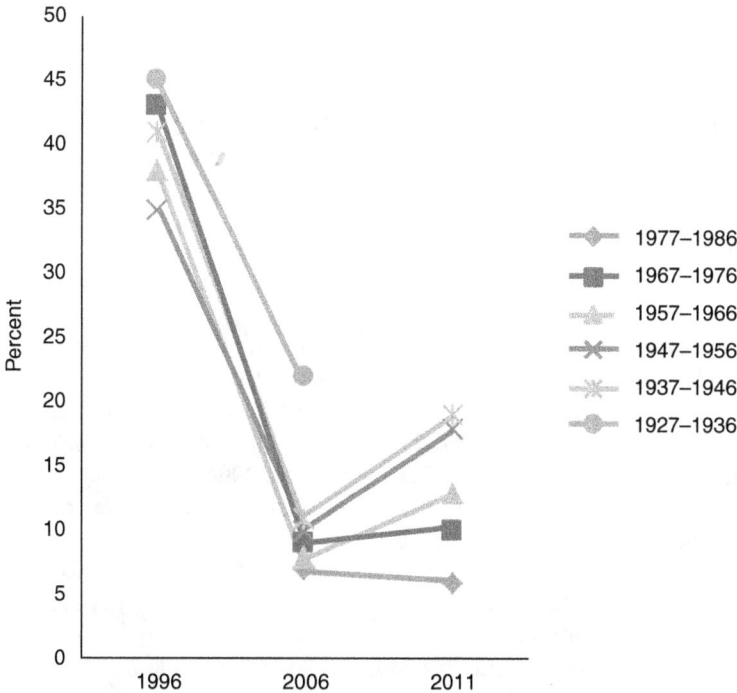

Figure 2.4 Trust in political parties by birth cohort (source: Korea Democracy Barometer (1996) and Asian Barometer Survey in Korea (2006 and 2011)).

between the oldest birth cohort and the other younger ones, suggesting that the effect of this period was weaker on the former than the latter. In 2006 the percentage of those cynical of political parties within all birth cohorts except for the oldest one converged while in 2011 it diverged somewhat. The percentage of those cynical of political parties remained the same within the two youngest birth cohorts while it increased within other older birth cohorts, suggesting some generational difference.

What happened especially during the period between 1996 and 2006 may be responsible for that sharp drop in institutional trust. One such event may be the 1997 economic crisis. After decades of uninterrupted high growth, ordinary Koreans experienced an economic shock of unprecedented severity (Jang 2003). This catastrophic economic downturn seems responsible for a simultaneous huge decline in institutional trust across all birth cohorts.

Normative regime orientations

Rejection of authoritarian rule

Disapproval of democratic performance and distrust in representative political institutions, however, did not encourage ordinary Koreans to embrace political authoritarianism. Not all common forms of authoritarian rule – strongman rule, single-party rule and military rule – remained within the clear recollection of adult Koreans. There has been no legacy of single-party rule in Korea. Although party politics was limited under authoritarian rule, Korea never institutionalized a one-party system, as in Taiwan. Even though the military played a key role in installing and maintaining authoritarian rule, direct military rule (meaning rule by military junta) was rather an exception. The type of regime remaining most vividly in the memory of the Korean people is that of strongman rule or civilian dictatorship backed by the military. Since strongman rule of the past is often associated with economic development, it could be viewed as a competing alternative to democracy.

As shown in Figure 2.5, public rejection of strongman rule proved to be wide. Those who disagreed with the statement 'We should get rid of parliament and elections and have a strong leader decide things' accounted for 85 per cent of the electorate in 1996, 80 per cent in 1997, 75 per cent in 1998, 81 per cent in 1999, 76 per cent in 2001, 85 per cent in 2003, 83 per cent in 2006, and 80 per cent in 2011. Citizen opposition to strongman rule declined after the economic crisis of 1997 but bounced back right after the 2002 presidential election. On average, four in five remained opposed to replacing the National Assembly and elections with civilian dictatorship. Strongman rule as an alternative to democracy has lost its appeal among most ordinary Koreans.

As presented in Figure 2.5, citizen opposition to military rule proved to be even wider. Those who disagreed with the statement 'The military should come in to govern the country' accounted for 84 per cent of the electorate in 1997, 85 per cent in 1998, 87 per cent in 1999, 79 per cent in 2001, 90 per cent in 2003,

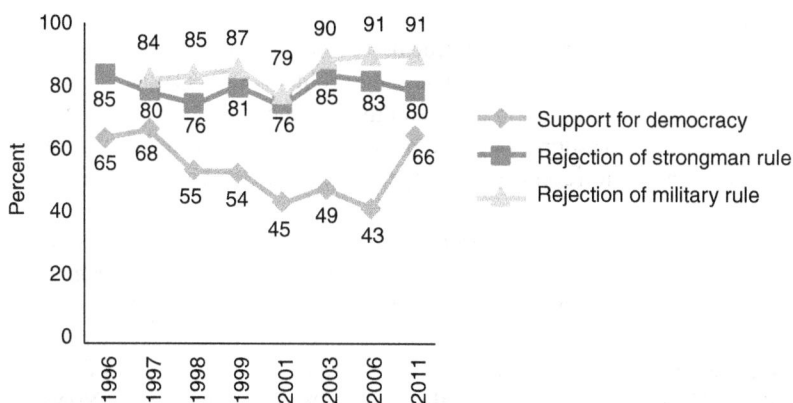

Figure 2.5 Trends in regime orientations (source: Korea Democracy Barometer (1996, 1997, 1998 and 1999) and Asian Barometer Survey in Korea (2003, 2006 and 2011)).

and 91 per cent in both 2006 and 2011. Perhaps a temporary decline in 2001 may have to do with popular anxiety about national security aroused by a left-leaning president's surprise visit to North Korea in 2000. Nonetheless, on average, nine in ten remained opposed to military dictatorship.

Lastly, citizen rejection of single party rule also turned out to be wide. In 2003, 87 per cent disagreed with the statement 'No opposition party should be allowed to compete for power' and in both 2006 and 2011, 88 per cent disagreed with the statement 'Only one political party is allowed to stand for election and hold office.' On average, nearly nine in ten remained opposed to party dictatorship.

In the midst of declining confidence in key democratic institutions, the Korean people's detachment from authoritarian rule remains stable and robust. The most common forms of authoritarian rule have little appeal among ordinary Koreans. It is evident that they no longer are viable alternatives to democracy.

Support for democracy

Despite unequivocal rejection of authoritarian rule, however, public commitment to democracy as a universal value has yet to be firmly entrenched. Over the last 15 years Koreans have been repeatedly asked to choose among the following three statements: 'Democracy is always preferable to any other kind of govern-ment', 'Under some circumstances, an authoritarian government can be prefer-able to an democratic one', and 'For people like me, it does not matter whether we have a democratic or a nondemocratic regime.' As presented in Figure 2.5, those who believed that democracy is always preferable steadily fell from 65 per cent of the electorate in 1996 to 54 per cent in 1998, 45 per cent in 2001, and 43 per cent in 2006 and then bounced back to 66 per cent in 2011, the level registered 15 years ago. A decade-long steady decline since the 1997 economic crisis was belatedly followed by a recent reversal, although whether this turn-around marks the beginning of a new trend remains to be seen. Similarly, citizen beliefs in the efficacy of democracy fluctuated for the last decade. Those who believed that democracy is capable of solving problems of society fell from 72 per cent in 2003 to 55 per cent in 2006 and then bounced back to 70 per cent in 2011. Although popular support for democracy has surged recently in the midst of a global 'democratic recession', it appears to be less robust, responding to unfolding events.

It is noteworthy that the largest drop in support for democracy occurred in the wake of the 1997 economic crisis, suggesting that economic performance has the greatest influence in citizen beliefs in democratic legitimacy. However, the sudden rise in the wake of the 2008–2009 global economic crisis challenges any simplistic economic accounts. No doubt the 1997 economic crisis had far more devastating effects on Koreans' lives than the 2008–2009 global one. Nonetheless, if economic performance mattered most, support for democracy should have also further declined or stayed low in the wake of the global economic downturn. Other events that occurred between 2006 and 2011 should be responsible for the upturn in support for democracy. An obvious candidate is the 2007 presidential election in which an unpopular incumbent president was replaced. It is possible that the collective experience of electoral accountability may convince ordinary Koreans that democracy is still better than its alternatives or 'a lesser evil' (Rose *at al.* 1998). What is evident though is that support for democracy had steadily declined during the period which conservatives called 'a lost decade' of left-leaning governments.

A further analysis suggests that the decline in support for democracy largely reflects period effects. Figure 2.6 shows the percentage of those expressing unconditional preference for democracy within birth cohorts. Between 1996 and 2001 support for democracy sharply declined within every birth cohort. Between 2001 and 2006 it slightly declined in every birth cohort except those born between 1937 and 1946. Between 2006 and 2011 it sharply increased within every birth cohort. The size of the decline between 1996 and 2001 varied much across birth cohorts. Similarly, the size of the increase between 2006 and 2011 varied much across birth cohorts. Both downward and upward shifts occurred simultaneously within all birth cohorts, indicating period effects. The magnitude of the downward shift was as large as the upward shift, which suggests that political performance may be as important as economic performance in engendering support for democracy.

The gaps between lines may indicate generational effects. In 1996 there was little difference between birth cohorts, suggesting little generational disagreement about the value of democracy. Yet, in 2001, there emerged some notable difference but the difference was not stable across time. In 2006 the percentage of those holding beliefs in democratic legitimacy within each birth cohort converged except for the oldest birth cohort. In 2011 a small difference remained even with the newly entering youngest birth cohort. The effect of generational change gradually disappeared. The downward shift between 1996 and 2001 was most marked within the oldest birth cohort (those born between 1927 and 1936)

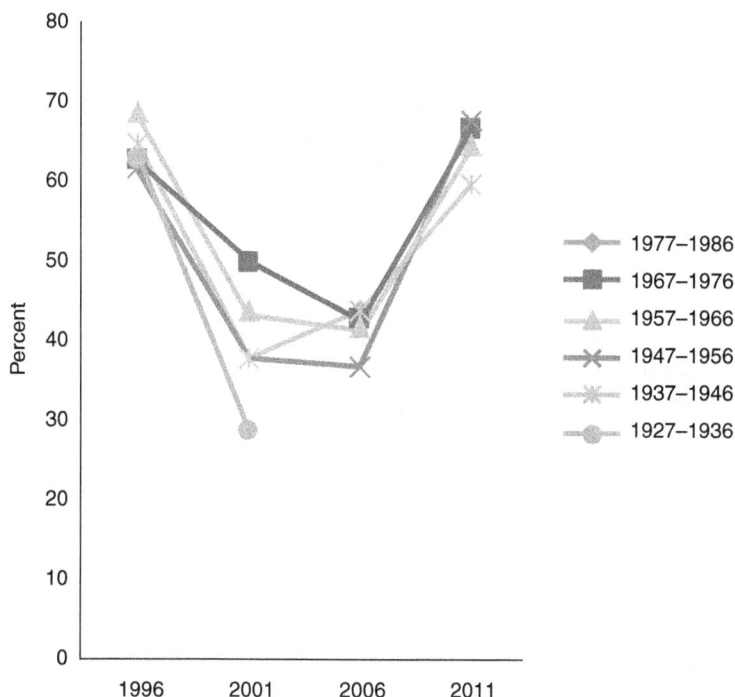

Figure 2.6 Support for democracy by birth cohort (source: Korea Democracy Barometer (1996 and 2001) and Asian Barometer Survey in Korea (2006 and 2011)).

while least marked, the youngest one (those born between 1967 and 1976), suggesting that support for democracy was more shallow among older generations.

As discussed above, the simultaneous downward shift which occurred between 1996 and 2001 may be largely attributable to the 1997 economic crisis. By contrast, the simultaneous upward shift which occurred between 2006 and 2011 may be attributable to the working of electoral accountability. That support for democracy increased rather than declined or stayed low even in the wake of the global economic downturn raises a question of whether economic performance matters most to support for democracy.

Overall, the results indicate a mixed picture of normative regime orientations among the Korean electorate. Nearly everyone rejected non-democratic forms of governance. Popular rejection of authoritarian rule remained unwavering or became even stronger. By contrast, support for democracy has fluctuated, responding to unfolding events and is yet to be firmly entrenched. Poor economic performance under democratic rule as compared to the economic success of authoritarian past seems to shaken citizen beliefs in the universal validity of democracy. Yet, the working of electoral accountability appears to strengthen a realist view of democracy as 'a lesser evil.'

Expectations and performance

Public evaluation of democratic performance is shaped by not only actual regime performance but also the criteria for evaluation citizens employ and the information to which they are exposed (Pharr and Putnam 2000). As citizens become more exposed to alternative sources of information, old and new media, they become better informed about regime performance. Hence, evaluation of democratic performance may reflect media effects as in advanced old democracies (Norris 2000). Setting aside citizen information, we here focus on citizen expectations, which determine criteria for evaluation. Citizen expectations, the outcomes they expect of democracy and the priorities they place on it, may differ across time and place. In 2006 when asked to choose the most essential characteristic of democracy, a third (36 per cent) chose a small income gap between rich and poor; another third (36 per cent), opportunity to change the government through elections; more than a tenth (15 per cent), freedom to criticize those in power; and a tenth (10 per cent), basic necessities like food, clothes and shelter for everyone. Ordinary Koreans seemed equally divided in their expectations of democracy. One half chose social justice and basic welfare while the other half, popular control and political freedom. This finding suggests that not only political goods but also socio-economic ones serve as equally important criteria in evaluating democratic performance. Such diverging or polarizing expectations of democracy tend to make it difficult for democratic government to satisfy its constituents.

If every policy area does not weigh equally in evaluation of democratic performance, it is advantageous to identify the most relevant policy dimensions (Roller 2005). In 2011 when asked to indicate the most important problem facing the country that government should address, more than two-fifths (43 per cent) mentioned management of the economy, which was followed by unemployment (15 per cent), and poverty (7 per cent). Two in three considered economic stability and security the most urgent problems to solve. This finding illustrates that economic and social performance may weigh more than political performance in Koreans' evaluation of democracy. Perhaps it is why the trends in popular evaluation of democracy did not coincide with the trend in experts' assessments of democratic governance.

To understand growing political disaffection in Korea, we may have to look at trends in objective indicators reflecting economic and social performance. Figure 2.7 shows trends in economic growth and unemployment, two key indicators of economic management, over the last two decades. The trends roughly coincided with the trends in support for democracy and institutional trust examined above. For eight years (1990–1997) prior to the economic crisis, the economy grew by an average of 7.7 per cent per year. The economy quickly recovered in 1999 after the IMF bailout and then economic growth had steadily declined until it turned around in 2010 (for a decade between 2000 and 2009, average growth rate was 4.4 per cent per year). Prior to the economic crisis, the unemployment

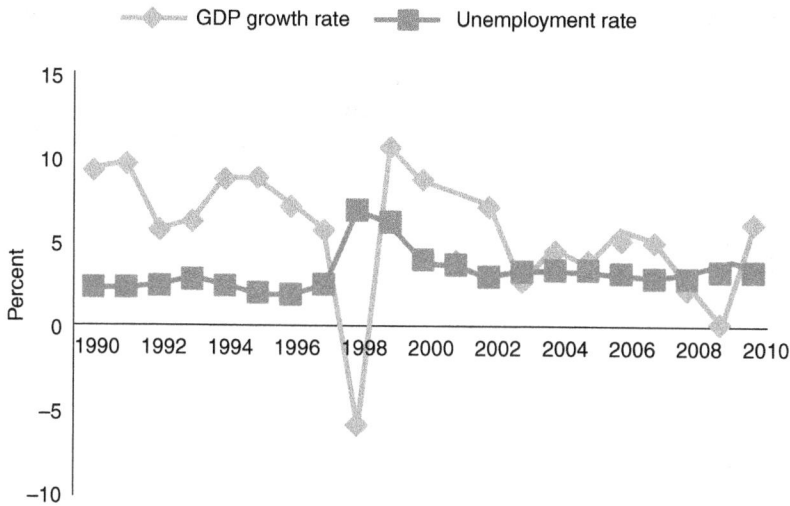

Figure 2.7 Trends in economic growth and unemployment (source: Korea National Statistical Office (available online at: http://kostat.go.kr)).

rate was low, averaging 2.4 per cent per year. In 1998 unemployment surged and then gradually declined but stayed higher than the pre-crisis level.

Figure 2.8 shows trends in two indicators of income distribution over the past two decades, which also roughly coincided with the trends in support for democracy and institutional trust. There existed a marked increase in income inequality in the wake of the 1997 economic crisis. Prior to the crisis, the Gini

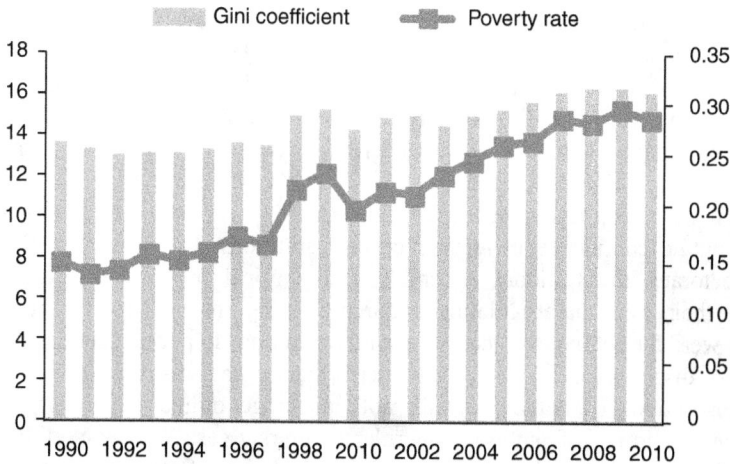

Figure 2.8 Trends in economic equality (source: Korea National Statistical Office (available online at: http://kostat.go.kr)).

coefficient stayed lower than 0.3. Since the economic crisis, income inequality has gradually deteriorated, with the coefficient rising above 0.3 The relative poverty rate, which indicates the percentage of persons living with less than 50 per cent of median household income, has also steadily risen since the economic crisis. Before the crisis, the rate was well below 10 per cent but for the last few years it hovered around 15 per cent, which was higher than most OECD countries.

Given that the quality of political performance assessed by experts has improved over the last two decades, the downward trends in support for democracy and trust in political institutions cannot be attributable to better political performance. The above analysis strongly suggests that Korean voters tend to penalize democratic governments for poor economic and social performance. A slow economy, increasing unemployment and widening disparities seem responsible for the erosion of confidence in representative institutions and ambivalence toward democracy. Korean democracy remains far short of its people's socio-economic expectations of democracy.

Conclusion

Despite recent global backsliding in democracy, Korea has successfully maintained and even improved democratic institutions and practices. It is regarded as a model of democracy in East Asia. Yet, ordinary Koreans have become increasingly cynical of political institutions, especially the National Assembly and political parties, remained sceptical of democracy as a universal value, and disengaged themselves from conventional politics. Their experience with democracy appeared to be far short of their expectations.

The analysis of a series of public opinion data demonstrates that Koreans have mixed views of democratic performance. They view the current political system as a democracy, if not a flawless democracy. Their satisfaction with the functioning of democracy remains modest, albeit unstable. Yet, not every institution or mechanism of democracy is adequately supplied in the eyes of the Korean electorate. In particular, equality of treatment, law-based governance, and citizen political participation are considered more lacking whereas freedom and electoral competition, less lacking.

The most notable phenomenon over the past 15 years has been a sharp decline in public confidence in representative institutions. In the eyes of the Korean electorate, the National Assembly and political parties have failed to perform their roles in articulating and representing their interests. These institutions were far behind even coercive state institutions in public confidence. Nonetheless, disapproval of democratic performance and distrust in representative institutions of democracy did not encourage ordinary Koreans to embrace various forms of authoritarian rule as alternatives. Yet, support for democracy has yet to be firmly entrenched. A sceptical view of democracy as the best form of government has persisted, responding to faltering economic performance.

Another notable finding is that the dramatic decline in support for democracy and institutional trust, particularly for the second decade of democracy can be attributable to the 1997 economic crisis, apparently strengthening an economic account of democratic legitimacy. A huge downward shift occurred within every birth cohort, indicating the effect of the collective experience of an economic disaster. Yet, a dramatic rebound in support for democracy in the midst of the recent global economic crisis warns against any simplistic economic accounts. The huge increase may be attributable to the collective experience of electoral accountability. What is interesting is that unlike support for democracy, institutional trust has not rebounded much. This finding suggests that electoral accountability matters not much to confidence in representative institutions while matters greatly to preference for democracy. Citizen trust in political institutions seems to reflect more economic and social policy performance.

Overall, core representative institutions of democracy, if not democracy itself, in Korea are in trouble. The recent political malaise in Korea has to do with poor performance of representative institutions. The National Assembly and political parties become the most salient targets of political cynicism. Much to our relief is that such institutional disaffection has not encouraged ordinary Koreans to entertain political authoritarianism. The new democracy in Korea faces similar political challenges old Western democracies face (Pharr and Putnam 2000). It increasingly encounters 'critical citizens' who are supportive of democracy as an idea but critical of the performance of political institutions (Norris 1999). Unlike advanced industrial democracies, however, Korean democracy also faces 'ambivalent citizens' who are sceptical of democracy as a universal value as well as critical of the performance of political institutions. The biggest flaw of Korean democracy in the eyes of ordinary people is that it is not as 'kinder, gentler' to everyone as they expect. To alleviate the political malaise in Korea today, political institutions need to be more responsive to and representative of diverging interests and expectations.

References

Altman, David and Perez-Linan, Anibal (2002) 'Assessing the quality of democracy: freedom, competitiveness and participation in eighteen Latin American countries', *Democratization*, 9(2): 85–100.

Chu, Yun-han, Diamond, Larry, Nathan, Andrew J. and Shin, Doh Chull (eds) (2008) *How East Asians View Democracy*, New York: Columbia University Press.

Dahl, Robert (1971) *Polyarchy: Participation and Opposition*, New Haven: Yale University Press.

Dalton, Russell J. (2004) *Democratic Challenges, Democratic Choices: The Erosion of Political Support in Advanced Industrial Democracies*, Oxford: Oxford University Press.

Diamond, Larry (2008) *The Spirit of Democracy: The Struggle to Build Free Societies throughout the World*, New York: Times Books.

Diamond, Larry and Morlino, Leonardo (2004) 'The quality of democracy: an overview', *Journal of Democracy*, 15(4): 20–31.

Diamond, Larry and Shin, Doh Chull (eds) (2000) *Institutional Reform and Democratic Consolidation in Korea*, Stanford: Hoover Institution Press.

Economist Intelligence Unit (2011) *Democracy Index 2011: Democracy under Stress*.

Freedom House (2012) 'Freedom in the World 2012'; www.freedomhouse.org/report/freedom-world/freedom-world-2012 accessed 22 April 2013.

Huntington, Samuel (1991) *The Third Wave: Democratization in the Late Twentieth Century*, Norman: University of Oklahoma Press.

Im, Hyug Baeg (2004) 'Faltering democratic consolidation in South Korea: democracy at the end of the 'three Kims' era', *Democratization*, 11(5): 179–198.

Jang, Jiho (2003) 'Economic crisis and its consequences', *Social Indicators Research*, 62/63: 51–70.

Kang, David (2003) 'Regional politics and democratic consolidation in Korea', in Kim, Samuel (ed.) *Korea's Democratization*, New York: Cambridge University Press, pp. 161–180.

Kim, Byung-Kook (2000) 'Party politics in South Korea's democracy: the crisis of success', in Diamond, Larry and Kim, Byung-Kook (eds) *Consolidating Democracy in South Korea*, Boulder: Lynne Rienner Publishers, pp. 53–85.

Kim, Samuel (ed.) (2003) *Korea's Democratization*, New York: Cambridge University Press.

Lee, Sangmook (2007) 'Democratic transition and the consolidation of democracy in South Korea', *Taiwan Journal of Democracy*, 3(1): 99–125.

Lijphart, Arend (1999) *Patterns of Democracy: Government Forms and Performance in Thirty-Six Countries*, New Haven: Yale University Press.

Marshall, Monty G. (2013) 'Polity IV Project: Political Regime Characteristics and Transitions, 1800–2012'; www.systemicpeace.org/polity/polity4.htm accessed 22 April 2013.

Morlino, Leonardo, Dressel, Bjorn, and Pelizzo, Riccardo (2011) 'The quality of democracy in Asia-Pacific: issues and findings', *International Political Science Review*, 32(5): 491–511.

Norris, Pippa (ed.) (1999) *Critical Citizens: Global Support for Democratic Governance*, Oxford: Oxford University Press.

Norris, Pippa (2000) 'The impact of television on civic malaise', in Pharr, Susan J. and Putnam, Robert D. (eds) *Disaffected Democracies: What's Troubling the Trilateral Countries?* Princeton: Princeton University Press, pp. 231–251.

Park, Chong-Min (2011) 'Political discontent in South Korea', *International Review of Sociology*, 21(2): 391–412.

Pharr, Susan J. and Putnam, Robert D. (eds) (2000) *Disaffected Democracies: What's Troubling the Trilateral Countries?* Princeton: Princeton University Press.

Roller, Edeltraud (2005) *The Performance of Democracies: Political Institutions and Public Policies*, Oxford: Oxford University Press.

Rose, Richard, Mishler, William, and Haerpfer, Christian (1998) *Democracy and Its Alternatives: Understanding Post-Communist Societies*, Baltimore: The Johns Hopkins University Press.

Schedler, Andrea, Diamond, Larry and Plattner, Marc F. (eds) (1999) *The Self-restraining State: Power and Accountability in New Democracies*, Colorado: Lynne Rienner.

Shin, Doh Chull and Lee, Jaechul (2006) 'The Korea Democracy Barometer Surveys: unraveling the cultural and institutional dynamics of democratization, 1997–2004', *Korea Observer*, 37(2): 237–275.

Torcal, Mariano and Montero, Jose Ramo (eds) (2006) *Political Disaffection in Contemporary Democracies*, London: Routledge.

Transparency International. *The Corruption Perception Index*; http://cpi.transparency.org/cpi2012/results/ accessed 22 April 2013.

World Bank. *Worldwide Governance Indicators*; http://info.worldbank.org/governance/wgi/index.asp accessed 22 April 2013.

3 From regime transition to liberal democracy

The case of Taiwan

Chung-li Wu and Shih-chan Dai

> Conflict, competition, organization, leadership, and responsibility are the ingredients of a working definition of democracy. Democracy is a political system in which the people have a choice among the alternatives created by competing political organizations and leaders.
>
> Schattschneider 1960: 138

Introduction

Over the last few decades, the transition from totalitarian and authoritarian regimes towards democracy – or in Huntington's (1991) usage, the third wave of democratization – has swept the developing world from Eastern Europe through Latin America to East Asia. One common characteristic of this phenomenon has been the breakdown of the incumbent political parties and the formation of opposition ones caused by democratic reforms initiated by the governing regimes (Dickson 1996; Huntington 1991, 1992; O'Donnell *et al.* 1986). Political development in Taiwan (the Republic of China, or ROC), in contrast, was not the consequence of regime collapse but of a measured process in which the Kuomintang (KMT, or the Nationalist Party) has remained the ruling political party in control of the central government, legislature, and most local governments, even though it temporarily lost power from 2000 to 2008. The case of Taiwan raises the question: How can an authoritarian, revolutionary-oriented political party transform itself into a democratic party in response to social change and local popular demands and still retain political dominance?

This chapter explores the transformation of the KMT from an authoritarian regime to a democratic political party by using four indicators: leadership ideology, membership structure, elite composition, and its policy towards the political opposition. Furthermore, this chapter reviews the KMT's China policies as contained in its manifestos/platforms since the early 1990s. This will help us determine whether manifesto formation in the KMT has been shaped by forces originating from democratization. The chapter also assesses the implications of this transformation and the prospects for KMT rule in a democratic Taiwan. The major argument is that there is potential for further change, although the prospects are still far from certain. As the pace of inter-party electoral competition accelerates, one should expect the KMT to further democratize its party organizations and to deregulate its China policies, and thereby to continue to win respectable majorities in elections or, simply put, to retain its governing position.

The transformation: the changing nature of the KMT

In 1949, the KMT government retreated from the mainland to Taiwan after it was defeated by the communists in the Chinese civil war. The KMT regime, under the leadership of Chiang Kai-shek, imposed authoritarian rule on the island from that time until the mid-1970s when rapid socio-economic change began. Its comprehensive domination of the ruling mechanism characterizes it as a highly authoritarian one-party state with elements of totalitarianism (Cheng 1989; Cohen 1991; Winckler 1984).

The KMT's authoritarian grip on Taiwan began to show signs of relaxation in the 1970s when Chiang's son, Chiang Ching-kuo, rose to political prominence. The process of controlled liberalization and democratization of the political system culminated in the abolition of martial law in 1987, an event that established a new arena for free and open political competition. Beyond any doubt, one aspect of Taiwan's transition from authoritarianism towards democracy was democratization within the KMT itself, which facilitated the party's pursuit of political openness. In discussing the change in the nature of the KMT, it is useful to focus on certain essential elements: leadership ideology, membership structure, elite composition, and party policy towards opposition movements.

Ideology of the party leadership

Leadership factors are regarded as important in developing democratization. Huntington (1991: 38–39) emphasized that point by citing Weiner's conclusion that democratization is related to the 'strategies available to those who seek a democratic revolution'. This advice appropriately highlights the crucial role of the leadership and political skill in bringing about democracy. Although the motives and decisions of ruling elites do not provide a complete explanation of political reform, they are an important ingredient. In some respects, the KMT regime has evolved from hard authoritarian through soft authoritarian to weak democracy over the past four decades (Winckler 1984: 482; Wu 1997). This evolution underscored the ideological distinctions among the three consecutive party leaders – Chiang Kai-shek, Chiang Ching-kuo and Lee Teng-hui.

Chiang Kai-shek ruled Taiwan from the time of the KMT government's retreat from mainland China in 1949 to 1975. According to Cheng (1989: 477–478), the control exercised by Chiang was similar to that of the leader of a Leninist state, with two exceptions: the existence of private ownership and the institutionalization of local elections. Chiang was always depicted as a godlike figure fighting a holy war against communism on behalf of justice. In his eyes, recovering the Chinese mainland from communist rule was the foremost goal of the party and nation (Wu 1997: 233).

The Chiang Ching-kuo era in Taiwan politics began in 1972 when the junior Chiang became premier, although his father remained the paramount leader. In 1975, Chiang Kai-shek died and was succeeded by Vice-President Yen Chia-kan. Although Yen served as president *de jure*, Premier Chiang Ching-kuo dominated the KMT regime. Finally, the National Assembly rubber-stamped Chiang the junior as president in 1978. Even though the junior Chiang came to power as his father's heir, his rule was rather different. Unlike his father, who tended to suppress all forms of political opposition, Chiang gradually liberalized the political system. One piece of evidence of his reformist orientation was his attitude towards the 'illegal' formation of the opposition Democratic Progressive Party (DPP) in September 1986. While the initial reaction of KMT leaders was divided, there was no arrest of the DPP founders. Over time, it became apparent that Chiang was inclined to tolerate, rather than suppress, the DPP. After Chiang's death in January 1988, Vice-President Lee Teng-hui, a native Taiwanese with a PhD from Cornell University, succeeded to the presidency and the KMT chairmanship. In a short time, Lee became popular among Taiwanese, a factor that enabled him to maintain the momentum of reform.

Although this account may not be conclusive, it does convey the rough contours of these leaders' perceptions and styles. There is evidence that the governing KMT, under the leadership of these three figures, was transformed from a revolutionary-oriented and authoritarian party into a democracy-oriented and pragmatic one. The transition to democracy under Chiang Ching-kuo and Lee Teng-hui was consistent with socio-economic transformation in Taiwan and changes in the international environment, which made it more difficult for the KMT to continue to rule in an authoritarian manner and to suppress the social and political demands of a new middle class. Beyond the thinking of the party leaders, actual changes in the structure of KMT membership also made an important contribution to reform within the party.

Structure of party membership

By the end of 1948, the KMT, still in control of the government of mainland China, had about four million members (Wu 1997: 235). There are no reliable membership figures for the period immediately after the party moved its headquarters to Taiwan in 1949 because the party apparatus was in paralysis. According to one study, the KMT had only some 34,000 members in 1949, or about 0.8 per cent of Taiwan's total adult population, and most of them had come from the mainland with the regime (Huang 1996: 114). As shown in Table 3.1, before the 1950 reconstruction movement, the KMT had a total of 80,043 members, slightly over 1 per cent of the population, rising to about 282,000 by the end of the reconstruction in 1952. Members were organized into around 30,000 party cells with an average of about six members each, and more than 49 per cent of KMT members were farmers, workers and merchants. Party branches were established throughout the island in villages, government offices, schools, businesses and the transportation sector. The ratio of party members to non-members in government

Table 3.1 Composition of KMT membership, 1948–1992

Year	Total membership	Taiwanese	% of total membership	Mainlanders	% of total membership
1948	4,080,293[a]	n.a.	n.a.	n.a.	n.a.
1950	80,043	n.a.	n.a.	n.a.	n.a.
1952	282,000[b]	n.a.	n.a.	n.a.	n.a.
1957	509,864	202,416	39.70	307,448	60.30
1963	667,000[b]	205,000[b]	30.73[b]	462,000[b]	69.27[b]
1968	919,327	358,537[b]	39.00[b]	560,790[b]	61.00[b]
1969	950,993	374,666	39.40	576,327	60.60
1972	1,198,418	553,215	46.16	645,203	53.84
1975	1,448,106	764,961	52.82	683,145	47.18
1977	1,686,724	954,145	56.57	732,579	43.43
1979	1,884,766	1,124,561	59.67	760,205	40.33
1980	1,934,011	1,180,352	61.03	753,659	38.97
1981	1,997,636	1,236,534	61.90	761,102	38.10
1982	2,070,683	1,300,772	62.82	760,911	36.75
1983	2,120,979	1,346,014	63.46	774,965	36.54
1984	2,187,973	1,408,980	64.40	778,993	35.60
1985	2,268,974	1,480,032	65.23	788,942	34.77
1986	2,356,042	1,552,025	65.87	804,017	34.13
1987	2,398,155	1,586,264	66.15	811,891	33.85
1988	2,422,195	1,619,538	66.86	802,657	33.14
1989	2,535,530	1,713,377	67.57	822,153	32.43
1990	2,546,429	1,735,223	68.14	811,206	31.86
1991	2,570,904	1,764,196	68.62	806,708	31.38
1992	2,617,651	1,810,392	69.16	807,259	30.84

Sources: Wu (1997: 236); see also Huang (1995: 102–103; 1996: 115).

Notes

All data are year-end statistics. According to records released by the Department of Organizational Affairs of the KMT Central Committee, the KMT had 2,653,471 members in 1993. Since the revision of the Household Registration Law in February that year, the KMT has not maintained statistics on the ethnic composition of its membership. Data for 1969 and 1972 include the Taiwan Area only; data for other years include both the Taiwan Area and the Fukien Area.

a The figure includes overall KMT membership in mainland China.

b The figures are estimates collected from the Reports on Party Affairs of the KMT National Party Congress.

agencies was 5:1 in the central government, 1:1 in the provincial government, and 8:13 in county and city governments.

Two conclusions can be drawn from the figures cited above. First, there was a significant expansion of party membership, and, in a sense, the composition of the membership reflected the KMT's social base. After its arrival in Taiwan, the KMT regime saw a need to build a new grassroots organization. Its strategy was to incorporate all sectors of society into the party. One of the guidelines of the reconstruction movement was to enlarge the membership to include farmers, workers, youth and the intelligentsia. While the KMT continued to gain members from diverse social backgrounds, it concentrated on a newly emerging group of educated youth, and by 1992, membership had risen to more than 2.6 million.

Second, the KMT transformed itself from a mainlander-dominated political party into a Taiwanese-based one. In the 1950s and 1960s, mainlanders constituted the majority of party members, with native Taiwanese representing about 39 per cent of the total membership from 1957 to 1969. By 1975, under Chiang Ching-kuo's 'Taiwanization' recruitment policy, ethnic Taiwanese constituted a majority of the party membership for the first time, and by 1977 they represented more than 56 per cent. By the 1990s, about 1.8 million party members (70 per cent) were native Taiwanese.

Composition of the party elite

Even more important than the recruitment of large numbers of Taiwanese into the party at the grassroots was the rise of Taiwanese elites into the KMT ruling circle. Changes in the ethnic composition of central party bodies – the Central Committee (CC) and the Central Standing Committee (CSC) – reflected the KMT's strategy of Taiwanization. In a sense, members of the CC and the CSC had a greater influence on national policy than did those working in government organs. While few Taiwanese held positions on the CC during the period 1952–1969, the proportion of Taiwanese members increased significantly after 1976 (see Table 3.2). The incorporation of Taiwanese elites into the central bodies followed Chiang Ching-kuo's re-election as chairman of the party at the end of 1976. Taiwanese representation on the CC rose to 14.6 per cent in 1976, steadily increasing to 34.4 per cent in 1988, the year that Lee Teng-hui became the party leader.

The composition of the CSC exhibited the same trend. There were no Taiwanese on the party's governing body from 1952 to March 1957 (see Table 3.3). Over the next three decades, the CSC continued to be dominated by mainland elites. The situation changed only when Chiang Ching-kuo succeeded to the chair and initiated the Taiwanization policy, widening Taiwanese membership and promoting native Taiwanese KMT loyalists to positions of political prominence. This policy, moreover, was an effective means of defusing mainlander-Taiwanese tensions. When Lee became the party chairman in 1988, native Taiwanese held a majority of the seats on the CSC for the first time.

The decreasing proportion of party members from the military with positions on the KMT's highest bodies reflected internal party democratization. In an authoritarian system, members of the ruling party from the military – the conservative wing – usually play a key role in the policymaking process, while those from representative bodies – the reformist wing – have little input. Depoliticization of the military and a strengthening of the influence of representative bodies in the political realm are generally therefore key indicators of a shift from authoritarianism towards democracy (Huang 1996: 117, 121; Linz and Stepan 1996; Tien and Chu 1996: 1142–1143). Likewise, as the proportion of military personnel in the KMT ruling circle was reduced, this had the effect of loosening mainlander dominance.

In the early days of KMT rule in Taiwan, the military had little influence in the central bodies of the party. The increase in the military's importance by the end

Table 3.2 Composition of the KMT Central Committee, 1952–1997

Date	National Congress	Total	Leader	Taiwanese	% of total	Military	% of total	Parliament representatives	% of total
19 October 1952	7th	32	CKS	1	3.1	10	31.3	5	15.6
23 October 1957	8th	50	CKS	3	6.0	11	22.0	15	30.0
22 November 1963	9th	74	CKS	4	5.4	16	21.6	14	18.9
8 April 1969	10th	99	CKS	6	6.1	16	16.2	16	16.2
17 November 1976	11th	130	CCK	19	14.6	21	16.2	15	11.5
3 April 1981	12th	150	CCK	29	19.3	15	10.0	30	20.0
12 July 1988	13th	180	LTH	62	34.4	21	11.7	37	20.6
17 August 1993	14th	212	LTH	114	53.8	8	3.8	69	32.5
27 August 1997	15th	230	LTH	142	61.7	7	3.0	61	26.5

Sources: Wu (1997: 238); see also Huang (1995: 104; 1996: 118).

Notes

CKS=Chiang Kai-shek; CCK=Chiang Ching-kuo; LTH=Lee Teng-hui.

Table 3.3 Composition of the KMT Central Standing Committee, 1952–1997

Date	Leader	Total	Taiwanese	% of total	Military	% of total	Representatives	% of total
23 October 1952	CKS	10	0	0.0	3	30.0	4	40.0
5 August 1954	CKS	10	0	0.0	2	20.0	5	50.0
3 March 1955	CKS	10	0	0.0	3	30.0	4	40.0
8 May 1956	CKS	10	0	0.0	1	10.0	5	50.0
3 March 1957	CKS	10	0	0.0	1	10.0	5	50.0
26 October 1957	CKS	16[a]	1	6.3	4	25.0	5	31.3
19 May 1959	CKS	16[a]	2	12.5	5	31.3	6	37.5
2 October 1960	CKS	16[a]	2	12.5	6	37.5	6	37.5
16 November 1961	CKS	16[a]	2	12.5	6	37.5	6	37.5
15 November 1962	CKS	16[a]	2	12.5	5	31.3	6	37.5
23 November 1963	CKS	16[a]	2	12.5	6	37.5	8	50.0
28 November 1964	CKS	18[a]	2	11.1	6	33.3	6	33.3
29 November 1966	CKS	19	2	10.5	6	31.6	8	42.1
23 November 1967	CKS	19	2	10.5	6	31.6	9	47.4
10 April 1969	CKS	21	2	9.5	5	23.8	7	33.3
10 March 1972	CKS	21	3	14.3	5	23.8	5	23.8
15 November 1973	CKS	21	3	14.3	4	19.0	5	23.8
19 November 1976	CCK	22	5	22.7	4	18.2	6	27.3
10 December 1979	CCK	27	9	33.3	6	22.2	5	18.5
6 April 1981	CCK	27	9	33.3	5	18.5	4	14.8
14 February 1984	CCK	31	12	38.7	4	12.9	6	19.4
29 March 1986	CCK	31	14	45.2	4	12.9	6	19.4
14 July 1988	LTH	31	16	51.6	3	9.7	9	29.0
23 August 1993	LTH	35[b]	20	57.1	3	8.6	9	25.7
22 August 1994	LTH	35[b]	21	60.0	3	8.6	8	22.9
23 August 1996	LTH	35[c]	21	60.0	2	5.7	10	28.6
28 August 1997	LTH	37[c]	24	64.9	2	5.4	13	35.1

Sources: Wu (1997: 239); see also Huang (1995: 105; 1996: 119–120).

Notes

CKS = Chiang Kai-shek; CCK = Chiang Ching-kuo; LTH = Lee Teng-hui.

a Includes Chen Cheng as the party vice chairman.
b Includes Li Yuan-tsu, Lien Chan, Hau Pei-tsun, and Lin Yang-kang as vice chairmen.
c Includes Li Yuan-tsu, Lien Chan, Yu Kuo-hua, and Chiu Chuang-huan as vice chairmen.

of the reconstruction movement was perhaps a result of heightened tensions between the two sides of the Taiwan Strait. Thus, although military representation on the CSC decreased between 1952 and 1957, it rose again in 1957 and remained at a high level (over 30 per cent) through 1969. During this time a prominent military official, Chen Cheng, served concurrently as Vice-President and Vice-Chairman of the KMT, consolidating the military's grip on society. When Taiwan became more secure by the end of the 1960s, the proportion of CSC members with military backgrounds fell, first to 23.8 per cent in 1969, then to 9.7 per cent when Lee became party leader, and then to its lowest level (5.4 per cent) in 1997.

Policy towards opposition movements

In authoritarian one-party systems, the ruling party's policy towards the political opposition is critical. Weiner and LaPalombara (1966: 401–403) summarize four strategies used by authoritarian parties to respond to opposition demands: repression, mobilization, limited admission, and full admission. The transformation of the KMT fits into such a framework, a gradual change from repression to full admission.

Prior to the early 1970s, the KMT regime adopted repressive policies towards its political opponents. Martial law made the formation of any opposition party a risky business. The abortive attempt to set up the China Democratic Party (CDP) was a case in point. In the summer of 1960, a group of liberal-oriented mainlander intellectuals, in association with some Taiwanese elites, attempted to form a new party. The CDP was headed by two mainlanders, Lei Chen and Fu Cheng, who published the journal *Free China Fortnightly* (*Ziyou Zhongguo*) to propagate liberal democratic thought. In September, before the birth of the new party, Lei and Fu were arrested and charged with associating with communist agents. Subsequent to this, the opposition movement quickly evaporated.

Another event illustrating the hostile attitude of the KMT towards any opposition was the Peng Ming-min incident. In 1964, Peng, a professor of political science at National Taiwan University, and two of his students prepared to distribute a manifesto entitled 'A Declaration of Formosan Self-Salvation' that questioned the government's policy of returning to the mainland and called for the replacement of the Chiang Kai-shek regime with a freely elected government. All of them were arrested and imprisoned (Peng 1972). After the KMT repressed these two groups, political opposition was silenced for almost two decades. The only surviving challenges to KMT authority came from individuals who ran against KMT candidates in local elections.

The early Chiang Ching-kuo era was a mixture of repression and mobilization, indicating that the governing authority was willing to permit or even encourage participation, but only within prescribed limits (Weiner and LaPalombara 1966: 403). After Chiang the junior assumed power following the death of his father, he allowed the opposition a limited amount of leeway to express anti-KMT thinking. The Chungli (1977) and Kaohsiung (1979) incidents were two serious clashes between the KMT regime and the opposition (Wu 1997:

241–242). In December 1979, most of those who had participated in the Kaohsiung uprisings were arrested, tried by a military tribunal on charges of sedition, and given long prison sentences.

During the period 1980–1986, Chiang's policy towards political opposition was a combination of mobilization and limited admission. In the 1972 local election, the term *dangwai* (outside the party) was used to refer to non-KMT candidates. Before 1981, the *dangwai* was by no means a fully-fledged opposition force. The opposition grew with the electoral competition that developed from the early 1980s, consisting of elections to the Legislative Yuan. By holding popular elections and expanding electoral participation from local to national level, the KMT gradually permitted the existence of opposition forces. Although the KMT government banned the formation of new political parties, it tolerated the activities of the *dangwai*.

In Chiang Ching-kuo's last years, his reformist attitude led him to adopt a mixed policy of participation towards the opposition. In 1986, the *dangwai* initiated the formation of the DPP. Instead of banning the DPP and arresting its leaders, Chiang promised to accelerate political reforms. Additionally, KMT officials, with Chiang's permission, held regular meetings with DPP leaders to facilitate communication (Dickson 1996). These decisions signalled Chiang's determination to transform the KMT and the political system itself from a non-competitive authoritarian regime into a competitive democracy. After the death of Chiang Ching-kuo in 1988, Lee Teng-hui continued the democratization process within the KMT.

In summary, the KMT has changed substantially over the years. Its transformation confirms the theory of Weiner and LaPalombara (1966) with respect to the evolution of one-party regimes. Since the 1970s, Taiwan has experienced rapid socio-economic development that is conducive to democratic transition; even the KMT leadership has had to respond to these social changes by incrementally modifying its policy towards the opposition. The KMT, over time, has transformed itself from an authoritarian and exclusionary party into a pragmatic and inclusionary one.

Changes to KMT manifestos on China policy

Given the significance of relations between the two sides of the Taiwan Strait in shaping people's perceptions of and support for a particular party in Taiwan, successive KMT leaderships have produced manifestos revealing specific stances on issues in this area (Fell 2002). As the KMT came under pressure from more competitive elections and from a more democratic party structure, we would expect its manifestos to become more responsive to popular demands, especially on topics that are usually highly constrained by ideological factors. The following pages provide an analysis of the evolution of the KMT's manifestos in four phases, each of which was marked by a change in the party leadership or in the party's China policy orientation. It will be seen how the transformation of the KMT's China policies correlates with its evolution into a more democratic party.

The first phase of Lee's presidency: 1988–1996

In order to demonstrate that the ROC was the only legitimate political entity representing China in the international community, Chiang Kai-shek insisted on a position of *hanzei bu liangli* (literally, 'the legitimate government does not coexist with rebels') (Tu 1996).[1] Even though the leaders of the People's Republic of China (PRC) began a peaceful propaganda campaign for reunification from the late 1970s, which included Deng Xiaoping's 'one country, two systems' formula of 1979 and the Message to Compatriots in Taiwan, released in 1982, the ROC's stance remained rigidly in line with Chiang Ching-kuo's 'three no's' policy (no compromise, no contact and no negotiation) (Huang and Qian 1994). However, after the lifting of martial law, the government permitted people in Taiwan to visit their relatives in China and further freed-up investment and tourism on the mainland (Weng 1997: 53–56).

After Lee Teng-hui succeeded to the presidency in 1988, the official position on national sovereignty was expressed in the Guidelines for National Unification, which stated that China would ultimately be reunified through a three-stage process. This stance was further solidified by the '1992 Consensus' which emphasized the principle that there was only one China. Although both the KMT government and the PRC adopted a 'one-China' stance, the two sides interpreted this principle in quite different ways (Romberg 2008). Two quasi-official bodies, Taiwan's Straits Exchange Foundation (SEF) and the mainland's Association for Relations across the Taiwan Straits (ARATS), were established in 1992 to take charge of relations between Taiwan and mainland China in both the private and public spheres.

The KMT adopted an amendment to its platform at the party's 13th national congress in 1993. In the 1988 version of the platform, the PRC was required to initiate internal reforms in five areas, while the 1993 version incorporated the principles stated in the Guidelines for National Unification.[2] Thus, the amended version sought stable and mutually beneficial relations with the mainland with a view to eventually realizing the unification of China. Strictly excluding any possibility of territorial secession, the 1993 party platform also called for the cooperation of citizens at home and overseas in support of the ROC's bid for participation in international organizations. In the uncertain climate after the transfer of Hong Kong and Macau to the PRC, the platform stated that the KMT should play an active role in protecting Taiwan's liberal way of life, and promote stability and prosperity by enacting special laws to increase interactions with the mainland.

Lee's second term: 1996–2000

During President Lee's second term, he seemed to change his views on both national sovereignty and interaction with mainland China. In an interview with the German broadcaster Deutsche Welle on 9 July 1999, Lee pointed out that the ROC and the PRC were at that time 'two states in one nation' and in a 'special state-to-state relationship'. It emphasized non-interference in administrative constitutional governance and ensured that both sides were separate political entities (Lee 1999).[3] In the same year, Lee also proposed the concept of 'new Taiwanese nationalism', which he explained thus: 'Regardless of your ethnic origin, be it aborigine, islander, or mainlander, once you live in Taiwan, have an emotional linkage with Taiwan, and are willing to sacrifice for Taiwan, then you are one of the New Taiwanese' (Yu 1999).

Concerning interactions with China, Lee reaffirmed his stance of 'cautious self-restraint' in response to Beijing's policy of encouraging Taiwanese investors in the mainland to put pressure on the Taiwan government to adopt a more relaxed strategy (Wu and Yen 1999). Worried that Taiwan was becoming more dependent on the mainland and that domestic industries were investing there rather than upgrading their operations at home, Lee asked the Ministry of Economic Affairs to impose restrictions on mainland investment and technological cooperation while at the same time offering alternatives such as the 'go south policy' (Chen 1996).

The revised version of the KMT party platform in 1997 stated that national unification was the common goal of all KMT members and that with this goal in mind, the KMT had, since the early 1990s, proposed various win-win solutions to replace zero-sum confrontation between the ROC and the PRC. The platform also stated that improved relations with mainland China should be achieved through increasing interactions and the building up of mutual respect between the two sides, while at the same time recognizing the status quo. The platform further advocated a policy of 'cautious self-restraint', lest reckless investment in mainland China should damage domestic economic growth. The government was urged to pursue policies that would be mutually beneficial and it was hoped that the PRC would discard its ideology of conflict and confrontation in order to facilitate friendly negotiations and interactions.

Power transition to Lien Chan, 2000–2005

Lee was expelled from the KMT for his role in the founding of the separatist Taiwan Solidarity Union in 2001. During the 2000 presidential election campaign, Lien Chan, the KMT candidate, promised that he would follow the principles laid down in the Guidelines for National Unification (Wu 2000). In April 2005, Lien was invited to Beijing by Hu Jintao, the general secretary of the Chinese Communist Party (CCP). The two sides issued the Joint Vision on Cross-Strait Peaceful Development (Kao and Wang 2008), in which the 1992 Consensus was mentioned in order to counter any appeal for Taiwan independence (Chan 2006).[4] This document led to the establishment of the Cross-Strait Economic, Trade and Cultural Forum in 2006, which continued to play an important role in shaping policy consensus between the two parties even after the KMT returned to power in 2008 (Wang 2007).

Back in Taiwan, Chen Shui-bian of the DPP won the 2000 presidential election, an event that symbolized the progress of democracy in terms of party politics (Fell 2005a: 129–133). Although the new administration introduced the 'mini three links' (limited postal, transportation and trade links between certain cities in Fujian Province and the islands of Kinmen and Matsu) under the slogan of 'pro-active liberalization with effective management', benign interactions between Taiwan and the PRC were not sustainable under Chen's leadership (Sheng 2002: 57–62). In 2002, Chen characterized the relationship as 'one country on each side [of the Taiwan Strait]' which was an explicit expression of Taiwan's statehood and broke the linkage between the mainland and Taiwan. His pro-independence stance became even more apparent when he abolished the National Unification Council and held two referendums, one in 2004 on cross-Strait security and the other in 2008 on Taiwan's proposed application for membership of the United Nations (Sheng 2002: 40–49).

The KMT's party platform was amended in two phases in July 2001 and August 2005. The main content of these amendments can be analysed as follows. First, it was stated that in order to guarantee national security, the two sides of the Strait should begin negotiations in line with the 1992 Consensus to create a win-win situation. In accordance with the Guidelines for National Unification, the KMT would put forward concrete policies for eventual unification through the establishment of a confederation, while ensuring that Taiwan's interests were not impaired. Second, with the precondition that Beijing would accept the 1992 Consensus and peaceful engagement, the KMT supported the establishment of mechanisms for institutional negotiations and interactions so as to actively seek opportunities for the achievement of common benefits rather than passive resistance.

Ma Ying-jeou's fusion of ruling party and government since 2008

After Lien Chan retired, Ma Ying-jeou took over the leadership of the KMT. Ma's status was enhanced when he won the presidential election in 2008. For Ma, the basic motif of cross-Strait relations has been the 'three no's' – no unification, no independence and no use of force. In Ma's view, guided by the 1992 Consensus, Taiwan and the PRC should maintain the status quo by pursuing reconciliation and a truce (Rigger 2008). During his 2012 campaign for re-election, Ma proposed the 'golden decade' policy and outlined a vision of cross-Strait relations in which a peace agreement with the PRC would be achieved within a decade. Ma also envisaged an increase in the intensity of cross-Strait interactions without either side questioning the other's sovereignty or jurisdiction (Xin 2010).

After Ma came to office, official negotiations between the two sides of the Taiwan Strait and other institutional mechanisms were re-established, as outlined in the KMT's 2009 platform. The most important events resulting from this were the 'Chiang-Chen summits' between the leaders of the SEF and ARATS, the first of which took place in June 2008. Specific topics such as cross-Strait charter flights and tourism were discussed and the agreements that were concluded served as the foundation for subsequent domestic legislation (Zhang 2011).

Among the breakthroughs were the establishment of the 'three links' and the signing of the Economic Cooperation Framework Agreement (ECFA) (Tung 2011: 133–135). The two signatories promised to lower tariffs for items such as machinery, petrochemicals, textiles and auto parts.

After the corruption case against Chen Shui-bian had dealt a severe blow to the DPP, Tsai Ing-wen took over the party's chairmanship in 2008 and stood as the party's candidate in the 2012 presidential election. In August 2010, Tsai and her future running mate, Su Jia-chyuan, announced a 'ten-year policy' covering such topics as national security, employment and cross-Strait trade. This platform and a statement issued by Tsai in February 2011 denied the existence of the 1992 Consensus and stressed that maintaining the status quo was the only 'consensus' agreed by the people of Taiwan. She also criticized the KMT's economic dependence on mainland China, inferring that such a one-dimensional, simplified path of development would certainly endanger Taiwan's future and sovereignty.[5]

The KMT revised its party platform in June 2007 and again in October 2009 after Ma Ying-jeou had been elected president. Promoting the normalization of relations with mainland China in terms of economic cooperation was the main aim of collaboration in transportation, trade and investment. The platform included such goals as the opening-up of tourism, agricultural exchanges, the limited recognition of educational qualifications conferred in China, mutual assistance in judicial matters, and cooperation on green-energy innovation. In addition to the adoption of military confidence-building mechanisms and the signing of a peace agreement, flexible and independent diplomacy coupled with the enhancement of national defence were seen as the foundations of peace between the two sides and the maintenance of Taiwan's sovereignty.

The above analysis provides only a rough idea of the correlation between the evolution of the KMT's China policies and its transformation into a more democratic party. Now, we will use five opinion surveys conducted by the ROC government's Mainland Affairs Council (MAC) since 2008 to examine how the KMT's efforts to adapt its China policies have been perceived by the public.[6] According to the 2008 Survey of Perceptions on Mainland Policies and Cross-Strait Negotiation, most people were positive about closer cooperation between Taiwan and China. More than 60 per cent of respondents had a positive view of direct cross-Strait flights, for example. In the 2009 survey on the second Chiang-Chen meeting, approximately 75 per cent of respondents were satisfied with the four agreements signed during the meeting and anticipated that they would have a positive impact on economic development. Nearly three-quarters of respondents to the survey on the third Chiang-Chen meeting thought that institutional consultation was an appropriate mechanism for dealing with cross-Strait issues. Another poll was conducted in December 2009, prior to the fourth Chiang-Chen meeting, in which more than 60 per cent of the respondents expressed satisfaction with the issues to be covered in the meeting. With the controversy over the signing of the ECFA in mind, the MAC released the poll on the fifth Chiang-Chen meeting after the talks had taken place. Even though the ruling and opposition parties held conflicting views concerning the legal status of the ECFA, with some DPP members even proposing a referendum on the subject, nearly 60 per cent of respondents expressed satisfaction with the agreement, and approximately 80 per cent agreed with the government's institutionalized approach to cross-Strait relations.

Although cross-Strait relations are ideological and highly controversial in Taiwan, the above survey data indicate that Ma's China policies have the support of at least 50 per cent of the population. The surveys also show that most people are interested in the benefits to be gained from cross-Strait cooperation and the ROC government's mainland policies. The KMT government thus gained legitimacy through its pursuit of cross-Strait cooperation and by responding to demands for a peaceful and mutually-beneficial relationship with the mainland.

The KMT's response to socio-economic problems

As Taiwan achieved a higher degree of democratic consolidation, electoral campaigns and manifestos became more responsive to popular demands. This is apparent in the above analysis of how the KMT's manifestos on relations with mainland China have been amended in line with changes in the political environment. But voters are concerned with other issues apart from cross-Strait relations – most notably, official corruption and the gap between rich and poor. Chang, Chu and Huang (2011) asked why Taiwan's democratic performance was highly rated in reports published by international organizations while its citizens gave it a low rating. Rather than the standards of democratic quality emphasized by experts, such as freedom, citizens tend to base their judgements on issues they care most about, such as controlling corruption, improving the rule of law, and providing more accountable and responsible government. Hence, we will explore below how Ma's manifestos for the 2008 and 2012 presidential elections responded to voters' demands for clean government and economic equality.

Clean government

Corruption had long been associated with the KMT, which had cultivated clientelist relationships with local factions in an effort to establish its legitimacy after its retreat to Taiwan. In response to criticism from the DPP, the KMT in recent years has advocated judicial independence as a way of countering corruption. In order to cultivate a 'clean' image, the KMT also announced that severe disciplinary action, including suspension of membership, would be taken against party members guilty of corruption (Fell 2005b). In these circumstances, it is not surprising that the issue of corruption was a focus of Ma's election campaigns in both 2008 and 2012.

The 2008 KMT presidential manifesto clearly stated that corruption had become even more of a problem since the DPP took office in 2000, and that clean government could only be achieved by both preventing and fighting corrupt practices. Relevant measures were proposed as follows. First, integrity committees were to be established at central and local levels under the supervision of the Judicial Yuan. These committees would issue periodic anti-corruption reports. Second, there was to be no political interference in the work of independent organs, such as the Control Yuan and the judicial sector. Further, the manifesto called for changes to current laws governing corruption. For example, heavier sentences were to be imposed on public servants who failed to declare all their assets.

In his 2012 election manifesto, entitled 'The Golden Decade', Ma Ying-jeou set out his vision for the future of the country. With respect to countering corruption, Ma's main goal was to increase the transparency and efficiency of the public sector. He promised measures to counter corrupt practices, plus the amalgamation of existing official anti-corruption networks to reduce such crimes as embezzlement, bribery and graft, and to increase the conviction rates for these crimes. The manifesto also included proposals for judicial reforms aimed at increasing the independence and accountability of the judiciary.

The gap between rich and poor

Owing to Taiwan's dependence on international trade for economic growth, its economic performance was negatively affected by the 2008 global financial crisis (Wang 2010). In response to rising demands for government intervention in the economy, Ma proposed a number of policy innovations. Besides traditional strategies, such as economic innovation and industrial upgrading, Ma promised to establish closer cross-Strait economic cooperation. Ma was also under pressure from social movements and non-governmental organizations to take care of the welfare of economically disadvantaged groups (Ho 2010). Since the 1980s, with higher rates of economic growth, an inevitable gap between rich and poor has opened up in Taiwan (Hsiao 2007). To tackle the problem of unequal distribution of wealth, Ma prioritized social welfare policies for the economically disadvantaged in both the 2008 and 2012 election campaigns.

To remedy problems originating from the polarized distribution of wealth in society, the 2008 campaign manifesto gave priority to poverty reduction. Members of low-income households were to be offered employment assistance, counselling, training, welfare-to-work, and loans to start their own businesses. Ma also proposed subsidies for education and housing to enable the children of such households to become economically self-sufficient as they grew up. An emergency relief fund financed by the Taiwan Lottery was to be provided for the unemployed. The 2012 manifesto included policy recommendations to remedy the unequal distribution of incomes in Taiwan society. To achieve social justice and to raise living standards for the poor, the manifesto set out four areas for improvement, namely housing, maternity services, employment and special arrangements for economically disadvantaged minority peoples. In this manifesto, the KMT promised to encourage more job opportunities for people from lower-income households. 'Justice in housing' was another important topic raised during the 2012 campaign. In order to combat real estate speculation,

Ma advocated a property purchase tax system based on actual selling prices. He also promised subsidized housing for people on low incomes or newly-weds.

Most of these policy proposals have been realized. For example, the April 2009 amendments to the Anti-corruption Act incorporated the crime of not declaring how one obtained one's assets, while the establishment of an Anti-corruption Agency under the Ministry of Justice and the passage of the Judges Act in July 2011 facilitated further action against corruption. As for economic equality, the main government actions include the imposition of a luxury tax in late 2011, the lowering of the poverty subsidy threshold, and the introduction of an employment promotion programme that provides subsidies for enterprises that hire those who find it difficult to obtain work.

Yet despite all these positive measures, the public did not give the government much credit for doing so. In various polls conducted by the TVBS Poll Center and the *United Daily News*, President Ma received a low approval rating on anti-corruption and administrative satisfaction (Survey Center at United Daily News Group 2012).[7] On the one hand, this may be a result of public dissatisfaction with political scandals or unfavourable policy changes.[8] In other words, distrust of the government is a short-term response to negative news rather than a long-term assessment of the government's effectiveness. These sentiments appear to have been aroused by intensive, if not exaggerated, reports in the mass media. On the other hand, it may be that despite his 2009 blueprint for reform that embodied the principles of democracy and anti-corruption, Ma has subsequently failed to bring about real structural change such as disposal of ill-gotten party assets. As the poll on party image shows, the KMT scores low in terms of integrity and pro-reform orientation.[9]

Conclusion

In Taiwan in the early 1950s, the KMT reorganized itself into a 'democratic revolutionary' party with strong authoritarian characteristics. The KMT's party organizations permeated Taiwanese society and ruled the island nation for five decades. Meanwhile, the party continued to adapt itself to the changing social and political environments. Through this process of evolution, the KMT regime moved from hard authoritarianism through soft authoritarianism to a weak democratic system. The ideological proclivities of the three consecutive KMT leaders – Presidents Chiang Kai-shek, Chiang Ching-kuo and Lee Teng-hui – contributed to this transition. In terms of its membership structure, the expansion of the grassroots ranks of the KMT consolidated the party's governing base. At the same time, the KMT was transformed from a mainlander-dominated party into a Taiwanese-based one. Taiwanization involved not only the recruitment of large numbers of ordinary native Taiwanese as rank-and-file members, but also the promotion of Taiwanese elites into the party's ruling circles. By the 1990s, Taiwanese held a majority of seats in the key party decision-making bodies. The party's policy towards the opposition has also changed over time from one of repression to one of mobilization and limited participation, and then to one of full participation. Faced with a plural social structure and increased electoral competition, the KMT has gradually adjusted its role and its structure from a Leninist-style party to an ordinary democratic party.

How has this authoritarian party been able to survive democratic reform? Over the past decades, the governing KMT, driven by socio-economic change, has adjusted its practices to enable it to interact with an array of new political groups and to deal with deeper social cleavages. Throughout the evolution of the KMT regime, the party has successfully appealed to the electorates by recruiting more Taiwanese elites into its leadership. At the same time, the KMT has gradually evolved from a revolutionary-oriented party into one that is oriented towards democratic elections. In line with Epstein's (1986) observations concerning the adaptation of US parties to adverse circumstances, the KMT may be said to have become 'porous' and 'permeable' to social change through its successive organizational reforms, as it has sought to retain the support of the majority of the electorate and maintain its political dominance. Yet, even though the KMT regime has survived the transition to democracy, it may lose its dominant position in the face of increasingly fierce electoral competition and democratic consolidation if it fails to democratize itself further and to do so at an even faster pace in the near future.

Now we return to the question raised at the beginning of this chapter, is Taiwan currently a consolidated democracy? If the answer is yes, then how can the KMT accommodate itself to these democratic changes? With the KMT regaining power after the 2008 presidential election, Taiwan passed what Huntington called the 'two-turnover test'. In addition to this, two-party competition remains stable under two different electoral systems for legislative elections. These political institutions and electoral outcomes demonstrate that Taiwan is institutionally close to a 'stable liberal democracy' as defined by Larry Diamond (1994). Besides, the political parties have also put forward policy proposals in areas such as relations with China and clean government as part of their party platforms and electoral campaigns in an effort to win the popular vote.

In addition to institutional factors, political parties in Taiwan still need to carry out further reforms in order to achieve democratic consolidation. As the 2012 survey data on party image shows, the public is still dissatisfied with the KMT's performance in terms of both integrity and responsiveness to popular demands. Although Ma, as chairman of the KMT, has repeatedly stressed the need for reform within the party, he has failed to put forward any concrete plans or policies. Nonetheless, despite its low approval ratings, the KMT still has advantages when it comes to attracting voters. In comparison with the DPP, it has more technocrats, is more flexible in dealing with mainland China, and has stronger personal networks that have developed from the old-time local factions and that can be mobilized for campaigning. Nevertheless, the results of recent presidential and legislative elections demonstrate that the KMT is not immune to challenges.[10] Ironically, even though the KMT regime has survived the transition to democracy, it may lose its ruling position in the wake of increasingly intensive electoral competition and democratic consolidation if it fails to accelerate the pace of future democratization. Despite the lack of mature civil society as a compelling driving force for party reforms, electoral competition is expected to further consolidate Taiwanese democracy in the far future to come.

Notes

1 This phrase reflects Chiang's uncompromising stance that the ROC was the only legitimate entity representing China.
2 These areas were political democratization, economic liberalization, the diversification of society, and cultural Sinicization.
3 The ROC and the PRC had closer trade and other ties than most independent countries on account of their shared history and ethnic and cultural heritage.
4 Sensitive issues, such as Taiwan's participation in the World Health Organization, were set aside for further discussion.
5 The analysis is based on content from the DPP's '10 iing' website. For more information, see http://10.iing.tw/ accessed 3 March 2013.
6 For details of the surveys, please visit the MAC's website: www.mac.gov.tw/np.asp?ctNode=6331&mp=1 accessed 3 March 2013.
7 These polls include 'Poll on Approval Rating before President Ma's Inauguration' (conducted on 15 May 2012) and 'Poll on President Ma's Satisfaction Rating after the Lin Yi-shih Bribery Case' (conducted on 21 July 2012). For the poll results, see www1.tvbs.com.tw/tvbs2011/pch/tvbs_poll_center.aspx accessed 3 March 2013.
8 For example, rising fuel and electricity prices and the political scandal arising from the Lin Yi-shih bribery case both had an impact on the poll results.
9 Full results of the TVBS poll can be found at www1.tvbs.com.tw/FILE_DB/PCH/201204/6pjdybsy03.pdf accessed 3 March 2013.
10 In the 2012 presidential election, for instance, though negatively affected by the TaiMed case and the Su Jia-chyuan farmhouse scandal, Tsai Ing-wen still garnered 45.63 per cent of the vote, while the incumbent Ma Ying-jeou obtained 51.6 per cent.

References

Chan, S. (2006) 'Taiwan in 2005: strategic interaction in two-level games', *Asian Survey*, 46 (1): 63–68.

Chang, Y., Chu, Y. and Huang, M. (2011) 'Procedural quality only? Taiwanese democracy reconsidered', *International Political Science Review*, 35(5), 491–511.

Chen, X. (1996) 'Taiwan investments in China and Southeast Asia: "Go west, but also go south"', *Asian Survey*, 36(5), 447–467.

Cheng, T. (1989) 'Democratizing the quasi-Leninist regime in Taiwan', *World Politics*, 41, 471–499.

Cohen, M.J. (1991) *Taiwan at the Crossroads*, Washington, DC: Asia Resource Center.

Diamond, L. (1994) 'Rethinking civil society: toward democratic consolidation', *Journal of Democracy*, 5(3), 3–17.

Dickson, B.J. (1996) 'The Kuomintang before democratization: organizational change and the role of elections', in H. Tien (ed.) *Taiwan's Electoral Politics and Democratic Transition*, Armonk, NY: M.E. Sharpe.

Epstein, L.D. (1986) *Political Parties in the American Mold*, Madison, WI: University of Wisconsin Press.

Fell, D. (2002) 'Party platform change in Taiwan's 1990s elections', *Issues & Studies*, 38(2), 31–60.

Fell, D. (2005a) *Party Politics in Taiwan: Party Change and the Democratic Evolution of Taiwan, 1991–2004*, New York: Routledge.

Fell, D. (2005b) 'Political and media liberalization and political corruption in Taiwan', *The China Quarterly*, 184, 875–893.

Ho, M. (2010) 'Understanding the trajectory of social movements in Taiwan (1980–2010)', *Journal of Current Chinese Affairs*, 39(3), 3–22.

Hsiao, H.M. (2007) 'Reflection on income inequality problem and the middle classes issue in Taiwan', *Taiwan Democracy Quarterly*, 4(4), 143–150 [in Chinese].

Huang, J. and Qian, A.X. (1994) 'One country, two systems, three law families, and four legal regions: the emerging inter-regional conflicts of law in China', *Duke Journal of Comparative & International Law*, 5, 289–328.

Huang, T. (1995) 'Electoral competition and the evolution of the Kuomintang', *Issues & Studies*, 31(May), 91–120.

Huang, T. (1996) 'Elections and the evolution of the Kuomintang', in H. Tien (ed.) *Taiwan's Electoral Politics and Democratic Transition*, New York: M.E. Sharpe.

Huntington, S.P. (1991) *The Third Wave: Democratization in the Late Twentieth Century*, Norman: University of Oklahoma Press.

Huntington, S.P. (1992) 'Foreword', in T. Cheng and S. Haggard (eds) *Political Change in Taiwan*, Boulder: Lynne Rienner.

Kao, C. and Wang, C. (2008) 'On development of cross-Strait relations: reviews and future perspectives', *Prospect Quarterly*, 9(3), 167–198.

Lee, T. (1999) 'Understanding Taiwan: bridging the perception gap', *Foreign Affairs*, 78(6), 9–14.

Linz, J.J. and Stepan, A. (1996) *Problems of Democratic Transition and Consolidation: Southern Europe, South America and Post-communist Europe*, Baltimore: Johns Hopkins University Press.

O'Donnell, G., Schmitter, P.C. and Whitehead, L. (eds) (1986) *Transitions from Authoritarian Rule: Prospects for Democracy*, Baltimore: Johns Hopkins University Press.

Peng, M. (1972) *A Taste of Freedom*, New York: Holt, Rinehart and Winston.

Rigger, S. (2008) 'Taiwan's presidential and legislative elections', *Orbis*, 52(4), 689–700.

Romberg, A.D. (2008) 'Cross Strait relations: in search of peace', *China Leadership Monitor*, 23, 1–19.

Schattschneider, E.E. (1960) *The Semisovereign People: A Realist's View of Democracy in America*, New York: Holt, Rinehart and Winston.

Sheng, L. (2002) *China and Taiwan: Cross-Strait Relations under Chen Shui-bian*, London: Zed Books.

Survey Center at United Daily News Group (2012) 'Before May 20, Administrative Satisfaction with Ma Reaches New Low', *United Daily News*, 18 May: Section A1; http://paper.udn.com/udnpaper/PID0001/216512/web/ accessed 2 March 2013 [in Chinese].

Tien, H. and Chu, Y. (1996) 'Building democracy in Taiwan', *China Quarterly*, 145: 1141–1170.

Tu, W. (1996) 'Cultural identity and the politics of recognition in contemporary Taiwan', *China Quarterly*, 148, 1115–1140.

Tung, C. (2011) *Taiwan's Strategy towards China: From Bandwagoning to Balancing*, Taipei: Showwe Information Co.

Wang, J. (2007) 'Hu Jintao's 'new thinking' on cross-Strait relations', *American Foreign Policy Interests*, 29, 23–34.

Wang, J. (2010) 'The strategies adopted by Taiwan in response to the global financial crisis, and Taiwan's role in Asia-Pacific economic integration', *Japan and the World Economy*, 22(4), 254–263.

Weiner, M. and LaPalombara, J. (1966) 'Conclusion: The impact of parties on political development', in J. LaPalombara and M. Weiner (eds) *Political Parties and Political Development*, Princeton: Princeton University Press.

Weng, S.J. (1997) 'Mainland China, Taiwan, and Hong Kong as international actors', in G.A. Postiglione and J.T. Tang (eds) *Hong Kong's Reunion with China: The Global Dimensions*, New York: M.E. Sharpe.

Winckler, E.A. (1984) 'Institutionalization and participation on Taiwan: from hard to soft authoritarianism?', *China Quarterly*, 99, 481–499.

Wu, C. (1997) 'From authoritarianism to democracy in Taiwan: socioeconomic change and political response', *American Review of Politics*, 18(Fall), 227–248.

Wu, C. and Yen, S. (1999) ' "Cautious self-restraint" versus "courageously going west?" An analysis of Taiwan's investment in mainland China', *Issues & Studies*, 38(7), 43–62.

Wu, Y. (2000) 'The impact of Taiwan's presidential elections on cross-Straits relations: vote-maximizing model and strategic triangle approach', *Prospect Quarterly*, 1(3), 1–33 [in Chinese].

Xin, Q. (2010) 'Beyond power politics: institution-building and mainland China's Taiwan policy transition', *Journal of Contemporary China*, 19(65), 525–539.

Yu, T. (1999) 'Relations between Taiwan and China after the missile crisis: toward reconciliation?', *Pacific Affairs*, 72(1): 39–55.

Zhang, B. (2011) 'Taiwan's new grand strategy', *Journal of Contemporary China*, 20(69): 269–285.

Part II

Flawed democracies, developing democracies and democratic consolidation

4 Indonesia's low-quality democracy consolidated

The dangers of drift and corrosion

Steven Drakeley

Addressing the Sixth Assembly of the World Movement for Democracy in Jakarta in April 2010, Indonesian President Susilo Bambang Yudhoyono declared democracy in Indonesia 'irreversible' (Yudhoyono 2010). The sceptics had been proven wrong, he asserted, and while acknowledging that challenges remain, such as eradicating 'money politics', he lauded the establishment of democratic institutions and the rule of law. SBY (as Indonesians refer to him) has good reason to brag about Indonesia's democratic achievements, but few observers give quite as much credit; indeed some denounce Indonesia's democracy as deeply flawed (Robison and Hadiz 2004; Klinken 2009). Although the 2014 elections will constitute a more conclusive test, Indonesian democracy does appear consolidated. It is now normalized, a 'daily fact of life' as SBY put it, or to employ Linz and Stepan's famous phrase (1996: 15) democracy is the 'only game in town' with regular changes of government accepted without challenge either on the streets or from the barracks. But SBY's claim for its irreversibility cannot be endorsed. Indonesia's democracy has flaws of such proportions that reversion to authoritarian government remains possible. Moreover, although consolidated, Indonesia's democracy is of a relatively low quality and the factors that make it so are deeply entrenched. In this chapter I will discuss the defects and their dangers to Indonesia's democracy, and consider its prospects.

Before proceeding it is appropriate to acknowledge the immense democratic progress made since the late 1990s, despite formidable opposition. Foremost is the free formation of political parties with equal rights to participate in the electoral process, allowed for the first time since the 1950s: a far cry from the previous condition of a thinly disguised one-party state. Importantly, an independent electoral commission (KPU) has been established, removing the power to administer elections from the government-controlled bureaucracy. Since President Soeharto's fall from power there have been three (substantially) free, fair and peaceful national elections, and numerous local and regional elections, producing results widely regarded as genuinely reflective of the voters' will. Again, this contrasts sharply with the heavily manipulated elections during Soeharto's 'New Order' regime. Furthermore, participants (mostly) abided by the 'rules of the game', losers accepted the results and peaceful power handovers occurred when appropriate. Second, the authoritarian and hitherto unchanged 1945

Constitution has been extensively amended, with human rights safeguards and numerous checks and balances inserted, including separation of the powers between executive, legislature and judiciary (Ellis 2007). Important here was the creation of a constitutional court and an independent judicial commission. Third, the political system has been radically decentralized with real powers devolved to directly-elected local level governments. Fourth, the principles of freedom of association and the right to strike and demonstrate now exist and are frequently exercised. Again this differs markedly from before when political and labour activists risked imprisonment, torture and 'disappearance'. Fifth and highly significantly, the previously tightly controlled media has been unshackled. Publishing permits together with the Information Ministry that issued them have been abolished, resulting in an explosion of fiercely competitive media outlets conveying a wide gamut of opinion. Finally, and crucially, the military have been pushed out of formal politics and the police force separated from the armed forces. Serving officers no longer held positions in the government or bureaucracy and the military's reserved places in national and local parliaments were abolished in 2004 when all seats at all levels of government became contested and direct presidential elections were introduced.

The contrast with the preceding decades is stark. Following the stuttering parliamentary democracy of the early 1950s, Indonesia experienced authoritarian rule from President Sukarno's declaration of martial law in March 1957, the prelude to his 1959 founding of 'guided democracy', until the seemingly permanent New Order's downfall in 1998. The latter's sudden demise was quite unexpected; but the swift transition to democracy astounded observers, most of whom expected an extended period of chaos and violence followed by the emergence of another authoritarian regime (Crouch 2010: 2). Optimists merely dared hope that the new regime would preside over cautious progress towards greater political pluralism, culminating eventually in a distant democracy. It is worth noting that Indonesia's stunning democratic transformation occurred well after the 'third wave of democratization' had ebbed (Diamond 2010: 21).

The authoritarian and economic threats

Given Indonesia's long authoritarian history, expectations of democracy's rapid reversion to another authoritarian regime were understandable. Not since the 1960s has there been any prospect of a leftist authoritarian regime, but concerns over the possibility of the emergence of some form of military-backed authoritarian regime were credible, even (albeit less plausibly) an extreme Islamist regime. Indeed, immediately following Soeharto's resignation, army elements contemplated a coup (Mietzner 2009a: 134–136). And for several years afterwards similar elements manipulated numerous outbreaks of interethnic and interreligious conflict (Kingsbury 2003). Either they sought to generate an atmosphere of sufficient crisis to make a military takeover palatable or, more likely, they aimed to block political reforms inimical to their interests. During the presidencies of Megawati Sukarnoputri and (former general) SBY, however, the military became reconciled to the emerging democratic status quo and their semi-depoliticized role within it, reassured that it would not entail chaos or national disintegration. Probably they also recognized the absence of support for overthrowing the new democracy. Currently no realistic prospect of a military takeover exists unless some massive crisis should engulf the nation. Under such circumstances, however, it is quite conceivable that a president might 'suspend' democracy with military backing, or that the military might assume power itself to 'maintain security and stability'.

Indonesia's extremist Islamist organizations would implement an authoritarian theocracy if they could. It is very unlikely, however, that they will ever be in a position to do so. Indonesia's Muslims (88 per cent of the population) have repeatedly shown through the ballot box that support for such a polity is very low. Moreover, Indonesia's mass Muslim organizations Muhammadiyah and Nahdlatul Ulama, together with all but some small Muslim-based parties, reject an Islamic state for Indonesia, let alone one that is not democratic. Islamist extremists are also badly hampered by disunity, disagreeing sharply over methods and the specifics of their utopian goal. Their miniscule chances of success rest upon a massive surge in support and obtaining backing or at least acquiescence from the military. The former is barely conceivable even in the event of a severe and protracted political crisis, and only massive popular support could possibly persuade the military to accept an Islamist regime. Although its traditional hostility towards Islamist politics has waned, it is implausible that the military would champion a cause it fought against for so long.

From where might a crisis of sufficient scale to propel Indonesia back to authoritarian rule come? Indonesia's famously complex ethnic and religious composition is one possible source. Since independence, numerous serious clashes between rival ethnic and religious groups have occurred and resentment of the numerically dominant Javanese (42 per cent) has contributed, as have religious differences, to several regionalist/separatist rebellions. Not surprisingly, the New Order regime justified its existence and policies partly on the supposed need for a strong state to manage such dangers. But, if anything, democracy has managed them better. The long-running rebellion in Aceh has ended with an apparently durable peace settlement and that in East Timor with the latter's (now amicable) departure from Indonesia. Only the conflict in West Papua drags on. Elsewhere a host of regionalist resentments have evaporated following the decentralization policies and accompanying extension of democracy to the local level. On the other hand, outbreaks of religious conflict have increased, partly because of the greater political space democracy allows extremists. But this should not be overstated. The friction does not reflect mainstream attitudes; indeed, overall the politicization of religious identity has been declining. Intimate relationships between particular parties and religious groups were common but Indonesian voters are now far less inclined to support parties based on ethnic or religious affiliations (Mujani and Liddle 2010: 95). This sentiment is also reflected in the shift to the middle ground on the previously highly divisive

Islamic versus secular state issue (Platzdasch 2009). Even overtly Muslim-based parties now emphasize their commitment to Indonesia's 'secular' state philosophy, the Pancasila, while simultaneously supporting a more Islamic Indonesia.

Economic problems are more likely to generate a major crisis. The notion often referred to as modernization theory, originally posited by Lipset (1959), that attainment of a certain level of economic development is a prerequisite for successful democracy, has been proven to be greatly overstated (Diamond 2008: 27). Yet generally speaking, low levels of economic development obviously make establishment and maintenance of a democracy significantly more difficult. Indonesian democracy's failure in the late 1950s is a case in point. But Indonesia is no longer the impoverished, underdeveloped country of that era. Per capita income tripled between the early 1970s and the Asian economic crisis in 1997–1998, producing a substantial middle class and greatly reduced poverty levels (UNDP 2000: 184). Growth dropped off dramatically for two years in tandem with the rest of Asia during this crisis, with attendant rises in the proportion of the population living in poverty, but it recovered to a respectable average level of 4.8 per cent between 1999 and 2008 (Diamond 2010: 29). More recently, Indonesia has been posting growth rates of around 6 per cent (6.5 per cent in 2011, 6.2 per cent in 2012, and 5.9 per cent projected for 2013), despite the Global Financial Crisis (World Bank 2013).

Although no major economic crisis looms on the horizon, they are rarely considerate enough to announce their coming. Worth recalling here is that all three of Indonesia's post-independence regime changes, including that which produced democracy, were strongly associated with economic crises. The latter case is particularly pertinent as it was the anger generated by the abruptly straightened circumstances of the new middle classes and of those tipped back into poverty that propelled the New Order's collapse. The perception took hold that the Soeharto regime was not only largely responsible for Indonesia's suddenly dire economic circumstances, but that its removal was necessary for recovery. This belief meshed with long simmering discontent over the refusal to even embark upon a process of democratization. A mirror image of this scenario, whereby an authoritarian regime replaces democracy in the event of sharply declining living standards during a future economic crisis is thus surely possible. Already there is much grumbling from those not prospering in the democratic era and nostalgia for the New Order with its average growth rates of 10 per cent is rising. This grumbling links with other complaints. It is well understood that Indonesia's impressive economic progress since the 1970s was accompanied by particularly high levels of social disparity. Certainly it spawned an explosion in Indonesia's middle class and lifted a significant proportion of the population out of poverty. But a tiny super rich elite also emerged and the yawning gulf between its living conditions and those of the vast majority fuels considerable resentment. The bitterness was muted while poverty levels were falling; it could be swallowed as the price of development. But ominously for democracy, the proportion living in poverty has barely shifted since and the equality gap has continued to widen, a fact lamented by SBY recently (Saragih 2013a). Of course it is not axiomatic that when an economic crisis strikes democracy will fall. More likely it will manage the stresses such a crisis will inevitably bring. But Indonesian democracy's prospects of surviving these pressures will be significantly reduced if it continues to wallow at the current low-quality level. Under such circumstances its legitimacy can far more easily be called into question and commitment to its defence is more likely to be half-hearted.

The elements of low quality and attendant corrosion

While there is no imminent prospect of a coup, Indonesia's military still interferes in politics. With the ever present implied threat carried by its capacity to apply force, it exerts subtle and sometimes overt pressures as a discrete interest group with excellent contacts in politics, business and the bureaucracy. A measure of the influence the military yet wields is the total failure of reformers to dent the culture of impunity it enjoys, despite serious past and ongoing human rights abuses. Central to the problem is its retention of two levers facilitating continued political influence: its territorial structure that mirrors the civilian bureaucracy from top to bottom and its substantial business arm. The former enables political meddling especially at the local level where it is subject to less scrutiny and where civil society and state administration are weaker. Here local elites, politicians, and army commanders often find a synergy in their respective 'business' interests and capacities. This phenomenon also links dangerously neatly with the military's economic activities. Although it no longer controls large legitimate enterprises, the military still owns many medium-sized businesses. Moreover, to compensate its reduced place in legitimate business it has expanded involvement in criminal enterprises and other black economy activities (Mietzner 2009a: 363–364). The survival of the military's business wing, albeit truncated, effectively means it retains a significant degree of financial independence, which coupled with its historically rooted sense of autonomy, ensures that it remains not quite an instrument of elected government. Thus, even if the conventional menace posed by the military to democracy is currently dormant, its substantial informal political capacity constitutes a significant indirect threat by weakening the democratic system. It distorts political outcomes, dilutes civilian political authority and obstructs good governance by contributing to the deficiencies of the law and its agencies.

Similarly, the threat to democracy posed by Islamist extremists lies not in their remote prospects of attaining power but in two side effects of the violent campaigns waged since the late 1990s in pursuit of this chimera. The more serious involves violence and intimidation carried out by Islamist militias against Christians and other groups, including 'liberal' Muslims and minority Muslim sects such as the Shia and Ahmadis. The human rights watchdog Setara Institute (2012) reported 264 violent attacks against minorities in 2012, up from 244 in 2011. Such attacks damage the civic community and aggravate Indonesia's problems with identity politics. If unchecked, large-scale religious conflict could ensue, just as the extremists intend. But most damaging to Indonesian society, the state and democracy, is the impunity with which these blatant violations of the law take place (Christianto 2012). The inability or unwillingness of the state to protect its citizens, uphold the rule of law, and meet this challenge to its authority sends unfortunate messages. It emboldens the perpetrators to escalate their campaigns and signals to the victims that the state is either too weak to protect them or is complicit with the extremists, thus encouraging minorities to withdraw from the general community and perhaps to resort to violence themselves. That the government appears incapable of maintaining law and order and the rule of law dilutes the legitimacy of democracy and renders disillusioned and frightened citizens more susceptible to the siren appeal of authoritarianism.

The bombing campaign (currently suspended) by tiny extreme Islamist groups neither directly threatens democracy nor the Indonesian state's viability, although it has damaged Indonesia's economy and international reputation. Indirectly, however, if resurrected and sustained, it could goad the state into repressive measures incompatible with a liberal democracy. Given Indonesia's history, the security services could readily resort once more to routine employment of illegal methods, thereby undermining the rule of law and human rights safeguards. There is already some sign of this problem emerging with Densus 88, the specialist anti-terrorist police unit, criticized recently by human rights and Muslim groups for a 'trigger-happy' trend (*The Jakarta Post* 2013a). On the whole, however, Indonesia has earned much praise internationally for tackling its terrorist problem in accordance with the principle of the rule of law, including through policing and rehabilitation. Arguably Indonesian authorities, constrained by fears of appearing Islamophobic, have been too soft. Comparatively lenient sentences have been handed down to convicted terrorists and their supervision during incarceration and after release has been woefully inadequate (International Crisis Group 2007, 2010a), deficiencies that also undermine the rule of law and encourage extremism.

More seriously, a complex set of problems associated with corruption and deficient governance are undermining Indonesia's democracy. Politicians, bureaucrats, police and the judiciary share a potent disincentive to tackle Indonesia's corruption-riddled and dysfunctional administrative machinery.[1] A vast and intricate political economy has evolved to feed off the lucrative spoils. In a context where almost nothing can be accomplished without navigating the byzantine-like bureaucracy, government ministers, chairs of parliamentary committees and even ordinary members of parliament are cast automatically in the role of 'fixers', courted by all who can hope to leverage them. Few so placed can resist the temptation to extract fees for their 'fixing' services; especially because rent-seeking from government positions is a normative, historically rooted practice. Strategically-placed personnel in the judicial and policing systems profit similarly from the administrative dysfunction and associated corruption as 'fixers' and also as protectors. Thus the endemic corruption in the legal, bureaucratic and political systems is mutually reinforcing. Corruption on this scale would dent any polity's legitimacy but is especially problematic for democracy. The patent dishonesty of those entrusted as the people's representatives, coupled

with the attendant catering only for the interests of the wealthiest and best connected citizens, directly contradicts core democratic principles, disenfranchises
the general citizenry, undermines the rule of law, and erodes public trust
(Diamond 2008: 165).

These circumstances encourage elite acquisition of parliamentary seats and
party leadership positions in order to promote their business interests. Accentu-
ated by deep-seated patron-client traditions, Indonesia's elite has a reputation for
venality and arrogance. As mostly rent seekers rather than entrepreneurs, they
are largely dependent for business success on their capacity to leverage the state.
This fact, as much as greed, compels them as politicians to subordinate the
national interest to their own, in the process contributing greatly to poor policy
outcomes and poor governance generally. Indonesia's political parties have thus
become dominated by wealthy individuals and elite cliques for whom the parties
are merely the political wings of their businesses, the vehicles for their enmeshed
political/business ambitions. Exactly the same pattern has emerged at the local
level where local elites have responded identically to the devolution of power
and democracy to their terrain (Hadiz 2010). Thus with few exceptions, the
parties now have very shallow roots, represent social interests far less than
before, and offer little in the way of distinct political programmes. This is the
downside of their otherwise welcome move away from the identity politics that
plagued Indonesia in the 1950s and 1960s (Sukma 2010: 65–66).[2] Moreover,
since business competition is waged largely in the political arena there is a very
high commercial premium for electoral success. This 'commercialisation of
electoral politics' (Tomsa 2010: 148) grossly inflates electioneering costs as
wealthy politicians and their parties literally 'invest' ever larger sums in their
'bids' to secure election. Concomitantly, competition for votes is waged less
now through mobilization of party organizations and more through political
advertising and image building with a heavy 'show business' feel and all the
'tricks' of professional pollsters and political consultants (Qodari 2010). Old-
fashioned 'pork' barrelling persists, but is increasingly dwarfed by vote buying,
often thinly disguised as payments for election 'volunteers' and 'expenses' for
attending rallies. Ironically, this phenomenon has been exacerbated by the introduction of direct elections aimed at empowering voters. The higher electoral
costs, combined with their institutional weakness, have increased the parties'
vulnerability to takeover by wealthy patrons and made it almost impossible for
citizens of ordinary means to run effectively for office. Naturally the patrons,
candidates and the parties themselves are all nudged further by these circumstances towards corrupt behaviour. Once in office, they channel public wealth
into private and party pockets in order to recoup electoral expenses.

Unsurprisingly, elite obstructionism impedes reforms intended to democratize
the political process or reform the judicial system. Highly relevant is the prevailing culture of elite impunity. Wealth and influence allows the elite to flout the
law, often escaping punishment for serious and sometimes highly public crimes.
Apparently they would rather preserve their impunity than secure the theoretical
benefits accruing from the rule of law and the attendant reduction in business

costs. In the absence of serious measures to address these problems, Indonesia's business elite continues to extend its dominance over the post-Soeharto political system, controlling its commanding heights just as they do those of the economy. Unless this trend is reversed, Indonesia will evolve into an oligarchic democracy similar to the Philippines. The tenacity of powerful corrupt elements in resisting reform was vividly displayed during long-running and high stakes public battles between the police and the Corruption Eradication Commission (KPK). In 2009, elements in the police (regarded as one of the most corrupt institutions in Indonesia) went so far as to fabricate charges of corruption against KPK personnel. The effort failed ignominiously when KPK wiretaps of the police plot were played in parliament and broadcast live on television. Generally the public enthusiastically back the KPK, while most members of parliament support the police presumably because they have much to hide from the KPK which has claimed many parliamentary scalps. The struggle continues. In 2012 for instance, parliament obstructed the disbursement of funds necessary for KPK to move from its cramped premises to a bigger building (Aritonang 2012a). SBY, who campaigned as a corruption fighter, has largely dodged opportunities to intervene, denting his already faded anti-corruption credentials.

Indonesia has made some gains in the battle against corruption, however, as the KPK exposes and charges prominent individuals on an almost daily basis. Accordingly, Indonesia has moved from near the bottom of (formerly) 182 countries (now 176) in Transparency International's corruption index to 118th in 2012 (Transparency International 2012). But these figures also show how much remains to be done, with Thailand 88th, Malaysia 54th and Singapore 5th. The public's support for the KPK demonstrates its avid desire for corruption to be tackled. But without meaningful progress, disenchantment with democracy will grow. According to the Indonesian Survey Institute the proportion of people who trust the government's corruption fighting efforts fell from 83.7 per cent in 2009 to 34 per cent in 2010 (Alford 2011: 9). Claims that an Islamist regime would eradicate corruption have faltered as the KPK has charged prominent Islamist politicians recently with serious corruption offences. Similarly, because corruption under Soeharto was even worse, the notion that an authoritarian regime could solve the problem has gained little traction. But in the 2014 election, 35 per cent of voters will be first timers, for whom the New Order is already a dim childhood memory (Hardjono 2012).

There are several other serious flaws in the political system. An emerging problem is a sharp decline in the quality of election management by an under-resourced KPU. This was manifested in severe deficiencies affecting the 2009 national ballot, including faulty voter lists, shortages of ballot papers, and slow vote counting, which could have undermined confidence in the result and led to political instability (Sukma 2010: 55–59; Schmidt 2010: 100–101, 116–117). So far national elections have been mostly peaceful, but violence could emerge at this level as it has in some local elections if electoral management does not improve (International Crisis Group 2010b). These problems have prompted calls for a return to indirect elections at the local level (Tadjoeddin 2012:

477–478). Other problems linked to the decentralization of power to regional governments include the emergence of 'bossism' and higher levels of corruption and other abuses by local authorities (Aspinall 2010: 27; Buehler 2010). Problems also exist around efforts to implement local sharia regulations which conflict with the Constitution and national laws (Bush 2008: 175).

That Indonesia's parliament, once a rubber-stamp club of New Order cronies, is now an arena of genuine national debate, rightfully contributes to Indonesia's democratic credentials. Its notoriously cumbersome processes, however, contribute to poor governance with much-needed laws delayed for years. Of much greater concern is the parliament's opaque decision-making process that prevents voters from holding their representatives to account and facilitates corruption. The main culprits are the absence of voting, the committee system, and the absence of procedural transcripts (Sherlock 2010: 164–169). Legislation is rarely debated in plenary sessions (as per most parliaments), but in closed-door committee sessions until a 'consensus' is reached. The consensus is usually arrived at by party caucus leaders and is not necessarily endorsed by even a majority of committee members (Sherlock 2010: 168). These practices, which promote back-room deal making including of a pecuniary rather than political nature, are an unfortunate legacy of the New Order and Guided Democracy. These regimes insisted they were implementing Indonesia's supposed tradition (highly dubious historically) of consensus decision-making, a useful ideological fig leaf that obscured their tyrannous natures. The survival of the consensus notion in contemporary Indonesian parliamentary practice is no mere anachronism; its perpetuation lies at the root of the parliament's democratic defects. Apart from those touched on above, this unfortunate process means that often badly drafted bills are inadequately scrutinized and their implications poorly understood (Sherlock 2007: 37–38). The resulting low quality legislation contributes to the common phenomenon whereby laws are not actually applied (Ziegenhain 2009: 44). Legislative tardiness is another consequence, as without a voting process to resolve matters each party effectively has a veto until its concerns are somehow met (Sherlock 2010: 168–169). Deficiencies in executive government agencies and poor coordination between them and the parliament are also problematic, as is the parliament's lack of resources and budgetary autonomy (Sherlock 2007: 37–40, 49, 52–53). Together these defects in parliamentary procedures, resources and culture result in a parliament 'of cabalistic or oligarchic control' that even struggles to conduct its core functions effectively (Sherlock 2010: 161).

Better-resourced and operating in a similar fashion for decades, the executive level of government functions more effectively. A major weakness, however, is the tendency for presidents to form 'rainbow' cabinets with ministries handed to most parties. Rarely is there optimum matching of talent to ministries and usually cumbersome and divided governments ensue, requiring constant deal making to achieve basic cohesion. This practice also encourages parties to operate 'their' ministries as silos that coordinate poorly with other ministries, and to utilize them for distributing 'spoils' and as sources for party funds and personal enrichment. A contributing factor to the 'rainbow cabinet' phenomenon is the enduring election pattern whereby several parties divide the bulk of the votes roughly evenly, and numerous small parties garner the rest. Without a clear winner the necessary coalition forming necessitates complex bargaining. New electoral regulations introduced to combat this problem reduced the number of parties eligible to stand for election and set parties a vote threshold of 2.5 per cent to win seats. Accordingly, in 2009, the number of parties represented in parliament fell from 17 to nine. That no fewer than 29 small and new parties failed to win seats should have discouraged them from trying again in 2014 (Mietzner 2009b: 8). But the expected response, parties amalgamating with (or rejoining) other parties did not occur, reflecting their natures as highly personalized vehicles of ambition. In early 2013, the KPU announced that only ten parties were eligible to run in the 2014 elections. 15 of the 18 disqualified parties have appealed. At the time of writing only two appeals appear likely to succeed. Media reports suggest that the larger parties have begun wooing the disqualified parties so a less fractured party system may emerge (Aritonang 2013b). Nevertheless, the essential problematic pattern is likely to persist with several parties continuing to win roughly equivalent numbers of seats. Albeit arguably necessary, the restrictive electoral regulations have costs for democracy. Thereby the small parties' supporters have effectively been disenfranchised. Moreover, the party system could become ossified as the regulations impede emergence of new parties, a danger illustrated by the fact that only one of the parties approved to run in 2014 is new (Aritonang 2013a).

The relationship between the executive and parliament is also problematic. A powerful parliament is a novelty for Indonesia after an absence of several decades. Consequently the two arms of government are still adjusting to the new constitutional requirements of 'joint agreement' for legislation as per Article 20 (2). Such friction will probably persist until the power relationship is resolved either by the Constitutional Court or through the gradual building of precedent. Already the Constitution has seen amendment in this area after the tussle between parliament and President Abdurrahman Wahid in 2001, which culminated in his removal from office on dubious grounds. Impeachment remains possible but now only for serious illegal wrongdoing and with confirmation from the Constitutional Court (Sherlock 2010: 162–163). There is also ambiguity over the presidential veto power. Formally there is no such power and presumably that was intended since Article 20 (5) states that a jointly approved bill becomes law after 30 days if the President does not sign it. But in practice the veto exists through the simple mechanism of executive inaction at various choke points in the process which prevent the required joint approval indefinitely (Sherlock 2007: 8). If a presidential veto is desired it should be formalized so that the president can be held to account by the public for exercising it. If not, then mechanisms must be introduced to prevent the president from subverting the Constitution's intention.

Each of the weaknesses and problems outlined above represents a serious and deeply embedded deficiency in Indonesia's democracy. Collectively their impact is magnified. It is the accumulation of these defects that consigns Indonesian democracy to a low-quality level. Moreover, together they mutually reinforce each other, producing a systematically defective and highly reform-resistant democracy that is best characterized as oligarchic.

Prospects

The outcome and process of the 2014 parliamentary and presidential elections will reveal much about the health of Indonesia's democracy. Political competition is heating up as SBY's authority declines towards the end of his tenure. In such a context of heightened political tension a repeat of KPU's 2009 deficiencies in 2014 risks significant political violence if the result is close. KPU's performance in the 2012 Jakarta gubernatorial elections bodes ill in this regard, with complaints about faulty voter lists evoking widespread suspicions of manipulation (Arditya 2012: 4; *The Jakarta Post* 2012b). While Indonesia's democracy appears to have attained considerable solidity how well it would cope with such pressures cannot be predicted. The risks are compounded if no viable successors emerge. SBY's presidency, now deep into its second and constitutionally final term, has provided an extended period of stability and relative competence after several years of political volatility. Three presidents in less than seven years before SBY was a rapid turnover for a country with only two presidents in half a century before 1998. SBY's calm demeanour, combined with his comfortable second term victory cooled the political temperature. Unfortunately, much of the apparent democratic progress and political stability could be illusory, a product of the SBY factor. If the next president is less competent and/or less democratic then volatility could return and many democratic gains could be reversed.

At present none of the likely candidates has standing comparable to that enjoyed by SBY before the 2004 and 2009 elections. Predicting just who the candidates will be is difficult because the electoral regulations stipulate that formal nominations can only be made after the 2014 parliamentary elections. This is because only parties or alliances of parties that win 25 per cent of the vote or 20 per cent of the seats at these elections can nominate candidates for president.[3] None of the existing parties are polling particularly well with recent surveys indicating an accentuation of the trend for disillusioned voters to look for individual candidates rather than their parties when voting (*The Jakarta Post* 2012e). The Functional Groups Party (Golkar) seems best placed with a recent poll giving it 19.7 per cent support ahead of the Indonesian Democratic Party of Struggle (PDIP) on 18.3 per cent and the Greater Indonesia Movement Party (Gerindra) on 13.9 per cent (Sukoyo 2013). These three parties have improved their positions at the expense of SBY's Democrat Party (PD) whose vote seems likely to collapse from almost 21 per cent in the 2009 election to around 6 per cent (Sukoyo 2013). This reflects SBY's declining popularity but mostly it reflects recent serious corruption scandals that have engulfed PD.

Given the regulations and the polls, the previous pattern of alliances of convenience for the presidential elections will be repeated, either before or more likely just after the parliamentary elections. Typically, one party will provide the presidential candidate and the other the vice-presidential running mate. Considerations will also be given to matching a candidate with strong Islamic credentials with one with a more 'secular' or minority religion profile, and a Javanese with a member of another ethnic group. Similarly, one or other member of the ticket is likely to have a military background. Reflecting the lack of genuine ideological or programmatic differences between the parties almost any possible alliance is imaginable. A number of permutations have already been suggested publicly, either by politicians 'flying kites' or making mischief, or by the media speculating. Amongst the potential alliances floated to date are an alliance between Golkar and PD, with the current Army Chief of Staff, General Pramono Edhie Wibowo, SBY's brother-in-law, running for the vice presidency (*The Jakarta Post* 2012d). Similarly, a visit to SBY by Prabowo Subianto encouraged speculation of a Gerindra–PD alliance (Saragih 2013b).

Prabowo, with 19.2 and 22.7 per cent support according to two recent polls (*The Jakarta Post* 2013c; Sukoyo 2013) is frequently mentioned as a potential candidate. As Soeharto's son-in-law and a former general with an appalling human rights reputation, his election would raise the twin spectres of the return to pre-eminence of the Soeharto family and the reintroduction of authoritarian rule. Aburizal Bakrie, announced as the candidate Golkar will nominate, has also been polling well (20.3 and 16.3 per cent in the same polls). Reputedly one of Indonesia's richest men, an Aburizal presidency would exemplify the notion of democracy's capture by the wealthy elite. His candidacy would be handicapped, however, by his association through his company PT Lapindo Brantas with the infamous 'mud volcano' environmental disaster in Sidoarjo East Java.[4] Fears that this handicap would severely dent Golkar's otherwise good prospects of the presidency are one of the factors behind moves to oust Aburizal from his position as Golkar party chairman and to replace him as Golkar's candidate with the nationally respected former party chairman and former Indonesian vice-president Jusuf Kalla (Sijabat 2013b). Another consideration here for Golkar 'number crunchers' might be that the parties most identified with Islam (Justice and Welfare Party, United Development Party, People's Awakening Party, and People's Mandate Party) might be persuaded to throw their support behind Kalla who has sound Islamic credentials, given that they are all languishing in the polls. None of them are expected to win more than 5 per cent of the vote, and their collective vote could be below the threshold where they could nominate an Islamic candidate of their own, even in the unlikely event that they could agree on one (Perdani 2013).

Other potential candidates include former president Megawati Sukarnoputri, on 13 per cent support, and former Armed Forces Commander and perennial candidate Wiranto on 13.2 per cent (Sukoyo 2013). The latter's prospects have been boosted by wealthy media proprietor Hary Tanoesoedibjo joining Wiranto's People's Conscience Party (Hanura) (*The Jakarta Post* 2013b). Potentially he can bargain his way to a vice-presidential candidacy with his respectable vote bank supplemented by his military credentials. A potential wild-card candidate is Joko Widoyo, the recently elected popular Jakarta Governor. Although he has ruled out running in 2014 (but not 2019), polls indicate he has considerable support (Parlina *et al.* 2013). As he is a PDIP member, Megawati could decide to back him rather than risk the personal humiliation of a third rejection. Whoever runs, the 2014 elections are unlikely to arrest the unpromising medium-term trends and could well accelerate them.

Indonesia's remarkably smooth transition to democracy was, ironically, achieved precisely because of the low quality of the democracy established (Aspinall 2010: 32). The defects and problems are the results of politically necessary compromises without which the transition would probably have foundered. Nevertheless, we should bear in mind that viewed comparatively, Indonesia's democracy appears in quite a favourable light despite its weaknesses (Aspinall and Mietzner 2010: 17). Indonesia is the most liberally democratic country in Southeast Asia and even advanced democracies share some of Indonesia's problems, if not to the same degree. Thus Indonesia has been designated 'free' since 2005 with a score of two for political representation and three for civil liberties, the same levels as India (Freedom House 2013). Moreover, those reformers who made the concessions were entitled to hope that once established the democratic system would self-generate further reforms and the quality of Indonesia's democracy would gradually improve. In some areas this has indeed happened and in the longer term these hopes may yet be fulfilled. But for now the reform project has stalled. Indeed (irony upon irony) far from withering away, most of the accommodations to established power and privilege as the price for a relatively peaceful democratic transition have consolidated in tandem with democracy. The central problem is that not only do the accommodations comprise serious obstacles to the construction of a higher quality democracy, but they are having corrosive effects that threaten further degradation, possibly to the point where democracy relapses to authoritarianism.

To elaborate, its low quality leaves Indonesian democracy vulnerable to the corrosion of disillusionment. The intractable nature of the flaws and problems raises the risk levels because without progress disillusionment is more likely. Problematically, that disillusionment is likely to result in acceptance and thus persistence of the substandard status quo. Furthermore, it will tend to allow those factors devaluing democracy (and the interests linked to them) to further subvert Indonesia's fledgling democratic institutions, potentially lowering the quality of democracy in a downward spiral. Thus the slow burn of disillusionment, if unchecked, prepares the ground for a possible return to authoritarian rule, potentially even for a rapid unravelling of democracy in a crisis. Distinctly possible, if the parliament and parties fail to reform and if the 2014 elections disappoint, is mounting pressure to return to a stronger and more authoritarian presidency, either by default or by specific constitutional change. While few would wish to return to a presidency with Soeharto's unchecked power, advocates for a shift some way in this direction, including from within powerful institutions such as the military, would likely gain an increased hearing. No doubt they would repeat the old argument that this form of governance is more in keeping with Indonesia's culture and history. While a stronger presidency is not inherently incompatible with democracy, in the Indonesian context the removal or reduction of the checks and balances associated with the constitutionally powerful parliament would probably result in far more arbitrary wielding of state power and a shift back towards centralization.

Indonesian democracy does, however, possess three important strengths. The first is its robust quality, a key indicator of which is the high turnover of elected representatives, starkly illustrated by the fact that fully 70 per cent of the current members of parliament were newly elected in 2009 (Sukma 2010: 59). Dissatisfied voters clearly have no hesitation in removing incumbents in pursuit of better representation. A prominent recent example is the serving governor of Jakarta's loss in the mid-2012 gubernatorial elections to Joko Widoyo, the former mayor of the Central Javanese city, Surakarta. That he was an 'outsider' with a Chinese Christian running mate obviously mattered less to voters in the Islamist stronghold of Jakarta than his track record of clean and effective administration. Amongst other things, this outcome further illustrates the finding of Mujani and Liddle (2010: 91–95), echoed by Sukma (2010: 71), that Indonesian voters make essentially rational and autonomous decisions. In other words, vote buying, exertion of influence by traditional authorities, occasional intimidation and communalist appeals have relatively little impact on the way that Indonesians vote. Indonesians want democracy, social harmony, honest representation and effective government and they vote for candidates deemed most likely to deliver it (Mujani and Liddle 2010: 91).

The frequent defeat of incumbents also clearly demonstrates the second strength: the absence of structural impediments in Indonesia's democratic system that could prevent voters from exercising their choices. A major reform in this regard was achieved in 2008 when the Constitutional Court ruled that candidates would be allocated seats in accordance with their individual vote tally rather than according to their position on their respective party lists. Indonesia's partially open party lists system was thereby transformed to a fully open one, empowering voters to choose not only their favoured party but their preferred candidates for that party within their electoral districts. Over time this monumental reform, if it is not reversed as some parties are seeking (Snyder 2012), should force candidates to lift their performance if they wish to retain or win seats. This is because the former practice whereby obtaining a favourable position on a party list would automatically deliver victory, no longer applies. Parties are thus also provided with an incentive to select candidates who can attract votes in their own right and with the talent to perform well enough to be returned to office. In theory, this reform should reduce the practice of 'seat buying'. The proportion of Jakarta-based politicians in parliament should also decline, since presumably voters will generally prefer local candidates. The parties are also thereby encouraged to build better local party machinery and local links, a countervailing force against the corrosive trends outlined above.

Partially undermining the positive impact of the reform is the failure to implement a much needed related reform. This is the introduction of individual voting in parliament, in both committee and plenary sessions, and accompanied by promptly and publicly available transcripts and voting records. This measure would greatly improve the public's capacity to punish their representatives for poor performance and for transgressions like corruption. Furthermore, it would enable scrutiny of the stances of parliamentarians and the parties on issues. The absence of voting and recording currently means that they can often evade taking a definitive public position on an issue and conceal their actual stance on legislation (Ziegenhain 2009: 46). Unfortunately it is unlikely that any reform along these lines will be implemented in the foreseeable future, and without it there is little prospect that Indonesia's dysfunctional and venal parliament will improve. This is dangerous because its reputation, along with that of the parties, has already sunk very low, tainting the democratic system (*The Jakarta Post* 2012a; Aritonang 2012b). The ramifications of failed parliamentary reform go further because a cleaner, more effective and representative parliament is a fundamental requirement for driving reform of other key institutions such as the judiciary, police and civil service. And while Indonesian voters have repeatedly replaced their elected representatives in pursuit of better representation and better governance, to date they have rarely succeeded in obtaining either, generating the early signs of disillusionment. The participation rate of 91 per cent in the 1999 elections was always unsustainable, a product of the enthusiasm for the first democratic elections since 1955. In 2009 the rate had dropped to 71 per cent (Tomsa 2010: 156n), still relatively high by international standards. But fears are growing that the participation rate could plummet in 2014 to 60 per cent, fears reinforced by the unexpectedly low voter turnout of 63 per cent in the 2012 Jakarta gubernatorial elections (*The Jakarta Post* 2012c; Hussain 2012).

The third strength of Indonesia's democracy is the relatively high level of support for liberal values. This is a vital prerequisite for the construction of a quality democracy, as it is illiberal democracies that are least likely to endure (Diamond 2010: 25). Arguably liberal values are particularly important in the Indonesian context given the ethnic and religious diversity and history of authoritarianism. Survey results confirm that most Indonesians appreciate the importance of mutual respect between segments of a society for democracy's viability, recognize the cardinal value of individual rights vis-à-vis the state, and are wary of authoritarian solutions (Diamond 2010: 39–42). An important related asset for Indonesian democracy is the strength of civil society. Indonesia has a plethora of strongly rooted and active NGOs which in addition to pursuing welfare measures act as watchdogs and advocates (Lussier and Fish 2012). This tradition indicates the depth of Indonesians' commitment to civic responsibility and democratic values.

Regrettably, Indonesian democracy is likely to deteriorate further over the next several years, consolidating further as an oligarchic, low quality democracy in the process. The collective and cumulative impact of the corrosive elements, particularly on levels of disenchantment, contains a latent but potent danger of a relapse to authoritarian government, although this is unlikely to eventuate without the precipitating effect of a major crisis. More likely Indonesia's low-quality democracy will stumble on indefinitely, rather like India's. An important saving grace is that although increasingly oligarchic, Indonesia's democracy is not authoritarian and so there is yet considerable genuine democratic space. Nor is there (and nor is there likely to be) a dominant party that has captured the state apparatus and so with the capacity to distort the electoral process as in the electoral authoritarianisms of Malaysia and Singapore. Indonesia's elections will probably remain genuinely competitive, even if the competition is merely between rival gangs of 'predatory interests' (Hadiz 2004: 619). Not only will this serve to preserve the democratic space for other voices but the competition for votes should continue to provide at least a limited brake on the unbridled pursuit of elite interests. My longer term view is even less gloomy. While authoritarianism has been a feature of Indonesia's post-independence history, nevertheless Indonesians have persistently fought to establish and maintain democracy, even throughout the long period of authoritarian rule, despite the attendant risks and costs to careers, liberty and lives. It is also striking that Indonesia returned to democracy immediately when circumstances allowed, emphatically contradicting the claims that Indonesians do not want democracy and that it is incompatible with Indonesian culture. Finally, Indonesia's positive longer-term economic prospects should underpin further efforts, which history suggests will surely come, towards improvements in its quality.

Notes

1 For the much-needed and difficult civil service reforms see Synnerstrom (2007).
2 Luke Barrett (2011) argues that while policy programmes are largely absent, nevertheless ideological divisions remain. But while they may be discernible they are very faint echoes of those that pertained 30 years ago.
3 At the time of writing, some parties (such as Gerindra) are seeking to lower the threshold, but the larger established parties prefer the status quo (Aritonang 2013c; Sijabat 2013a).
4 The mudflow, a natural gas well blowout began in May 2006 and now covers more than 25 square kilometres, swallowing villages, roads and rice fields. Lapindo's denial of responsibility has added greatly to the damage to Aburizal's popularity.

References

Alford, P. (2011) 'SBY steps up effort to fight corruption', *The Australian*, 19 January.
Arditya, A.D. (2012) 'Problems with voter roll are "beyond control" of local KPU', *The Jakarta Post*, 4 July.
Aritonang, M.S. (2012a) 'House rejects KPK office due to poor performance', *The Jakarta Post*, 13 July.
Aritonang, M.S. (2012b) 'House ends session with loads of unfinished work', *The Jakarta Post*, 27 October.
Aritonang, M.S. (2013a) 'Same old story in 2014 elections', *The Jakarta Post*, 9 January.
Aritonang, M.S. (2013b) *The Jakarta Post*, 11 January.
Aritonang, M.S. (2013c) 'As polls near, Gerindra intensifies call for lower threshold', *The Jakarta Post*, 4 February.
Aspinall, E. (2010) 'The irony of success', *Journal of Democracy*, 21(2), 20–34.

Aspinall E. and Mietzner M. (2010) *Problems of Democratization in Indonesia: An Overview*, Singapore: ISEAS.

Barrett, L. (2011) 'Something to believe in: ideology and parties in Indonesian politics', *Review of Indonesia and Malaysia Affairs*, 55(1 and 2), 69–94.

Buehler, M. (2010) 'Decentralisation and local democracy in Indonesia: the marginalisation of the public sphere', in E. Aspinall and M. Mietzner (eds) *Problems of Democratisation in Indonesia*, Singapore: ISEAS.

Bush, R. (2008) 'Regional sharia regulation in Indonesia: anomaly or symptom?' in G. Fealy and S. White (eds) *Expressing Islam: Religious Life and Politics in Indonesia*, Singapore: ISEAS.

Christianto, D. (2012) 'Impotent govt lets FPI run rampant: Top criminologist', *The Jakarta Post*, 5 August.

Crouch, H. (2010) *Political Reform in Indonesia after Soeharto*, Singapore: ISEAS.

Diamond, L. (2008) *The Spirit of Democracy*, New York: Times Books.

Diamond, L. (2010) 'Indonesia's place in global democracy', in E. Aspinall and M. Mietzner (eds) *Problems of Democratisation in Indonesia*, Singapore: ISEAS.

Ellis, A. (2007) 'Indonesia's Constitutional Change Reviewed', in R.H. McLeod and A. MacIntyre (eds) *Indonesia: Democracy and the Promise of Good Governance*, Singapore: ISEAS.

Freedom House (2013) 'Freedom in the World 2013', London; www.freedomhouse.org/report/freedom-world/freedom-world-2013 accessed 2 August 2013.

Hadiz, V.R. (2004) 'Indonesian local party politics: a site of resistance to neo-liberal reform', *Critical Asian Studies* 36(4), 615–636.

Hadiz, V.R. (2010) *Localising Power in Post-Authoritarian Indonesia*, Stanford California: Stanford University Press.

Hardjono, R. (2012) 'The new Indonesia: 67 million first-time voters in 2014', *The Jakarta Post*, 19 January.

Hussain, Z. (2012) 'High hopes for voter turnout in Jakarta Polls', *The Jakarta Globe*, 29 October.

International Crisis Group (2007) 'Deradicalisation and Indonesian prisons', *Asia Report*, 142, 19 November.

International Crisis Group (2010a) 'Indonesia: Jihadi Surprise in Aceh', *Asia Report*, 189, 20 April.

International Crisis Group (2010b) 'Indonesia: Preventing Violence in Local Elections', *Asia Report*, 197, 8 December.

Kingsbury, D. (2003) *Power Politics and the Indonesian Military*, London and New York: RoutledgeCurzon.

Klinken, G. van (2009) 'Patronage democracy in provincial Indonesia', in O. Tornquist, N. Webster and K. Stokke (eds) *Rethinking Popular Representation*, New York: Palgrave McMillan.

Linz, J. and Stepan, A. (1996) *Problems of Democratic Transition and Consolidation: Southern Europe, South America, and Post-Communist Europe*, Baltimore: Johns Hopkins University Press.

Lipset, S. (1959) 'Some social requisites of democracy: economic development and political legitimacy', *The American Political Science Review*, 53, 69–105.

Lussier, D.N. and Fish, S.M. (2012) 'Indonesia: the benefits of civic engagement', *Journal of Democracy*, 23(1), 70–84.

Mietzner, M. (2009a) *Military Politics, Islam and the State in Indonesia*, Singapore: ISEAS.

Mietzner, M. (2009b) *Indonesia's 2009 Elections: Populism, Dynasties and the Consolidation of the Party System*, Sydney: Lowy Institute for International Policy.

Mujani, S. and Liddle R.W. (2010) 'Voters and the new Indonesian democracy', in E. Aspinall and M. Mietzner (eds) *Problems of Democratisation in Indonesia*, Singapore: ISEAS.

Parlina, I., Aritonang, M.S. and Dewi, S.W. (2013) 'Jokowi plays down presidential aspirations', *The Jakarta Post*, 8 February.

Perdani, Y. (2013), 'Grim outlook for Islamic parties', *The Jakarta Post*, 11 March.

Platzdasch, B. (2009) *Islamism in Indonesia: Politics in the Emerging Democracy*, Singapore: ISEAS.

Qodari, M. (2010) 'The professionalisation of politics: the growing role of polling organisations and political consultants', in E. Aspinall and M. Mietzner (eds) *Problems of Democratisation in Indonesia*, Singapore: ISEAS.

Robison, R. and Hadiz, V.R. (2004) *Reorganising Power in Indonesia*, London and New York: Routledge.

Saragih, B.B.T. (2013a) 'Equality gap "continues to widen", says SBY', *The Jakarta Post*, 22 January.

Saragih, B.B.T. (2013b) 'Prabowo, SBY deal looking more likely' *The Jakarta Post*, 13 March.

Schmidt, A. (2010) 'Indonesia's 2009 elections: performance challenges and negative precedents', in E. Aspinall and M. Mietzner (eds) *Problems of Democratisation in Indonesia*, Singapore: ISEAS.

Setara Institute 'Report on Freedom of Religion and Belief in 2012'; www.setara-institute.org/en/content/report-freedom-religion-and-belief-2012-0 accessed 29 July 2013.

Sherlock, S. (2007) 'The Indonesian Parliament after Two Elections: What has Really Changed', Canberra: CDI Policy Papers on Political Governance, Australian National University.

Sherlock, S. (2010) 'The parliament in Indonesia's decade of democracy', in E. Aspinall and M. Mietzner (eds) *Problems of Democratisation in Indonesia*, Singapore: ISEAS.

Sijabat, R.M. (2013a) 'Presidential threshold could still be challenged: Mahfud', *The Jakarta Post*, 30 January.

Sijabat, R.M. (2013b) 'Senior Golkar members move to oust Aburizal', *The Jakarta Post*, 7 March.

Snyder, J. (2012) 'Tough choices ahead on the road to democratic consolidation', *The Jakarta Post*, 20 January.

Sukma, R. (2010) 'Indonesia's 2009 elections: defective system, resilient democracy', in E. Aspinall and Mietzner M. (eds) *Problems of Democratisation in Indonesia*, Singapore: ISEAS.

Sukoyo, Y. (2013) 'Prabowo favoured in 2014 Presidential Election if Joko Declines Run: Poll', *The Jakarta Globe*, 16 July; www.thejakarta globe.com/news/prabowo-favoured-in-2014-presidential-election-if-joko-declines-run-poll// accessed 28 July 2013.

Synnerstrom S. (2007) 'The civil service: towards efficiency, effectiveness and honesty' in R.H. McLeod and A. MacIntyre (eds) *Indonesia: Democracy and the Promise of Good Governance*, Singapore: ISEAS.

Tadjoeddin, M.Z. (2012) 'Electoral conflict and the maturity of local democracy in Indonesia: testing the modernisation thesis', *Journal of the Asia Pacific Economy*, 17(3), 476–497.

The Jakarta Post (2012a) 'After one month recess, house members still too lazy to show up', 14 May.

The Jakarta Post (2012b) 'Jakarta's Civil Registration Agency "to blame" for vote list fiasco', 12 June.

The Jakarta Post (2012c) 'Lower turnout confounds pollsters', 12 July 2012.

The Jakarta Post (2012d) 'Golkar mulls picking SBY's family members', 21 October.

The Jakarta Post (2012e) 'Parties of no value in presidential election', 23 October.

The Jakarta Post (2013a) 'Muslim groups want Densus 88 dissolved over rights abuses', 1 March.

The Jakarta Post (2013b) 'I have the right to defend myself, says Wiranto', 18 March.

The Jakarta Post (2013c) 'Megawati back in the game', 18 March.

Tomsa, D. (2010) 'The party system after the elections: towards stability', in E. Aspinall and M. Mietzner (eds) *Problems of Democratisation in Indonesia*, Singapore: ISEAS.

Transparency International (2012) 'Corruption Perceptions Index 2012'; www.transparency.org/cpi2012/results/ accessed 21 March 2013.

United Nations Development Programme (2000) 'Human Development Report 2000'; http://hdr.undp.org/en/reports/global/hdr2000 accessed 29 July 2013.

World Bank 'Country Data'; www.world bank.org/en/country/Indonesia accessed 20 July 2013.

World Bank 'Indonesia Economic Quarterly', 2 July 2013; www.worldbank.org/en/news/feature/2013/07/02/indonesia-economic-quarterly-adjusting-to-pressures accessed 29 July 2013.

Yudhoyono, S.B. (2010) 'Keynote Speech Sixth Assembly of the World Movement for Democracy', *World Movement for Democracy*; www.wmd.org/assemblies/sixth-assembly/remarks/keynote-speech-dr-susilo-bambang-yudhoyono accessed 31 October 2012.

Ziegenhain, P. (2009) 'The Indonesian legislature's impact on democratic consolidation', in M. Bunte and A. Ufen (eds) *Democratization in Post-Suharto Indonesia*, London and New York: Routledge.

5 Thai democracy at a dangerous crossroads

Pavin Chachavalpongpun

Introduction

At dusk, on 19 September 2006, the military staged the 18th coup since Thailand was transformed from an absolute monarchy to a constitutional monarchy in 1932. Tanks rolled onto the streets of Bangkok and were greeted with cheers from the crowd. Bangkok residents were seen offering flowers to Thai soldiers for toppling the elected government of Prime Minister Thaksin Shinawatra. Two years later, the royalist yellow-shirted People's Alliance for Democracy (PAD) organized months-long protests against the elected Thaksin-backed regimes of Samak Sundaravej and Somchai Wongsawat. The PAD members carried the portraits of revered King Bhumibol Adulyadej and proclaimed themselves as guardians of the monarchy against the perceived threat posed by Thaksin and his cohorts. The PAD was successful in creating a state of ungovernability by seizing Thailand's Suvarnabhumi Airport but failed to remove Thaksin's proxies from politics. The Constitutional Court intervened in the crisis and finally stripped Samak and Somchai of their premierships on rather absurd grounds.[1] And in May 2010, the military launched a brutal crackdown against the pro-democracy Red-Shirt demonstrators at the behest of the Abhisit Vejjajiva government, resulting in almost 100 people killed and over 2,000 injured. In a move deemed as retaliation against the state, the Red Shirts allegedly committed arson attacks against public property. Many in the Thai capital praised the Abhisit government's harsh measures against the Red-Shirt protesters. They were convinced that some of the Red Shirts were members of an underground terrorist network. These three incidents raise a crucial yet disturbing question: What has gone wrong with Thai democracy?

Since the military coup in 2006, the Thai crisis has shown no sign of subsiding. All sides of the Thai conflict, while seeking to delegitimize their political adversaries through various means, have claimed to strive towards protecting democracy, even when some of their actions were highly despotic. This chapter attempts to answer the above question, in order to foretell the future of democracy in Thailand. It argues that democracy is still seen by the people as a desirable form of government despite the fact that more Thais have increasingly lost their faith and trust in the electoral system. The establishment forces, known to consist of the military, the bureaucracy and those associated with the monarchy have frequently overturned election results in the past whenever they found them unacceptable and threatening to their position of power, either through military coups, judicial intervention or through the use of undemocratic non-state actors to bring down a supposedly ominous regime. These factors are responsible for what Larry Diamond has called the 'democratic recession' (Diamond, 2008). Meanwhile, these establishment forces have insisted on maintaining their own kind of democracy – a paradigm that celebrates the benevolence of the rulers who possess seemingly highly ethical authority. In this paradigm, the monarchy sits on top of the apex of the Thai political structure. Although the role of the Thai King is immense in politics, the subject itself is untouchable and protected by the stiff lèse-majesté law. As the current reign is in its twilight years, anxiety has deepened as to what will happen to Thailand in the post-Bhumibol period.

Democratic transition in Thailand has been a lengthy process. Thailand may have abolished its absolute monarchy in 1932, but democratic consolidation has proven an arduous task because of the consistent interference of actors outside of the constitution who have continued to maintain the old status quo at the expense of weakening electoral politics. This chapter argues that to consolidate Thai democracy, a paradigm shift is urgently needed. Simultaneously, faith and trust in the electoral system must be restored.

In order to understand better the complexity of the Thai case, it is imperative to analyse it from the perspective of a network politics. For a decade now the Thai political domain has served as a battlefield between the two power networks; one with the establishment forces and one with Thaksin. Somewhat crudely, whereas the former represents 'old politics' dominated by the palace and the army, the latter represents the work of electoral politics based on popular support. The 2011 election, which brought a newly founded pro-Thaksin party, Pheu Thai, back to power, is part of the ongoing trend in the restoration of faith and trust in electoral politics. Yet there are many hurdles ahead for the consolidation of democracy. The challenge for the establishment forces is to come to terms with new, uncompromising bottom-up demands: a fairer distribution of political power and national wealth. Failing to respond to such demands could perpetuate political violence and further polarize Thai society, pushing it deeper into a state of democratic recession.

Desirable but not attainable

Democracy in Thailand is still desirable even though it might not be immediately attainable in the current political circumstances. It is desirable, I submit, because it represents the best political option for promoting justice, equal rights, and an equal say in a society that has traditionally been structured by rigorous hierarchy and social status. Retrospectively we can see that the economic boom that began in the mid-1980s effectively reshaped the Thai social structure and gradually opened up a space for Thais across different social strata to play a more significant role in politics. The rapid increase in prosperity among the urban workforce, brought on by the demand for skills as a result of the economic boom, enhanced their self-importance and their sensitivity to the political and economic environment (Pasuk and Baker 2002: 463). But the impact reverberated more in the agrarian sector where the rural poor were introduced to modern life, new technology, higher education and information of more relevance. Increasingly they called for new policies that would provide them with opportunity and access to public resources, particularly public funds and political power. Yet such calls long fell on deaf ears. Into this space stepped a new breed of Thai politician – the billionaire-turned-prime minister Thaksin, who came to power in 2001. He saw the advantage in harnessing the changing face of Thai society, implementing a series of populist programmes designed to empower his supporters in the far-flung regions of Thailand. Economically, Thaksin fulfilled their dreams, for instance by handing out cash to facilitate local businesses and by strengthening the country's niche markets to raise their international competitiveness. Politically, Thaksin provided them with a sense of state ownership by reiterating the power of the electoral process. The rural residents, long marginalized in the Thai political landscape, for the first time felt that their vote was actually meaningful. In his interview with *The Times* in 2009, three years after the coup, Thaksin stressed,

> We won a landslide – half of parliament's seats – and we formed a coalition government. And it was the first time in Thai history we stayed for a four-year term without the House being dissolved. And it is the first time in Thai history that the prime minister was re-elected for a second term. And the first time in Thai history that we won 377 seats, so that we could form a government without needing a coalition – 76 per cent of the parliament's seats at that time.... But that became my problem – because I was too popular, being loved by the people too much. That was where my problem comes from.
>
> (Perry 2009)

The problem Thaksin was talking about became the key accelerator of the Thai democratic recession that has been seen in recent years. During Thaksin's premiership, his mounting political power and popularity upset the traditional elites immensely. Further irritating them, Thaksin was keen to redefine the Thai social structure and shift the political status quo. Under Thaksin, the Thais no longer needed to rely on their benevolent rulers, but rather on an elected regime. Undoubtedly, Thaksin's eagerness was perceived as a threat to the old power in Thailand. His new power structure emerged as a challenge to the old paradigm: this challenge and the reaction to it became the root cause of the current crisis. The Thai academic, Somsak Jeamteerasakul, argued that at the core of the crisis lies the gigantic contest between two power blocs, one centred on the elective institutions (e.g. parliament, political parties, and politicians) and the other on the non-elective ones, with the monarchy at the latter's peak.[2] I would not assert that the Thaksin regime was in every sense democratic, since it was also blighted by multiple forms of bad governance, including widespread corruption and human rights abuses. However, it is important to underscore that Thaksin's government was elected and hence legitimate, and that it continued to receive overwhelming popular support. This hard fact, coupled with Thaksin's self-appointed role as an agent of change, led the establishment forces to take up extra-constitutional methods to get rid of Thaksin and subsequently thereby to reverse the consolidation of Thai democracy. Ironically, the coup leader, General Sonthi Boonyaratglin, rationalized the military coup as the only way to save democracy from Thaksin's 'immoral' regime (*Handbook on Thailand's Political Situation* 2007).

However, getting rid of Thaksin has only reinforced the pro-democracy movement in Thailand. It is true that some of the anti-government Red-Shirt members are supporters of Thaksin. Lately, however, the movement has gone beyond performing as a mere proxy of the former prime minister. Today, the Red Shirts have a more elaborate pro-democracy agenda and, like Thaksin, continue to challenge the traditional elites and demand the decentralization of power. After the emergency decree was finally lifted in December 2010, the Red-Shirt movement returned to the streets of Bangkok to protest against the Abhisit government, considered a puppet of the old power.[3] The return of the Red Shirts has once again signified that democracy is still much needed, even when such a need exposes a dark paradox lurking in the minds of the Red Shirts. This paradox is based on an ambivalent view of the Red Shirts – they have been increasingly frustrated by the weakness of the electoral process, although they acknowledge that democracy remains the only hope as the political solution.

Enemies of democracy

What are the 'real and present dangers' to Thai democracy? The establishment forces have resorted to diverse strategies and tools as part of safeguarding their power interests. Such strategies and tools serve to demoralize Thai democracy and these are the sources of democratic recession in the kingdom. First, the military's incessant meddling in politics represents the greatest threat to Thai democracy. The army has made no secret about the possibility of staging another coup should the Thai political situation get out of control, a view allegedly endorsed by the current Army Chief, General Prayuth Chan-ocha. As is widely known, the Thai military lacks professionalism, and indeed fails to maintain an apolitical stance. In Thailand, the military has been tasked to serve the elites' interests, when in fact defending national sovereignty should have been its first priority. Traditional elites have tied the notion of national security tightly with the royal institution, thus inviting the military to become directly involved in politics. Thitinan Pongsudhirak argued that the military has drawn a line in the sand and defined the fault line of Thai politics around the monarch (Thitinan, 2010a). This process has consolidated the military's position in the political domain, as manifested in 2008 when it stage-managed the formation of Abhisit's coalition government following the abrupt dissolution of the ruling People's Power Party (PPP), led by Prime Minister Somchai, who happens to be Thaksin's brother-in-law.

The politicized judiciary also poses a threat to democracy. A number of incidents suggest that the Thai courts have been exploited as a political tool in castigating the elites' opponents and protecting their allies. For example, in 2008, the Court decided to end the political deadlock by removing two prime ministers in Thaksin's camp – a decision made in favour of the elites and the yellow-shirted PAD. Pro-democracy activists compared such action to the Court 'staging a coup through legal channels'. But when the military-backed Democrat Party, Thailand's oldest political party, was accused of receiving more than US$8.4 million in illegal donations from a private company for use in the 2005 general election and not declaring it, the Constitutional Court dismissed the dissolution case citing that the complaint filing process lodged by the Election Commission had been unlawful.[4] In the period leading up to the Court's verdict, a series of video clips were leaked on YouTube, showing a member of parliament from the Democrat Party appearing to lobby the secretary of the Court president, Chai Cholaworn, to go easy on the party, adding more suspicion about the Constitutional Court's supposedly non-political role. To the Red Shirts, the decision was self-evidently political. The verdict was seen to further aggravate the political situation since it reaffirmed the existence of social injustice and double standards in Thai society.

The military and the politicized Constitutional Court are not the only two instruments employed to undermine Thai democracy. The emerging anti-democracy non-state actors have done great damage to Thailand's democratization, too. The PAD played 'mob politics' in order to put pressure on the Thaksin government and its successors, while often stirring up a sense of nationalism against both its domestic and foreign enemies (Cambodia in particular). It is apparent that the PAD has aligned itself with the Bangkok elites and hence identified Thaksin and his supporters as a menace to 'democracy' and the monarchy. In reality, the PAD itself is hardly a true champion of democracy. Evidence of this is overwhelming in the PAD's version of 'democracy', referred to as 'new politics'. The concept states that 30 per cent of a future parliament would consist of elected members while the remaining 70 per cent would be appointed. The PAD explains that with this new political model, future politicians would be able to exercise their powers more responsibly with clear limits – an obvious anti-Thaksin measure. Whatever purpose it may serve, the 'new politics' concept will certainly be a real setback to Thai democracy.

Lastly, in discussing the challenges of Thai democracy, the following questions must be asked: Is the monarchical institution compatible with democracy? Can it be used to run a modern state? As the political crisis has increasingly intensified, more aggressive approaches have been adopted by hardcore royalists to ward off their enemies, at the same time as they have been re-glorifying the royal institution. Consequently, the sacralization of the monarchy and the belief in righteous rule backed by extra-constitutional interventions is at an all-time high. Meanwhile, more lèse-majesté cases have been recorded. Lèse-majesté, or the crime of injury to the royalty, is defined by Article 112 of the Thai Criminal Code, which states that defamatory, insulting or threatening comments about the king, queen and regent are punishable by 3–15 years in prison. The increasing frequency of lèse-majesté cases over the past few years suggests that Thailand's claim to be the 'land of the free' is highly questionable. There are at least two reasons behind the law's application. One is to prop up a weakened monarchical institution and disguise the uncertainty of the royal succession. The other is to attempt to control society, conserve elitist privileges, prolong the military's role in politics, obstruct democratization and cope with the technological revolution in cyberspace. But ironically the more the traditional elite employ the law for political purposes, the more they weaken the monarchical institution. The lèse-majesté law is used to protect not only the monarchical institution but also a much broader system known as the 'network monarchy' – a term for describing the structure of power through which the Thai monarchy asserts its political interests (McCargo 2005: 499–519). The law serves to obscure the functions of the royal institution and to defend the members of the network monarchy from public scrutiny – so long as their actions are justified by the pretence of safe-guarding the monarchy. This process runs parallel with the unending sacraliza-tion and re-glorification of the monarchy. The strategy allows political opponents to be accused of disparaging the centuries-old institution and be labelled 'enemies of the state'.

Interestingly, before the 2006 coup, allegations of lèse-majesté primarily served as an inter-elite means to eliminate one's enemies. For example, Thaksin accused the Democrat Party of committing lèse-majesté by exploiting the mon-archy in its election campaign. Similarly, Thaksin and Sonthi Limthongkul, a leader of the PAD, also pointed the finger at each other for not respecting the royal institution. The politicization of the lèse-majesté law has effectively set a dangerous precedent as it has been turned into a weapon undermining political opponents. After the coup, with the political space much more open – and with the prerogative state coming under threat – the royalists began to target virtually anyone with different political leanings. Thirty-three charges of lèse-majesté came before the Courts of First Instance in 2005, and the number increased almost fourfold to 126 in 2007. This number jumped to 164 in 2009 and tripled to 478 by 2010. The most dramatic increases came under Abhisit Vejjajiva's Democrat government. According to one estimate, there may have been hun-dreds jailed for lèse-majesté in this post-coup period (Streckfuss 2011: 22–53). The dramatic spike in cases seems to have occurred after a pro-elite group – con-sisting of the PAD, the Democrat Party and the military – urged all Thais to display their absolute and unwavering loyalty to the monarchy. In this line of thinking, treason seems to lurk around every corner, and the lèse-majesté law is a powerful device to silence political dissent. According to the global anti-censorship network Global Voices, the Abhisit government had blocked at least 113,000 websites deemed threatening to the monarchy.[5] All these approaches have provoked a deeper rift in society. The re-glorification plot concentrates on the need for Thais to depend on the monarchical institution and its defenders as the ultimate moral authority, especially during a Thai crisis, giving them a legitimate right to interfere in politics, even when this means an interruption to democracy. While objectives like these clearly explain the law's misuse, the reason for singling out particular enemies is more elusive. As one example, in May 2011, Thailand's Centre for the Resolution of Emergency Situations drew up a stupefying 'mind map' (which identifies those who may want to overthrow the monarchy or *lom chao*) that presented an obscure and convoluted chart supposedly mapping linkages between the monarchy's enemies – but without any clear explanation. Kanit Na Nakorn, Chairman of the Truth for Reconciliation Commission of Thailand, stated that all trials connected to political conflict before and after the 2006 coup should be halted and reviewed. He also suggested that the government should reconsider whether to prosecute cases that expand the law's interpretation too broadly, such as those dealing with a so-called conspiracy to topple the monarchy. The discursive employment of lèse-majesté law has certainly hindered Thai democratization.

The 2011 election

After tumultuous years of political conflict triggered by unending street protests and the eventual military coup of 2006, Thailand's second election in the post-coup period took place in July 2011. The first election in this period took place in December 2008, and produced the overwhelming victory of the PPP led by Samak. Samak's government did not last long, however. Unwisely, he did not give up his sideline job as a weekly TV celebrity chef, and he was accused of a conflict of interest and subsequently forced to resign. Pro-Thaksin groups immediately condemned the Thai Constitution Court's decision for undermining a democratic institution, perceiving it as an attempt to overturn the election result that had brought Samak to power in the first place (Mydans 2008). But the forced resignation of Samak failed in its objective because another proxy of Thaksin, Somchai, assumed political power. Somchai's nomination by fellow parliamentarians to succeed Samak was regarded as an act of unremitting defiance against Thaksin's enemies in high places. Undeterred, the traditional elite later employed the same tactic to oust the Somchai government. The Constitutional Court ordered Somchai to step down from the premiership on the grounds that one of PPP's executive members had committed electoral fraud (Thitinan 2010b). The elimination of Thaksin's proxies in this way, now usually referred to as 'judicial coup', revealed the dark underbelly in Thai politics: the Thai elite were still not prepared to accept the shift away from the old status quo. They had no faith in and respect for electoral democracy because this type of political system threatened their vested interests. After the departure of Somchai, the Thai elite, along with the military, lent their support for the formation of a minority government under the leadership of Abhisit Vejjajiva from the opposition Democrat Party. The Abhisit government outlived those of Samak and Somchai, unsurprisingly thanks to strong backing from the army and the palace (Crispin 2010). Yet his term from early 2009 to July 2011 was marked by bloody confrontations and persistent instability. Abhisit was constantly challenged by anti-government Red-Shirt members. During this period, the Thai political crisis slipped even deeper towards the abyss. The election of July 2011, which has produced an unpalatable result in the eyes of the elite, could indeed worsen the fragile state of Thai politics.

It was an unpalatable result because despite the deployment of every kind of political tool – from the military coup to the judicial coup – against Thaksin's surrogates, the elite were apparently unable to be free of them. Yingluck Shinawatra, 44, the youngest sister of Thaksin, led the Pheu Thai and managed to win a landslide election in July 2011. Her triumph unveiled two political facts. First, Thaksin, although having been in self-exile for almost five years, had remained hugely popular. The electoral success of Yingluck and the Pheu Thai was possible partly owing to Thaksin's remaining influence in politics as well as to the rise of the Red-Shirt movement. Moreover, the elite were in no position to compete with their opponents in the game of electoral democracy. They had never valued electoral politics that had not served them well. It is noteworthy that the Democrat Party of Abhisit, which allied itself so closely with the military and the palace, had not won a single election since 1992. Thus, the victory of Yingluck, much celebrated as a victory of electoral democracy, has seriously jeopardized the old political consensus, which, in the past, allowed the traditional elite to maintain firm control over politics. Political analysts have already posed some pertinent questions: Is it likely that Yingluck will be overthrown in much the same way as her predecessors? Will her premiership, underpinned by massive popular support, be able to further strengthen Thai electoral politics? And how will her rise to power shape Thailand's democratization?

The July 2011 election was politically meaningful for a host of reasons. The most obvious was that it returned power to the people after 30 months of the military-backed Abhisit rule (Croissant 2002: 15). The deep polarization in Thai politics has for the first time in the country's recent memory given birth to a loose two-party system under which one party represents the middle/lower class and the other the elitist class. The fact that the Pheu Thai Party has emerged as a dominant political entity reconfirms that the power distribution within this two-party system is increasingly disproportional. The Pheu Thai won an absolute majority in the last election, which witnessed the highest voter turnout in Thai history (75.03 per cent), thus signalling not just the return of public confidence in electoral democracy but also the undisputed legitimacy of the Pheu Thai. With deep political polarization, a fairly strong regional pattern of voting took place; voters in the north and northeast regions offered their support to the Pheu Thai, whereas some parts of Bangkok and the south remained firmly Democrat Party territories. But this phenomenon masked a certain irony in Thai politics: the Thais may now enjoy vibrant electoral politics, but Thai democracy continues to be vulnerable.

The victory of the Pheu Thai Party

The return of Thaksin's clan to politics has posed an emerging threat to the Bangkok establishment. But it is too early for the enemies to strike at the newly-formed government, considering that the Pheu Thai Party earned an enormously popular mandate. Shawn Crispin of the *Asia Times* reported that as early as February 2011, the military and the palace already realized that they would not be able to compete with Thaksin through the electoral system and were therefore ready to conclude a deal with him. The meeting between them reportedly took place in Brunei. Each side agreed not to interfere in the other's affairs; for example, the army would allow the Pheu Thai to set up a government in exchange for a vow from Thaksin not to pursue political revenge or legal prosecutions of the top military officials behind the 2006 coup and the 2010 crackdown, and to refrain broadly from intervening in military affairs, including the annual reshuffle that determines the army's leadership (Crispin 2011). So far no one from either the Thaksin camp or the Bangkok elite has come out to confirm that such an agreement, now dubbed by the Thai media the 'Brunei Declaration' exists.

With or without the 'Brunei Declaration', there has been one question in the people's minds: Given that the Pheu Thai's election victory defied all the odds in Thai politics that had for so long been manipulated by the traditional elite, what exactly inspired so many Thais to vote for Pheu Thai? The relentless use of illegal methods, both through the military and judicial coups, had unfortunately created a clear barrier between the pro- and anti-Thaksin groups. For supporters of the former, the existence of social injustice and double standards was a key driving force behind their support for the Pheu Thai Party; this was reflected by the Red Shirts' persistent demand to bring those who killed the protesters in May 2010 to justice. More significantly, it was clear that there had been a serious flaw in the Thai political system in which non-elective institutions employed their resources to constantly challenge the elected ones. A myriad of incidents point to a distrust of elections on the part of the elite and its reliance instead on undemocratic methods ranging from the toppling of the Thaksin government in an unlawful coup to the removal of Samak and Somchai through the courts. The historian Thongchai Winichakul argues, 'The distrust of elections in fact goes a long way back.... It is rooted in the nationalistic conservatism that distrusts democracy as alien to Thai culture which honours hierarchical relations and venerates the monarchy as the highest authority in the land' (Thongchai 2008: 27). The fact that the yellow-shirt PAD seized the House of Government and the Suvarnabhumi Airport in 2008 and that it has not yet been prosecuted has enraged the pro-Thaksin movement. While the Thai Rak Thai Party and the PPP were forced to dissolve on political grounds, as claimed by the pro-Thaksin supporters, the case of the Democrat Party, which was accused of misuse of political party development funds, was dismissed by the Constitutional Court. Ultimately, the violent crackdowns on the Red Shirts in May 2010, in comparison with the no-action approach of the military against the Yellow Shirts when they occupied the airport, were projected as the security forces adopting double standards. For many pro-Thaksin supporters, the only way to strengthen democracy and to eliminate such double standards and social injustice is to restore the faith in and respect for the electoral process. This has been one of the key agendas pursued by the Red-Shirt movement: promoting electoral democracy as part of its motivation to shift the old consensus whereby the traditional elite, most of whom have espoused an anti-Thaksin position, had long dominated Thai politics. The emergence of the Red-Shirt movement, as a chief supporting unit of the Pheu Thai, played a large role in the victory of the party.

The rise of the Red-Shirt Movement

Social and political injustice compelled factions of Thaksin supporters at the grassroots to form a loose alliance initially with an anti-coup agenda, later known as the United Front for Democracy against Dictatorship (UDD).[6] Since its formation in the aftermath of the coup until the period before the election of 2011, the Red-Shirt movement has grown in strength, despite being accused of – and some core leaders arrested for – committing terrorist acts in the confrontations in May 2010. It is, however, important to clarify that while many of the Red-Shirt members are loyal supporters of Thaksin, some are pro-democracy and even disapprove of Thaksin's past policies. What holds these groups together is their common objective: to contest the existing elite-centric political system (Thitinan 2009: 39). This proved to be a key ingredient that made the victory of the Pheu Thai possible.

While it is difficult to analyse the Red-Shirt movement in terms of its organization and strategies, it is clear that the UDD still represents the core organization for an uncountable number of the Red Shirts. In this context, it is useful to discuss the UDD's objectives in order to explain its success in encouraging the residents in Thaksin-influenced regions to vote for the Pheu Thai. Those objectives were to achieve democracy and sovereignty belonging to the people; to unite all people to fight against the aristocracy/elite network; to be non-violent; to resolve economic problems of the people; to establish a 'true rule of law' and eliminate double standards; and to cancel the 2007 Constitution (drafted by the military government of Surayud) and reintroduce the 1997 People's Constitution, which gave more power to civilian government (UDD 2011). The conflict between the Red-Shirt movement and the traditional elite has sparked a fierce ideological debate over how Thailand's democracy should develop; their clash truly benefited the Pheu Thai. The movement has undoubtedly aspired to empower the electoral system and to remove the double standards, which of course meant the reduction of the entrenched power of the traditional elite. On the contrary, in defending their vested interests, the Thai elite have exploited the monarchy as a political apparatus to attack the Red-Shirt enemies. They have accused the Red-Shirt members of tilting towards republicanism. In April 2011, Army Chief General Prayuth Chan-ocha assigned an army officer to file a complaint against a number of Red-Shirt UDD leaders for committing lèse-majesté (Pavin 2011). The UDD leaders denied the allegations and pledged never to have pursued a *lom chao* (overthrowing the monarchy) campaign. Even Thaksin has repeatedly pronounced his continued loyalty to the much revered institution (Plate 2011).

In scheming to win the 2011 election, the Pheu Thai cooperated closely with the Red-Shirt movement. The Pheu Thai has served as a 'sanctuary' for some of the top leaders of the Red Shirts. Jatuporn Prompan is a member of the Pheu Thai. Nattawut Saikua was a member of the dissolved PPP and a spokesman in the Somchai government. Veera Musigapong was a member of the Thai Rak Thai executives; he was a leading member of the Red-Shirt movement but gradually faded from the scene after his release from prison in February 2011. (Veera and other UDD leaders were arrested in the aftermath of the May 2010 violent demonstrations.) The Pheu Thai cunningly used the Red-Shirt movement to solidify its connections with the communities in different constituencies across the country. The party captured and played along with the theme of 'political inclusion', arguing that the elite had incessantly interfered in politics, ignored the will of the majority, and undermined electoral democracy. The grassroots were the main source of legitimacy for the Pheu Thai and the justification for their political activities. Now that the election has ended, the question emerges: What does the electoral triumph of the Pheu Thai mean to Thai democracy? It is true that the Pheu Thai won an undisputed victory in July 2011. But because the party has represented Thaksin and often fought to redeem his reputation, its democratic credentials have sometimes been doubted. Regardless of this dilemma, the fact that the majority of Thais turned up to cast their votes revived a healthy state of electoral politics. More importantly, the belief among voters that an election might indeed change their lives was contributory to the ongoing democratization process. Because the Pheu Thai promoted the principle of a one-person, one-vote system, its electoral achievement could be perceived as a major step towards consolidating Thai democracy. Its pro-democracy platform, no matter how imperfect it has been, appealed not just to the Red Shirts, but also to the 'colourless' members of society. The arrival of the Pheu Thai in power thus opened a new chapter in the Thai political system in which the 'vote' counts.

The Yingluck era

Since the assumption of Yingluck's premiership in 2011, her Pheu Thai Party has shown a certain interest in strengthening democratic institutions, such as through the amendment of the current 2007 constitution, which was drafted by the military-appointed members in the aftermath of the 2006 coup. But the process has not been plain sailing. The opposition Democrat Party has continued to closely cooperate with extra-constitutional forces – the old establishment, the military and the Yellow Shirts – to challenge the Yingluck government. Numerous allegations against the Yingluck government have been made, one of which is that she attempted to enact the amnesty bill so as to bring her fugitive brother home. The opposition even accused the government of conspiring to amend certain Articles that would weaken the position of the monarchy – an act deemed disloyal to the much revered institution.

In the current period, it is clear that the old pattern of political struggles has re-emerged, with the traditional elite resorting to non-parliamentary means to overthrow the elected government and thus belittle the people's aspiration for long-lasting democracy. The role of the judges is more significant than any time before in Thai history. They have become essential instruments in determining the fate of successive governments. It is evident that the Thai Court has been highly politicized and has worked to protect the political interests of the traditional elite. In the game of electoral politics, the traditional elite realize that they are unable to compete with Thaksin and his proxies. In the past 12 years, the Shinawatras and their loyalists have dominated Thai politics, winning every election, the last one bringing Yingluck to power. Hence, the only tactic left is to rely on extra-constitutional elements to eliminate Thaksin and his political nominees. But staging another coup would be too devastating and the military would be condemned by the international community. It would also shatter foreign investors' confidence in Thailand's economy, of which the Thai traditional elite possess fairly large stakes.

Today, the old elite are now turning to the royalist judges in defending their political interests. It shows the extent to which Thai politics is still very much manipulated by the old powers, whose only objective is to safeguard the political status quo, even at the expense of obstructing the democratization process. But they have been operating with increased difficulty, particularly with the more hostile response from society at large. Many Red Shirts are now identifying themselves not just as pro-Thaksin forces, but also as a pro-democracy movement. The fact that they staged months-long demonstrations on the streets of Bangkok from March to May 2010, which ended tragically with the brutal crackdowns at the hands of the state, reaffirms that the Thai consciousness of democracy has been heightened. Available social media networks have become the new frontier for many Thais to express their views on politics. In my recent interviews with a number of Red Shirts in Ubon Ratchathani, in the northeastern region of Thailand, they said passionately that if there was another military coup, then they would travel to Bangkok to stage demonstrations against the military. They said that the people have awoken, known in Thai as *ta sawang*, and would not allow the traditional elite to hold electoral democracy hostage again.[7] The *ta sawang* phenomenon is the latest response from the majority of Thais vis-à-vis the domination of power of the old elite.

How can Thai democracy be consolidated?

This chapter argues that political reform is imperative in expunging critical hurdles to Thai democracy. As part of the reform, political leaders will need to ensure that the military detaches itself from politics. This will be an uphill task because of the mutual benefits found between the military and the traditional elites. Whereas the former needs the latter to legitimize its political role, the latter needs the former to protect its power position. Over the decades, the militarization of politics has been gradually normalized with the army's occasional interventions in political affairs, especially when Thailand was ruled by weak civilian governments. But when strong civilian governments were installed, like those of Chatichai Choonhavan (1988–1991) and Thaksin, the military immediately felt vulnerable and often reacted by taking extreme measures, mostly a coup. But the Thai political situation is more complex today. The Thais have become more 'politically conscious'. Even those from far-flung regions of Thailand have refused to remain subservient to the military and the political elites in Bangkok. For the military, the issue today is therefore no longer about whether Thailand has a weak or strong government, but about how to manipulate the notion of democracy and how to perpetuate its power in politics. The fact that there has been a split within the military, with the majority remaining supportive of the traditional elites and a tiny portion becoming increasingly sympathetic towards the Red Shirts – the so-called watermelon soldiers – has added another layer of difficulty in separating the military from politics.

Next, the debate on the future of the monarchical institution needs to be encouraged. This is because of the inexorable connections among the monarchy, the pace of democratization and the stability of Thai politics. The monarchy-centric paradigm has competed fiercely with that of electoral democracy and has relied heavily on extra-constitutional elements to sustain its existence. Therefore, a part of the problem with Thai democracy is that the royal institution does not operate to enhance the function of democracy, but instead obstructs it. Can all sides in the Thai conflict depoliticize the monarchy? If yes, then they must be courageous enough to initiate an honest discussion on the reform of this much-revered institution. A key question is: How can the monarchy stay above politics and yet not be alienated from Thailand's political life? They must also be prepared to raise untouchable issues, such as the royal succession and the power transition inside the walls of the palace. But if all political factions are unable to depoliticize the monarchy, then Thai democracy will remain at risk, since any future political decisions will continue to be based on the approval of the monarchy, not the majority of Thais. If democracy is the only exit to the Thai political impasse, Thai elites, either in the government or those outside the constitutional frameworks, will have to let democracy run its own course. Thongchai Winichakul recently suggested that for a short-term solution, discussing the royal succession issue is imperative. The reflexive accusation against political opponents that they are a threat to the throne must end. For a long-term solution, as Thongchai maintained, the royalist democracy or the rule by the high moral authority must come to an end and democracy must be allowed to run its own course.[8]

Ultimately, to stop the process of democratic recession, faith and trust in the electoral process need to be reinstated. In December 2010, Prime Minister Abhisit told the Thai media that he would dissolve parliament during the first quarter of that year and call for an election. Almost at the same time, key members of the opposition Puea Thai Party flew to Beijing to meet with Thaksin, reportedly to lay out several election strategies. The focus here is on the obvious conundrum: Who will win and how to undermine opponents? But an election in the future will become meaningless if trust and faith among voters is still not present. The 2006 coup only served to damage Thailand's electoral process.

The coup makers might have claimed to be saving Thailand from corrupt politicians – they painted Thaksin as a major hindrance to Thai democracy – but staging a military coup did not contribute to the country's ongoing democratization either. Eliminating political enemies in this way only reduced the legality of the electoral process. Rebuilding trust and faith in the electoral system is part of the solution to the protracted political crisis. If the Abhisit camp is genuine about bringing a close to the political conflict, it must reassure voters that the results of the election will be respected, regardless of which political party comes out on top. Simultaneously, it needs to convince its backers in high places not to resort to unconstitutional means even if they find the election results unpalatable. More importantly, it is now time for traditional elites to recognize that the Thai political landscape has changed significantly and that they are no longer the only stakeholders in the political and economic domains. The political space has opened up in the past decade, and this has allowed Thai voters, especially in remote provinces, to directly participate in politics and to claim ownership of their own country. Unless the elites grasp the new rules of the game, elections will remain largely a fraudulent expression of Thai democracy.

Conclusion

This chapter began with a provocative question: What went wrong with Thai democracy? To make the question gloomier, a recent report released by watchdog group Freedom House (2013) showed that Thailand is among 25 countries listed as declining in levels of freedom. The Thai case is intensely complicated, certainly more than Larry Diamond would have imagined. There is a clash between two political paradigms: an electoral democracy and a righteous rule led by non-elected benevolent leaders. But because the latter has successfully made a lifelong deal with other extra-constitutional actors, specifically the military, it is capable of undermining pro-democracy forces with guns and dubious laws. As a result, Thailand's democracy has gone into recession. To prevent Thai democracy from backsliding further, indeed to improve it, political reform is fundamental. In this process, the military and the judiciary must be depoliticized. Equally significant is the fact that Thais must be able to openly discuss the issue related to the royal institution without fear of retribution. This chapter concludes that faith and trust among Thai voters in the electoral process must be revived. All parties in the conflict will have to accept election results, and more importantly, a new paradigm shift in which democracy is the only commandment in politics.

I support Andrew Walker and Nicholas Farrelly's suggestion that 'Thailand's royal family, military and judiciary will have to respond to this (election) result very carefully.... To move against this government, either through legal manipulation or a more open display of force, would be lunacy. The millions of voters who turned out for Yingluck simply will not tolerate yet another electoral decision being overturned.' (Walker and Farrelly 2011). This observation suitably sums up the delicate situation in Thai politics with one force extolling the rule of democracy and the other seeking to maintain its political power in the hands of a tiny elite group. The latter, while capable of sustaining the old status quo that allowed them to dictate power in the past, have been faced with a new kind of threat in the form of mass-based electoral politics led by a new kind of political leadership, exemplified by Thaksin. In recent years, electoral politics was often rendered rather meaningless as the traditional elite continued to weaken it through periodic military coups. On the other hand, since 2001, Thaksin has proven that electoral politics could be employed to diminish the Bangkok elite's control of political power. He took advantage from the gap between different classes in society, widening the political space for the poorer classes to express their needs and desires, and giving them a sense of belonging. Through this, they came to know that they could govern their own destiny only through the electoral process. Thus, when another coup took place again in 2006, it crushed their hopes. As they recovered their equilibrium, they began to protest against the coup and demanded that the Bangkok elite share power with them. The emergence of the Red-Shirt movement acted as a catalyst in the process of challenging the old consensus. An emerging new consensus places electoral politics at its centre.

The 2011 election was a driving force behind the shift of the old status quo. The election triumph of the Pheu Thai served as a referendum for many players and ideologies. For one thing, it served to corroborate that most Thais now wanted a 'real' democracy to return to Thailand, through the legitimate electoral process based on a one-person-one-vote principle. In the past five years, the traditional elite have tried desperately to disparage electoral politics through different versions of coups. But the move has proven counterproductive and became an inspiration for the pro-democracy fronts to fight back through both ballot boxes and violence on the streets. Thailand is entering a new phase in which the people's political consciousness is ever more powerful. It will certainly make the staging of a future coup more difficult, if not impossible. Moreover if one were to occur, the response to it would probably involve large-scale violence with potentially terrible and unpredictable consequences for Thai society and the Thai polity: a dangerous crossroads indeed.

Notes

1 Samak was charged with conflict of interests since he maintained his cooking television programme while serving as prime minister. Meanwhile, the Court ordered the dissolution of Somchai's party, the People's Power Party, which was the reincarnation of Thaksin's Thai Rak Thai Party, because one of its executive members was found guilty of committing electoral frauds.

2 His statement can be found at http://asiapacific.anu.edu.au/newmandala/2010/12/03/legitimacy-crisis-in-thailand/ accessed 19 January 2011.

3 Thailand finally lifted the state of emergency that had been in place since April 2010 in Bangkok and three surrounding provinces. The emergency law empowered the military to take charge of security. The government first imposed it in April shortly after anti-government red-shirted demonstrators broke into the country's parliament. The Abhisit government gradually lifted the decree in provinces where it thought security threats had diminished.

4 'Peud Kham Winichai Sanratthathammanoon Yokkhamfong Khadiyoobphakprach-athipat Doei-la-iard' [Exposing the Verdict of the Constitutional Court in the Dissolution Case of the Democrat Party: In Details], *Matichon Online*, 29 November 2010 www.matichon.co.th/news_detail.php?newsid=1291030368&grpid=no&catid=02 accessed 21 January 2011.
5 At http://advocacy.globalvoicesonline.org/2010/06/18/thailand-government-shuts-43000-more-websites-for-lese-majeste-plans-to-block-3000-more-total-up-to-113000/ accessed 21 January 2011.
6 The Red-Shirt social movement first called itself the Democratic Alliance against Dictatorship (DAAD) to reflect its anti-coup identity. It came into being following the coup in late 2006.
7 Interview with a group of Red Shirts leaders at Red Shirt villages in Ubon Ratchathani, 22 June 2012.
8 Speech of Thongchai Winichakul on the topic 'Is the End of Thailand's Crisis in Sight?' at the Regional Outlook Forum organized by the Institute of Southeast Asian Studies, Singapore, 12 January 2011.

References

Crispin, Shawn W. (2010) 'Bloody desperation for Thailand's Reds', *Asia Times*, 17 March; www.atimes.com/atimes/Southeast_Asia/LC17Ae01.html accessed 13 October 2011.

Crispin, Shawn W. (2011) 'The deal behind Thailand's polls', *Asia Times*, 30 June; www.atimes.com/atimes/Southeast_Asia/MF30Ae01.html accessed 13 October 2011.

Croissant, Aurel (ed.) (2002) *Electoral Politics in Southeast and East Asia*, Singapore: Friedrich-Ebert-Stiftung, Office for Regional Co-operation in Southeast Asia.

Diamond, Larry (2008) *The Spirit of Democracy: The Struggle to Build Free Societies throughout the World*, New York: Henry Holt and Company.

Freedom House (2013) 'Thailand: Freedom in the World 2013'; www.freedomhouse.org/report/freedom-world/2013/thailand accessed 24 July 2013.

Handbook on Thailand's Political Situation (2007) News Division, Department of Information, Ministry of Foreign Affairs of Thailand, 6 June.

McCargo, Duncan (2005) 'Network monarchy and legitimacy crises in Thailand', *Pacific Review*, 18(4), 499–519.

Mydans, Syth (2008) 'Thai court forces Premier from office over TV cooking show', *New York Times*, 9 September.

Pasuk Phongpaichit and Baker, Chris (2002) *Thailand: Economy and Politics*, Oxford: Oxford University Press.

Pavin Chachavalpongpun (2011) 'Thailand's military on the offensive', *Wall Street Journal*, 20 April.

Perry, Richard Lloyd (2009) 'Thaksin Shinawatra: the full transcript of his interview with *The Times*', *Times Online*, 9 November 2009; www.timesonline.co.uk/tol/news/world/asia/article6909258.ece accessed 19 January 2011.

Plate, Tom (2011) *Conversations with Thaksin: From Exile To Deliverance: Thailand's Populist Tycoon Tells His Story*, Singapore: Marshall Cavendish.

Streckfuss, David (2011) 'Freedom and silencing under the neo-absolutist monarchy regime in Thailand, 2006–2011', in Pavin Chachavalpongpun (ed.) *Thailand's Fearlessness: Free Akong*, Bangkok: Prachatai Press, pp. 22–53.

Thitinan Pongsudhirak (2009) 'After the red uprising', *Far Eastern Economic Review*, 172(4), 39.

Thitinan Pongsudhirak (2010a) 'Meaning and implications of General's rise', *Bangkok Post*, 5 October.

Thitinan Pongsudhirak (2010b) 'Thailand's misrule by law', *Wall Street Journal*, 15 December.

Thongchai Winichakul (2008) 'Toppling democracy', *Journal of Contemporary Asia*, 38(1), 11–37.

UDD (2011) *Khem Mung Khong Nor Por Chor Deang Thang Prates* [Future Direction of the UDD] Bangkok.

Walker Andrew and Farrelly, Nicholas (2011) 'Prime Minister Yingluck Shinawatra', *East Asia Forum*, 4 July; www.eastasiaforum.org/2011/07/04/prime-minister-yingluck-shinawatra/ accessed 11 October 2011.

6   The limits of post-plunder reform in the Philippines' oligarchic democracy

Nathan Gilbert Quimpo

When Benigno Simeon Aquino III ran for the Philippine presidency in 2010, his platform, 'A Social Contract with the Filipino People', highlighted two major agenda items: fighting corruption and reducing poverty. His campaign slogan, 'If no one is corrupt, no one will be poor!'– encapsulated and linked these two top concerns. After nine years ridden with corruption and fraud scandals under President Gloria Macapagal Arroyo, Aquino's slogan resonated among many Filipinos, becoming a household catchphrase and helping him win the election by a wide margin.

As president, Aquino has embarked on a programme of reforms that hews closely to his electoral platform. He has made good on his campaign pledge to fight corruption. He constituted a Cabinet of predominantly professional-technocratic officials, including some reputedly reform-oriented figures, and he has called on those in the public service to follow the 'straight path'. In line with the call for 'transparent, accountable and participatory governance', Aquino and his Cabinet have undertaken such reforms as a more transparent way of preparing the national budget and the adoption of technologies facilitating public disclosure of data. To break the atmosphere of impunity, the Aquino administration has arrested, jailed and prosecuted former top government officials on various malfeasance charges, including Arroyo herself. Incarcerated – under 'hospital arrest' as she has been undergoing medical treatment for a bone ailment – she is now being prosecuted on charges of plunder, corruption and electoral fraud. Two close allies of Arroyo, Ombudsman Merceditas Gutierrez and Supreme Court Chief Justice Renato Corona, both deemed to be too 'soft' or partial in cases involving the Arroyo administration, were impeached by the House of Representatives. In April 2011, Gutierrez resigned ten days before the Senate, sitting as an impeachment tribunal, could try her. In May 2012, after a four-month trial that was broadcast live and widely followed, Corona was convicted of betrayal of public trust and culpable violation of the Philippine constitution for failing to disclose to the public his statement of assets, liabilities and net worth as required by law. In national surveys, the Aquino government has generally received high approval ratings in its efforts to fight corruption.

Some of Aquino's reform measures, however, such as those related to rapid and sustained growth and to poverty reduction, have not – or at least not yet – achieved the desired results. In terms of economic growth, Aquino, at least in his first two and a half years in power, has fared much better than his predecessors, but the growth rates have not been consistently high. After surging to 7.6 per cent in 2010, the Philippines' GDP growth rate dropped to a feeble 3.7 per cent in 2011, then bounced back to 6.6 per cent in 2012, one of the strongest economic growths in Asia last year. Despite massive infusions of funding for a conditional cash transfer programme and other poverty reduction projects, poverty remains widespread, perhaps even worsening.

With the seemingly iron-willed determination that the Aquino administration has shown in pursuing its reform agenda, it would appear that the Philippines is now well on the way to recovering from the depredations of the Arroyo period and to addressing the deficiencies in its democracy and rule of law, and may now have a better chance at achieving rapid and sustained growth and reducing poverty. This chapter takes a much more circumspect view. It argues that while the Aquino government has made significant gains in the fight against corruption, it has barely dented the core problem in the Philippines' oligarchic democracy: entrenched political families that maintain their stranglehold on wealth and power through patronage and various other means and who hamper faster economic development. It argues further that the Philippines has merely reverted from a predatory regime to a clientelist regime and that many of the conditions that gave rise to the politics of plunder under Arroyo and her predecessor President Estrada remain. The challenge for the Aquino government is to prevent the return of the predatory regime by prevailing upon the reformers in the establishment and their allies in civil society to undertake much more thoroughgoing initiatives aimed at combating ingrained cultures of patronage and impunity and strengthening the rule of law.

Descent to predatory politics

The Philippine state has been characterized as a 'weak state' captured by powerful political families (McCoy, 1993), a 'patrimonial state' (Kuhonta 2008) or, more specifically, a 'patrimonial oligarchic state' (Hutchcroft 1998). The roots of the Philippines' oligarchic state can be traced to the country's colonial past. The Spanish and American colonizers worked closely with, and nurtured, the local elite, allowing its members to compete in municipal elections in the latter part of Spanish colonial rule, and then in provincial and national legislature elections in the early years of American colonial rule. Patronage and clientelism suffused the electoral politics of Philippine 'colonial democracy'. As early as the first national legislative elections in 1907, notes Paredes (1988), a complex network of clientelist dyads featuring both factional competition and alliance emerged at all levels of Philippine society extending all the way to Washington, DC. These clientelist ties deepened in the decades thereafter, well into the Commonwealth period (1935–1942; 1945–1946).

Since gaining independence, the Philippines has generally been regarded as a democracy except during the authoritarian interregnum under Marcos

(1972–1986). Political and social scientists, however, have often appended somewhat depreciatory adjectives to the country's democracy, to wit: 'cacique democracy' (Anderson 1988), 'elite democracy' (Bello & Gershman 1990; Timberman 1991), 'oligarchical democracy' (Sidel 2008), and 'bourgeois democracy' (Thompson 2010). In all the above characterizations of the Philippine state/democracy, the country's politics is described as being dominated or controlled by factions of the entrenched politico-economic elite that resort to patronage and various other means to maintain their hold on wealth and power.

Apart from experiencing democratic and authoritarian regimes, the Philippines has experienced two regime types in terms of how its oligarchic elite has wielded power to promote its economic ends: clientelist and predatory. A clientelist regime is one based on pyramids of dyadic alliances in which politicians and their supporters exchange favours, usually material benefits for political support. A predatory regime is one in which the usual clientelist exchange of favours has degenerated into rampant corruption, a systematic despoliation of state resources, and the perversion of state institutions into instruments of plunder, repression or propaganda (Quimpo 2009). The clientelist electoral regime that emerged after independence underwent a crisis in the 1960s and the early 1970s when elections were much more marred by campaign overspending, corruption, fraud and violence – or 'guns, goons and gold'. With Marcos' declaration of martial law in September 1972, the old order gave way to a predatory authoritarian regime. Former Senate President and opposition figure Jovito Salonga (2003: 231) explains the authoritarianism-predation relation this way:

> What then was the need for martial law? Partly to prolong [Marcos'] stay in office beyond 1973 ... and partly to expand what the conjugal dictatorship [of Ferdinand and Imelda Marcos] had already accumulated. The partnership made sure that under the constraints of martial law – among other things, a controlled, captive media, an abolished Congress, a subservient judiciary and the blind, unwavering support of the military – they could continue robbing the country blind without any danger of being found out.

Marcos suppressed freedom of speech, of association, and of the press and other civil liberties, and he clamped down on all opposition. In a war against communist and Muslim rebels, government security forces killed or maimed tens of thousands of rebels and their sympathizers. They arrested, detained, tortured or caused the involuntary disappearance of tens of thousands of political prisoners. Furthermore, Marcos sought to control all the agencies of government and to exploit them as instruments for plundering the country's resources. The dictator and his cronies used various means to acquire and secure ill-gotten wealth: the creation of monopolies in vital industries and placing them under the control of cronies; the awarding of loans by government banking or financial institutions to favoured private individuals; the outright takeover by Marcos' relatives or associates of large enterprises; the issuance of presidential decrees and orders favouring certain individuals and enterprises; the use of shell corporations and dummy companies to launder money and invest in real estate; and depositing funds with the use of pseudonyms, numbered accounts and code names in banks in the Philippines and overseas (Salonga 2000). According to Transparency International (TI), Ferdinand Marcos stole as much as US$5–10 billion during his two decades in power (Denny 2004).

Marcos' fall and the restoration of democracy under the leadership of President Corazon Aquino in 1986, far from casting out or weakening oligarchic rule, simply brought back the clientelist electoral regime of old. The anti-Marcos traditional elite made a political comeback, and they were soon joined by many ex-Marcos loyalists who had managed to refurbish themselves, as well as ambitious new politicians who, once elected into office, quickly embarked on building their own political dynasties. In an open letter to President Aquino III shortly after his electoral victory in 2010, the famed novelist F. Sionil Jose (2010) wrote of the role played by the president-elect's mother, Corazon:

> And, finally, your mother. We loved her – she united us in ousting an abominable dictator. But she, too, did not leave a shining legacy for her presidency was a disaster. She announced a revolutionary government but did nothing revolutionary. She promised land reform but did not do it. And most grievous of all – she transformed the EDSA I revolution [the 1986 'people power' uprising] into a restoration of the oligarchy.

Political decay in the clientelist order soon set in again. By the early 1990s, writes MCoy (1993: 10), the country's 'powerful political families' were resorting to various tactics and methods to maintain themselves in power, but most especially to 'rent-seeking' and political violence. In the 'synergistic' interaction between the state and the oligarchic elite, 'the privatisation of public resources strengthens a few fortunate families while weakening the state's resources and its bureaucratic apparatus'. In many provinces, warlords – powerful, semi-autonomous politicians who had reinforced their positions with 'private armies' – emerged or revitalized. Corruption in high places grew worse.

The short-lived Estrada presidency marked the transition from clientelist to predatory regime. Corruption scandals beset the Estrada administration throughout its short span. What greatly incensed many and mainly brought about his downfall was his involvement in a nationwide illegal numbers game (*jueteng*) racket in which he netted PHP545 million in protection money. Opposition leaders sought to impeach him for *jueteng* racketeering, as well as for kickbacks from the tobacco excise tax, undue intervention in an insider trading case, and unexplained wealth as manifested by the lavish lifestyles of his mistresses and extended family. Estrada survived the impeachment attempt but was soon forced out of office by 'People Power II' in January 2001. Since he was not in power long enough, he was unable to pervert government institutions into instruments of plunder as Marcos had done. TI estimates that Estrada looted US$78–80 million from the government's coffers (Denny 2004). Convicted in September 2007, he was granted executive clemency by Arroyo several weeks later.

Although Arroyo, who succeeded Estrada, had vowed to bring about 'new politics', 'high moral standards' and 'leadership by example' at her inauguration, her nine-year administration proved even more nefarious than her predecessor's. It was ridden with corruption and fraud scandals involving her close associates and allies, including some in which Arroyo herself, her husband and/ or other close kin were implicated. The most controversial and notorious of these scandals were the 'Hello Garci' scandal (2005) in which Arroyo and election commissioner Virgilio 'Garci' Garcillano were apparently tapped talking over the phone about the rigging of the 2004 presidential election, and the NBN-ZTE scandal (2007) in which a US$329 million National Broadband Network (NBN) contract with China's ZTE Corp. involving First Gentleman Jose Miguel 'Mike' Arroyo was reportedly overpriced by US$130 million to cover kickbacks. In an editorial, the *Philippine Daily Inquirer* (2009) described corruption under Arroyo as 'humongous', with virtually every major project involving the government 'honeycombed with graft and corruption', and with sums running in the hundreds of thousands or even billions of pesos.

Worse, Arroyo bequeathed, in the words of Doronila (2009), 'a legacy of ruined political institutions underpinning Philippine democracy'. She managed to put Congress under her thumb – and defeat all attempts at impeachment – through patronage, especially in approving the release of pork barrel funds. To control the bureaucracy, she stacked it with loyalist appointees, many of them unqualified. Through congressmen, governors and line agencies, she extended 'governance by patronage' to local governments. Political parties, long notorious for lacking programmes and ideologies, served as conduits and cover for patronage and plunder (Quimpo 2010). The military and the police became subservient instruments. As exposés of big-time corruption in the Armed Forces of the Philippines (AFP) and the Philippine National Police (PNP) have shown, top military and police officials were only too happy to partake in the largesse. The Commission on Elections (Comelec) ceased to be an independent and impartial body, as revealed by the investigations into the cases of large-scale fraud in the 2004 and 2007 elections. Instead of fighting corruption, the Ombudsman, according to the *Philippine Daily Inquirer* (2010), 'shielded the former president, her family, close associates and officials from charges of corruption, enrichment in office and abuse of authority'. The independence and integrity of the Supreme Court became questionable. Consisting mostly of Arroyo appointees, it consistently delivered pro-Arroyo decisions. Arroyo transformed the very institution of the presidency itself into the ultimate tool for patronage and predation by utilizing its broad powers in making appointments and in disbursing government funds.

With the pervasive corruption and the large-scale perversion of state institutions, Arroyo's administration brought the predatory regime into full fruition. According to a Pulse Asia survey conducted in late 2007, Filipinos rated Arroyo as 'the most corrupt' among the five Filipino presidents of the past two decades, surpassing even Marcos and Estrada. Unlike Marcos, who resorted to authoritarian rule to plunder the country's resources, Arroyo maintained an electoral democracy and exploited the weaknesses of a patronage-based 'democratic' system.

An important factor helping Arroyo to survive politically and finish her term was the state of the economy. Despite all the scandals, the Philippine economy grew at a faster pace under Arroyo (2001–2009), registering an annual GDP growth rate of 4.5 per cent, compared to 3.9 per cent under Corazon Aquino (1986–1991), 3.8 per cent under Fidel Ramos (1992–1997) and 2.4 per cent under Estrada (1998–2000) (Lopez 2010).

Tens of millions of Filipinos did not benefit from such growth, however, as levels of poverty and inequality remained high. Far from cutting by half the percentage of Filipinos living in poverty by 2015 in line with the Philippines' commitment to the Millennium Development Goals, the Arroyo government managed to reduce poverty only from 33 per cent of the country's population in 2000 to 29.7 per cent in 2009. The rich-poor gap in the Philippines widened, becoming the most pronounced in Southeast Asia. In 2010, the Philippines registered a Gini coefficient of 44 per cent, higher than Thailand's 42.5 per cent, Indonesia's 39.4 per cent, Malaysia's 37.9 per cent and Vietnam's 37.8 per cent (Ho 2011). While real wages in Asia in general rose continuously in 2000–2010, those in the Philippines remained stagnant, constrained by the lack of competition due to the increase of monopolies and oligopolies in the country (Asian Development Bank 2011).

Political violence increased sharply under Arroyo, highlighted by the killings of many activists and journalists, the escalation of election-related violence, and the proliferation of private armies. In the course of the government's counter-insurgency campaigns, hundreds of members of left-wing activists were summarily killed or 'disappeared' in 2001–2010. According to the Commission on Human Rights (CHR), summary killings under Arroyo claimed 1,254 victims. Only six cases of extrajudicial killings, according to Human Rights Watch (2010), were successfully prosecuted, with 11 defendants convicted, none of whom were military men, despite many testimonies of military involvement. During Arroyo's term, a total of 103 journalists were killed for various reasons: exposing malfeasances such as corruption, taking sides in local disputes, or themselves being involved in corruption. The Philippines thus earned the notoriety of being among the most dangerous places for journalists (Quimpo 2012). After declining in the 1990s, election-related violence, reflecting the fierce battle for spoils of rival political clans, rose sharply again under Arroyo. With at least 100 people killed in election-related violent incidents in every general and midterm election between 2001 and 2010, Philippine elections have probably become the most violent in the world. Arroyo's presidency also witnessed a proliferation of private armies and death squads that were beholden to local warlords and outside of national government control. According to the PNP, 112 private armies are spread throughout the country (Agence France-Presse 2010). One of the primary factors for their growth was the proliferation of 'loose firearms' – unlicensed and unregistered guns – estimated by the PNP to number over a million. The worst single case of political violence under Arroyo was the infamous Maguindanao massacre of November 2009, in which at least 57 people – journalists, as well as relatives and supporters of a political rival – were brutally murdered by the private army of Maguindanao Governor Andal Ampatuan, Sr, the top warlord in the southern Philippines and a staunch ally of Arroyo.

Money politics, apart from political violence, intimidation and fraud, increasingly distorted Philippine election results under Arroyo. Among the most notorious forms of money politics are vote buying, which has become more flagrant, campaign overspending, and the use of state resources, as well as of grey money from *jueteng* and drug lords, for campaigning (Quimpo 2012).

Social Weather Stations (SWS) surveys indicated that in the wake of the scandals during the Arroyo presidency, Filipinos' satisfaction with the way democracy works in the country plunged and support for authoritarian rule rose. Shortly after Arroyo's highly contested victory in the 2004 presidential elections, only 44 per cent of Filipinos expressed satisfaction, in contrast to the 70 per cent peaks reached in October 1992 and July 1998 after the election of Ramos and Estrada, respectively. In September 2006, a record low of 49 per cent of respondents stated that 'democracy is always preferable to any other form of government', and in March 2006, a record high of 26 per cent said that 'under some circumstances, an authoritarian government can be preferable'. Less than six months after Aquino assumed the presidency, Filipinos' satisfaction rating for democracy hit 69 per cent, clearly a recovery from the Arroyo era ebb and just one per cent shy of the 1992 and 1998 peaks. Preference for authoritarianism, however, established a new record: 27 per cent (GMANews. TV 2010).

Reforms and the fight against corruption under Aquino

Given the severity of corruption and poverty the Aquino government's decision to prioritize addressing these two problems may well be important for the consolidation and deepening of democracy in the Philippines. A good democracy, state Diamond and Morlino (2005: xiv), has a strong and vibrant rule of law in which, among other things, '[t]he law is equally enforced toward everyone', and '[c]orruption is minimized, detected, and punished, in the political, administrative, and judicial branches of the state.' Warren (2004: 328–329) argues that corruption 'usually indicates a deficit of democracy', elaborating that corruption 'breaks the link between collective decision-making and people's powers to influence collective decisions, thus [reducing] the reach of democracy; ... undermines the culture of democracy, [often making people] cynical about public speech and deliberation; [and] undermines democratic capacities of association within civil society by generalizing suspicion and eroding trust and reciprocity'. As mentioned earlier, corruption under Arroyo reached such proportions that it made a shambles of many of the country's democratic institutions. 'Poverty', contends Huntington (1991: 311), 'is a principal and probably the principal obstacle to democratic development.' When vast numbers of the citizenry are poor and uneducated, and thus unlikely to build strong civil society organizations, writes Ruhl (1996), achieving democratic consolidation is difficult. On the whole, democratization has been reversed more often in countries where the poverty rate has been high (40 per cent of the population) than in countries with a low rate (20 per cent) (Kapstein and Converse 2008).

In pursuing his 'Social Contract with the Filipino People', Aquino has embarked on reforms in five 'key result areas', the first two reflecting the strongly anti-corruption and poverty reduction thrust of his electoral platform.

- *Transparent, accountable and participatory governance.* Following the principle of 'daylight in governance', the Aquino government has adopted various budgeting-related measures to eliminate or reduce waste and corruption, such as 'zero-based budgeting'; fleshing out lump-sum funds; public disclosure of budget information through the Internet; and consultations with civil society organizations in the crafting of the budget and auditing of infrastructure projects. It has enforced strict adherence to public bidding rules. It has also promoted the enhanced use of information and communications technology in government operations to 'promote arms-length transactions [and] reduce human intervention' (Aquino 2011). The strategic objectives of the government's Good Governance and Anti-Corruption (GGAC) Plan for 2012–2016 are to curb corruption, to improve the delivery of public services, and to enhance the business and economic environment. The Plan also seeks to contribute to greater fiscal discipline and further promote public input in the preparation of the national budget through a 'bottom-up' approach.
- *Poverty reduction and empowerment of the poor and vulnerable.* To reduce poverty incidence to 16.6 per cent by 2015 in line with the Philippines' Millennium Development Goals, the Aquino administration has considerably increased allocations for social services and poverty reduction, constituting a third of the government's budget in 2012 and 2013. The centrepiece programme of the poverty alleviation efforts is a conditional cash transfer (CCT) programme that aims to provide a 'life vest' to Filipinos 'drowning in extreme poverty' (Department of Budgeting and Management, 2012). Under this programme, indigent families receive as much as PHP1,400 a month for six years provided that their children go to school, attend classes regularly and receive proper immunization, and mothers avail of maternal health-care services. With about three million indigent household beneficiaries now covered, the government seeks to enroll all 4.3 million indigent households into the programme by 2016. The government has also undertaken measures for the expansion and improvement of education quality, better health-care facilities and thorough implementation of the universal health-care programme, and greater investment in housing assistance, potable water, rural electrification, etc.
- *Rapid, inclusive and sustained economic growth.* In order to spur rapid economic growth, the government has increased spending for infrastructure, as well as sought to entice private capital into public-private partnerships for key infrastructure and development projects. It has also embarked on fiscal consolidation to narrow the fiscal deficit and to improve the country's debt

profile. In dealing with the perennial problem of low revenues, the government has undertaken tax collection reform involving intensified implementation of tax laws and programmes. In the agriculture sector, the government has boosted irrigation development, the centrepiece programme in its drive to attain self-sufficiency in food staples, as well as built arterial roads, and promoted the use of genuine certified seeds, the search into higher yielding crop varieties and other technologies.

- *Just and lasting peace and the rule of law.* The government signed a preliminary peace agreement with the Moro Islamic Liberation Front (MILF) in October 2012 and is now working towards a final peace pact that would hopefully bring to an end the decades-old armed conflict in southern Philippines. Peace negotiations have been reopened with communist rebels. The government has also launched programmes seeking to enhance the capabilities of the military and the police to address external and internal threats. In December 2012, Aquino signed a human rights law criminalizing enforced disappearances, the first of its kind in Asia. It makes the abduction of people suspected of anti-government activity by agents of the state punishable by life imprisonment.
- *Integrity of the environment and climate change adaptation and mitigation.* Apart from intensifying reforestation efforts, the government has greatly increased funding for the identification of key disaster risk areas, timely and accurate weather forecasting and improved disaster risk management planning.

In addition to pushing for reforms in the five key result areas, the Aquino administration has successfully worked for the passage of the Reproductive Health Bill in the face of strong opposition from the Catholic Church hierarchy. The government hopes that the new law, which provides for free or cheap contraceptives to poor couples and institutionalizes sex education, will bring down high maternal mortality rates and promote responsible parenthood.

At the World Economic Forum (WEF) in Davos, Switzerland, in January 2013, Aquino credited the reforms for such achievements as the country's high growth rate in 2012, the Philippines Stock Exchange index breaking its own record high 70 times under his administration, and the Philippines' jump from 85th in 2010 to 65th in 2012 in the WEF's global competitiveness rankings. For the first time ever, the country has received investment-grade rating from Fitch and Standard & Poor, two of the world's major ratings agencies.

The fight against corruption has dominated the government's actions in the first two years of Aquino's term. In his very first executive order, Aquino established a 'truth commission', headed by former Supreme Court Chief Justice Hilario Davide, Jr, to investigate allegations of official wrongdoing and impunity committed during the previous administration. What was envisaged to be Aquino's central anti-corruption initiative, however, was soon stymied. Arroyo's allies questioned the legality of the commission, contending that only Congress could establish such a commission and that its functions overlapped with those of the Ombudsman. In December 2010, the Supreme Court, headed by Corona, ruled that the 'truth commission' was unconstitutional.

The tide started to turn in Aquino's favour in early 2011 during an investigation by both houses of Congress into a controversial plea bargaining agreement between the Office of the Ombudsman and the former AFP comptroller, Major General Carlos Garcia, accused of stealing PHP303 million from government coffers. Instead of being charged with the non-bailable crime of plunder, Garcia was allowed to plead guilty to the lesser charge of direct bribery and money laundering, to return only PHP135 million of his loot, and was released on bail. At the Senate investigation, a former AFP budget officer, Colonel George Rabusa, exposed large-scale embezzlement of military funds by top generals, especially the diversion of hundreds of millions of pesos of military slush funds for 'welcome' and 'send-off' money for chiefs of staff. A former Commission on Audit accountant corroborated Rabusa's story. As the investigation deepened, former AFP chief Angelo Reyes, who was among those tagged as a 'welcome-send-off' recipient, committed suicide.

The AFP corruption case helped pave the way for the impeachment and subsequent resignation of Ombudsman Gutierrez. In 2009, Gutierrez had survived an attempt to impeach her for gross inaction on several large-scale corruption cases. The next year, the drive for her ouster revived. In the wake of the AFP corruption case, the Senate Blue Ribbon Committee echoed the demand for her impeachment, this time for 'neglecting, weakening and complicating' the plunder case against Garcia. Gutierrez's resignation in April 2011 provided a big boost to Aquino's anti-corruption efforts. The 'truth commission' was no longer needed. The Ombudsman's office could once again serve as the anti-corruption body it was constitutionally mandated to be. Although six cases of 'plunder' had been filed against Arroyo at the office of Ombudsman Conchita Carpio-Morales, who replaced Gutierrez, no formal charges had yet been filed against the former president in court. Only when Arroyo tried to leave the country in November 2011, ostensibly for medical treatment abroad, did the Aquino government's resolve become clear. Upon orders by Secretary De Lima, immigration officials prevented Arroyo, who was in a wheelchair and wearing a head and neck brace, from boarding her plane in a dramatic airport scuffle. Three days later, electoral sabotage charges were filed against Arroyo and two others at a regional trial court and she was arrested. A few weeks later, corruption charges were filed against her, her husband and close associates in connection with the anomalous NBN-ZTE deal. Released on bail in July 2012, she was rearrested and re-confined ten weeks later on a charge of plunder – a non-bailable offence – for allegedly using state lottery funds amounting to PHP366 million for personal gain.

To Aquino and his allies, the conviction of Chief Justice Corona was crucial not just for the administration's anti-corruption agenda but also for the restoration of the judiciary's independence and for judicial reform. Aquino had always questioned Corona's appointment. Arroyo picked Corona, who once served as her chief of staff and spokesman, to head the Supreme Court in the last few weeks of her presidency despite a constitutional prohibition on 'midnight appointments'. What triggered the impeachment of Corona was the Supreme Court's issuance of a temporary restraining order that very nearly allowed Arroyo to escape from prosecution. 'Corona's designated role in GMA's play-book', writes Joel Rocamora (2012), lead convener of the government's National Anti-Poverty Commission and a member of Aquino's Cabinet, 'was to use the Supreme Court to prevent her from going to prison … [Aquino] understands that, without removing Corona, the Court would remain a court of last resort for reactionaries. Any person or organization resisting reform but facing defeat in other arenas could always look forward to being defended by the Corona Court.'

Since the arrest of Arroyo, more cases of large-scale corruption and fraud have been filed in court and more investigations ordered. The former chairman of the Comelec, Benjamin Abalos, Jr, has been jailed on corruption and electoral sabotage charges in connection with the NBN-ZTE scandal and the 2007 elections. Former Governor Andal Ampatuan, Sr, already behind bars and being tried for the Maguindanao massacre, also faces charges on the electoral sabotage case. Ombudsman Carpio-Morales has laid charges against ten retired and active Philippine Navy officers for the 1995 murder of Ensign Philip Andrew Pestaño for opposing the use of a Navy vessel to transport illegal lumber. The Justice Department has recommended to the Ombudsman the filing of plunder charges against eleven top military officials, including two former AFP chiefs of staff, in connection with the *'welcome-send-off'* scandal. Carpio-Morales has ordered a reinvestigation of the so-called 'euro generals' case, in which the former Interior Secretary and top PNP officials were said to have diverted police funds for a junket of the PNP generals to Europe. Graft cases have also been filed by the Ombudsman against five former officials of the Presidential Commission on Good Government, including its former chairman, for leasing vehicles worth PHP12 million without public bidding.

A major setback in the fight against corruption has been the non-passage of the Freedom of Information (FOI) bill that Aquino had earlier declared a priority measure. Although the right of the people to information on matters of public concern, including access to official records and documents on official acts, transactions and decisions, is contained in the Bill of Rights of the 1987 Philippine Constitution, it needs an implementing law, which Congress has perennially failed to pass. In the latest enactment attempt, the Senate passed the FOI bill in December 2012, but it floundered again in the Lower House. A Malacañang spokesperson resignedly admitted that the House discussions still had not thoroughly threshed out the FOI issue and that it still needed 'extensive deliberation' (Salaverria and Burgonio 2013).

Elite hegemony unaddressed

While the Aquino government has made major gains in the fight against corruption and fraud, it has made little progress in many of its other reform efforts. The fluctuation in annual GDP growth rates has contradicted the government's projection of rapid and sustained economic growth. Extra cautious that infrastructure projects do not become mired in corruption as in previous administrations, the Aquino government has been slow in pursuing its public–private partnerships (PPP) programme, which it identified early on as one of its key strategies for achieving fast, inclusive growth. As of January 2013, only two projects had actually been awarded: a connector road project and a school infrastructure project.

Deep structural problems remain. Asian Development Bank senior economist Norio Usui (2012: viii) attributes the Philippines' perennial slow economic growth and its chronic problems of high levels of unemployment, and poverty and low level of investment' to sluggish industrialization. He explains that the Philippine economy, which has long been led by services, has grown even more reliant on services, especially given the country's booming business process outsourcing industry. He believes, however, that such a course is unsustainable. What needs to be done is 'to develop a stronger industrial base to enable the economy to "walk on two legs" of industry and modern services, to create productive job opportunities for the growing working-age population'.

A particularly sore point for the administration is poverty reduction, avowedly one of its top two priorities. Thus far, official government statistics have not registered any significant change in poverty incidence and the rich-poor gap under Aquino. According to a 'self-rated poverty' survey of SWS, the number of Filipinos who consider themselves 'poor' has in fact risen, from 48 per cent in September 2010 to 54 per cent in December 2012. Both figures are several notches above the all-time low of 43 per cent recorded in March 1987 and March 2010. Hunger incidence also increased slightly from 15.9 per cent in September 2010 to 16.3 per cent in December 2012. According to official government statistics, annual unemployment rates under Aquino have hovered at 7 per cent. SWS, however, has come up with much higher figures, which show that joblessness has risen under Aquino. Adult unemployment, which had been above 20 per cent in most of SWS's quarterly surveys from May 2005 to December 2011, spiked to a record high 34.4 per cent in March 2012 before sliding down to 29.4 per cent in August 2012. The decline in the Philippines' GDP growth rate in 2011 was a major let-down. To bring down poverty incidence to 16.6 per cent by 2015, the Aquino administration had early on targeted an average annual economic growth of 7–8 per cent. To explain continuing high poverty levels, presidential spokesman Ramon Carandang clarifies that it would take some years before the effects of the government's poverty reduction programmes would be felt (Mendoza 2012).

Aquino's approach to poverty reduction appears to lack depth. Since being inducted into office, he has continued to harp on about his campaign message linking the fight against corruption with the fight against poverty. In February 2012, he stated, 'By curbing corruption, we can reduce poverty.' (Aquino 2012). While this slogan may have been election-winning, it is a rather simplistic purported solution to poverty. Conditional cash transfer, with its education and health ingredients, could well serve as investment in human capital. Without a well laid out industrialization plan that opens up jobs, however, CCT could end up as nothing more than dole-outs for indigent families. Abelgas (2012) compares it to a Marcos-era initiative intended to be only a stopgap response to joblessness:

> While the World Bank described [the CCT program] as a 'prudent safety net' for poor families during tough economic times, the danger here is that like the overseas workers program, [it] is boosting the mendicant mentality among Filipinos and that like the OFW [overseas Filipino workers] program, which was launched as a temporary program during the oil crisis in the 70s, the CCT program might become a permanent policy that would instill dependency and complacency among the poor Filipinos.

Many of the Aquino government's reform efforts, especially those against corruption and fraud, may be laudable. The main weakness in Aquino's reform efforts, however, is that they do not fully confront the core problem in the Philippines' oligarchic democracy: the stranglehold on wealth and power by an elite few. Corruption and fraud are not the only means, nor necessarily the main means, by which the rich and powerful maintain their hold. Such other means as patronage, political dynasty-building and political violence have remained largely unaddressed. When the political winds change, they could easily lead back to humongous corruption and fraud.

Under the Philippines' patronage-based politics, Arroyo took advantage of the weak political party system and the strong presidency to gain and maintain control of Congress and most local governments and to engage in what many regard as plunder. Since political parties in the Philippines are merely instruments of convenience, turncoatism is a common phenomenon. Very much aware of the president's effective control over disbursement of funds, especially pork barrel funds, opposition politicians switch to the president's party or coalition in droves at the start of his or her term. When an impeachment motion was initiated against Arroyo in 2005, her coalition already had a very large majority in the House of Representatives. Nonetheless, to make sure that none of them would waver, she cut off pork barrel disbursements to pro-impeachment congressmen.

Various reforms to combat patronage, such as strengthening political parties, abolishing pork barrel, and curbing presidential powers, have often been advanced in the past. Aquino is not pursuing any of them, at least for now. A bill for political party reform was reintroduced at the Senate, but Aquino did not give it tangible support. Mobilizing legislative support for party reform or pork barrel abolition would be a difficult, uphill battle. Aquino's coalition enjoys an overwhelming majority in Congress. But this majority, far from being a body of anti-patronage stalwarts, is mainly the result of the usual party-switching opportunism during presidential changeovers. A Congress studded with patronage politicians cannot be relied upon to pass anti-patronage legislation. In fact, to ensure congressional support for his initiatives, Aquino has inflated the budget for pork barrel from PHP6.9 billion in 2010 to PHP22.3 billion in 2011 – a whopping

223 per cent increase – and to PHP24.89 billion in 2012 (Mangahas 2012). With Aquino continuing with his anti-corruption drive and battling with powerful political figures, it would be a most inopportune time to pursue the curbing of presidential powers. A shift from a presidential system of government to a parliamentary system, as many reformers have advocated, would require a constitutional amendment, something Aquino is very much disinclined to attempt during his term, as this would open him to the charge of manoeuvring to extend his stay in power.

Political dynasties, expressly prohibited by the Philippine Constitution, have flourished in the post-authoritarian era. Tasked with enacting the enabling legislation to ban political dynasties, legislators have been building or perpetuating them instead. A study by Mendoza *et al.* (2011) reveals that 70 per cent of the jurisdiction-based legislators in Congress belong to political dynasties. Dynasty-building has reached epidemic proportions, as politicians at all levels of government, once elected to public office, try to get their relatives ensconced in other government positions, elective or appointive, or to succeed them. 'The [2013] election season,' noted the *Philippine Daily Inquirer* (2013) in an editorial, 'is turning out to be an unprecedented showcase of dynastic hubris, with members of historically well-entrenched political families indicating their intent to seek important posts with hardly any or a minimum of qualifications and track record of public service, or any record, for that matter, of competence and vision.' Aquino has not taken any initiative to push for enabling legislation for the dynasty ban. He himself belongs to two of the country's most powerful political dynasties, the Cojuangcos (mother's side) and the Aquinos (father's side).

Historically, the concentration of land in the hands of a few landowners in the Philippines has engendered deep grievances among landless and dependent farmers and farm workers that have sometimes led to armed resistance. Since 1955, every Philippine president has pursued his or her own version of land reform, yet huge tracts of agricultural land remain under the ownership or effective control of powerful political families. 'Landowners just wanted the [agrarian reform] program stopped,' economist Solita Monsod (Mercado 2008) points out. 'Over the last 20 years, they managed, through every means fair or foul, to keep over 80 per cent of their land safe from redistribution. And they wanted to make that permanent.'

The government's perennial poor performance in agrarian reform has actually worsened under B. Aquino. In 2011, the Department of Agrarian Reform (DAR) achieved only 54.6 per cent of its land acquisition and distribution target. Under pressure from farmers' groups and Catholic bishops, Aquino promised in June 2012 to speed up land acquisition and distribution and to allocate the necessary funds for this. DAR's accomplishment rate in land acquisition and distribution in 2012, however, further declined, falling to below 25 per cent – the worst record in DAR history. Agrarian reform advocates have called for the sacking of DAR Secretary Virgilio de los Reyes, but Aquino has stood by him. Close to a million hectares still needs to be processed before the expiration of the agrarian reform programme in June 2014. It seems unlikely that the task will be accomplished.

The lack of support may have something to do with the interests of his mother's landed clan. Farmers and farm workers of the Cojuangcos' Hacienda Luisita, a 4,916-hectare sugar plantation, had for decades fought to gain ownership of the land they tilled. In November 2011, the Supreme Court made an historic decision to distribute the estate's lands to the farmers. The Cojuangcos filed a motion for reconsideration, but the Supreme Court ruled with finality in April 2012 reaffirming its earlier decision.

The Aquino administration has become embroiled in a controversy over the resolution of an issue dating back to the Marcos era: the coconut levy fund. From 1973 to 1982, Marcos imposed a levy on coconut farmers purportedly to create a levy fund for protection against global market fluctuations and for the development of the coconut industry. The levy proceeds ended up in the hands of Marcos cronies such as Eduardo Cojuangco, an estranged uncle of the current president, and Juan Ponce Enrile, the current Senate president who broke with Marcos in 1986. For three decades, coconut farmers' organizations pressed for a recovery of the levy fund. Finally, in September 2012, the Supreme Court upheld a lower court ruling that a 24 per cent chunk of shares in Cojuangco's San Miguel Corporation were illegally acquired through coconut levy proceeds and should therefore be awarded to the government to be used for the benefit of coconut farmers. This chunk, now worth a total of PHP70 billion, is the single biggest recovery of illegally acquired wealth of Marcos and his cronies. An inter-agency Presidential Task Force on the Coco Levy Fund favours using the levy money for the rehabilitation and modernization of the industry and for a poverty alleviation programme for the poorest coconut farmers. Some militant farmers' organizations, however, have demanded that the levy money be distributed directly to coconut farmers in cash and other benefits.

Since Aquino assumed the presidency, the level of political violence has significantly decreased. According to the CHR, extrajudicial killings dropped from about 130 victims per year during Arroyo's term (January 2001–June 2010)[1] to 114 victims in the first two and a half years of Aquino's term (Human Rights Watch 2013). Despite such a decrease and the 2012 landmark legislation on enforced disappearances, Human Rights Watch (2012) has strongly criticized Aquino for his unfulfilled promise to punish security forces responsible for human rights violations. 'The Aquino government,' the group points out, 'has not successfully prosecuted a single case of extrajudicial killing or enforced disappearance, including those committed during his presidency.' Human Rights Watch has challenged the government to show its resolve in combating impunity by arresting retired army Maj. Gen. Jovito Palparan, implicated in the abduction, torture and execution or disappearance of leftist activists. Palparan remains at large despite a PHP1 million reward for information leading to his capture.

Under the Arroyo presidency, human rights violations were mainly attributed to the government's security forces – the military, police and paramilitary forces. Under Aquino, the CHR has put the blame for continuing human rights violations primarily on politicians' 'private armies' (ABS-CBN News 2012). Members of the Ampatuan clan and its 'private army', who were already arrested and jailed during the Arroyo era, are now being tried in court for the Maguindanao massacre. Despite Aquino's electoral campaign promise and subsequent instructions to dismantle 'private armies', they continue to operate with impunity.

The high incidence of political violence in the Philippines is very much related to the oligarchic nature of the country's politics. Extrajudicial killings have been perpetrated against leftists – legal activists as well as communist insurgents – who oppose the rule of an entrenched elite few, and against journalists, a good number of whom expose the corruption and abuses of those in power. Electoral contests for power between factions of the elite sometimes become so intense that they can end up in grisly bloodletting, as the Maguindanao massacre most graphically illustrated.

Can Aquino really do much more than just fighting corruption?

In his post-election open letter to Aquino, F. Sionil Jose (2010) challenged the president-elect to be a revolutionary, not in the bloody sense, but in the tradition of the 1986 uprising, and 'to destroy the most formidable obstacle to our progress – the oligarchy to which you and your family belong'. Jose bluntly told him, 'To succeed, you have to betray your class.'

Perhaps Aquino is just biding his time and he will embark on more substantive political reforms at a later time, possibly after the resolution of the cases against Arroyo, or possibly after the May 2013 midterm elections, which afford the opportunity for Aquino-backed reformers to win seats in Congress and the local governments.

There are no indications, however, that Aquino is grooming more reform-oriented politicians to run in 2013 in place of the usual patronage-type ones. His own Liberal Party, which accommodated large numbers of political turncoats after his election, is once again heavily dominated by traditional politicians belonging to powerful clans. The drive to strengthen the party in terms of its political programme and organization, very visible in the years prior to Aquino's victory, has evaporated. The Liberal Party is once again an amorphous, non-ideological, non-programmatic, catch-all party, in an even more amorphous, non-ideological, non-programmatic, catch-all ruling coalition.

Conclusion

After the depredations of the Estrada-Arroyo era, President Aquino, making good on his anti-corruption and anti-poverty electoral platform, has undertaken a reform programme that highlights good governance and poverty reduction. The Aquino government's reform measures have repaired a lot of damage to the country's democratic institutions and considerably brought back transparency and accountability in the public sector. Moreover, its fight against corruption and fraud has taken on very high public officials once regarded as untouchable, headed by no less than former President Arroyo herself.

While the reforms in themselves may be commendable, they do not go far enough. Aquino appears to be well aware of the dangers, declaring recently, 'Without structural reform, another corrupt president might one day take the reins of power; another chief justice might one day again betray the public trust' (Chiu 2013). The Aquino government's reluctance to pursue deeper reforms to combat patronage, political dynasty building and political violence, however, indicates that it is not – or at least, not yet – willing and ready to challenge the power elite in the Philippines' oligarchic democracy. Even if Aquino were to 'betray' his class, he would still run up against quite a wall. Many of the major political reforms would require legislative action or even constitutional change. It would be too much to expect that Congress, which is packed with patronage politicians and members of political dynasties, some of whom belong to warlord clans with private armies, would be supportive of such reforms.

From a predatory regime, the Philippines has reverted to a clientelist order, similar to that under C. Aquino and Ramos. Unless reformers within the ruling coalition vigorously push for deeper political reforms, the country will remain an oligarchic democracy. Aquino's reforms could very well be carried on and deepened by a worthy successor. But if a Marcos- or Arroyo-type politician wins the next presidential election, the Philippines could again find itself in the clutches of a predatory regime.

Note

1 Email communication with Byron Bocar, a CHR official, 28 November 2011.

References

Abelgas, Val G. (2012) 'Walls of poverty', *Pinoy Weekly*, 9 May; http://thepinoyweekly. com/?p=5626 accessed 24 July 2013.

ABS-CBN News (2012) 'Private armies tagged in rights abuses', 25 January; www.abs-cbnnews.com/nation/01/25/12/private-armies-tagged-rights-abuses accessed 24 July 2013.

Agence France-Presse (2010) 'Private armies hold RP politics at gunpoint', 2 July; www.abs-cbnnews.com/nation/07/02/10/private-armies-hold-rp-politics-gunpoint accessed 25 July 2013.

Anderson, Benedict (1988) 'Cacique democracy in the Philippines: origins and dreams', *New Left Review*, 169, 3–31.

Aquino, Benigno Simeon III (2011) 'The President's Budget Message', 26 July; www. dbm.gov.ph/?page_id=779 accessed 24 July 2013.

Aquino, Benigno Simeon III (2012) 'Speech at the Cabinet Workshop on Anti-corruption Strategies', 21 February; www.pcoo.gov.ph/speeches2012/speech2012_feb21.htm accessed 24 July 2013.

Asian Development Bank (2011) 'Key Indicators for Asia and the Pacific 2011', Manila: Asian Development Bank.

Bello, Walden and Gershman, John (1990) 'Democratization and stabilization in the Philippines', *Critical Sociology*, 17(1), 35–56.

Chiu, Patricia Denise (2013) 'Aquino cautions vs. corrupt future leaders', GMA News, 31 January; www.gmanetwork.com/news/story/292798/news/nation/aquino-cautions-vs-corrupt-future-leaders accessed 24 July 2013.

Denny, Charlotte (2004) 'Suharto, Marcos and Mobutu head corruption table with $50bn scams', *Guardian*, 26 March; www.theguardian.com/world/2004/mar/26/indonesia. philippines accessed 4 August 2013.

Department of Budgeting and Management (DBM) (2012) 'Budget ng bayan: Tungo sa paggugol na matuwid'; http://budgetngbayan.com/ accessed 24 July 2013.

Diamond, Larry and Morlino, Leonardo (2005) *Assessing the Quality of Democracy*, Baltimore: Johns Hopkins University Press.

Doronila, Amando (2009) 'Era of quick solutions for storm rehab', *Philippine Daily Inquirer*, 26 October; http://opinion.inquirer.net/inquireropinion/columns/view/20091026-232251/Era-of-quick-solutions-for-storm-rehab accessed 25 July 2013.

GMANews.TV (2010) 'SWS: satisfaction with democracy nears record highs', 22 December; www.gmanetwork.com/news/story/208854/news/nation/sws-satisfaction-with-democracy-nears-record-highs accessed 24 July 2013.

Ho, Abigail L. (2011) 'Philippines leads in income inequality in ASEAN, says study', *Philippine Daily Inquirer*, 22 July; http://business.inquirer.net/8377/philippines-leads-in-income-inequality-in-asean-says-study accessed 24 July 2013.

Human Rights Watch (2010) 'Philippines: ending killings should top Aquino's agenda', 12 July; www.hrw.org/news/2010/07/12/philippines-ending-killings-should-top-aquinos-agenda accessed 24 July 2013.

Human Rights Watch (2012) 'Philippines: two years under Aquino, abuses go unpunished', 27 June; www.hrw.org/news/2012/06/27/philippines-two-years-under-aquino-abuses-go-unpunished accessed 24 July 2013.

Human Rights Watch (2013) 'World Report 2013'; www.hrw.org/world-report/2013/country-chapters/philippines?page=1 accessed 24 July 2013.

Huntington, Samuel P (1991) *The Third Wave: Democratization in the Late Twentieth Century*, Norman: University of Oklahoma Press.

Hutchcroft, Paul D. (1998) *Booty Capitalism: The Politics of Banking in the Philippines*, Ithaca: Cornell University Press.

Jose, F. Sionil (2010) 'An open letter to Noynoy', *Philippine Star*, 23 May; www.philstar.com/sunday-life/577141/open-letter-noynoy accessed 26 July 2013.

Kapstein, Ethan B. and Converse, Nathan (2008) 'Why democracies fail', *Journal of Democracy*, 19(4), 57–68.

Kuhonta, Erik Martinez (2008) 'Studying states in Southeast Asia', in Kuhonta, Dan Slater and Tuong Vu, *Southeast Asia in Political Science: Theory, Region and Qualitative Analysis*, Stanford: Stanford University Press, pp. 30–54.

Lopez, Virgil (2010). 'Aquino urged to pick "fresh economic team"', *SunStar Manila*, 19 June; www.sunstar.com.ph/manila/aquino-urged-pick-fresh-economic-team accessed 24 July 2013.

Mangahas, Malou (2012). 'PDAF racket rocks "*daang matuwid*"', Philippine Center for Investigative Journalism, 17 July; http://pcij.org/stories/pdaf-racket-rocks-daang-matuwid/ accessed 24 July 2013.

McCoy, Alfred W. (1993) 'An anarchy of families': the historiography of state and family in the Philippines', in McCoy, A.W. (ed.) *An Anarchy of Families: State and Family in the Philippines*, Madison: University of Wisconsin Center for Southeast Asian Studies, pp. 1–32.

Mendoza, Ronald U., Beja, Jr., Edsel L., Yap, David Barua, and Venida, Victor (2011) 'An Empirical Analysis of Political Dynasties in the 15th Philippine Congress', Asian Institute of Management, Working Paper 12–001, 9 September; http://papers.ssrn.com/sol3/papers.cfm?abstract_id=1969605 accessed 24 July 2013.

Mendoza, Shielo (2012) 'SWS: self-rated poverty in March highest for Aquino gov't', Yahoo Southeast Asia Newsroom, 3 May; http://ph.news.yahoo.com/sws--self-rated-poverty-highest-for-aquino-gov-t.html accessed 25 July 2013.

Mercado, Juan (2008) 'Country of mad men', *Philippine Daily Inquirer*, 23 December; http://opinion.inquirer.net/inquireropinion/columns/view/20081223-179506/Country-of-mad-men accessed 25 July 2013.

Paredes, Ruby R. (1988) 'Introduction: The paradox of Philippine colonial democracy', in Paredes, R.R. (ed.) *Philippine Colonial Democracy*, New Haven: Yale University Southeast Asia Studies.

Philippine Daily Inquirer (2009) 'Legacy of corruption', 28 July; http://opinion.inquirer.net/inquireropinion/editorial/view/20090728-217534/Legacy-of-corruption accessed 25 July 2013.

Philippine Daily Inquirer (2010) 'Impeach the Ombudsman', 13 September; http://opinion.inquirer.net/inquireropinion/editorial/view/20100913-291965/Impeach-the-Ombudsman accessed 25 July 2013.

Philippine Daily Inquirer (2013) 'Dynastic hubris', 1 February; http://opinion.inquirer.net/46085/dynastic-hubris accessed 24 July 13.

Quimpo, Nathan Gilbert (2009) 'The Philippines: predatory regime, growing authoritarian features', *The Pacific Review*, 22(3), 335–353.

Quimpo, Nathan Gilbert (2010) 'The presidency, political parties and predatory politics in the Philippines', in Kasuya, Yuko and Quimpo, N.G. (eds) *The Politics of Change in the Philippines*, Manila: Anvil Publications, pp. 49–74.

Quimpo, Nathan Gilbert (2012) 'Country report: Philippines', in Dizard, Jake, Walker, Christopher and Tucker, Vanessa (eds) *Countries at the Crossroads 2011: An Analysis of Democratic Governance*, New York: Freedom House and Rowman & Littlefield, pp. 533–560.

Rocamora, Joel (2012) 'Remove that crown of thorns', ABS-CBN News, 5 January; www.abs-cbnnews.com/blogs/insights/01/05/12/remove-crown-thorns accessed 24 July 2013.

Ruhl, J. Mark (1996) 'Unlikely candidates for democracy: the role of structural context in democratic consolidation', *Studies in Comparative International Development*, 31(1), 3–23.

Salaverria, Leila B., and Burgonio, T.J. (2013) 'Another setback for FOI bill', *Philippine Daily Inquirer*, 23 January; http://newsinfo.inquirer.net/345365/another-setback-for-foi-bill accessed 24 July 2013.

Salonga, Jovito V. (2000) *Presidential Plunder: The Quest for the Marcos Ill-gotten Wealth*, Quezon City: National College of Public Administration and Governance, University of the Philippines.

Salonga, Jovito V. (2003) *The Intangibles that Make the Nation Great*, Mandaluyong: Regina Publishing.

Sidel, John T. (2008) 'Social origins of dictatorship and democracy revisited: colonial state and Chinese immigrant in the making of modern Southeast Asia', *Comparative Politics*, 40(2): 127–147.

Thompson, Mark R. (2010) 'After populism: winning the "war" for bourgeois democracy in the Philippines', in Kasuya, Yuko and Quimpo, Nathan Gilbert (eds) *The Politics of Change in the Philippines*, Manila: Anvil Publications, pp. 22–46.

Timberman, David G. (1991) *A Changeless Land: Continuity and Change in Philippine Politics*, New York: M.E. Sharpe.

Usui, Norio (2012) *Taking the Right Road to Inclusive Growth: Industrial Upgrading and Diversification in the Philippines*, Mandaluyong: Asian Development Bank.

Warren, Mark E. (2004) 'What does corruption mean in a democracy?' *American Journal of Political Science*, 48(2), 328–343.

7 Developments in Cambodian democracy

Democratic consolidation or authoritarian durability?

Melissa Curley

Introduction

It is well known that Cambodia endured violent political upheaval from the late 1960s to the early 1990s. Neighbouring Vietnam, Cambodia was drawn into the Vietnam War, and from 1975–1979 suffered the genocide regime of Pol Pot under the Khmer Rouge (KR) (see Chandler 2003). A period of Vietnamese backed rule followed under Hun Sen, known as the People's Republic of Kampuchea (PRK) (1979–1989), and the State of Cambodia (1989–1993) during which civil war lingered on. Following the end of the Cold War, Cambodia's civil war was partially resolved by the 1991 Paris Peace Agreement, which then tasked the United Nations (UN) with rebuilding Cambodia into a multiparty democracy. It was hoped the state would thus 'transition' to a liberal democracy, according to the transition paradigm (Linz and Stepan 1996), whereby with the right institutions and features of governance, countries could move out of authoritarianism and into the spectrum of democracy. The United Nations Transitional Authority in Cambodia (UNTAC) oversaw Cambodia's transition from 1991–1993, the largest and most ambitious attempted to date.

The success or otherwise of the UNTAC mission and Cambodia's democratic credentials is a matter for ongoing debate (McCargo 2005; Un 2006; Richmond and Franks 2007; Paris 2009). Since the mid to late 2000s, however, a consensus has formed that the ruling Cambodian People's Party (CPP) dominates the political and economic decision-making process (Chandler 2010; Un 2012), with widespread recognition that corruption and nepotism exist in the party-state apparatus (Broadhurst and Bouhours 2008; Ear 2013). As such, faith in the ability of the Cambodian elite to continue on the path to 'democratic consolidation' has waned, with some using the Cambodia case as a critique of the 'liberal peace' project itself (Richmond and Franks 2007). Executive capture and influence over the judicial system, and the extent of the fusion between state and party power, are two recurrent themes in the literature on Cambodian democratization.

This chapter reviews developments in Cambodian politics from 2008 onwards. During this period, the Cambodian government and the CPP enjoyed increased political power via gains in the 2008 national election, and consolidated its control of local government communes. After the Global Financial crisis, however, an economic downturn in 2009 hit the export-orientated garment industry hard, resulting in the loss of around 30,000 jobs (Chandler 2010: 230). On the domestic front, apart from countering political opponents, the government also faced complex transnational problems, such as managing the outbreak of H5N1 (bird flu), and irregular migration in the form of both trafficking in persons and migrant smuggling.

Three areas are deemed significant during the period under review which relate to the key theme of this book – that is, the state of democracy in Cambodia. These are: the electoral process and the party system, state-civil society relations, and the rule of law and justice system. Analysis of these three arenas provide a window into how the CPP and its leaders have maintained and consolidated political power, and mobilized the judicial system to intimidate political opponents and stifle political speech and activities which run counter to the government's political and economic agenda. State-civil society relations is an important site where local and international actors are pushing the government (at times via the courts) to increase the accountability and transparency of government decision-making and resource allocation, with mixed results.

The chapter argues that a slide from the rule of law to rule *by* law is occurring in Cambodia, and is a serious negative development for further democratic consolidation. The judicial system continues to be influenced by the ruling political elite, which uses its powers to support a range of politically-motivated decisions. The Cambodian Criminal Justice System (CCJS) therefore is faced with, and poses, a number of serious challenges to the promotion and consolidation of democracy. The specific challenges include the limited availability of resources in policing and legal arenas, lack of capacity and adequate training, lack of legal representation for victims, as well as other pressing crime issues, such as drug trafficking and youth violence (Broadhurst and Bouhours 2008). Nevertheless, the presence of opposition figures willing to speak out, and strong opposition to the government's attempt to further 'regulate' non-governmental organizations (NGOs), are positive points.

Perspectives on transition and their application to Cambodia

The nature of democratization in Southeast Asia itself has a vast literature which draws from debates about the context and history of post-colonial Southeast Asian polities, in relating to monarchical systems and historical patterns of governance and rule (Chandler 1983; Reid and Castles 1975) and wider debates about democratic transition and consolidation (Diamond 2008; Levitsky and Way 2010). The most relevant aspects of such debates pertain to how the democratization process in Southeast Asia has been conceptualized.

Detailed treatments of the conceptual and theoretical differences between transitional democracy, competitive authoritarianism, or hybrid regimes are well documented. It is worth briefly reviewing this debate, as it has influenced the way Cambodia's democracy has been 'categorized'. In recent times, points of difference have centred around the utility of 'transition' as a conceptual frame (due to its teleological assumptions about temporal movement along a spectrum), whether and how democratic 'quality' relates to regime change, and understanding the dynamics of authoritarian features within non-democracies.

In examining the latter part of the third wave of democratization, Diamond proposed the need for the category of 'hybrid regimes' (Diamond 2002) where a combination of democratic structure and institutions, and aspects of authoritarianism and illiberal forms of politics, were simultaneously present. Diamond (2008) also conceptualized the issue of quality as democracies consolidate, stressing the need to think beyond static definitions and procedures that could account for 'democracy'.

He categorized Cambodia within other Southeast Asian polities as '[an] electoral (hegemonic) authoritarianism', along with Singapore and Thailand. Indeed if one compares contemporary Cambodian politics to Diamond's criteria, the case for a match appears to be strengthening. These criteria are regular elections, but where only one party can win; limits on press freedom; restrictions on criticizing the government; unfair financial assistance available to one party; and the screening out of 'unsuitable' candidates and parties.

Levitsky and Way (2010), however, contend that a further category is required to account for the proliferation of non-democratic regimes after the Cold War. In their major study of 35 post-Cold War 'hybrid' regimes, they argue that the regime category of 'competitive authoritarian' better captures the nature of 'democracy' in their sample group, where multiparty elections were held, but where 'electoral manipulation, unfair media access, abuse of state resources, and varying degrees of harassment and violence skewed the playing field in the favour of incumbents' (2010: 3). They add a fifth variable to the well-established 'procedural minimal' definition of democracy (following Dahl) which displays four key attributes: (1) free, fair and competitive elections, (2) full adult suffrage, (3) protection of civil liberties and freedom of speech, press and association; and (4) absence of non-elected tutelary authorities (such as militaries and monarchies) that constrain elected officials' power to govern (Levitsky and Way 2010: 5–6). Their fifth variable, (5) 'the existence of a reasonably level playing field between incumbents and opposition', is designed to measure the degree of incumbent manipulation of state institutions and resources.

A new category is necessary, they contend, because no existing term adequately captures the range of characteristics of both democracy and authoritarianism. Furthermore, they suggest it avoids the production of 'misleading' labels which stem from classifying hybrid regimes as different 'subtypes of democracy' – such as those used by Diamond and Zakaria. This debate speaks to the tension inherent in assumptions about democratic transition, and the need to take the 'nondemocratic nature of regimes seriously' (Schedler in Levitsky and Way 2010: 15).

Levitsky and Way, however, define Cambodia as a 'competitive authoritarian' regime, noting in addition to the features of an 'electoral authoritarian' regime, the degree to which the opposition lacks a level playing field. Further, their interest in examining the dynamics of authoritarian regimes, including the role and centrality of informal institutions, succession politics, and party behaviour (where parties have electoral and regime objectives), make their approach insightful in the Cambodian context. Cambodia's democracy also interests scholars as part of the post-conflict reconstruction agenda that has become so salient in the 1990s and beyond. Cambodia's experience with democratization is also pertinent to the question of how Asia-Pacific states manage and manipulate political reform. As Reilly notes, Asian citizens and political elites are engaged in a discussion over issues such as the relative merits of presidentialism versus parliamentarism; decentralization, federalism, or regional autonomy; the development of political parties and party systems; and the design of constitutional structures (2007: 59).

Reviewing Cambodia's democratic progress post-2008

Electoral and party politics

Contrasting narratives of how post-conflict stability was achieved influence contemporary discussions about Cambodia politics and political parties (Hughes 2006; 2009). On the one hand, the 1990 Paris Agreements and the subsequent UNTAC peacekeeping mission of 1991–1993 is credited, by the UN and the international community, with heralding a new democratic and inherently more stable period for Cambodians. On the other hand, CPP party members and loyalists attribute this stability to a functioning state structure, with its roots in the PRK period after Vietnam ousted the Khmer Rouge in 1979. Underlying that apparatus are the personal loyalties and connections forged between state officials and party members. Contemporary administrative or governance reforms that are seen by central elites to undermine those relationships are viewed by CPP loyalists as having the potential to unravel stability gains so hard won in the 1980s. From this perspective, the CPP provides a strong centralizing force whose capabilities cannot be matched by the smaller, more fragmented political parties that are accused by the CPP of being less connected with the 'grassroots'. This narrative views stability based on long-held client-patron relations as a stabilizing and fundamentally good aspect of present government structures (Gainsborough 2012).

Cambodia held its fourth national general election in July 2008, which generally consolidated the CPP's power. Although 53 political parties were registered nationally in 2008, only 12 contested the election, with only five parties winning seats. These were the CPP, the Sam Rainsy Party (SRP), the newly formed Human Rights Party (HRP), FUNCINPEC, and the Norodom Ranariddth Party (NRP). Space does not allow a detailed discussion of the election and evaluations of its electoral procedures; however, a number of important points relating to democratization should be noted. As Thayer (2009) argues, the 2008 election resulted in a further consolidation of CPP power, securing 98 per cent of the communes, and 58 per cent of the popular vote. The CPP won 90 seats out of the

123 contested. The SRP consolidated its position in the National Assembly marginally, by gaining 26, compared to 24 seats in the previous election. The HRP won three seats, FUNCINPEC two seats, dropping drastically from its previous 26, and the NRP two seats. Notably, voter turnout (75 per cent) was the lowest for national elections since 1993 (Thayer 2009).

Although monitored by numerous international agencies the election was marred by opposition claims that voter lists had been manipulated. During the election, the four major opposition parties rejected the preliminary election results, claiming that up to a million voters countrywide had been left off voter lists (Thayer 2009). In August the SRP and HRP filed complaints with the Constitutional Council and lobbied the international community about the conduct and outcome of the election. As Thayer argues, 'while virtually all of the major international and domestic election monitoring organizations found faults and irregularities in the conduct of the election, none concluded that the election was not free and fair' (2009: 90). A number of commentators noted that overt political violence, killings, threats and intimidations diminished, and that the campaign and election was more peaceful than in the past.[1] However, such positivity was tempered by the reality that opposition groups were subject to ongoing intimidation throughout the campaign.

Two themes emerge from the literature that analyses elections and political parties in Cambodia since the 2007 commune elections and 2008 national election. The first is the increasing fusion between the party and state power; the second is the ongoing weakness of the opposition. In terms of party/state fusion, the ongoing political consolidation of CPP power via the electoral process, including at the commune level (see Hughes 2010), means that key areas of the state's administrative and security apparatus are increasingly at the party's disposal, and are being harnessed 'to undermine the work of political opponents' (de Zeeuw 2010: 1187). As Broadhurst and Bouhours argued in 2008, state institutions and their agents struggled to function independently of CPP politics: 'The merging of CPP and the state now seems complete and the regime exercises administration more in terms of traditional patron/client relations than rational allocation of resources' (2008: 185–188).

The historical role of patron-client relations is also a theme in Gainsborough's analysis of the 'non-democratic trajectory' of Cambodia, Vietnam and Laos. He suggests that the political culture of Cambodia is underpinned by 'heavy doses of elitism and paternalism' where 'cultural assumptions about the proper relationship between the state and its citizens, or between rulers and the ruled, contrast starkly with what is taken for granted in the West' (2012: 38–40). While such analyses point to societal and historical barriers to democratic consolidation in Cambodia, others look to the ability of legislatures to provide accountability.

In his analysis of the role of legislatures under electoral authoritarianism, Case (2011a) outlines the mechanisms through which Hun Sen has limited the opposition's capacity to impose accountability on the government. These include the legislature's institutional autonomy being 'circumscribed by executive decree, dissolution, and impoundment powers' (Fish and Kroenig in Case 2011a:

52–53), and 'by placing many of his family members in positions of influence' to establish alternative mechanisms for feedback (Case 2011a: 53). International aid has also been implicated in the CPP consolidation of power, as de Zeeuw argues:

> The channelling of massive international aid packages through party-controlled government agencies seems to have boosted the organisational development of ... the CPP. However necessary for peace-building..., the consequence was that ... the CPP could expand their control over the state, media and other institutions virtually unchecked and thereby strengthen their position vis-à-vis other parties.
>
> (2010: 1187)

The second theme in the literature on elections and political parties has emphasized the weakness of the political opposition. While the constraints faced by the opposition parties have been noted, their own internal weaknesses and declining levels of domestic appeal need to be acknowledged (Un 2011; de Zeeuw 2010). Following years of disruption and exile, as in the case of Sam Rainsy, the appeal and popularity of the SRP has been damaged. Coupled with the recognition that the CPP is 'genuinely popular' in many areas (as demonstrated by opinion polling), major opposition parties SRP and the HRP must combat state interference in their activities and address their own institutional weaknesses.

The pessimistic scenario for the electoral process and political parties in the future is that this emerging uneven form of party competition continues to grow. The likely result is a cycle of CPP power consolidation (the power of incumbency) alongside deteriorating conditions for political parties in opposition to improve their internal functions, and overall institutionalization. While those challenges should not be underestimated, as Case suggests, what stands out in Cambodia's legislature will be 'an opposition still motivated to use it' (2011a: 57). Thus the ability and willingness of opposition parties to challenge the government via electoral process and the legislature will be important areas for ongoing analysis. Worryingly, however, the movement towards a 'rule by law' rather than 'rule of law' (Un 2012) provides the government with additional legislative options to control political statements and media commentary.

State–civil society relations

One of the enduring legacies of the UNTAC period has been the emergence of a large and vibrant NGO and international NGO (INGO) presence in Cambodia, albeit concentrated in Phnom Penh. Equating 'civil society' in Cambodia with externally funded NGOs is problematic. Civil society in Cambodia is a diverse combination of externally funded organizations (many staffed by international and local personnel), local NGOs with Cambodian leadership, Buddhist organizations, union and labour groups, and locally-based community-based organizations (CBOs). Since 2008, however, it is clear that the government's intolerance towards political party activism and unfavourable legal decisions has extended to NGOs that speak out particularly against human rights abuses, breaches of the land law, and environmental degradation. As noted above, while the CPP has been happy to allow international and local agencies to implement aid projects to build capacity and improved outcomes in areas such as health, education, poverty reduction, or human trafficking, it has been less tolerant of civil society activism in areas related to key business interests of the political elite and their connections.

Proposed law on associations and NGOs

International and local NGOs and religious groups have functioned without heavy state regulation in the post-UNTAC period, bar registration requirements for legal and tax/revenue purposes. Detailed regulations governing NGO activity, which characterize other East Asian states such as China or Vietnam, where NGOs must have a nominated government agency as their partner, and where their activities and disbursements of money are monitored, have not featured in Cambodian state-civil society relations. While discussed since 1994, it was not until 2009 that the government moved to draft a Law on Associations and NGOs (hereafter 'NGO Law'). While the government claims that the draft law is required to promote, enable and strengthen civil society, and to better manage NGO activity in administrative terms, civil society groups and some international diplomats and agencies are sceptical (Human Rights Watch 2011). Cambodian human rights NGO LICADHO have been the most active in commenting on and criticizing the draft law. Responding to the first draft, LICADHO argued that the law contained 'numerous problematic provisions, some of which violate the rights to freedom of association and expression guaranteed under the Constitution and international law – such as provisions for NGOs to be suspended or dissolved if they are deemed to have conducted activities for undefined "political interests"' (2009b: 3).

Following much criticism from international and local NGOs after the release of the first draft, and a government consultation, a second draft was released by the Ministry of Interior in March 2011. Despite a number of changes, LICADHO continued its criticism and opposition to the NGO Law citing at least five major problems, including (1) significant restrictions to freedom of association, (2) burdensome requirements and a 'difficult and intimidating' process for organizations to register, (3) excessive powers granted to government officials that would 'favour arbitrary decision-making', (4) intrusive requirements for organizations to report to the government, and (5) unreasonable restraints placed on foreign NGOs that would 'likely lead to a greater politicization of aid to Cambodia' (LICADHO 2011: 2–3).

The international community is also concerned about the proposed NGO Law. Numerous statements from Hun Sen and other government officials suggest an increasing distaste and intolerance for NGO activities that encroach into CPP political territory. As National Assembly President, Heng Samarin put it: 'Today, so many NGOs are speaking too freely and do things without a framework. When we have a law, we will direct them.' (LICADHO 2009b: 3). While there are good arguments for increased donor coordination within Cambodian development projects, and areas where increased transparency within NGOs may be warranted, the concern that vaguely defined articles of the NGO Law will be used at the discretion of the executive is justified.

Land policy and land rights conflicts

Citizens' land rights and the government's actions to grant land titles to major business interests for development purposes has emerged as a major tension point. Despite the existence of the 2001 Land Law, it is estimated that over 130,000 people have been evicted from their homes in Phnom Penh, with around 250,000 rural people forced off land that has been expropriated by the government (Chandler 2010: 232). In development terms, the land expropriation has increased landlessness and inequalities in overall landownership, in a country that was already extremely unequal. Thus, up to 30 per cent of Cambodia's land is owned by just 1 per cent of the population, and some 25 per cent of people are completely landless (Heder 2011: 211). A further 40 per cent of rural households own less than 0.5 hectares, which is less than half the minimum area estimated to provide basic nutritional needs (ibid.); 80 per cent of households with land 'have no secure title and are easily displaced' (Hughes 2008: 71). As Heder notes, the government enacted legislation in the new Land Expropriation Law in 2009 which increased opportunities for so called 'land-grabbing' and has resulted in popular resistance by self-organized groups of villagers. While the case of Boeung Kak Lake residents in Phnom Penh is well known, there are many other examples in rural areas, such as Koh Kong, Pursat and Kampong Chhnang (Um 2011: 59–61). Ominously, the military has been involved in repressing resistance to land retitling and forced eviction, adding weight to claims that Cambodian politics is becoming more militarized (LICADHO 2009a: 20–26). The case of a military style operation in Kratie province in May 2012, involving villagers protesting land claims, in which a 14-year-old girl died, is a case in point (Mu Sochua 2012).

Legal action against hundreds of villagers has been another tool to resolve land disputes favourably for government-linked interests. Hun Sen's decision to cancel the World Bank's US$24 million land-titling project, which had issued around 1.1 million titles since 2002, gave further evidence of the connection between political elites and the expropriation and exploitation of land (Chandler 2010: 232; Hughes 2008: 71–72). While economic growth has increased, with the exception of 2009 (post-global financial crisis), the benefits are not reaching the rural population where over 80 per cent of Cambodia's population live. In sum, the growing concern is that government wealth is not being redistributed for the benefit of the poorest. Government attention to agricultural policy has been inadequate (Um 2008: 113–115), such that Cambodia has one of the least developed agricultural sectors in Southeast Asia.

Not surprisingly, NGOs and lobby groups have spoken out against govern-ment action in this area, also acting on behalf of villagers and urban dwellers evicted from their land. Human Rights organizations such as LICADHO, Human Rights Watch, and Amnesty International have criticized evictions, while Amnesty's 2010 report cited 'forced evictions and legal actions against housing rights defenders among their principle issues of concern' (Um 2011: 60). As Um summed up:

> The issues of transparency and accountability are most troubling in the area of land ownership. Despite important strides made on land registration and on crafting measures to protect land tenure, land grabbing and systematic circumvention of existing laws and provisions continue to engender wide-spread dislocation of communities, forced evictions and other forms of viol-ence directed at vulnerable populations.
>
> (2011: 59)

This is one such area that the proposed NGO Law would likely target.

Environmental activism

Like land ownership, Cambodian forests are also a lucrative source of income for the government, for both legal and illegal logging enterprises. NGO activities around environmental degradation, and particularly illegal logging, have been another area where the government has sought to intimidate activists and stifle criticism. In 2007 the INGO Global Witness published a report – 'Cambodia's Family Trees' – documenting the destruction of 29 per cent of Cambodian forest cover in five years to a 'kleptocratic elite' (Global Witness 2007). The report alleged connections between the owners and exploiters of Cambodian land and forest resources with Hun Sen's family members, and was subsequently banned by the Cambodian government (Hughes 2008: 71). Another event captured inter-national attention in 2012 when a well-known environmental activist and founder of the NGO Natural Resource Protection Group, Chut Wuthy, was mur-dered. He was attempting to film illegal logging activities in Koh Kong province near the construction site of the 338-megawatt hydropower plant being built by China Huadian. The project is one of four dams that have been criticized because of logging activities and potential negative impact on wildlife and local liveli-hoods of villagers (*The Economist* 2012: 32). The investigation into Wuthy's murder, by a member of the Cambodian military, who then reportedly killed himself, has been fraught with inaccuracies and led to further accusations of governmental manipulation of the investigation's findings (LICADHO 2012; Global Witness 2012).

Land rights and environmental activities, along with human rights (see Ear 2013), represent areas where the government has clashed most with Cambodian civil society. It is also true that the government has deeply entrenched relation-ships with international aid donors and local organizations, established since the early 1990s, which has facilitated some positive gains in infrastructure, aspects of child and maternal health and sanitation, and combating the sexual exploitation and trafficking of women and children, for example. Nevertheless, such aid relationships are complex, and recent evidence illustrates how seemingly neutral 'good governance' reform initiatives promoted by international aid agencies may consolidate existing power hierarchies (Rodan and Hughes 2012). The fact remains that the government is now more willing and able than before to use judicial processes to protect its interests, particularly when civil society actors speak out against, and support legal claims in the courts, alleging corruption and nepotism. This is explored in more detail below.

Rule of law and the Cambodian Justice System

Political interference in the judiciary, political corruption, lack of capacity, and the deliberate manipulation of vaguely worded legislation for political purposes, are frequently noted in analyses of the justice system in Cambodia. Un's ethnographic research on the workings of the Cambodian judicial system provide some of the most detailed analysis of political interference and corruption. His analysis combines a knowledge of historical and patron-client relations to provide insight into why the CPP has only initiated ad hoc and ineffectual reforms, and why problems in the judiciary are endemic. On the latter point, he cites two major reasons: first, corruption is a practice that judges participate in on a routine basis to get to, and stay in, office; and second, judges are susceptible to removal from the bench for 'offensive' decisions (Un 2009). The judiciary therefore becomes 'a tool of the ruling party/parties to legitimize their actions and strengthen the executive power at the expense of the principle of check and balances' (2009: 95). Further to this, lack of material resources and low levels of trust between law enforcement and judicial police (which is rooted in 1980s' PRK politics) mean that cooperation between the courts and law enforcement is poor.

Un suggests that the government's attempts to 'reform' or 'crackdown' on judicial corruption (such as the 'mission iron grip' exercise) is a mere smokescreen to cover up widespread social injustice and corruption and to make a scapegoat of the judiciary (2009). Corruption of course stems from its prevalence in the wider state apparatus, where it is recognized to be a factor in undermining growth, diverting resources from public coffers, undermining investor confidence, and fuelling social inequalities and tensions (Um 2011: 57–59).

Lack of capacity and other legal issues

Lack of capacity in the CJS includes limited resources in terms of materials but also training and budget for the most basic expenses, such as petrol for police to travel to investigation locations. However, as Chinnery's analysis of the 2001 Land Law illustrates, people's access to justice following land-grabbing and evictions is severely limited by a number of factors. She cites such issues as vaguely-worded legislation, inadequate supporting legislation and guidelines, and the government's failure to demarcate land, that prevent claimants from seeking a fair hearing for their land rights claims to avoid eviction, or to seek compensation after it occurs (2009: 167). Furthermore, her analysis details how problems within the court system, including the deliberate misapplication of the 2001 Land Law, lack of court independence, and inadequate investigative procedures, result in very limited legal options for people evicted from their land.

The much anticipated trial of Khmer Rouge leaders, which commenced in 2007, captured significant international attention. While the Extraordinary Chambers in the Courts of Cambodia (ECCC) has achieved one high-profile conviction, there have been claims of political interference and disagreements over further prosecutions that have caused the most disruption.

Extraordinary Chambers in the Courts of Cambodia (ECCC):
2007–2012

Although two infamous 'show trials' of former Khmer Rouge suspects was conducted in Cambodia *in absentia* in 1979, there had long been calls for the perpetrators of the Cambodian genocide to be brought to justice.[2] While talks to establish a criminal tribunal started in August 1999, the ECCC did not commence proceedings until 2007 after suffering many setbacks and disagreements about its structure and composition, specifically over the 'pairing' of international judges and prosecutors with domestic appointees (Magliveras 2002).[3]

The ECCC is structured with a Trial Chamber and a Supreme Court Chamber. The Trial Chamber includes three Cambodian judges and two international judges, and the Supreme Court Chamber has four Cambodian judges and three international judges. Noteworthy is the 'supermajority' requirement, 'with decisions requiring the affirmative vote of a majority of the judges in each chamber plus one' (Williams 2004: 234–235). As Williams notes, the Cambodian ECCC is the only example of a hybrid tribunal not to have a majority of international judges.[4] This chapter cannot discuss in detail the events of the ECCC to date. Rather, the analysis reviews the ECCC in terms of (1) political interference, (2) corruption, (3) victim participation and (4) capacity building. It illustrates how the disagreements and public arguments between international and domestic judges, and between international judges and Hun Sen, provide substantial evidence of corruption and political interference.

Despite these factors, capacity building and the participation of victims as 'civil parties' in the ECCC, have been cited as positive factors for the legal system, and for the truth and reconciliation process, respectively. While some commentary supports the view that the ECCC has facilitated capacity building in the Cambodian legal system (see e.g. Form 2009; Bertelman 2010), it struggles to mitigate elite power and influence in contemporary Cambodian politics. Nevertheless, the long-term benefits are difficult to predict.

The ECCC commenced proceedings against five suspects, known as Cases 001 and 002 in 2007.[5] Only crimes committed within the period from 17 April

1975 to 6 January 1979 are within the temporal jurisdiction of the Extraordinary Chambers, reflecting the accepted duration of Khmer Rouge rule (Williams 2004: 238). The jurisdiction of the Extraordinary Chambers does not extend to the human rights violations of the Khmer Rouge either before or after that date. In what is considered the tribunal's legacy to date, in July 2010 Kaing Guek Eav (or 'Duch'), was found guilty of crimes against humanity for the killing of up to 13,000 prisoners when he was head of the S21 detention facility in Phnom Penh.[6] 'Duch' (Case 001) is possibly the most well-known perpetrator of violence under the Khmer Rouge reign, beyond Pol Pot himself. This verdict and appeal received international attention and commentary on its implications for international criminal law (Dubler 2010; Jain 2010; Ryngaert 2008; Un and Ledgerwood 2010; Bari 2011; Wilson 2011), and also conferred a degree of success on the ECCC.[7] However, the subsequent Cases – 003 and 004 – have become the most significant obstacles to the ECCC's continued functioning and legitimacy.[8]

Political interference

From the outset, Hun Sen publicly stated that he did not support the prosecution of lower ranking members of the Khmer Rouge regime, and instead wanted the process to focus on a group of four to five senior KR leaders who were already well known and 'tried in the court of public opinion'. Disputes between the international and domestic personnel relating to the continuation of Cases 003 and 004 have led to the high profile resignations of two international co-investigating judges, Siegfied Blunk and his replacement, Swiss national Laurent Kasper-Ansermet. McAuliffe provides some useful analysis on the reasons for Hun Sen's reticence, beyond the often quoted one of 'causing instability'. He suggests that most of the current leading CPP figures began their careers as mid-low ranking KR cadres who later rebelled. While there is no evidence that these members would meet the ECCC's personal jurisdiction of 'most responsible for crimes', McAuliffe argues that 'the shackles placed on the ECCC are borne less of a desire to shield CPP figures from prosecution than to save them from embarrassing testimony from their former associates if there were more trials that delved deeper into the KR apparatus' (2010: 118).

Serious division arose when the International ECCC Co-Prosecutor Robert Petit moved to investigate more people, a decision opposed by Cambodian prosecutor Chea Leang. Hun Sen publicly opposed additional investigations in a speech on 18 March 2009 'on the basis that it would undermine the peace settlement in Cambodia' (McAuliffe 2010: 135). In April 2011 investigations into Case 003 were closed, and in June 2011 concerns were raised that the investigation was stalled and then finally closed down by the Cambodian government, and that a proper investigation had not occurred. However, the UN defended the decision to close the case, denying media speculation that it had directed the investigating judges to stop Case 003.[9] In October 2011, International Co-Investigating Judge Blunk resigned over the handling of the case, and was replaced by Laurent Kasper-Ansermet. In January 2012 the Supreme Council of the Magistracy, Cambodia's judicial appointments authority (which, although nominally independent, has been moved within the control of the Cambodian government's Ministry of Justice), indicated that it would not approve Kasper-Ansermet. However, this was strictly unnecessary as he had already been approved by the Council as a reserve co-investigating judge. On 21 January 2012, the UN responded to Cambodia's rejection of the replacement international co-investigating judge, 'deploring' the decision and calling on the government to appoint him immediately. A UN statement said the decision not to appoint Laurent Kasper-Ansermet as a joint investigating judge was 'a matter of serious concern', and a breach of a 2003 agreement between Cambodia and the UN on prosecuting former Khmer Rouge officials (*New York Times* 21 January 2012).

Judge Kasper-Ansermet resigned on 19 March 2012 'because his Cambodian counterpart You Bunleng had thwarted attempts to investigate former members of the 1970s regime' (BBC 19 March 2012). Kasper-Ansermet said he considered that the present circumstances no longer allow him to properly and freely perform his duties, and further described the ECCC as 'dysfunctional' and 'riven with petty intrigues and carrying a political taint that keeps it from investigating well-documented crimes of well-known Khmer Rouge alumni who are living openly and freely in Cambodia' (McDonald 2012). In July 2012, it was confirmed that a replacement international co-investigating judge, Mark Harmon of the USA, and a reserve international co-investigating judge, Olivier Beauvallet of France, had been approved by the Cambodian government (ECCC 2012).

Corruption

Although most negative international attention has focused on political interference with the investigative and prosecutorial process, corruption allegations have also been made at various stages of the proceedings, particularly in relation to 'kickbacks' paid by Cambodian employees in return for their employment in relatively well-paid ECCC positions. Indeed, the president of the Trial Chamber of the ECCC, Nil Non, has publicly admitted accepting payments from litigants in his previous judicial roles. Bertelman notes that speaking to an American journalist in 2002, Nil Non reportedly said:

> [Y]es, it happens to me as it does to others ... but it is not through any efforts on my part. However, if people after a trial feel grateful to me and give me something, that's normal, I don't refuse it. I've settled the case for them and they feel grateful.
>
> (Bertelman 2010: 374)

The act of gift giving and reciprocation is central to Khmer society, and its influence in electoral politics is well known (Hughes 2006). It comes as no surprise that well-established systems of reciprocation – such as payment for appointment to jobs – could occur at the ECCC. Numerous sources and rumours have emerged about the hiring process of staff at the ECCC, and that Cambodian court personnel, including judges, paid a percentage of their salary to Cambodian government officials (Skilbeck 2008: 429–430). However, sources to confirm any allegations rarely want to be publicly named for fear of reprisal.[10]

Issues of corruption were also raised, unsuccessfully, by defence counsel (see Bertelman 2010), resulting in a restriction on funding to the ECCC in 2008 after the United Nations Development Programme (UNDP) froze contributions to the Cambodian side of the court. Ironically, funding restrictions may prove counterproductive in reducing corruption in the Cambodian context for a number of reasons, such as the degree to which 'contributions by states can and should be conditioned', and donor demands that are too specific could come to 'encroach upon the appearance of independence of the court' (Bertelman 2010: 376). While political interference and corruption allegations dominated critiques of the ECCC, victim participation in the process and the potential for capacity building are cited as two significant positives.

Victim participation

One particularly groundbreaking aspect of the ECCC is the participation of victims as 'civil parties' giving them some representational rights before the tribunal. The Victims Unit, a subdivision of the ECCC, was established to handle subsidiary charges. The Cambodian Code of Criminal Procedure (CPC) is the authoritative legal basis for victim participation (not the ECCC Statute) and thus the CPC 'regulates the rights of the victim and their opportunity to appear in court as civil parties' (Form 2009: 909–910).

A number of legal commentators have emphasized the reconciliation opportunities that have arisen from giving victims a robust role (Mohan 2008; Form 2009; Blair 2009). Blair, for example, argues that the ECCC, 'despite all its flaws, has taken a remarkable step forward in making international tribunals more open, more inclusive, and more responsive to the needs of victims than any institution that has come before it' (2009: 551). Furthermore, Form emphasized the role of civil parties as a forward-looking aspect of transitional justice. He suggests that 'the influence of victims on the procedural order of events can positively influence acceptance of the tribunal within the population. Even if it is only a small intervening group, it connects the court with the rest of the victim population' (Form 2009: 913). Despite these positives, concerns have been expressed that the ECCC failed to recognize the differential suffering of some ethnic minorities, such as the Khmer Krom (Mohan 2008), and about the suitability more generally of a victim-oriented approach to international criminal justice (Mohan 2009).[11]

Capacity building

One of the 'secondary benefits' of the ECCC's hybrid structure was thought to be the potential for Cambodian legal practitioners to learn 'best practice' from their international counterparts (Form 2009: 915–916). Many international aid workers and policymakers saw the participation of the international community in the ECCC as an opportunity to consolidate the rule of law within Cambodia. Apart from this general aspiration, the judiciary's participation in the tribunal was seen to potentially increase the legitimacy in the domestic arena and improve the public identification with and accessibility to the process (Bertelman 2010: 364; Lieberman 2005: 165). Those familiar with Cambodia's CJS, however, recognized that any longer-term capacity building would 'not happen by chance'; they would require formalized institutional change, adequately funded, at the least, leaving aside concerns about political interference (Skilbeck 2008: 444).

Conclusions about the ECCC's capacity building legacy may yet be premature. However, there is some recognition that the expectations in this regard, given the political realities in Cambodia, need to be tempered. As Kelsall has noted, 'it is important to be both more honest about the political agenda being promoted and more realistic about its feasibility in Cambodia' (2009: 168).

In sum, intense international scrutiny of the Khmer Rouge tribunal in Cambodia fed into the assessment of democratic regression (or stagnation at best), via its role in consolidating 'the rule of law', in two major ways. First, analysis of the ECCC provides evidence of the government's political involvement and investment in the ongoing deliberations of the tribunal. Public comments by Hun Sen and other high profile exchanges, such as between international and domestic co-prosecutors, only served to highlight significant challenges in the way the CCJS operates (BBC News Asia 2012; ECCC 2011). Kelsall's critique of the viability of the ECCC as a law and development project highlights the pitfalls of relocating Western models of law:

> [A]dvocates of rule of law extrapolate from Weberian sociology and the imagined experiences of Western capitalism to the rest of the world, promoting as a result a formalist model of law detached from the social and political connections that form actual legal systems everywhere.
>
> (Upham in Kelsall 2009: 167)

The presence of the ECCC and scrutiny of it provided plenty of evidence of ongoing structural problems in the relationship between political elites and the judiciary, and the way that social and party connections continue to play a formative role in the workings of the Cambodian CJS. This contributed to the view that the rule of law and democracy was struggling to 'move forward', even in the presence of regular 'elections'.

Second, the potential for legal and judicial reform to improve the rule of law where political influence is present has been seriously questioned. In reference to Cambodia, Golub noted: 'Although technical progress can take place even in the face of undue influences, where such influences are widespread they tend to trump the value of the technical change' (quoted in Ear 2007: 274).

Conclusion

Any assessment of Cambodia's democratic progress should first consider from where it has come. Watchers of Cambodian politics recognize that people suffered enormously during the Khmer Rouge period, and that attempts to reconfigure democratic institutions upon an essentially communist system were always going to be difficult. Therefore, recognition of what is a *realistic* expectation for Cambodian democracy two decades after UNTAC is now being debated more openly (Öjendal and Sedara 2011). Perhaps this has been prompted through recognition that building Western institutions of rule of law and governance upon a traditional system of patron-client relations was always going to make 'transition' to democracy a flawed temporal expectation. Others remain bitterly disappointed that the investment into electoral mechanisms and the political opposition has not achieved a better 'quality' democracy (Brinkley 2011).

Regardless, this chapter has argued that the slide from rule of law to rule *by* law is occurring in Cambodia (following Un 2011), which represents one of the most concerning negative developments for future democratic consolidation, or improvements in democratic 'quality'. The judicial system continues to be influenced by the ruling political elite, which uses its powers to support a range of politically-motivated decisions. The increasing fusion of party/state power is a further development of ongoing concern, as weaker political parties struggle to work within an uneven framework, and where they may be open to legal action for speaking out against the government. The proposed NGO Law, if implemented, could well provide the government with new legal avenues to monitor or suppress groups that express oppositional sentiments. However, the diversity of civil society and ongoing presence of a political opposition that is still motivated to hold the government to account, despite such obstacles, is positive.

In sum, the struggle to consolidate democracy in Cambodia is mirrored in some other East Asian polities covered in this collection. The transition to democracy in East Asia has been 'particularly arduous' and even where it may look to be completed, significant barriers to hinder further consolidation await (Case 2011b: 370). As one Cambodian academic expressed it, in relation to the CPP holding over 90 per cent power at the grassroots level: 'They have the big sail but also the big boat' (Interview 1: with author). The CPP will face increased responsibility for its actions, such as land-grabbing, if recent protests by evicted people are anything to go by. The degree to which Cambodian citizens are willing and able to hold the government to account, and demand greater transparency in policy and decision-making, will be a key factor for democratic quality going forward.

Cambodia held national elections in late July 2013, with the opposition Cambodian National Rescue Party (CNRP) led by Sam Rainsy, faring far better than many observers expected. At the time of writing, some opposition MPs were disputing the election result, with Hun Sen vowing to continue his leadership of government, despite allegations of vote rigging.

Notes

1 Um (2008: 107–109) also argues this was the case in the April 2007 commune elections.
2 For the use of trials *in absentia*, in general, and in relation to Cambodia, see Starygin and Selth (2005). For the 1979 trial, see Skilbeck (2008: 442).
3 For a more in-depth discussion of pre-commencement issues, see Linton (2006); Luftglass (2004); Lieberman (2005); Bowman (2006).
4 For more in-depth discussion of the workings of the ECCC and the Special Law pertaining to it, see the ECCC website available online at www.eccc.gov.kh/en/organs, and Williams (2004).
5 These were: Kaing Guek Eav charged as the head of the S21 detention facility with crimes against humanity for the killing of up to 13,000 prisoners; Nuon Chea, charged with crimes against humanity and grave breaches as the Deputy Secretary of the Communist Party of Democratic Kampuchea; Ieng Sary, charged with crimes against humanity and grave breaches in his capacity as Minister of Foreign Affairs; Ieng Thirith, charged with crimes against humanity in her capacity as Minister of Social Action; and Khieu Samphan, charged with crimes against humanity and grave breaches of the Geneva Conventions in his role as Head of State of Democratic Kampuchea from 1976 (from Skilbeck 2008: 442). The proceeding against Ieng Sary was dropped after his death on 14 March 2013.
6 He was sentenced to 35 years imprisonment, which was subsequently increased to life imprisonment, following the appeal.
7 Case 002 is continuing, although now only against two defendants.
8 For an update on Cases 003 and 004 see the ECCC website: www.eccc.gov.kh/en/crime-sites-cases-003-and-004.
9 For international commentary on the decision, see BBC (15 June, 2011) and Mydans (2011).
10 For further discussion about the development of a code of ethics in the ECCC, see Kelsall (2009).
11 For further discussions about the participation of civil parties, administrative issues, ECCC outreach work, and the connection between victim participation and national reconciliation see Bertelman (2010), Werner and Rudy (2009), Yesberg (2009) and Sokol (2011).

References

Bari, M Ehteshamul (2011) 'Dispensation of justice by the Extraordinary Chambers in the Courts of Cambodia: a critical appraisal', *Journal of East Asia & International Law*, 4(1), 193–216.
BBC (2011) 'Khmer Rouge Tribunal: UN rebuffs Cambodia criticism', 15 June.
BBC (2012) 'Judge quits Cambodian UN-backed Khmer Rouge Trial', 19 March.
BBC News Asia (2012) 'Cambodian Khmer Rouge Trial judges argue in public', 9 January.
Bertelman, Hanna (2010) 'International standards and national ownership? Judicial independence in hybrid courts: the Extraordinary Chambers in the Courts of Cambodia', *Nordic Journal of International Law*, 79, 341–382.
Blair, James P. (2009) 'From the numbers who died to those who survived: victim participation in the Extraordinary Chambers in the Courts of Cambodia', *31 University of Hawai'i Law Review*, 507, 551–552.
Bowman, Herbert D. (2006) 'Not worth the wait: Hun Sen, the UN, and the Khmer Rouge tribunal', *UCLA Pacific Basin Law Journal*, 24(1), 51–80.

Brinkley, Joel (2011) *Cambodia's Curse. The Modern History of a Troubled Land*, Philadelphia: Public Affairs.

Broadhurst, Rod and Thierry Bouhours (2008) 'Policing in Cambodia: legitimacy in the making?' *Policing & Society*, 19(2), 174–190.

Case, William (2011a) *Executive Accountability in Southeast Asia: The Role of Legislatures in New Democracies and under Electoral Authoritarianism*, Hawaii: East West Centre, Policy Studies 57.

Case, William (2011b) 'What ails democracy in East Asia', *Australian Journal of International Affairs*, 65(3), 360–370.

Chandler, David (1983) 'Going through the motions: ritual aspects of the reign of King Duang of Cambodia (1848–1860)', in L. Gesick (ed.) *Centers, Symbols, and Hierarchies: Essays on The Classical States of Southeast Asia. Monograph Series No. 26*, New Haven, Connecticut: Yale University Southeast Asia Studies.

Chandler, David (2003) *A History of Cambodia*, 3rd ed., Chiang Mai: Silkworm Books/ Westview Press.

Chandler, David (2010) 'Cambodia in 2009: *plus c'est la même chose*', *Asian Survey*, 50(1), 228–234.

Chinnery, Suzanne (2009) 'Access to justice? Forced evictions in Cambodia', *Asian Law*, 11, 167–189.

de Zeeuw, Jeroen (2010) ' "Sons of war": parties and party systems in post-war El Salvador and Cambodia', *Democratization*, 17(6), 1176–1201.

Diamond, Larry (2002) 'Thinking about Hybrid Regimes', *Journal of Democracy*, 13(2), 21–35.

Diamond, L. (2008) *The Spirit of Democracy: The Struggle to Build Free Societies Throughout the World*, New York: Times Books.

Dubler, Robert (2010) '*Kaing Guek Eav alias Duch*, Judgment, ECCC, Case No 001/18– 07/2007/ECCC/TC (26 July 2010)', *Australian International Law Journal*, 17, 247–252.

Ear, Sophal (2007) Does aid dependence worsen governance?' *International Public Management Journal*, 10(3), 259–286.

Ear, Sophal (2013) *Aid Dependence in Cambodia*, New York, Chichester: Columbia University Press.

ECCC (2011) 'Statement by the International Co-Investigating Judge', 10 October; www. eccc.gov.kh/en/articles/statement-international-co-investigating-judge accessed 24 July 2013.

ECCC (2012) 'Deployment of New International Co-Investigating Judge', 30 July; www. eccc.gov.kh/en/articles/deployment-new-international-co-investigating-judge accessed 18 February 2013.

Form, Wolfgang (2009) 'Justice 30 years later? The Cambodian Special Tribunal for the Punishment of Crimes Against Humanity by the Khmer Rouge', *Nationalities Papers*, 37(6), 889–923.

Gainsborough, Martin (2012) 'Elites vs Reform in Laos, Cambodia, and Vietnam', *Journal of Democracy*, 23(2), 35–46.

Global Witness (2007) 'Cambodia's Family Trees'; www.globalwitness.org/library/ cambodias-family-trees accessed 1 March 2013.

Global Witness (2012) 'Cambodian Court Denies Justice to Family of Murdered Activist Chut Wutty', Press Release; www.globalwitness.org/sites/default/files/library/GW%20 Press%20Release%20-%2022.10.12.pdf accessed 24 July 2013.

Heder, Steve (2011) 'Cambodia in 2010: Hun Sen's Further Consolidation', *Asian Survey*, 51(1), 208–214.

Hughes, Caroline (2006) 'The politics of gifts: tradition and regimentation in contemporary Cambodia', *Journal of Southeast Asian Studies*, 37(3), 469–489.

Hughes, Caroline (2008) 'Cambodia in 2007: development and dispossession', *Asian Survey*, 48(1), 69–74.

Hughes, Caroline (2009) *Dependent Communities. Aid and Politics in Cambodia and East Timor*, Ithaca: Cornell University Press.

Hughes, Caroline (2010) 'Cambodia in 2009: the party's not over yet', *Southeast Asian Affairs*, 2010, 85–99.

Human Rights Watch (2011) *Cambodia: Revise or Abandon Draft NGO Law*, Human Rights Watch, 23 December.

Interview 1 (2011) Interview with Dr Kim Sedara, (Phnom Penh), September.

Jain, Neha (2010) 'Introductory Note to Extraordinary Chambers in the Courts of Cambodia: Co-Prosecutors' Notice of Appeal Against the Judgment of the Trial Chamber in the Case of Kaing Guek Eav *Alias* Duch', *International Legal Materials*, 49, 1683–1688.

Kelsall, Michelle Staggs (2009) 'Symbolic, Shambolic or Simply *Sui Generis*? Reflections from the Field on Cambodia's Extraordinary Chambers', *Law in Context*, 27(1), 154–178.

Levitsky, Steven, and Lucan A. Way (2010) *Competitive Authoritarianism: Hybrid Regimes After the Cold War*, Cambridge: Cambridge University Press.

LICADHO (2009a) '*Land Grabbing & Poverty in Cambodia: The Myth of Development*', (May); www.licadho-cambodia.org accessed 24 July 2013.

LICADHO (2009b) '*Is An NGO Law in Cambodia Justified?*' (June); www.licadho-cambodia.org accessed 24 July 2013.

LICADHO (2011) '*Draft Law on Association & NGOs: An Updated Analysis of the Second Draft*' (March); www.licadho-cambodia.org accessed 24 July 2013.

LICADHO (2012) 'Conclusion of Two Cases Related to Chut Wutty Slaying Leave More Questions than Answers', Press Statement; www.licadho-cambodia.org accessed 24 July 2013.

Lieberman, Michael (2005) 'Salvaging the remains: the Khmer Rouge tribunal on trial', *186 Military Law Review*, 164, 165.

Linton, Suzannah (2006) 'Safeguarding the independence and impartiality of the Cambodian Extraordinary Chambers', *Journal of International Criminal Justice*, 4(2), 327–341.

Linz, Juan, and Alfred Stepan (1996) *Problems of Democratic Transition and Consolidation: Southern Europe, South America, and Post-Communist Europe*, Baltimore: Johns Hopkins University Press.

Luftglass, Scott (2004) 'Crossroads in Cambodia: the United Nation's responsibility to withdraw involvement from the establishment of a Cambodian tribunal to prosecute the Khmer Rouge', *Virginia Law Review*, 90(3), 893–964.

Magliveras, Konstantinos D. (2002) 'Difficulties and status of efforts to create an international criminal court in Cambodia', *Asia-Pacific Journal on Human Rights and the Law*, 2(105), 110–135.

McAuliffe, Padraig (2010) 'The limits of co-operation and judicial independence: resolving the question of "how low do you go?" in the Khmer Rouge Trials' bicephalous prosecution', *The University of Tasmania Law Review*, 29(2), 112–144.

McCargo, Duncan (2005) 'Cambodia: getting wway with authoritarianism?' *Journal of Democracy*, 16, 98–112.

McDonald, Mark (2012) 'The torturous path to justice in Cambodia', *New York Times Blogs*, 27 March.

Mohan, Mahdev (2008) 'Reconstituting the "Un-Person": The Khmer Krom & the Khmer Rouge Tribunal', *Singapore Year Book of International Law*, 12, 43–55.

Mohan, Mahdev (2009) 'The paradox of victim-centrism: victim participation at the Khmer Rouge tribunal', *International Criminal Law Review*, 9, 733–775.

Mu Sochua (2012) 'Senseless Kratie killing reflects a bitter truth', *Phnom Penh Post*, 23 May.

Mydans, Seth (2011) 'Conflicts imperil further Khmer Rouge trials', *New York Times*, 17 June.

New York Times (2012) 'Cambodia: UN assails rejection of Khmer Rouge Tribunal judge', 21 January.

Öjendal, Joakim and Kim Sedara (2011) *Real Democratization in Cambodia? An Empirical Review of the Potential of a Decentralisation Reform*, Swedish International Centre for Local Democracy, Working Paper No. 9.

Paris, Roland (2009) 'Understanding the coordination problem in post-war state building', in R. Paris and T.D. Sisk (eds) *The Dilemmas of State Building. Confronting the Contradictions of Post-war Peace Operations*, London: Routledge.

Reid, Anthony and L. Castles (eds) (1975) *Pre-colonial State Systems in Southeast Asia: the Malay Peninsula, Sumatra, Bali-Lombok, South Celebes*, Kuala Lumpur: Council of the Malaysian Branch of the Royal Asiatic Society.

Reilly, Benjamin (2007) 'Political engineering in the Asia-Pacific', *Journal of Democracy*, 18(1), 58–72.

Richmond, Oliver and Jason Franks (2007) 'Liberal hubris? Virtual peace in Cambodia', *Security Dialogue*, 38(1), 27–48.

Rodan, Gary and C. Hughes (2012) 'Ideological coalitions and the international promotion of social accountability: the Philippines and Cambodia compared', *International Studies Quarterly*, 56, 367–380.

Ryngaert, Cedric (2008) 'The doctrine of abuse of process: a comment on the Cambodia Tribunal's decisions in the Case against Duch (2007)', *Leiden Journal of International Law*, 21, 719–737.

Skilbeck, Rupert (2008) 'Defending the Khmer Rouge', *International Criminal Law Review*, 8, 423–445.

Sokol, David S. (2011) 'Reduced victim participation: a misstep by the Extraordinary Chambers in the Courts of Cambodia', *Washington University Global Studies Law Review*, 10, 167–186.

Starygin, Stan and Johanna Selth (2005) 'Cambodia and the right to be present: trials *in absentia* in the *Draft Criminal Procedure Code*', *Singapore Journal of Legal Studies*, 170, 170–188.

Thayer, Carlyle A. (2009) 'Cambodia: the Cambodian People's Party consolidates power,' *Southeast Asian Affairs*, 85–101.

The Economist (2012) 'Blood trail. The forest witnesses an unsettling death', 5 May.

Um, Khatharya (2008) 'Cambodia: a decade after the coup', *Southeast Asian Affairs*, 107–120.

Um, Khatharya (2011) 'Cambodia: hopes, trials, and tribulations', *Southeast Asian Affairs*, 53–70.

Un, Kheang (2006) 'State, society and democratic consolidation: the case of Cambodia', *Pacific Affairs*, 79(2), 225–245.

Un, Kheang (2009) 'The Judicial System and Democratization in Post-Conflict Cambodia', in Joakim Öjendal and Mona Lilja (eds) *Beyond Democracy in Cambodia: Political Reconstruction in a Post-Conflict Society*, NIAS Press, pp. 70–100.

Un, Kheang (2011) 'Cambodia: moving away from democracy', *International Political Science Review*, 32(5), 546–562.

Un, Kheang (2012) 'Cambodia in 2011: a thin veneer of change', *Asian Survey*, 52(1), 202–209.

Un, Kheang and Judy Ledgerwood (2010) 'Is the trial of "Duch" a catalyst for change in Cambodia's courts?' *Analysis from the East-West Center*, No. 95.

Werner, Alain and Daniella Rudy (2009) 'Civil party representation at the ECCC: sounding the retreat in international criminal law?' *Northwestern University Journal of International Human Rights*, 8, 301–349.

Williams, Sarah (2004) 'The Cambodian Extraordinary Chambers – a dangerous precedent for international justice?' *International and Comparative Law Quarterly*, 53(1), 227–245.

Wilson, Paul (2011) 'Observations of the Cambodian Trial of "Duch"', *Current Issues in Criminal Justice*, 22(3), 473–482.

Yesberg, Kate (2009) 'Accessing justice through victim participation at the Khmer Rouge Tribunal', *Victoria University of Wellington Law Review*, 40(2), 555–579.

Part III

Democratization under hegemonic party regimes

8 Democracy and change in Malaysia

When do authoritarian controls backfire?[1]

William Case

For more than three-and-a-half decades Malaysia operated one of the most stable political regimes in East Asia. Skillfully purveying an adjustable mix of authoritarian controls and democratic procedures, its government perpetuated a sturdy hybridity that some analysts have labelled as electoral authoritarianism (Schedler 2006). Under this regime type, the government reliably refreshed its extraordinary two-thirds parliamentary majority, necessary for unilaterally amending the constitution, through eight consecutive general elections.

But in Malaysia's contest held in 2008, the incumbent government was dealt such a startling setback that while it clung to office, it lost its extraordinary majority in parliament and control over four of the country's 13 states while failing to regain a fifth. There had been no economic crisis or elite-level ructions beforehand. Accordingly, the regime's institutions and the ruling party's apparatus had remained unchanged in their form and general functioning. And they had been defended by the government with its customary rhetoric and campaign appeals, stressing its respect for participation and choice, but underscoring the need also amid late-industrialization and societal pluralism for curbs on competitiveness. But while these institutions and the rhetoric that legitimated them had long reproduced electoral victories, their attractiveness appeared now to be fading. Though they had earlier helped the government in justifying its continuity in power, they were reinterpreted now by many citizens as masking party corruption and ethnic exclusion. Further, this erosion was in many ways deepened by the most recent election held in May 2013, with the government this time winning less than half of the popular vote.

Thus, in the context of what are best understood as 'liberalizing electoral outcomes' (Howard and Roessler 2006), there are reasons for thinking that Malaysia's regime has shifted in character from an electoral to 'competitive' authoritarian regime, one in which despite the persistence of many controls, government turnover is more imaginable. Indeed, as the 2013 election approached, speculation mounted that the opposition could win outright, a trajectory that might finally have amounted, so long as the new government that formed stayed true to its reformist pledges, to a process of 'democratization-by-election' (Lindberg 2009). In these circumstances, the government seemed unsure over when to dissolve parliament, its hesitation contrasting sharply with the confidence with which it had instantly called snap elections in the past.

Malaysia's record thus permits us to address a number of questions about democracy's meaning in an authoritarian context and the dynamics of democratic change. What are the key dimensions of electoral authoritarianism? How has this regime type been reinforced in Malaysia by a single dominant party? What historical and structural grounding has this regime and dominant party possessed? How specifically have electoral procedures and parliamentary activities enhanced this regime type's resilience? Why has the tide seemed recently to change, with the same sets of mechanisms that had long placated social constituencies now so alienating many citizens that they join in mass protests against the government and cast their votes for the opposition? And finally, how effectively has the government responded with new strategies by which to ward off democratic change?

It bears underscoring that these pressures have been accumulating in non-crisis conditions. Malaysia has confronted no economic shock, violent sectarian upheavals, serious secessionist pressures, or intense international conflict. Further, ruling elites have displayed no sudden surge in fractiousness. The country's record thus offers a rare vantage point from which to examine the intrinsic tensions which, in cumulating over time, can poise even the hardiest of electoral authoritarian regimes for fuller democratization – galvanized, perhaps, by the very elections that had once given this regime its resilience.

Electoral authoritarianism in Malaysia

Malaysia's particular variant of political hybridity has variously been badged as a 'quasi-democracy', a 'semi-democracy', and as 'neither authoritarian nor democratic' (Crouch 1993). But this investment in typological hair-splitting, while evincing the intellectual curiosity that Malaysia's regime type aroused, has finally been redeemed. As Andreas Schedler (2006: 3) declares, hybrid regimes, in falling short of democracy's requirements, must be framed as a subtype of authoritarian rule. He writes that 'electoral contests are subject to state manipulation so severe, widespread, and systematic that they do not qualify as democratic'. It is in this context, then, with the competitiveness of elections meaningful, but not so great that government turnover usually occurs, that Schedler coined the notion of electoral authoritarianism. Levitsky and Way (2010) later introduced 'competitive authoritarianism', depicting instances in which while the playing field remained 'uneven', an opposition victory grew more imaginable. A main aim of this chapter, then, is to investigate the pressures for change from one subtype to the other, setting the stage for democratization-by-election.

But in order to first to gauge electoral authoritarianism as it has been practiced in Malaysia, it is useful to recall Robert Dahl's (1972) twin dimensions of polyarchy – liberal participation and electoral contestation. A regime is at least minimally democratic when both of these dimensions are present. It slips into some form of authoritarian rule when either of them are seriously impaired. Let us review the ways in which in Malaysia both of these dimensions, though at some level functional, are grievously distorted.

On a liberal axis of free communication and organization, Malaysia's Home Ministry has usually permitted opposition parties, professional associations, labour unions, and non-governmental organizations (NGOs) to form. In addition, opposition parties have been able to win parliamentary seats, while advocacy groups hold forums through which to vent mass-level grievances, sometimes prompting the government to increase responsiveness. Accordingly, Malaysia has acquired over time a reasonably vibrant civil society, especially in its urban areas.

However, the government has also reacted by systematically containing civil society, preventing advocacy groups from gaining such transformative weight that they might more profoundly shape public policy. The government begins by registering and monitoring NGOs through provisions of the Societies Act. Moreover, after identifying these groups, the government has sometimes weakened them by instigating the formation of competing fronts. For example, Malaysia's independent Bar Association, the Malaysian Trades Union Congress, and a plethora of revivalist Muslim *dakwah* (missionary) movements came respectively to face the state-sponsored Islamic Lawyers Association, the Malaysian Labour Organization, and the Malaysian Islamic Advancement Office (JAKIM), thereby co-opting leaders, dispersing resources, and dividing memberships.

Further, when strategies of registration and obfuscation have failed, the government has turned more resolutely to coercion. To discourage journalists who operate outside the state-aligned media, it long imposed the Printing and Printing Presses Act and the Official Secrets Act, resulting in the suspension of newspaper licences and arrests. And to deter opposition leaders, activists, and bloggers, it has relied on stifling defamation suits and even a principle of 'preventive detention', enshrined until recently in the dreaded Internal Security Act (ISA). Thus, while civil society in Malaysia has enjoyed some freedom of communications and autonomy in organization, its leaders have largely been barred from significantly shaping policy outputs.

In terms of electoral contestation, Malaysia's government has regularly held polls at the federal and state levels. In addition, balloting, vote counting, and reporting have, at least until the contest in 2013, been regarded as reasonably fair, ensuring that election day presents a snapshot of propriety. In these conditions, opposition parties have been able to contest vigorously, thereby gaining seats in parliament and state-level assemblies. However, until recently, they have also been prevented from gaining enough seats that they could hope plausibly to form a new federal government. Competitiveness has been hindered by severe district malapportionment and gerrymandering, a highly partisan deployment of state workers and resources, hurried campaign periods, a skewed usage of the media, and on-the-spot 'development' grants that amount nearly to vote buying. Balloting has also been sullied by error-ridden electoral rolls, with the names of some registered voters transferred without notice across polling stations, while falsely registered 'phantom' voters descend without warning on targeted constituencies, abuses that go unchecked by a pliable Election Commission. In these conditions, Harold Crouch (1996: 75) once observed that 'the Malaysian electoral system ... was so heavily loaded in favour of the government that it was hard to imagine that the ruling coalition, as long as it remained united, could be defeated in an election'.

Historical and structural grounding

Samuel Huntington denied the durability that hybrid regimes might attain, baldly asserting that 'the halfway house does not stand' (1991: 174–175). In his view, such regimes were destined to tip forward into greater democracy or lurch back into harder authoritarianism. But electoral authoritarianism in Malaysia, even more than through intrinsic resilience, has found grounding in countervailing sets of historical legacies and structural features. Accordingly, the quavering democracy that Malaysia inherited from the British during the 1950s contracted during the next decade into electoral authoritarianism. The section below briefly explores the historical and structural bedrock upon which the regime came to rest.

Through British colonial rule, Malaysia acquired a strong bureaucratic apparatus, an independent judiciary, and professional security forces, contributing mightily to state building. It also gained a Westminster parliamentary system and multiple political parties, thereby fostering rule of law and accountability. Such British 'tutelary' experience has been interpreted as highly favourable for the formation and persistence of political democracy (Weiner 1987). However, through a strong colonial state, Malaysia was also bequeathed a countervailing set of elite-level entitlements and prerogatives, developmental imbalances, social rivalries, and elite-level entitlements and prerogatives. A British 'vice-regal' tradition thus took hold, understood as damaging in its imperiousness to democracy's prospects (Diamond 1989). Hence, little more than a decade after independence, politics in Malaysia shifted from what once was hailed as a finely-tuned 'consociationalist' variant of democratic politics to a 'control model' that amounted to a hybrid form of authoritarian rule (Lijphart 1977; Lustick 1979). But though Malaysia's democratic institutions, constructed hastily by the British atop infirm legacies and structures, were in this way weakened, they were never wholly extinguished, therein settling into the hybridity of electoral authoritarianism.

In brief, the British forged a 'classic' divided society in which indigenous and hence nominally 'sovereign' Malay sultans and civil servants oversaw Malay smallholders and fishermen. At the same time, they relied upon migrant Chinese and Indians to work in extractive industries, though regarded these labourers as sojourners who remained politically excluded. Accordingly, a tense structural pattern emerged wherein politically favoured, but collectively poor Malays were pitted against more economically assertive, but disenfranchised non-Malays.

Finally, when negotiating independence and a gradual transfer of power, the British engaged a small group of communal leaders through a series of face-to-face meetings, thereby exalting elite standings. They did little, then, to conjoin the broader ethnic segments of plural society in ways that might instill any shared sense of citizenship and democratic participation (Means 1976: 122–124).

Thus, to the extent that a local business community and non-bureaucratic middle class began to take shape, it remained almost exclusively Chinese, deepening grievances among the Malays who began during this period to migrate to the cities in large numbers. Meanwhile, in presiding over these arrangements, elites collaborated through a trio of ethnically delineated political parties – the United Malays National Organization (UMNO), the Malay(si)an Chinese Association (MCA), and the Malay(si)an Indian Congress (MIC) – then secured iterated electoral victories through a coalition that they framed as the Alliance.

But in 1969, opposition parties finally gave vent to mounting societal grievances. Many Malays, decrying UMNO's failure to better their economic prospects, alongside the Chinese, lamenting the MCA's inability to raise their political standings, voted for more communalist parties. The Malays thus veered toward the Pan-Malaysian Islamic Party (PAS), while the Chinese embraced the Democratic Action Party (DAP) and Gerakan (People's Movement of Malaysia). The Alliance was gravely weakened at the federal level, while the opposition parties gained power in two state assemblies. The Malays were taken aback by UMNO's eroded paramountcy. In turn, the Chinese celebrated, holding 'victory' processions throughout Kuala Lumpur. Gangs of Malays and Chinese then clashed, culminating in a watershed event of ethnic rioting known locally as the May 13th incident (von Vorys 1973). The UMNO-led government swiftly declared emergency rule.

In the aftermath of this upheaval, new elites gained ascendancy in UMNO and set to reconfiguring Malaysia's political economy. In consequence, little more than a decade after the British had withdrawn, the democratic institutions that they had bestowed were truncated in ways that corresponded more closely with mixed historical legacies and structural tensions. Through political incentives and sanctions, UMNO drew most of the opposition parties into its coalition, rechristened now as Barisan Nasional (National Front) (BN), then greatly increased its dominance (Mauzy 1983). Central to this strategy, UMNO seized the economic ministries from the MCA then penetrated the state bureaucracy more broadly, nearly fusing the party and administrative apparatuses. Next, to fulfill its new developmental agendas, UMNO created an array of state agencies through which to pursue concerted policies of industrial deepening. Further, in easing the resentments of Malay constituencies over their puny stakes in business, UMNO unveiled a vast affirmative action programme labelled the New Economic Policy (NEP). Thus, the new agencies and enterprises promoted by the state articulated with ethnic quotas swelled with Malay recruits. Further, their material appetites now whetted, new corporate and middle class Malays drew deeply from a stream of state licences and contracts, discounted bank loans and equities, and an opaque privatization of state assets (Gomez and Jomo 1999). This new political economy, wherein UMNO absorbed most opposition, laid claim to the bureaucratic apparatus, then gained the patronage and populist resources with which to perpetuate its single-party dominance, was colourfully summed up by the new prime minister, Tun Razak: 'This government is based on UMNO and I surrender its responsibilities to UMNO in order that UMNO shall determine its form' (Funston 1980: 225).

Single-party dominance

As a regime type, electoral authoritarianism may be preceded by a range of power configurations, including military-backed governments, sultanistic forma-tions, and shifting clientelist arrangements. But the frailties of these entities ensure that their electoral authoritarian front, whatever strength it may intrinsic-ally possess, remains vulnerable at base, ever at risk of democratic opening or descent into hard authoritarianism. In Malaysia, however, electoral authoritarian rule has found better grounding, firstly in the historical and structural factors elaborated above. But it has also gained an institutional armature in UMNO's single-party dominance. One of the oldest parties in Southeast Asia, UMNO has, especially since 1969, prised open conduits to patronage and populist resources that are delivered respectively to party elites and broad Malay constituencies, distributions that have been sanctioned by the NEP.

In one of the best studies of single-party dominance and authoritarian dur-ability, Jason Brownlee (2007) develops an historical-institutional theory. This enables him to document UMNO's origins and trajectory, the nationalist appeals that have reproduced ethnic support at the mass-level, and the patronage that has perpetuated elite-level loyalties. We will return later to evaluate his contention that after constituencies have been incorporated, elections themselves make little additional difference. It may be too that with respect to elite cohesion, Brownlee has exaggerated the regard for shared party ideals, while understating the import-ance of patronage benefits. But most relevant at this point is Brownlee's remind-ing us that electoral authoritarian regimes like Malaysia's gain much resilience from what he depicts as UMNO's 'ruling party' status.

Agency, elections and legislatures

As Samuel Huntington (1968) recorded in *Political Order in Changing Soci-eties*, most newly decolonized and democratized countries during the 1960s–1970s, in finding that societal demands exceeded their capacity for mediation, lapsed back into authoritarian rule. In Southeast Asia, then, Burma, Thailand, Indonesia, Singapore and the Philippines succumbed to a 'second reverse wave', resulting in military governments, a developmental state, and a personal dictator-ship. Malaysia, however, avoided any such hard landing. Its regime equilibrated instead into electoral authoritarianism. Indeed, in striving purposively for polit-ical hybridity, Tun Razak intoned that 'democratic government is the … most acceptable form of government. So long as the form is preserved, the substance can be changed to suit conditions of a particular country' (quoted in Zakaria 1989: 349).

But why did Razak take pains to retain democracy's form, it not all its substance, therein permitting a limited but significant degree of electoral competitiveness and legislative functioning to persist? As we have seen, the parameters set by countervailing historical and structural factors are important. So too are the properties of a dominant, but accommodative single-party system. But legacies, structural forces, and institutional capacities are hardly determinative. Agency also matters, prompting Razak to observe what leaders of other countries in Southeast Asia who had turned to hard authoritarianism would only later rediscover, specifically, that elections and legislatures, by fabricating an imagery of popular consent and procedural rightness, can more readily gain compliance among citizens.

Accordingly, through partial transitions, Singapore, Indonesia, Thailand, and Cambodia would gradually institute hybrid regimes, keeping a lid on civil liberties but permitting at least limited electoral and legislative activity. Further, at the poles of the spectrum of hybridity taking shape, the Philippines embarked on yet fuller democratization, while Burma, though benighted by the world's most enduring military government, experimented briefly, if disastrously with elections in 1990, then again in 2010. In this context, Carl Trocki (1998: 8) concluded that 'democratic forms, including elected legislative bodies and executives, regular elections, political parties, written constitutions, and formal guarantees of political and individual human liberties have become part of the legitimizing apparatus of most Southeast Asian countries'.

Thus, within Southeast Asia, Malaysia stands out as an early exemplar of electoral authoritarianism, assuming a posture that neighbouring countries would come in some ways to emulate. But notwithstanding this record, as new scholarly debates took place over authoritarian durability, scepticism crept in about elections and legislatures as separable causal forces. Brownlee (2007: 30–32), while highlighting the role of dominant single-parties in mobilizing mass-level support and elite-level loyalties, dismisses elections as merely a 'symptom', passively reflecting the extent to which they have prevented elite-level defections beforehand. Kenneth Greene (2007), in an influential analysis of contemporary politics in Mexico, suggests similarly that contests are won or lost long before election day. In his 'resource' theory of hyper-incumbency advantage, elections reveal only the degree to which dominant parties have kept control over public sector resources and state patronage, forcing the opposition parties that it confronts to the ideological fringes.

But as this chapter will demonstrate, even limited electoral competitiveness poses independent effects, helping mainly to sustain, but in some instances to subvert, incumbent governments. Elections provide opportunities for the government to re-energize constituencies, with ministers finally departing the capital city to stump round the hinterland, casting a glow over their party's local hopefuls, while dispensing the grant money that can bedazzle rural audiences.

In addition, the polling and vote-counting stations that are set up, when intricately arrayed, enable the government better to identify supportive locales and opposition strongholds. But more broadly, elections can provide a government with legitimating cover, encouraging among citizens a perception of procedural rightness that quickens their compliance.

Thus, while elections held under conditions of electoral authoritarianism might reliably return an incumbent government to power, they display enough uncertainty that its leaders can plausibly assert that citizens have been given a choice. As Mahathir Mohamad, Malaysia's prime minister during the 1980s–1990s, used to taunt his opponents, 'if you don't like me, defeat me in my district'. But it is perhaps the comments made by the current de facto law minister in the Prime Minister's Department, Nazri Aziz, that best convey the usefulness that an incumbent government discovers in waging elections under electoral authoritarianism. In responding to a local social movement, Bersih 2.0, that had mounted a large street protest in July 2011 demanding reforms in electoral procedures, Nazri intoned,

> Who are the NGOs supporting them? I don't know them. They just represent, what 50, 100, 200 people? They said 50,000 came [to the Bersih 2.0 rally]. What is that compared to the representatives like me, elected by the *rakyat* (i.e. the people)?
>
> (Hazlan 2012)

Thus, while some analysts may remain sceptical over the extent to which elections add to the durability of electoral authoritarianism, Malaysia's leaders have shown few such doubts.

This scepticism among scholars over elections and authoritarian durability extends also to the legislatures that convene after elections have been held. In an early study, Mishler and Hildreth (1984) argued that 'legislatures have remarkably little influence, positive or negative, on the stability of authoritarian governments or regimes'. In their view, quite 'different attributes' are what make authoritarianism durable, with the 'use of coercion ... principal among them'. Schedler (2009: 9) has equally dismissed the impact of parliamentarians, noting that within their frail chambers, they remain 'easy objects of control'.

However, Gandhi and Przeworski (2006) counter that at the very least, a legislature serves as an institutional 'forum' through which 'dictators' can help to stabilize their regimes by co-opting opposition through policy concessions and rent-sharing. Ellen Lust (2009: 128) provides apt illustrations, arguing that parliamentarians in these conditions are all too glad to accept rents: 'perks ... the glamour and prestige of being in parliament ... cars, drivers, offices ... immunity from prosecution.' More substantively, Boix and Svolik (n.d) show that by imposing at least some accountability on a government, a legislature can firm power-sharing arrangements between the executive and topmost allies in the cabinet, bureaucracy and military. Specifically, in describing an arena wherein informational asymmetries over the volume, value and distributions of public resources are levelled, Boix and Svolik contend that the legislature can help to resolve the 'commitment and monitoring problems' that often erode all trust within authoritarian coalitions. Accordingly, even where unusually autocratic, an executive may 'prefer a subservient legislature to no legislature at all' (Ziegenhain 2008: 15).

There is evidence that in Malaysia, the UMNO-led government permits at least mild accountability to be imposed on the executive by its legislature. The prime minister and his line ministers appear in Parliament periodically in order to introduce budgets and major bills. And as Muhamad Fuzi Omar (2008: 38) reports, opposition legislators respond by making shrewd use of the debates and question time that follow, often generating 'heated exchanges'. Additional strategies through which to confront the government have included the opposition's proposing inventive motions by which to cut the salaries of targeted ministers by an irksome 'ten dollars', a process that under Standing Orders automatically triggers debate; heckling and booing in reaction to vexing statements made by government MPs, or loud 'table thumping' in support of fellow opposition members' sharp ripostes; and walkouts, usually mounted over perceptions of the Speaker's procedural unfairness (Case 2011: 41–48). More substantively, the opposition has sometimes gained information that enables it to expose executive abuses in Parliament. Its findings are then publicized through press conferences which, even if ignored by mainstream outlets, are widely disseminated through new media, including the blogs that are vigorously mounted by Malaysia's opposition MPs.

But on balance, it is much less the opposition than the government that benefits from parliamentary activity. Even when appearing to make concessions over legislative functioning, the government manipulates processes and outputs in ways that ensure its maintaining the upper hand. Accordingly, by operating a forum in which societal demands can be raised and accountability imposed, only to be contained and diluted, the government reduces the coercion necessary for gaining compliance among citizens. As one example, in seeming to bow to the popular pressures that had been articulated by Bersih 2.0, the government set up a parliamentary select committee during late 2011 in order to consider changes to electoral procedures. But though the committee was comprised of members from both the government and opposition, it finally adopted only a few of the recommendations that Bersih had made, prompting the movement's leaders to threaten renewed street protests. However, by stressing the rightfulness of parliament, Nazri Aziz (Hazlan 2012), the law minister, was able to reply with indignation:

They do not have any business to go to the streets. We have a system of elected representatives that represent the rakyat. A system to go through if you want to improve things. If they want to influence change, they should use the system.... Who are they? They are nobody.

Pressures for democratic change

Implicit in electoral authoritarianism is a promise that more democratic days lie ahead. Indeed, Malaysia's blueprint for 'full' economic development, Vision 2020, unveiled during Mahathir's tenure, specified the country's democratic aspirations. So too has a more recent agenda for reform, the Government Transformation Program (GTP), devised by the current prime minister, Najib Razak. But over time, such pledges, rather than encouraging patience, might finally heighten popular demands for quicker delivery. Further, these pressures need not be triggered by exogenous crises. Though functioning for long periods, electoral authoritarianism's very procedures may come gradually to alienate rather than to placate many citizens, while also amplifying this alienation through electoral campaigning and voting. In this context, the impact of elections changes sharply, in Schedler's (2006: 49) phrase from 'regime-sustaining' to 'regime-subverting', a process which might amount to democratization-by-election.

The sections below review the prime ministerships of Mahathir's successors, Abdullah Badawi and Najib Razak. They show that Abdullah and Najib, in recognizing that the resonance of electoral authoritarianism had begun to fade, pledged new reforms over accountability and responsiveness, as well as greater ethnic equality. But in raising expectations that were never fulfilled, they hastened processes of alienation, leading to their governments' respective electoral setbacks in 2008 and 2013.

Abdullah Badawi

In 2003, Mahathir passed the baton to his deputy, Abdullah. At this juncture, then, Malaysia continued its recovery from economic crisis, while deftly avoiding any crisis over succession. And Abdullah set swiftly to bolstering his own standing in preparation for the next election, due by 2004. Recognizing that the patronage flows that UMNO mediated through which to perpetuate elite-level cohesion had begun to alienate citizens, including many urban middle-class Malays, he embarked on a comprehensive campaign to tamp down corruption. And in recognizing also that ethnic distributions overseen by UMNO in order to generate support among rural Malays, made manifest in crude quotas, had begun more seriously to aggrieve the non-Malays, he pledged even-handedness, promising 'to be a prime minister to all Malaysians'.

In seeking to curb corrupt practices, Abdullah unveiled a new Code of Ethics, while requiring that Barisan parliamentarians declare their assets. And in also addressing the links between the bureaucracy and rapacious business conglomerates, Abdullah vowed to restore integrity. In his first prime ministerial address to parliament, he declared 'our resolve to have a civil service that is corruption-free should not be weakened by unhealthy practices in the private sector ... that contribute to this disease' (*Malaysiakini* 2003).

As the election approached, the government appeared to begin seriously enforcing Abdullah's new strictures. To recount, the minister for Land

Cooperatives, Kasitah Gaddam, was arrested, allegedly for having been involved in an illegal sale of shares in a state-owned enterprise. Eric Chia, a former managing director of the state-owned steel company, Perwaja Terengganu, was also charged, suspected of having approved illicit payments to a Japanese partner.

Abdullah turned next to Malaysia's police force, widely criticized for its 'corruption, brutality, and poor service' (*Malaysiakini* 2004). Indeed, with a record besmirched by corrupt practices, soaring crime rates, and frequent deaths in custody, the Royal Malaysian Police had probably become the most distrusted element in the state apparatus. An unprecedented review body was thus created, formally denominated as the Special Commission to Enhance the Operations and Management of the Royal Malaysian Police, and ordered to make recommendations within a year.

In this context, when the general election was held in March 2004, the UMNO-led Barisan won its greatest victory ever, capturing a record 63.5 per cent of the popular vote which, when transcribed through a plurality system of single-member districts, snared 90 per cent of the seats in parliament. The government also wrested away control over the state assembly in Terengganu, one of those that had been held by PAS, while making deep inroads in Kelantan, PAS's northern stronghold. The margins were so great that they were first attributed to Abdullah's own likeability, heralded as the 'Pak Lah factor'. But the results can be read more specifically as surging popular support for his efforts to rein in corruption. As Lim Kit Siang, chairman of the opposition DAP, conceded, 'the new PM's anticorruption drive is populist and making it very difficult for us this time around' (Lopez 2004: 13).

Nonetheless, there had been fears even before the election had been waged that while efforts to curb corruption might re-energize support among ordinary citizens, they would inversely deepen resentments within in UMNO. One journalist speculated, then, that 'long accustomed to patronage in the form of contracts and licenses from the government in return for political support, the warlords of UMNO could work against the party in the coming elections' (ibid.).

Thus, in trying shortly after the contest had been won to reassure party elites over patronage, Abdullah slowed his drive against corruption. As an adviser to the prime minister confided, 'we can't take on the whole system – that's too hard. But we are hoping for a demonstration effect' (Vatikiotis and Jayasankaran, 2004: 23). Accordingly, Abdullah did little after the election to shake up his cabinet. Among four ministers deemed widely to be corrupt, two were left in place, while the remaining pair were simply shifted to other portfolios (Jayasankaran 2004: 20). This included Nazri Aziz, shunted from the Ministry of Entrepreneur Development, where he was suspected of having corruptly issued taxi licences, to the Prime Minister's Department. An aide to Abdullah then defended this modest reshuffle as 'the best we could do' (ibid.). In addition, although charges over corruption continued to be made for a time against various public officials, they came now to target low-level functionaries for smaller offences. The Code of Conduct remained laxly administered. The asset declarations required of parliamentarians were never publicly disclosed.

Later in the year, UMNO prepared to hold its internal party election. Abdullah and his deputy, Najib Razak, had secured their positions beforehand through an ad hoc party ruling. Lesser aspirants, however, in vigorously seeking the party posts that are linked to parliamentary nominations and bureaucratic spoils, defied Abdullah's ban on 'campaigning' in order to bid freely for delegate support. In this context, unregulated vote buying and gift giving enabled enfeebled 'has-beens' to edge out some front-runner candidates, yielding 'shock results' that could only be explained by the party's distributions of patronage, widely disparaged as 'money politics'. But as one delegate queried afterward, 'What's the fuss about? Whatever money given helps us recoup some cost. I do not think the leadership should be too worried' (Pereira 2004a: 10). And in view of the determination with which candidates and delegates pursued positions and payoffs, Abdullah seemed even to concur, plaintively asking 'What can I do?' (Pereira, 2004b: 10).

Over the coming years, corruption among party officials appeared to grow still more brazen. In a much publicized case in 2006, an UMNO parliamentarian, Mohd Said Yusof, his company having been discovered by Customs to have smuggled illegally-sawn timber through an obscure port on Malaysia's west coast, was reported to have asked agents to 'close one eye'. And in defending himself afterward before parliament and the media, he made plain the futility of Abdullah's efforts to instill probity in the party, querying 'I don't know whether my company was involved. Maybe yes, maybe no. If yes, so what? Why can't an MP take care of his own interest' (Beh 2006). At the same time, the trials of top officials and tycoons soon fizzled. Eric Chia was acquitted, with Lim Kit Siang, leading the parliamentary opposition at this stage, characterizing the outcome as a 'major setback, as Abdullah's anti-corruption drive has never really taken off' (*Malaysiakini* 2007a). The police review commission came to little, with its surprisingly robust recommendations over the formation of an independent complaints commission largely rejected. And suspicions even rose over the business dealings of Abdullah's own family members, with his son, Kamaluddin, and his son-in-law, Khairy Jamaluddin, benefiting handsomely from state contracts and investments. In these circumstances, Tian Chua, a leader of the opposition People's Justice Party (PKR), opined that 'Abdullah has learned that this is the way to do business in UMNO if you want to stay in power' (Gatsiounis 2007).

But if Abdullah's new orientations laid the complaints of UMNO leaders against him to rest, we see the ways also in which they now tested the patience of ordinary Malay citizens. In polling conducted by the Merdeka Centre a month before the fateful election of March 2008, more than 60 per cent of respondents agreed that while 'UMNO and BN say that they are fighting for Malay rights, they spend more time making money for themselves and giving contracts to friends and family members' (Merdeka Center 2009). But before scrutinizing the election, let us turn now to the question of how Abdullah's standing fared among the non-Malays.

After coming to power, Abdullah, in vowing to be a prime minister to all Malaysians, declared let all citizens of Malaysia, without feeling inferior, without feeling side-lined, irrespective of race or religion, rise to become statesmen in our land. We are equal, we are all Malaysians. No individual in this country is more Malaysian than another.

(New Straits Times 2004)

Yet just as Abdullah had abandoned his efforts to curb corruption, so too did he yield to communalist pressures. At UMNO's general assembly in 2005, UMNO's Youth leader, Hishammuddin Hussein, called for the inclusion of what he termed the 'Malay Agenda' in the 9th Malaysian Plan, a major planning document. At the 2006 assembly, televised nationally, Hishammuddin, serving now also as education minister, concluded his rousing speech by suddenly drawing a *keris*, a traditional long bladed Malay dagger, then waving it over his head. At the assembly in 2007, Hishammuddin repeated this provocative action, delighting the 2,500 delegates in attendance, but surely unnerving non-Malay audiences. Afterward, Abdullah meekly defended this display, stating that 'the *keris* is a weapon, but it is a weapon to protect yourself and your friends' (*Malaysiakini* 2007b).

Throughout the year, other incidents took place that also deepened the suspicions of the non-Malays over what many of them perceived as 'creeping Islamization'. In July, Najib Razak, the deputy prime minister, reiterated a claim once made by Mahathir, avowing that 'Islam is the official religion and we are an Islamic state' (Reuters 2007). A number of sharia court rulings on apostasy followed, resulting in forced family separations and Islamic 'rehabilitation'. And the government of the key state of Selangor ordered the demolition of several Hindu temples, shortly before celebration of the major Hindu holiday, Deepavali, in order to make way for a development project.

Thus, during 2007–2008, it became clearer that Abdullah was unable to stanch the flows of state patronage, essential for maintaining elite cohesion in UMNO. At the same time, the NEP's populist benefits were viewed as unfairly distributed at the mass-level, even by many ordinary Malays, therein threatening UMNO's constituent support. And the non-Malays grew more alienated still amid fears of intensifying Islamism.

In broad terms, then, societal grievances mounted over government corruption and policy unfairness. And efforts by Abdullah to contain them by using the ISA, as well as his government's anticipated manipulations of upcoming elections, only exacerbated discontent. At this juncture, then, the very dimensions of electoral authoritarianism and the dynamics of single-party dominance, while for so long having perpetuated the regime and the government's tenure, began now to invigorate the opposition. In ways that would surprise Brownlee and Greene, then, the election itself began to exert impact, though along lines that were less favourable to regime continuity than to change. Put simply, authoritarian controls had started to backfire, precipitating a trajectory that if not yet amounting to democratization-by-election, resulted at least in a liberalizing electoral outcome.

The clearest evidence for this lay in the emergence of a new social movement labelled Bersih – a Malay word for 'clean', but also an acronym for Coalition for

Clean and Fair Elections. Though this movement incorporating some 60 NGOs declared sundry grievances over corruption and social inequality, it focused most intently on the government's electoral manipulations. In late 2007, Bersih was denied a permit by the police to hold a public rally in Kuala Lumpur. Yet the movement's leaders, including Anwar Ibrahim, a former UMNO deputy prime minister who, after having been purged and serving a jail sentence now led a new opposition vehicle, the PKR, as well as top officials in PAS, pressed ahead. They took care, however, to portray Bersih as conforming to Malaysia's rightful political and socio-cultural order, thereby encouraging perceptions that it was the government's conduct that was improper. Specifically, after demands for elect-oral reforms were announced, Bersih's leaders and an estimated 60,000 fol-lowers converged on the royal palace to petition the country's king, high symbol of constitutional restraint and arbiter of traditional Malay culture.

To be sure, illegal public protests have regularly punctuated Malaysia's polit-ical record, with upsurges taking place during the late 1980s and the late 1990s. But their pace grew quicker during 2007–2008, with James Chin and Wong Chin Huat (2009: 79) observing that 'to have such big protests within a short span was unheard of'. Their character also grew qualitatively different. Earlier protests had sprung from economic shocks, shortfalls in patronage, and new fractious-ness between elites in UMNO, motivating rival leaders in the party to mobilize followers in top-down ways, often through strident communalist appeals. But during 2007–2008, there was neither any economic crisis nor surge in elite frac-tiousness. Rather, popular protest was driven by the ways in which elites were maintaining their privileges and their party's paramountcy, wholly unrestrained by Abdullah's reformism. It is an indication also of these protests' spontaneity and bottom-up autonomy that they began to breech the communal walls that had for so long precluded collective action. Interethnic participation in protests organized by the PKR, PAS and even the DAP rose markedly. Most notably, protests were increasingly joined by 'low income Malays', decrying the patron-age that a 'conspicuously consuming elite' so casually extracted through the NEP (Baradan 2007: 10).

Barisan won Malaysia's 12th general election, held in March 2008, but was dealt a severe setback. Its portion of the popular vote, ranging typically from 55–60 per cent, fell to a bare majority nationally, even less on the peninsula. Thus, notwithstanding the distortive effects of a plurality-based single member district system, Barisan won only 140 of parliament's 222 seats, leaving it shy for the first time since electoral authoritarianism had been instituted of a two-thirds parliamentary majority. Just as strikingly, it lost control for the first time also of four state governments, while failing to retake Kelantan, the stronghold of PAS.

To be sure, in voting against Barisan, many citizens were simply continuing with their protest that had begun in the streets, rather than fully embracing the opposition. But more positively, it appeared that among the estimated 5 per cent of Malay voters who had swung against the government, the 65 per cent of Chinese voters who supported the opposition, and the 52 per cent of Indian voters who, while once staunch government loyalists, now did the same, a greater sense of interethnic cooperation had taken root in order to combat corruption and social inequality. In this context, the PKR, in appealing to reform-minded Malays, but also addressing some of the grievances of the non-Malays, served as a linchpin between the Islamic PAS and the secular, largely Chinese DAP. After the election, they drew closer in a coalition labelled Pakatan Rakyat (People's Alliance), enabling them to form new governments in the states that they controlled. And Anwar, after winning a parliamentary by-election, emerged as opposition leader. It was in this context that some local analysts hailed the beginnings of a competitive 'two-party system' (Baradan 2008).

Najib Razak

In April 2009, Abdullah stepped down, unable to resolve the sharpening dilemma that confronted him. He had rightly diagnosed corruption and social inequity as diminishing UMNO's appeal among many citizens. But in promising reforms, he met stout resistance from the elites in UMNO who benefited from the party's distributions of state patronage and its patterns of ethnic exclusion. Thus, in highlighting UMNO's failings, but failing utterly to mitigate them, Abdullah deepened societal alienation. And indeed, electoral authoritarianism and single-party dominance themselves became issues, with many citizens motivated by the constraints on elections to use what competitiveness remained to vote resolutely against the government in protest. A great irony thus emerges from the blindness of elites in UMNO, for they blamed Abdullah for their electoral setback and then pushed him from power.

Abdullah was succeeded by his deputy, Najib Razak, who soon faced the same conundrum. Seeking to rein in corruption, Najib initiated a variety of new campaigns, including the GTP, one of whose National Key Results Areas targeted patronage flows (Pemandu 2011). Further, in seeking to maintain support among the Malays, but also to assuage the non-Malays, he initiated a campaign entitled '1Malaysia: People First, Performance Now' by which to instill greater harmony among Malaysia's ethnic communities and more efficiency in service delivery (Prime Minister's Department, n.d.). This was coupled with an Economic Transformation Program (ETP) that promised a meritocratic and more business-driven approach to economic development. Through a series of consultative 'labs', a number of priority areas, branded as National Key Economic Areas, were identified. Most notable in this exercise, though, was the imposition of a ban on undercapitalized firms, often owned by Malay entrepreneurs, from bidding on large and technologically complex government projects. Moreover, in addressing wider resentments over the limits on civil liberties, Najib responded to a large demonstration by Bersih in 2011 by pledging to repeal the ISA, as well as many restrictions on public protest.

In these circumstances, Najib's personal popularity surged, especially among the non-Malays. But his campaign against corruption, ethnic exclusion, and authoritarian controls soon triggered resentment among many elites and second-echelon division leaders in UMNO and the indigenous businessmen, often contractors, with whom they collaborated. In reacting to the '1Malaysia' campaign over greater national unity, Najib's deputy prime minister and deputy UMNO president, Muhyiddin Yassin, asked 'How can I say I am a Malaysian first and a Malay second? All Malays will shun me and say it's not proper.... It is not wrong for any leader to struggle for the interest of his own race' (Chapman 2010). A new social movement, Perkasa, (literally 'powerful'), then lent organizational strength to these sentiments. Led by an arch Malay chauvinist, Ibrahim Ali, and recruiting mostly from among rank-and-file UMNO members, Perkasa had been formed in the wake of the 2008 election. Dedicated expressly to defending the Malay 'special rights' that are encoded in Article 153 of the constitution, it organized demonstrations and large meetings through which to pressure Najib over his reforms, even presenting several memoranda to him demanding that Malay-owned companies continue to be favoured in awarding state contracts. Najib relented, announcing that the authoring of the ETP had not yet been completed and that Perkasa would be consulted. Further, there was little mention of the programme when the budget and the 10th Malaysian Plan were announced in 2011. Instead, the planning document stressed an ongoing need to advance the 'Malay Agenda'.

Meanwhile, corruption scandals continued to erupt, the most spectacular of which involved the gross misuse of a government loan that had been extended to the family members of the Minister for Women and Family Development, Sharizat Jalil. Sharizat's husband and son had been appointed as top executives in the National Feedlot Corporation, a state enterprise tasked with increasing livestock production. They were revealed to have used an accompanying loan to purchase luxury condominiums and cars, triggering much public disillusion. Indeed, even some division leaders in UMNO began to lament that the scandal was harming their own electoral prospects.

A backdrop of ethnic exclusion also remained intact, marked by a series of insensitive ministerial statements, aggressive sharia court rulings, Islamist protests, and even church burnings. Further, the limits on civil liberties and electoral competitiveness, though modified, remained in place. Perkasa loudly demanded that the ISA be retained, mainly in order to arrest those who might dare to question Malay special rights. Indeed, it called for the detention of the deputy education minister, Wee Ka Siong, after he had criticized the awarding of government scholarships to favoured Malay students. To be sure, after the Bersih demonstration in 2011, which was violently suppressed by police, Najib was prompted by the outcry that followed to make amends. Thus, the ISA was repealed – though replaced by new provisions for shorter-term, though still preventive, detention. And a new Peaceful Assembly Act was passed, removing the need for protesters to obtain permits – yet still enabling police to block particular protests.

Three years after coming to power, Najib's personal approval ratings remained reasonably robust. Many citizens appeared still to value his reformist aims, as well as recognize the momentous obstacles he faced in trying to implement them. But in consequence, UMNO itself remained widely despised for its recalcitrance. Thus, when the recommendations made by the parliamentary select committee were selectively passed by the government into law, resentments over electoral authoritarian procedures were ignited anew among Bersih leaders and followers. Yet another round of protest followed in April 2012, bringing many thousands of demonstrators into the streets of Kuala Lumpur.

Nearly a year later, barred by the constitution from delaying any longer, Najib finally dissolved parliament, presaging the election in May 2013. Precise voting patterns were highly complex and await further analysis, but key trends can be identified. Pakatan Rakyat, in trying to make further inroads into territory held by Barisan, descended upon Malaysia's southern states and across to Sabah and Sarawak. Chinese voters responded by completing their swing begun in 2008, with an estimated 80 per cent of them supporting Pakatan. Further, they were joined by more ethnic Malays than in 2008, especially in urban areas. This convergence of support across ethnic lines enabled the opposition to capture 52 per cent of the popular vote overall, while consolidating its grip on two important state assemblies. However, as Pakatan moved to the south and east, PKR and PAS lost to UMNO candidates many seats in the northern Malay 'heartland' that they had previously held. Thus, while UMNO's chief non-Malay partner, the MCA, was nearly wiped out, UMNO made enough gains that when combined with the support that it retained in Sabah and Sarawak, then magnified by electoral manipulations, especially malapportionment, it was able to lead Barisan in claiming a thin victory. However, as UMNO did this, its having won less than half the popular vote further strained the hybrid regime, more fully revealing its coercive components. Malaysia's regime thus held in 2013 but was battered by yet another liberalizing electoral outcome.

Conclusions

In addressing democracy and democratization in Malaysia, this chapter's main aim has been to show how they have long been avoided but seem increasingly to be within reach. To recount, analysis showed first how the hybridity of practiced electoral authoritarianism drew institutional strength from single-party dominance, while finding grounding in countervailing sets of historical legacies and structural features. It gained resilience too from its own adjustable dimensions of liberal participation and electoral contestation. Indeed, the regime's democratic content, involving at least limited electoral competitiveness and parliamentary accountability, helped reinforce its authoritarian character.

But after decades of operation, some of the very dynamics that had underpinned electoral authoritarianism now undermine it, therein imbuing it with greater competitiveness. The patronage flows upon which single-party dominance depends, sating the appetites of UMNO elites who might otherwise make trouble, and populist distributions, commanding the loyalties of mass-level Malay followers, have begun testing the patience of liberal middle-class Malays today, while deepening the alienation of most non-Malays. In addition, caps on liberal participation and electoral contestation, while once finding justification in the tensions inherent to a divided society, are increasingly decried today for their protecting elite interests. The very limits on assembly, elections, and parliamentary functioning, then, now rouse the opposition and ordinary citizens to make more vigorous use of them.

Thus, in elections held in 2008 and 2013, the incumbent government was dealt such setbacks that though it held onto office, its grip on parliament was shaken. Institutions had remained unchanged in their form and functioning. But while they had long aided the government in managing underlying structural pressures, they and the electoral authoritarianism that they had helped underpin came now to inflame the grievances of many citizens. In this context, then, it appeared that Malaysia's regime had shifted in character from an electoral to competitive authoritarian regime, one in which despite the procedural impediments still in place, government turnover grew imaginable, a change that were it to occur might amount to democratization-by-election. Malaysia offers rare analytical vantage, then, in which to investigate the inherent tensions that may cumulate over time to destabilize even the hardiest types of political hybridity.

Note

1 The work described in this paper was fully supported by a grant from the Research Grants Council of the Hong Kong Special Administrative Region (Project No. 9041396).

References

Baradan Kuppusamy (2007) 'Leaders urge return to moderation after protest in Malaysia', *South China Morning Post*, 27 November, 10.

Baradan Kuppusamy (2008) 'Two-Party System Takes Shape in Malaysia', *Asia Times On-line*, 10 April; www.atimes.com/atimes/Southeast_Asia/JD10Ae01.html accessed 24 July 2013.

Beh Lih Yi (2006) 'I Asked Customs to Close One Eye', *Malaysiakini*, 4 May; www.malaysiakini.com/news/50630 accessed 24 July 2013.

Boix, Carles and Milan Svolik (n.d.) 'The Foundations of Limited Authoritarian Government: Institutions and Power-sharing in Dictatorships'; www.princeton.edu/~cboix/boix-svolik-2009.pdf accessed 26 January 2013.

Brownlee, Jason (2007) *Authoritarianism in an Age of Democratization*, Cambridge: Cambridge University Press.

Case, William (2011) *Executive Accountability in Southeast Asia: The Role of Legislatures in New Democracies and Under Electoral Authoritarianism*, Honolulu: East West Center.

Chapman, Karen (2010) 'Muhyiddin: I am Malay First and Malaysian at Heart', *The Star Online*, 1 April; http://thestar.com.my/news/story.asp?file=/2010/4/1/nation/5976477&sec=nation accessed 24 July 2013.

Chin, James and Wong Chin Huat (2009) 'Malaysia's electoral upheaval', *Journal of Democracy*, 20(3), 71–85.

Crouch, Harold (1993) *Malaysia: Neither Authoritarian nor Democratic, in Southeast Asia in the 1990s*, Sydney: Allen and Unwin.

Crouch, Harold (1996) *Government and Society in Malaysia*, Ithaca: Cornell University Press.

Dahl, Robert (1972) *Polyarchy: Participation and Opposition*, New Haven: Yale University Press.

Diamond, Larry (1989) 'Introduction', in Larry Diamond, Juan J. Linz, and Seymour Martin Lipset (eds) *Democracy in Developing Countries: Asia*, Boulder: Lynne Rienner.

Funston, John (1980) *Malay Politics in Malaysia*, Kuala Lumpur: Heineman.

Gandhi, Jennifer and Adam Przeworski (2006) 'Cooperation, cooptation, and rebelion under dictatorships', *Economics and Politics*, 18(1), 1–26.

Gatsiounis, Ioannis (2007) 'Anti-Graft War Backfires in Malaysia', *Asia Times*, 21 March; www.atimes.com/atimes/Southeast_Asia/IC21Ae01.html accessed 24 July 2013.

Gomez, Edmund Terence and Jomo K.S. (1999) *Malaysia's Political Economy: Politics, Patronage and Profits*, Cambridge: Cambridge University Press.

Greene, Kenneth F. (2007) *Why Dominant Parties Lose: Mexico's Democratization in Comparative Perspective*, Cambridge: Cambridge University Press.

Hazlan Zakaria (2012) 'Nazri: If Bersih 3.0 Takes to Streets, They'll Face the Music', 19 January; www.malaysiakini.com/news/187031 accessed 24 July 2013.

Howard, Marc Morje and Philip G. Roessler (2006) 'Liberalizing electoral outcomes in competitive authoritarian regimes', *American Journal of Political Science*, 50(2), 365–381.

Huntington, Samuel P. (1968) *Political Order in Changing Societies*, New Haven: Yale University Press.

Huntington, Samuel P. (1991) *The Third Wave: Democratization in the Late Twentieth Century*, Norman, OK: University of Oklahoma Press.

Jayasankaran, S. (2004) 'Not so fast', *Far Eastern Economic Review*, 8 April, 20.

Levitsky, Steven and Lucan A. Way (2010) *Competitive Authoritarianism: Hybrid Regimes After the Cold War*, Cambridge: Cambridge University Press.

Lijphart, Arend (1977) *Democracy in Plural Societies*, New Haven: Yale University Press, pp. 150–157.

Lindberg. Staffen (ed.) (2009) *Democratization by Election: A New Mode of Transition*, Baltimore: Johns Hopkins University Press.

Lopez, Leslie (2004) 'Abdullah Gains in Corruption Fight', *Far Eastern Economic Review*, 4 March, 13.

Lust, Ellen (2009) 'Competitive clientelism in the Middle East', *Journal of Democracy*, 20(3), 122–135.

Lustick, Ian (1979) 'Stability in deeply divided societies: consociationalism versus control', *World Politics*, 33 (April): 325–344.

Malaysiakini (2003) 'Pak Lah Pledges Democracy in Maiden Parliamentary Speech', 3 November; http://m.malaysiakini.com/news/17707 accessed 24 July 2013.

Malaysiakini (2004) 'Ex-CJ Dzaiddin to Head Royal Police Commission', 4 February; www.malaysiakini.com/news/18559 accessed 24 July 2013.

Malaysiakini (2007a) 'Eric Chia Acquitted', 26 June; www.malaysiakini.com/news/69108 accessed 24 July 2013.

Malaysiakini (2007b) 'PM Defends Keris at UMNO Assembly', 7 November; www.malaysiakini.com/news/74468 accessed 24 July 2013.

Mauzy, Diane K. (1983) *Barisan Nasional; Coalition Government in Malaysia*, Petaling Jaya: Marican and Sons.

Means, Gordon P. (1976) *Malaysian Politics*, London: Hodder and Stoughton, 122–124.

Merdeka Center (2009, incorrectly dated 2007) '12th General Elections – Observations on Issues, Voting Directions and Implications'; www.merdeka.org/v2/index.php?option =com_content&view=article&id=90:12th-general-elections-observations-on-issues-voting-directions-and-implications&catid=35:research accessed 15 September 2012.

Mishler, William and Anne Hildreth (1984) 'Legislators and political stability: an exploratory analysis', *Journal of Politics*, 46(1), 25–59.

Muhamad Fuzi Omar (2008) 'Parliamentary behavior of the members of opposition political parties in Malaysia', *Intellectual Discourse*, 16(1), 21–48.

New Straits Times (2004) 'Unleash Your Potential', 31 August.

Pemandu (2011) 'Government Transformation Programme'; www.pemandu.gov.my/ gtp/?page_id=31 accessed 24 July 2013.

Pereira, Brendan (2004a) 'Battling Money Politics Entails Tougher Crackdown', *New Sunday Times*, 26 September, 10.

Pereira, Brendan (2004b) 'Show Us Proof, Says Abdullah,' *New Straits Times*, 25 September, 1.

Prime Minster's Department (n.d.) '1Malaysia: Rakyat Didahulukan, Pencapaian Diutamakan'; www.1malaysia.com.my/wp-content/uploads/2010/09/1MalaysiaBooklet.pdf accessed 24 July 2013.

Reuters (2007) 'Islamic State Label Sparks Controversy in Malaysia', 25 July; http:// groups.yahoo.com/group/beritamalaysia/message/95823 accessed 24 July 2013.

Schedler, Andreas (2006) *Electoral Authoritarianism: The Dynamics of Unfree Competition*, Boulder: Lynne Reinner.

Schedler, Andreas (2009) 'The New Institutionalism in the Study of Authoritarian Regimes', CIDE, no. 215; http://ovd.cide.edu/publicaciones/status/dts/DTEP%20215. pdf accessed 24 July 2013.

Trocki, Carl A. (1998) 'Democracy and the state in Southeast Asia', in Carl. A. Trocki (ed.) *Gangsters, Democracy, and the State in Southeast Asia*, Ithaca: Cornell Southeast Asia Program, pp. 7–16.

Vatikiotis, Michael and S. Jayasankaran (2004) 'Softly, Softly Go Reforms', *Far Eastern Economic Review*, 3 June, 23.

von Vorys, Karl (1973) *Democracy without Consensus*, Princeton: Princeton University Press.

Weiner, Myron (1987) 'Empirical democratic theory,' in Myron Weiner and Egun Ozbudun (eds) *Competitive Elections in Developing Countries*, Durham: Duke University Press.

Zakaria Haji Ahmad (1989) 'Malaysia: quasi-democracy in a divided society', in Larry Diamond, Juan J. Linz, and Seymour Martin Lipset (eds) *Democracy in Developing Countries: Asia*, Boulder: Lynne Rienner, pp. 347–381.

Ziegenhain, Patrick (2008) *The Indonesian Parliament and Democratization*, Singapore: ISEAS.

9 Democratization and embracing uncertainty in post-2011 Singapore

Netina Tan[1]

Introduction

The resilience of Singapore's hegemonic party rule is often viewed as an anomaly in the age of democracy. Despite the country's ideal socio-economic preconditions for democracy, the People's Action Party (PAP) has ruled the country uninterruptedly since 1968. But in recent years, the PAP's formidable grip on power appears to be slipping. In its 2011 general election (GE), the docile opposition won a five-man Group Representative Constituency (GRC) for the first time since the scheme was launched in 1988. Voters rewarded the opposition with nearly 40 per cent of the vote and six seats in Parliament – the best the opposition has achieved in three decades. Consequently, a five-person PAP team that included a popular Foreign Minister and a woman Minister was booted out of office. More surprisingly, old guards such as Minister Mentor Lee Kuan Yew and Senior Minister Goh Chok Tong resigned from the Cabinet. Three months later, in an American style presidential election (PE), four candidates held public rallies, mobilized support online and debated on national TV. Unlike the past two uncontested PEs, Singapore's first-past-the-post (FPTP) electoral system threw up a winner with no clear mandate. After nine days of heated campaign, Dr Tony Tan, the government endorsed candidate, finally won, but only narrowly. In the following two years, the PAP suffered two more humiliating defeats in two by-elections, boosting the number of opposition members of parliament (MP) to a total of seven.

To many observers, the series of elections since the 2011 GE signified the decline of the PAP's hegemony and the dawn of liberal democracy in Singapore. The term 'new normal' is now widely used to describe the country's changed political landscape, where an awakened electorate demands more political pluralism and participation. But will the 'new normal' bring about democratization and party alternation in Singapore?

Since taking office in 2004, Prime Minister Lee Hsien Loong has initiated political reforms and loosened Internet control to appease the changing aspirations of the electorate. Yet, liberalization is not democratization. While democratization entails liberalization, liberalization may or may not lead to full-scale democratization (Huntington, 1991: 9). As Mainwaring and Scully (1995: 20) remind us, for hegemonic party systems to democratize, deinstitutionalization must first occur. Deinstitutionalization refers to the abandonment of rules without being replaced by the same alternative institutional pattern. The intertwining of the party and state institutions must be dismantled before a hegemonic party system can democratize. No such process of deinstitutionalization has taken place in Singapore.

As the electoral authoritarianism literature tells us, institutional sources of hegemonic party persistence usually stem from the ruling party's 'hyper-incumbency advantage', access to state resources and use of electoral engineering strategies to entrench an uneven playing field which systematically impair the opposition's ability to organize and compete for national office (Greene 2007; Levitsky and Way 2002, 2010; Magaloni 2006; Schedler 2010). Likewise in Singapore, the ruling PAP remains the strongest party and enjoys incumbency advantage. Five decades of the PAP's rule have fused the lines between the party and state (Mauzy and Milne 2002; Seah 1985). Long-term incumbency has allowed the ruling PAP to dominate state institutions and gain easy access to state resources to build a vast network of para-political organizations for partisan purposes (K.P. Tan and A. Tan 2003). In addition, electoral engineering or selective tweaking of electoral rules has over time tilted the electoral arena so that it systematically disadvantages the resource-poor opposition (Norris 2004; Reilly 2007; N. Tan in press). Without dismantling of the strong party-state fusion and changes in the electoral system toward a more proportionate model, it is unlikely that Singapore will abandon its hegemonic party system and embrace liberal democracy in the near future.

To assess Singapore's prospects for democracy, this chapter begins by introducing Singapore's hegemonic party regime and tracing the government's liberalization efforts. Next, it considers how demographic changes and loosening of Internet control emboldened the opposition and intensified electoral competition. It argues that despite the decline in the PAP's credibility and electoral margins, the country's hegemonic party system remains institutionalized. Evidence drawn from the media, electoral and public opinion survey data show that the opposition parties have yet to emerge as credible alternatives at the national level, and the PAP will most likely remain the strongest party for some time to come.

Singapore's hegemonic party system

There are about 27 registered political parties in Singapore. But in reality, most parties are dormant between elections and only an average of six to seven parties contest elections. Singapore has held 11 GEs since its independence in 1965. Legislative assembly elections were competitive in the 1950s and early 1960s, but since 1968, the PAP has won every seat in every election until 1981 when a by-election broke the monopoly. Opposition legislative representation has not exceeded four, until the 2011 GE. See Table 9.1 for the GE results.

Scholars have difficulties classifying Singapore's regime as opinions are split over the yardstick used to assess the quality of its democracy (Diamond and

Table 9.1 General election results in Singapore

GE	Total seats	PAP's vote share (%)	PAP's seat share (% in brackets)	Opp. parties' vote shares (%)	Opp. parties seat shares (% in brackets)
1968	58	86.7	58 (100)	13.3	0 (0)
1972	65	70.4	65 (100)	29.0	0 (0)
1976	69	74.1	69 (100)	25.1	0 (0)
1980	75	77.7	75 (100)	22.3	0 (0)
1984	79	64.8	77 (97.5)	35.1	2 (2.5)
1988	81	63.2	80 (98.8)	36.8	1 (1.2)
1991	81	61.0	77 (95.1)	39.0	4 (4.9)
1997	83	65.0	81 (97.6)	35.0	2 (3.4)
2001	84	75.3	81 (97.6)	24.7	2 (2.3)
2006	84	66.6	82 (97.6)	33.4	2 (2.3)
2011	87	60.1	81 (93.1)	39.9	6 (6.9)

Source: Singapore Elections official website (www.eld.gov.sg/homepage.html) retrieved 1 April 2013 and Singapore Elections website www.singapore-elections.com retrieved 1 April 2013.

Morlino 2004). Labels stretching across both the democratic and authoritarian spectrums such as soft authoritarianism (Means 1996); competitive, authoritarian hybrid regime (Mauzy 2006); stable semi-democracy (Case 2002); semi-democracy (Diamond 1999); communitarian democracy (Chua 1995); and illiberal democracy (Zakaria 1994; Hussin 2000) have been used.

In terms of regime type, Singapore under the PAP's rule is best viewed as an electoral authoritarian hybrid regime where regular elections are conducted under relatively free but unfair conditions (Diamond 2002; Levitsky & Way 2002; Van de Walle 2006). The PAP maintains its legitimacy at the ballot box and elections are largely free from fraud or ballot rigging. However, the methods it uses to disadvantage the opposition, such as announcing constituency boundary changes three months before the elections, restrictions on freedom of expression, and organization of public rallies and the use of libel suits to intimidate opposition leaders reinforce the view that the electoral process is free but not fair (Mauzy 2002: 253). For example, the US Department of State 2010 Human Rights Report on Singapore also observed that '[E]lections were generally fair and free of tampering; however, the PAP placed formidable obstacles in the path of political opponents.... The government has broad powers to limit citizens' rights and handicap political opposition, which it used' (US Department Of State 2011).

While debates ensue over the definitions and range of political liberties encompassed by democracy, it is widely agreed that even the procedural, minimalist conception requires a minimum level of freedom of speech, press and assembly for elections to be competitive and participation to be meaningful (Diamond 1999: 8). Constraints on political freedoms and civil liberties have led independent watchdog organizations such as Freedom House and the Economist Intelligence Unit's *Democracy Index* to exclude Singapore as a liberal democracy (Freedom House 2013). Likewise, others such as the Bertelsmann Index have classified Singapore as a 'hybrid' country (Bertelsmann Index 2012), while Reporters Without Borders has consistently ranked the country poorly for its limited press freedom and compliant media. In the 2013 Press Freedom Index, Singapore was placed 149th out of 179 countries (Reporters Without Borders, 2013).

In Singapore, electoral competition is skewed as the ruling party enjoys an asymmetrical amount of power and resources over its challengers. Electoral competition is skewed not because of electoral fraud but rather because of unequal access to state institutions, electoral engineering and control over the media outlets (see Greene 2007; Levitsky and Way 2010; N. Tan in press). Unlike the resource poor opposition parties, the PAP has developed a sophistic-ated fund raising capacity over its five decade of rule. For example, through the People's Association (PA) – a statutory board formed to promote social harmony and cohesion – the PAP has been able to make use of the networks of grassroots organizations under the PA's umbrella for partisan purposes. The opposition parties, on the other hand, are excluded or unable to gain similar access to the state-funded facilities and activities. Opposition parties are disadvantaged as they face barriers in their fundraising, recruitment and outreach activities. Com-plaints by opposition leaders about difficulties in using public sites in their con-stituencies and the close links between the PAP and the PA are commonly heard and reported online (S. Lim 2011; Singh 2011).

Apart from these institutional barriers, the PAP also relies on selective coer-cion such as media control and other legal means to deny legal opposition parties a fair and authentic chance to compete for power. For example, all Singapore's mainstream media are owned by the Singapore Press Holdings, which is in turned controlled by the Ministry of Information and the Arts. The compliance of editors and reporters are informally encouraged by 'OB' (out-of-bounds) markers (George 2012). More recently, a well-known academic who has pub-lished widely on media freedom in Singapore was denied tenure in the local uni-versity, raising further concerns about the lack of academic and media freedom in the country (Salimat 2013).

Hegemonic party systems are characterized by the practice of manipulating political institutions and the constitution to disadvantage opposition and to manufacture legitimacy. Singapore's party system befits Sartori's hegemonic party system as: (1) the opposition parties are 'second class, licensed parties' which cannot compete with the PAP on equal terms; (2) the PAP outdistances the other parties with more than a two-thirds supermajority; and (3) alternation of power is not envisaged (2005: 204–205). As Magaloni's work on Mexico's Institutional Revolutionary Party reminds us:

> Autocracies strive to sustain oversized governing coalitions rather than min-imally winning ones because, first, as argued earlier, they want to generate an image of invincibility in order to discourage party splits. A second reason why hegemonic-party autocracies aspire supermajorities is to control insti-tutional change to their advantage. In order to manipulate institutional

change, these autocracies need supermajorities – most countries require legislative supermajorities, a popular referendum, or a combination of the two to change the constitution.

(2006: 15)

The PAP has turned to electoral engineering strategies to increase its winning margin and legislative presence (N. Tan in press). In fact, electoral engineering began as far back as 1963, when the Constitution was amended to prevent party switching – a practice endemic in the 1950s when dissenting PAP legislators would cross the floor to form opposition parties such as the United People's Party and Barisan Sosialis to challenge the PAP in the House (Thio and K. Tan 2009). Its legislative supermajority boosted the PAP's 'image of invincibility' and enabled the government to pass bills easily without the need for much debate or negotiations with the opposition.

From 1959 to 1987, Singapore's electoral system was based on the FPTP system in single-member constituencies (SMCs) of a Westminster, unicameral Parliament. Since 1984, a series of constitutional amendments that introduced schemes such as the Non-Constituency Member of Parliament (NCMP), GRC, Nominated Member of Parliament (NMP) and Elected Presidency[2] have transformed the country's electoral system.[3] Singapore's electoral system now consists of a mixture of SMC and party block vote or GRCs of four to six candidates based on a one-man-one-vote system and simple plurality. To ensure more legislative debate in a one-party dominant Parliament, an NMP scheme that appoints nine non-partisan MPs based on the recommendation of a Special Select Committee of the Parliament was also institutionalized, while the number of non-elected opposition MPs under the NCMP scheme was increased from six to nine. The 12th Singapore Parliament now consists of 87 elected MP seats and 12 non-elected MPs.

As Przeworski (1986: 58) reminds us, democratization is a process of institutionalizing uncertainty, of subjecting all interests to uncertainty. Democratization occurs when no group can intervene in the electoral process and when outcomes of conflicts violate the group's self-perceived interests. The critical point in democratization is the replacement of a government that is selected in a free, open and fair election. Power alternation is the ultimate litmus test of a regime's alienation of control over outcomes of conflicts (Geddes 2003: 71). Yet whether Singapore will embrace party alternation and electoral uncertainty is unclear. To date, Singapore's PAP leaders continue to reject the idea of alternation and at times, even the principle of one-man-one-vote. For example, Lee Kuan Yew warned: 'Singapore cannot afford revolving door style of government where leaders change every five years' (Popathal 2007). Likewise, his son, PM Lee Hsien Loong has argued that change has to come from within the PAP and that party alternation 'seldom works because having two or more parties has not guaranteed good governance or progress ... it is not a political system which is working properly. And I don't think you want that kind of political system in Singapore' (Li 2008). The disdain for party alternation thus raises the possibility of the government sending in the military in the event of a 'freak election' (C. Lim 2009). Without the experience of party alternation, we will not know whether the ruling party will ever give up power peacefully in the event of defeat (Van de Walle 2006: 10).

Managed liberalization

PM Lee initiated some controversial policy changes since taking office, raising expectations of democratization in the country. To begin with, he pushed through a highly divisive bill to legalize gaming and built two integrated resort and casinos, despite strong opposition from both the PAP and the public in 2005 (Koh 2005; Szep 2005). By 2008, he loosened rules governing public speeches and demonstrations at the Speakers' Corner and removed the need for police permits for indoor political demonstrations. More significantly, he also lifted the archaic ban on political films and videos (provided they passed the censorship board), political podcasts and vodcasts before elections. In addition, political films that were banned under the Films Act are now permitted. Election campaign recordings can also be posted as long as they are not 'dramatized' or published 'out of context' (Mydans 2011). These changes mean that videos taken at election rallies could now be uploaded onto the Internet without the need to go through the Film Censors Board.

To encourage legislative debate, PM Lee introduced more non-PAP presence in the House by institutionalizing the NMP scheme that appoints non-elected members of parliament and raising the number of the NCMPs or 'best opposition loser' from six to nine. In another clear move to appease criticisms that the GRC scheme disadvantaged the opposition, the sizes of some larger size multi-member constituencies were reduced, while the number of single member constituencies was increased from nine to twelve in 2011. And further demonstrating the government's willingness to review its tough laws, it surprised many by relaxing its mandatory death penalty and allowing judges the discretion to impose life sentences for certain drug trafficking and murder cases (Grant 2012; BBC 2012). Refer to Table 9.2 for a summary of the political reforms under PM Lee Hsien Loong.

Why did the PAP voluntarily make concessions and liberalize? Will these political concessions bring about freer and fairer party competition and liberal democracy? Liberalization refers to the 'partial opening' of an authoritarian system. Usually, it entails a mix of policy and social changes that could include release of political prisoners; return of political exiles; opening up of issues for public debate; improved income distribution; loosening of media censorship; renewal of civil society; and toleration of political opposition. In *The Third Wave*, Huntington (1991: 127–128) suggested four reasons for liberalization. First, he contends that liberalization occurs because autocrats calculate that the cost of staying in power, either through more repression or unsolvable problems, has reached the point where a graceful exit from power was more desirable. Second, reforms occur because autocrats want to reduce the risks they face (such

Table 9.2 Key political reforms under Lee Hsien Loong's government

Year	Key changes	Stated purpose
2004	Rules governing Speakers' Corner loosen. Indoor political activities permitted. Societies Act amended to allow automatic registration of non-specified societies.	To encourage political participation.
2008	Rules governing overseas voting relaxed. Outdoor political demonstrations allowed at Speakers' Corner.	Indoor political demonstrations no longer need permit.
2009	Films Act amended.	To allow political party films, manifestos and factual documentaries.
2009	NMP scheme institutionalized. No. of NCMP increased from 6 to 9. No. of SMCs increased from 9 to 12. Sizes of larger GRCs reduced.	To allow more alternative voices in the House.
2009	Public Order Bill introduced.	To give the police more powers over the control of outdoor political events.
2010	'Cooling off day' or campaign ban on the eve of polling day introduced.	To prevent 'emotional voting' and 'risk of public disorder'
2012	Mandatory death penalty changed.	Judges reserve discretion to impose life sentence on drug traffickers and murder cases.

Sources: Compiled by author based on various media reports.

as death) if they were to lose power. Third, they may also be so confident of their hold on office that they would organize genuine elections and facilitate more competition just so to renew their legitimacy. Finally, autocratic reformers may also come to believe that democratization benefits their country and that democracy is the 'right' form of government, just as in other countries.

It is improbable that the PAP leaders initiated reform because of the fear of retribution or doubted their inability to resolve crises. Most Singaporeans respect their leaders and place a lot of trust in their technocratic leadership. In fact, a survey by 2006 East Asia Barometer shows Singaporeans to have the highest level of confidence in government institutions and their ability to manage crises (East Asian Barometer 2006). Apart from the global financial crisis that slowed growth, spiked inflation and income inequality, there is no looming crisis that is driving the PAP leaders to initiate reform. As mentioned, senior PAP leaders are not fans of liberal democracy. It is unlikely that the belief in democracy as the 'right' form of governance has motivated political change. Currently, there is no indication that the PAP government wants full participatory, competitive elections that would cause the leadership to lose power. After ruling out three possible reasons for the reforms, legitimacy renewal seems to be the most likely motivation for liberalization in Singapore.

Experiences from hegemonic party transitions in Mexico and Taiwan show that liberalization could stretch over decades without immediate transition to fully competitive and open electoral politics (Cheng and Lin 1999). Indeed, diffusing opposition and dissent without resorting to full democratization is a common feature of liberalization. As transitology scholars such as O'Donnell and Schmitter (1986: 9) remind us, liberalization is not the same as democratization. Liberalization can result in a liberalized autocracy (*dictablanda*) or a limited democracy (*democradura*). Leaders could tolerate and even promote liberalization in the belief that by opening up certain spaces for individuals and groups, they can relieve pressures and obtain support and information without altering the structure of authority. In view of the changing demography and difficulty in controlling all media channels in the era of the Internet, the PAP's conciliatory moves are perhaps pre-emptive strategies to create 'a kinder, gentler, more secure and stable authoritarianism without altering fundamentally the nature of the system' (Huntington, 1991: 129).

The 'new normal'

The political ground in Singapore has shifted since 2011. Some have described the winds of change in the country as the 'new normal' – where an awakened and more vocal electorate is unafraid to voice its desires for a new leadership that is free of arrogance, complacency and insensitivity to the people's needs (Ong 2011c). The country's changing demography, Internet accessibility and connectivity have helped to embolden the dissenters, and increased opposition mobilization and support. In the 2011 GE, the total electorate increased by 8.8 per cent to 2.3 million, out of which a quarter were below 35 years old while about 100,000 were first time voters. Public opinion surveys show that younger voters want more political participation and are less willing to accept that a hegemonic party government is best for the country (Saad 2011). Despite the government's ability to shield the economy from the brunt of the global financial crisis and boost double-digit growth rate in 2010, Singaporeans remained unhappy.[4]

During the 2011 GE, Singaporeans vented their unhappiness through the ballot box. The depth of the anti-government sentiments stunned the PAP. As Minister Vivian Balakrishnan said, the PAP was 'swimming against a national tide and against an energized opposition' (Ong 2011b; Teo 2011). The PAP was shocked and dismayed by the unprecedented drop in their vote shares, which hit an historic low of 60.1 per cent. Unlike in the past, Singaporeans showed no fear as they packed the opposition rallies, demanding more inclusiveness, political pluralism and fairness. Accountability became a key electoral issue. The government's open-door immigration policy that exacerbated inflation, the income gap and overcrowdedness had fuelled mass resentment. And concerns over the rising cost of living, housing prices, immigration policy, income inequality, investment in casinos and high ministerial salaries dominated opposition rallies.

Capitalizing on the disaffection, the opposition lobbied hard for the electorate to vote for them to check a government that is increasingly seen to be arrogant and out of touch with the common people. Indeed, Singapore's Gini coefficient, a measure of inequality, had risen from 0.444 in 2000 to a high of 0.48 by 2010 (Singapore Statistics 2011). With 1.4 million foreigners constituting a third of the country's labour force, the privilege the government placed on the 'foreign talent' while neglecting the country's own in terms of housing and jobs, as well as the requirement for national service, are now highly contentious. Besides, the traditional PAP ethnic minority supporters were also reportedly split because of Lee Kuan Yew's insensitive statement in his new book about Malays' non-integration (Hussain 2011).

With the Internet being accessed by more than 78 per cent of Singaporeans, the new media has become an alternative channel for expression and communication (Channel NewsAsia 2011). Singaporeans are the heaviest Internet users in the region, averaging 25 hours online per week and with an estimated three million Facebook members and 900,000 local Twitter users in the country. Statistics from online monitoring companies show that for the first 26 days of April – the day before Nomination Day – there were 44,000 blog postings, Tweets, and Facebook updates related to elections (Chou 2011). Extensive and rapid online coverage of the opposition added pressures on the pro-government mainstream media, pushing the national newspaper and TV stations to cover more news on the opposition.

Meanwhile, Internet savvy opposition parties such as the Singapore Democratic Party (SDP), the Reform Party (RP) and the National Solidarity Party (NSP) wasted no time in using social media as a new tool to promote their candidates and party platforms. Young opposition women candidates such as charismatic and Internet-savvy Nicole Seah soon became a new media sensation. In fact, she led a team of virtual unknowns from the NSP to challenge former PM Goh Chok Tong in his Marine Parade GRC, nearly embarrassing him, with a respectable 43 per cent vote share. A reason for the PAP's poor showing in Marine Parade was largely due to the Party's miscalculation in fielding a young candidate, Tin Pei Ling, who received online flak for flaunting a branded handbag and behaving childishly in an interview. Her marriage to the principal private secretary of the PM also fuelled criticisms of nepotism and cast the PAP in a negative light. The polar opposite experiences of these two young candidates demonstrate the power of social media on electoral campaigning in Singapore's 'new normal' politics.

Traditionally, the PAP has had the monopoly over the media to set the agenda and terms of debate. But as the 2011 GE shows, the relaxation of rules governing online election advertising and campaigning has widened the space for opposition mobilization. During the campaign, opposition parties were better connected with supporters – posting on blogs, websites, Tweeting and providing video coverage of rallies. All the seven contesting parties maintained their own websites, while many candidates managed social media accounts. In fact, a Singapore Democratic Alliance (SDA) team raised a total of S$80,000 (US$62,824) electoral deposit through an online appeal, while the SDP leader Dr Chee Soon Juan, who was convicted of 'making an address in a public place without a licence' in 2006 was able to avoid jail time by raising S$20,000 through an online donation drive (AsiaOne 2011a). While social media improved opposition coordination, post-election surveys found that the effects of the new media remained limited. The survey results show that 70 per cent of the voters still turned to mainstream media for election news (Chang 2011). Hence, whether the new media will be a 'game-changer' in the next GE remains to be seen.

One step forwards, two steps back

Looser rules governing media and public demonstrations have encouraged more political participation. Yet, critics remained unconvinced. Political reforms have been dismissed as window dressing that came 'too little, too late' (A. Au 2009). Indeed, the government is wont to dance the 'one-step forwards, two-steps backward' reform routine, often flip-flopping on the terms of regulation. This is most evident in its treatment of online media and controversial speeches. After banning Facebook, Twitter or podcasts in the 2006 GE and declaring 'a quiet counter-insurgency' against its online critics, it later changed its tune and declared a 'light touch' to regulate new media (Au Yong and Wong 2011). The next year, the government changed its mind again, retracted its 'light touch' and reviewed its policies on online conduct. The constant shifts in position show the government's frustration and cluelessness in dealing with online dissent and controversial speech (Ramesh 2011).

Without clear guidelines to control online behaviour, some PAP leaders returned to the old ways of clamping down, initiating lawsuits threatening bloggers and political commentators for defamation (TOC 2012). In February 2012, the Law Minister, the PM and his brother threatened to sue a well-known political commentator and editors of Temesek Review Emeritus, a socio-political website, for defamatory remarks. Later, a popular blogger, Alex Au was forced to apologize and retract his blog posts that were deemed to have 'scandalized the judiciary' and cast doubts on Singapore's judicial independence for questioning the appropriateness of charges against a local plastic surgeon for giving false information and a speeding offence (AsiaOne 2012).[5]

In practice, the authorities do block some online content through directives to licensed service providers and they monitor online material regularly. Online contents that contain postings with inflammatory religious or racist undertones are blocked or shut down. For example, the police charged a blogger and three teenagers for racially sensitive remarks on Facebook in 2009. In 2010, it warned a pastor for making disparaging remarks about other religions on YouTube. Later, editors of the website New Asia Republic were held for questioning for re-posting pictures offensive to Muslims in 2011 (Au 2012b). While the policing of online racial and religious remarks, governed under the Maintenance of Religious Harmony Act and Sedition Acts, was aimed at preserving social harmony, the gazetting of a website, The Online Citizen (TOC), as a political association and the arrest of the Temesek Review editor over an election exit poll were widely seen as politically motivated.[6]

Singapore will not experience an Arab-Spring styled uprising. However, to avoid the possibility of any freak incident, the government is staying vigilant and putting up safeguards. For example, after lifting the ban on demonstrations at the Speakers' Corner, a Public Order Bill was swiftly passed to give the police more powers over the control of outdoor political events and to direct the public to stop filming law enforcement activities and search anybody believed to be in possession of a film or picture without warrant. The new bill reveals the government's insecurity and fear of large crowds that have turned up at opposition election rallies. In May 2010, additional measures such as the 'cooling-off day' rule were introduced to ban campaigning on the eve of polling day to prevent 'emotional voting' and 'risk of public disorder' (AsiaOne 2011b).

Despite liberalization efforts, the PAP government is still uncomfortable with political activism. For example, the Singapore Law Society's attempts to expose a human rights lawyer's, M. Ravi's, bipolar disorder illness[7] during his appeals in courts against the PM's 'unfettered discretion' to call a by-election brought the bar into disrepute (Chan 2012).[8] The ugly counter-suits between Ravi and the Law Society thus raise concerns about the political motivations behind the suits and legal procedures in the country (Loh 2012).

The constant post-hoc amendments and overzealous interpretations of the rules by the authorities have constrained liberalization efforts. Despite the relaxation of rules governing public speeches and new media during elections, some political demonstrations and public forums still face difficulties obtaining permits. For example, the organizers of 'Slutwalk' – a protest against sexual violence within the confines of the Speakers' Corner – had to apply for a police permit under the Public Order Act (A Au 2011). Furthermore, the organizer of Singaporeans For Democracy (SFD) was investigated under the Public Order Act for holding a private forum on Lee Kuan Yew and liberal democracy. Despite repeated appeals, the SFD's attempt to organize an anti-racism rally at Speakers' Corner on International Human Rights Day was rejected by the police in 2011. The arbitrary rule changes and selective repressions and harassments by the authorities show that the regime is unprepared to fully liberalize and accommodate the uncertainties of contentious politics and dissent that come with political pluralism.

Institutionalized hegemonic party system

In the 2011 GE, a total of 83 opposition candidates, nearly double the 47 candidates from the last election, contested. Unlike in the past, many overseas educated and well-qualified candidates stood under the opposition flags. For the first time in Singapore's electoral history, the opposition Workers' Party (WP) had a psychological breakthrough and won a GRC. Despite a rise in the electoral deposit to S$16,000 for each candidate, seven opposition parties fielded candidates in an unprecedented 82 out of 87 seats. The opposition would have contested all 87 seats if not for the disqualification of a multimember team from the SDA for being 35 seconds late in submitting the nomination form. The disqualification of the opposition resulted in a 'walkover' of a five-member team led by former Senior Minister Lee Kuan Yew in Tanjong Pagar GRC.

Despite the PAP's declining mass support, the hegemonic party system in Singapore remains stable and institutionalized. With only seven elected seats in the House, the opposition has a long way to go before it could emerge as a credible alternative. Unlike the PAP, opposition parties are still largely personality driven, fraught with power struggles and under-institutionalized. Institutionalization refers to a 'process by which organizations and procedures acquire value and stability' (Huntington 1965: 394). Party institutionalization implies that the party as an organization is valued in its own right, rather than merely as an instrument for the achievement of a political goal (Gunther, Montero and Linz, 2002: 196). Besides the WP, most opposition parties in Singapore are organizationally weak.

An institutionalized party system is widely seen to have: (1) regular and stable inter-party competition; (2) rooted parties in society; (3) party organizations that matter; and (4) parties with electoral legitimacy (Mainwaring and Scully 1995: 4). Apart from the WP, most opposition parties do not fare well in the last three dimensions.[9] In fact, most opposition parties lack stable roots and have short life spans. Aside from the WP, the Singapore Malay National Organization (PKMS) and the PAP, none of the pre-independence parties exist today. Most opposition parties are small and lack funding and resources to build party organizations. In terms of party newsletters, only the PAP and WP have regular printed party publications. Out of the seven contesting parties, only the WP and the NSP have functioning committees and town councils. In contrast, the PAP has 87 party branches sprawled across the island (N. Tan 2013).

Even the WP, the oldest and strongest opposition party, suffers from party disciplinary problems. For example, the WP had to expel its long-time member and newly-elected MP, Yaw Shin Leong for refusing to defend allegations of his extramarital affairs. His expulsion triggered a by-election at Hougang constituency and raised concerns about the WP's candidate selection process (Saad 2012). This was later followed by the WP's expulsion of another veteran member Poh Lee Guan for putting himself up as a candidate in the by-election without party endorsement (Ong 2012). Despite a series of faux pas that shows the WP's internal problems, the WP's new candidate, Png Eng Huat, won comfortably with 62 per cent of votes against the PAP challenger in the by-election, and the WP retained its seat in the House. Besides, the overwhelming victory of the WP's woman candidate, Lee Lilian over the PAP candidate in Punggol East by-election in January 2013, demonstrates the people's growing disaffection for the PAP, strengthening the opposition cause (Chia 2013).

Yet, despite the PAP's declining electoral legitimacy and vote share, it remains the dominant party of choice. With its track record of good governance and the high level of trust in the PAP's record in maintaining growth, it is unsurprising that it continues to command a respectable 60 per cent of the national vote. Furthermore, the support for the PM remains high as his popular vote share received a boost from 66.1 per cent to 69.3 per cent, signalling approval for his humility in apologizing for the Government's mistakes in the escape of the terrorist Mas Selamat and flooding of downtown Orchard Road (AsiaOne 2011c).

Besides, the PAP was also successful in wrestling back a single member seat in the former opposition stronghold Potong Pasir from opposition leader Chiam See Tong in the 2011 GE. Singaporeans want political diversity and opposition voice. Yet no opposition parties have emerged as PAP's credible replacement (see Przeworski 1986: 52). Voting for the untested and inexperienced opposition party comes with risks. In fact, a survey by the Institute of Policy Studies in Singapore has found 'efficient government' to be Singaporeans' top concern. (Wong 2011) The mixed 2011 GE results show that a large proportion of Singaporeans are unprepared to abandon the PAP model of governance and embrace the uncertainties that come with party alternation. As Slater has suggested, in strong states such as Singapore, the prospects for democratization also depend on the expectations of the masses of instability after democratization (2012: 20). The unwillingness to bet on an untested party or worries about weak economic performance after alternation could hold some Singaporeans back from embracing change. Presently, Singapore's low electoral volatility score, an indicator of party system institutionalization, shows that the hegemonic party system is well institutionalized. Electoral volatility measures change over successive elections in the balance of party support or the ability of parties to maintain their social bases. Based on Pedersen index calculations,[10] Singapore's electoral volatility still stands at 12.7 for the last 11 elections (1968–2011), a low score compared to the regional volatility average of 24.1 for 14 Asian party systems (Hicken and Kuhonta 2011).

Party-state fusion

One of the key institutional sources of Singapore's hegemonic party resilience lies in the fusion of the party-state apparatus. Long-term incumbency and access to state resources have helped the PAP lay a vast network of para-political organizations that fused party-state lines. In particular, the creation of the People's Association (PA) has been the PAP's most effective strategy of controlled mobilization. Established as a statutory board, the PA draws on state resources to build a sprawling network of Community Centres (CC), Citizens' Consultative Committees (CCC), Community Club Management Committees (CCMC), Residents' Committees (RC) in housing and Neighbourhood Committees (NC) in residential estates for political purposes.[11] The CCs provide a wide range of recreational, social and sports courses, activities, programmes and facilities in the local constituencies, while the CCMCs run the CCs. On the other hand, the CCCs act as institutionalized feedback mechanisms for the masses to relay messages from the ground to the government. Through these vast grassroots organizations, led by technocrats or bureaucrats, the PA co-opts local talents and directs them to the Government's socio-political development programmes (Seah 1987: 174). These grassroots organizations provide community and welfare services and foster political good will for the PAP. While they are supposed to be non-partisan, the overlapping memberships of political and apolitical organizations often result in its heavy politicization. For example, the PA is anchored in the government structure. The Chairman of its board of management is the PM and the Deputy Chairman is a Cabinet minister. The scandal revolving around the opaque transactions of the town council computer system to a PAP-owned company raises questions about conflict of interest and flow of state assets into partisan hands (Au 2012a).

The institutionalization of the PA for partisan aims is typical in one-party states. As Huntington and Moore observed decades ago: '[T]he institutionalization of a one-party system indeed is a process whereby the party devolves its functional overload upon a variety of governmental and autonomous or quasi-autonomous groups' (1970: 515). In reality, the para-political organizations serve the community and national development role of the government and free the PAP of the burden of organizing educational, sports and welfare activities at the grassroots level. While the network of grassroots organizations are set up as non-political, quasi-state institutions, the opposition parties are often excluded and prevented from using them to hold activities and mobilize support. Opposition leaders thus complained of unfair treatment and exclusion from the use of public funded space. As WP leader, Sylvia Lim, said in Parliament:

> Under the Town Councils Act, the incumbent MP of a constituency will be in charge of the Town Council which controls the use of common space. As for the Community Clubs, these are in the hands of the People's Association. It is next to impossible for an opposing candidate to be allowed to use a space to organize activities or dialogues. We have applied for permission to use spaces in PAP wards, and received expected rejections.
>
> (S. Lim 2010)

Indeed, since winning the Aljunied five-person GRC, the WP has complained of difficulties in taking over the office lease of the Town Council Office and organizing activities because of the politicization of the grassroots organizations (S. Lim 2011). Unless the opposition is in a position to duplicate a similar set of grassroots organizations or dismantle the party-state fusion (Singh 2011), it will be an uphill task for them to make significant headway to challenge the PAP in providing equivalent public services and reach out to the masses. As Ho Khai Leong rightly observes: 'The PAP-dominated party system will continue in Singapore, not because of a lack of demand for democratization from below, but because the state institutions built by the PAP have been effective in providing what seem to be essential goods and services for the populace' (2010: 73).

Conclusion

Diffusing dissent without resorting to full democratization is often a feature of liberalization. This chapter has suggested that the PAP's 'top-down' political reforms were initiated to diffuse the rising pressures and uncertainties that come with demographic change in the Internet era. It is also argued that the calibrated reforms and post-hoc rule changes show that the PAP regime is unprepared for a fully open and free political environment that could lead to party alternation. The strong party-state fusion and uneven playing field in the electoral arena mean that the opposition parties will continue to face an uphill task in challenging the PAP at the national level.

As Przeworski reminds us, a regime does not collapse unless and until some alternative is organized in such a way that presents a real choice for individuals (1979: 52). The opposition parties such as the WP and the SDP have made significant leaps in the recent election. However, institutional barriers, lack of funding, and organizational weaknesses continue to prevent them from presenting themselves as credible alternatives. Despite the shifts in mass sentiment and decline in mass support, the PAP remains the strongest party because of its massive party organization, access to state funding, incumbency and institutional advantage.

The political reforms have not altered the nature of Singapore's political system in any fundamental way. There are many concrete steps that still need to be taken before free and fair elections can occur. To begin with, the setting up of an independent Electoral Commission will be necessary to show the regime's commitment to this end. Presently, the PM's office controls both the Elections Department and the Electoral Boundaries Review Committee that provide the electoral boundaries report only weeks before an election. The de-linking between the Executive and the Elections Commission is necessary to lay a more level playing field and ensure fairer rules and timeframe for parties to prepare their bases before elections. In addition, PAP party leaders also need to refrain from the use of defamation suits against the opposition leaders and dissenters. Extending more rights for peaceful demonstrations and freedom of expression in the media could also foster a culture of political activism (Diamond 2006). More importantly, to ensure parties have equal and fair access to state resources, the quasi-statutory boards such as the PA and the umbrella of para-political organizations ought to be reorganized and staffed with non-partisan members.

The departure of Lee Kuan Yew and Goh Chok Tong signified the end of the strongman era and a new space for the younger leaders to remake themselves. As Schlesinger said: 'a party which does not respond to the electoral market will by definition lose to parties which do, and over the long run in a society where people are free to form new parties, it will find itself supplanted by responsive parties' (1984: 384). To appeal to the demanding younger electorate, the PAP needs to overhaul its old formula of organizing, campaigning, candidate selection and communicating with supporters. If the PAP does not adapt and meet the aspirations of the new electorate, it will eventually lose power. Singapore possesses all the ideal socio-economic preconditions for liberal democracy such as good governance, ethics of transparency, commitment to public service and rule of law. Yet, these are necessary but insufficient conditions for democratization. Strategic choices made by state and societal actors are also important in moving a regime forward during transitions (O'Donnell and Schmitter, 1986: 4–5).

A key indicator of this will be the deinstitutionalization of the party-state apparatus followed by an overhaul of its electoral system to a more proportionate one. Besides, risk-averse leaders and voters must also learn that democratic pluralism is a messy, disorderly and contentious business. To move forward, all need to embrace the uncertainties that come with truly free, fair and competitive elections.

Notes

1 This research was first presented at the 'Democracy in Eastern Asia' Panel, Association for Asian Studies Conference in Toronto on 16 March 2011, and supported by the Social Sciences and Humanities Research Council of Canada.
2 See (K.P. Tan and Lam 1997) for the rationale for introducing direct Presidential Election in 1993 that gives the President limited reserve powers over government expenditure, financial reserves and appointments to key public office.
3 For the mechanical and psychological effects of electoral laws on Singapore's hegemonic party system, see (N. Tan in press).
4 In a Gallup World Poll in 2010, Singapore was ranked 83 out of 150 countries in terms of overall satisfaction with life (Gallup 2010).
5 For the exchanges between Au and the Attorney-General Chambers, see A. Au (2012c).
6 Under the Political Donations Act, gazetted political associations and candidates are prohibited from accepting donations from foreign sources. Singapore law also bans the publication of opinion polls during elections and exit polls on Polling Day before the results are declared (Ong 2011a).
7 Ravi faced the threat of having his legal licence suspended and being committed to the mental institution if he were found mentally unfit to practice. He was later found fit to practice (Wong 2012).
8 A notable and colourful lawyer, Ravi has undertaken many controversial cases such as the mandatory death penalty, the constitutionality of Section 377A, the law that criminalizes male-male sex, and an opposition leader's challenge to the constitutionality of the Singapore government's loan to the International Monetary Fund (A. Au 2012a).
9 For a detailed study of the institutionalization of Singapore's party system, see Wong (2012).
10 Pedersen index measures the volatility by taking the sum of the net change in the percentage of votes gained or lost by each party from one election to the next, divided by two $((\Sigma \, |vit - vit+1|)/2)$.
11 For an excellent critique of the use of the community development councils to mute the antagonistic tendencies of civil society, see Tan & Tan (2003).

References

AsiaOne (2011a) 'Chee Soon Juan Escapes Jail Term'; http://news.asiaone.com/News/AsiaOne+News/Singapore/Story/A1Story20110210-262836.html accessed 25 July 2013.
AsiaOne (2011b) 'No Campaigning Allowed on Cooling-off Day and Polling Day'; www.asiaone.com/News/AsiaOne+News/Singapore/Story/A1Story20110504-277166.html accessed 4 January 2012.
AsiaOne (2011c) 'Singapore PM Says Sorry', 4 May; http://news.asiaone.com/News/AsiaOne+News/Singapore/Story/A1Story20110504-276990.html accessed 10 May 2011.

AsiaOne (2012) 'Yawning Bread Case: AGC Defends Contempt-Of-Court Law'; http://news.asiaone.com/News/Latest+News/Singapore/Story/A1Story20120718-359729.html accessed 25 July 2013.

Au, A. (2009) 'Minimum Nine Opposition MPs from Now On'; www.yawningbread.org/arch_2009/yax-1030.htm accessed 13 August 2012.

Au, A. (2011) 'Police have Nightmare About Boobs', *Yawning Bread*, 13 November; http://yawningbread.wordpress.com/2011/11/13/police-have-nightmare-about-boobs/ accessed 30 December 2011.

Au, Alex (2012a) 'PAP Mis-AIMed, Faces Blowback', *Yawning Bread*; http://yawningbread.wordpress.com/2012/12/29/pap-mis-aimed-faces-blowback-part-2/ accessed 3 April 2013.

Au, A. (2012b) 'The Ghosts of Absent Lawyers', *Yawning Bread*; http://yawningbread.wordpress.com/2012/07/23/the-ghosts-of-absent-lawyers/#more-7831 accessed 1 September 2012.

Au, A. (2012c) 'Using Power to Give Immunity to the Powerful', *Yawning Bread*; http://yawningbread.wordpress.com/2012/07/15/using-power-to-give-immunity-to-the-powerful/ accessed 3 September 2012.

Au, Yong J. and Wong, T. (2011) 'Green Light for New Media Use at GE', 15 March; www.straitstimes.com/BreakingNews/Singapore/Story/STIStory_645270.html accessed 14 March 2011.

BBC (2012) 'Singapore Plans Changes to Mandatory Death Penalty', BBC, 10 July; www.bbc.co.uk/news/world-asia-18778442 accessed 1 September 2012.

Bertelsmann Index (2012) 'Bertelsmann Transformation: Country Reports'; www.bti-project.org/countryreports/aso/sgp/ accessed 17 April 2013.

Case, W. (2002) *Politics in Southeast Asia: Democracy or Less*, Richmond, Surrey: Curzon.

Chan, R. (2012) 'Appeal Filed Against Hougang By-Election Case Decision', *Straits Times*, 3 September; www.straitstimes.com/breaking-news/singapore/story/appeal-filed-against-hougang-election-case-decision-20120903 accessed 3 September 2012.

Chang, S. (2011) 'GE Not an 'Internet Election', AsiaOne, 5 October; http://news.asiaone.com/News/AsiaOne+News/Singapore/Story/A1Story20111005-303216.html accessed 25 July 2013.

Channel NewsAsia (2011) 'Singaporeans Heaviest Internet Users in Southeast Asia', Channel NewsAsia; http://news.xin.msn.com/en/singapore/article.aspx?cp-documentid=5502733 accessed 25 July 2013.

Cheng, T. and Lin, C. (1999) 'Taiwan: a long decade of democratic transition', in James Morley (ed.) *Driven by Growth: Political Change in the Asia-Pacific Region*, Armonk, NY: M.E. Sharpe Inc., pp. 224–254.

Chia, A. (2013) 'Why Punggol East Voters went with WP', *TODAYonline*, 27 January; www.todayonline.com/singapore/no-title-0 accessed 27 January 2013.

Chou, H.H. (2011) 'GE2011 Hot on the Internet', *Straits Times*, 28 April; www.straitstimes.com/GeneralElection/News/Story/STIStory_662345.html accessed 28 April 2011.

Chua, B.H. (1995) *Communitarian Ideology and Democracy in Singapore*, London: Routledge.

Diamond, L. (1999) *Developing Democracy: Toward Consolidation*, Baltimore, Maryland: Johns Hopkins University Press.

Diamond, L. (2002) Thinking about hybrid regimes. *Journal of Democracy*, 13(2), 21–35.

Diamond, L. (2006) 'Public Lecture by Professor Larry Diamond Reports', *IPS*; www.spp.nus.edu.sg/ips/LarryDiamond_retirement_reports_reviews.aspx   accessed   11 September 2012.

Diamond, L. and Morlino, L. (2004) The quality of democracy, *Journal of Democracy*, 15(4), 20–31.

East Asian Barometer (2006) 'East Asian Barometer', East Asian Barometer Second Wave Survey: Singapore, Taiwan, Department of Political Science, National Taiwan University; www.asianbarometer.org/newenglish/surveys/SurveyResults.htm accessed 30 December 2011.

Freedom House (2013) 'Freedom in the World 2011 Survey'; www.freedomhouse.org/report/freedom-world/freedom-world-2011 accessed 25 July 2013.

Gallup (2010) 'Global Wellbeing Index 2010 – Country Rankings', *Geographic*; www.geographic.org/country_ranks/global_wellbeing_index_2010_country_ranks.html accessed 29 December 2011.

Geddes, B. (2003) *Paradigms and Sand Castles: Theory Building and Research Design in Comparative Politics*, Ann Arbour: University of Michigan Press.

George, C. (2012) *Freedom from the Press: Journalism and State Power in Singapore*, Singapore: NUS Press.

Grant, J. (2012) 'Singapore to Reconsider Death Penalty', *Financial Times*, 9 July; previously available at www.ft.com/cms/s/0/56879c74-c9c8–11e1-a5e2–00144feabdc0.html#axzz25ERK16wz accessed 1 September 2012.

Greene, K. (2007) *Why Dominant Parties Lose: Mexico's Democratization in Comparative Perspective*, N.Y.: Cambridge University Press; http://isbndb.com/d/book/why_dominant_parties_lose accessed 24 July 2013.

Gunther, R., Montero, J.R. and Linz, J.J. (2002) *Political Parties: Old Concepts and New Challenges*, Oxford: Oxford University Press.

Hicken, A. and Kuhonta, E.M. (2011) Shadows From the Past: Party System Institutionalization in Asia. *Comparative Political Studies*, 44, 572.

Ho, K.L. (2010) Political consolidation in Singapore, in *Management of Success: Singapore Revisited*, Singapore: Institute of Southeast Asian Studies.

Huntington, S.P. (1965) 'Political development and political decay', *World Politics*, 17(3), 386–430.

Huntington, S. (1991) *The Third Wave: Democratization in the Late Twentieth Century*, Norman: University of Oklahoma Press.

Huntington, S. and Moore, C.H. (1970) *Authoritarian Politics in Modern Society: the Dynamics of Established One-Party Systems*, N.Y.: Basic Books.

Hussain, Z. (2011) 'What Signals Did 2 Million Voters Send in GE 2011?' *Straits Times*.

Hussin, M. (2000) 'Illiberal democracy and the future of opposition in Singapore', *Third World Quarterly*, 21(2), 313–342.

Koh, G. (2005) 'Casino Debate: Laying Out All the Cards', *Stratis Times*, 15 January.

Levitsky, S. and Way, L. (2002) 'The rise of competitive authoritarianism', *Journal of Democracy*, 13(2), 51–65.

Levitsky, S. and Way, L. (2010) 'Why democracy needs a level playing field', *Journal of Democracy*, 21(1), 57–68.

Li, X.Y. (2008) 'Change Must Come to PAP, Rather than a Two-party System', *The Straits Times*, 16 November; http://news.asiaone.com/News/AsiaOne+News/Singapore/Story/A1Story20081116-101017.html accessed 25 July 2013.

Lim, C. (2009) 'Sir, Would You Send in the Army?'; http://catherinelim.sg/2009/09/03/sir-would-you-send-in-the-army/ accessed 28 December 2011.

Lim, S. (2010) 'Constitutional Amendment Bill'; http://v2.wp.sg/2010/04/constitutional-amendment-bill/ accessed 2 January 2012.

Lim, S. (2011) 'Media Release on Use of Public Sites at Aljunied GRC', *Workers' Party*; http://wp.sg/2011/08/media-release-on-use-of-public-sites-at-aljunied-grc/ accessed 2 January 2012.

Loh, A. (2012) 'M Ravi Files Lawsuits Against Wong, Law Society', *Public House*; http://publichouse.sg/categories/community/item/697-m-ravi-files-lawsuits-against-wong-law-society accessed 3 September 2012.

Magaloni, B. (2006) *Voting for Autocracy: Hegemonic Party Survival and Demise in Mexico*, New York: Cambridge University Press.

Mainwaring, S. and Scully, T. (1995) *Building Democratic Institutions: Party Systems in Latin America*, Stanford: Stanford University Press.

Mauzy, D.K. (2002) 'Electoral innovation and one-party-dominance in Singapore', in Hsieh, J.F. and Newman, D. (eds), *How Asia Votes*, NY: Chatham House Pub., pp. 234–254.

Mauzy, D.K. (2006) 'The challenge to democracy Singapore's and Malaysia's resilient hybrid regimes', *Taiwan Journal of Democracy*, 2(2), 47–68.

Mauzy, D.K. and Milne, R.S. (2002) *Singapore Politics Under the People's Action Party*, London & New York: Routledge.

Means, G.P. (1996) 'Soft authoritarianism in Malaysia and Singapore', *Journal of Democracy*, 7(4), 103–117.

Mydans, S. (2011) 'In Singapore, Political Campaigning Goes Viral', *NY Times*; www.nytimes.com/2011/05/06/world/asia/06iht-singapore06.html accessed 15 October 2011.

Norris, P. (2004) *Electoral Engineering: Voting Rules and Political Behaviour*, NY: Cambridge University Press.

O'Donnell, G. and Schmitter, P.C. (1986) *Transitions from Authoritarian Rule: Tentative Conclusions About Uncertain Democracies*, Johns Hopkins University Press, Baltimore.

Ong, A. (2011a) 'Man Arrested Over Election Exit Poll on Website', *Straits Times*, 16 October; www.straitstimes.com/BreakingNews/Singapore/Story/STIStory_723923.html accessed 23 October 2011.

Ong, A. (2011b) 'PAP Wins Holland-Bukit Timah GRC', *Straits Times*, 8 May; www.straitstimes.com/GeneralElection/News/Story/STIStory_666127.html accessed 31 December 2011.

Ong, A. (2011c) 'The New Normal in Politics', *Straits Times*, 30 July; www.scribd.com/doc/61256247/ST-The-New-Normal-in-Politics accessed 29 December 2011.

Ong, A. (2012) 'Workers' Party Expels Veteran Member Poh Lee Guan', 18 July; www.straitstimes.com/BreakingNews/Singapore/Story/STIStory_823686.html accessed 18 July 2012.

Popathal, A. (2007) 'S'pore Cannot Afford Revolving Door Style of Govt: MM Lee', *ChannelNewsAsia*, 4 April; www.channelnewsasia.com/stories/singaporelocalnews/view/268475/1/.html accessed 28 December 2011.

Przeworski, A. (1979) *Some Problems in the Study of the Transition to Democracy*, Latin American Program: Wilson Center.

Przeworski, A. (1986) Problems in the study of the transition to democracy, in O'Donnell, G., Schmitter, P.C. and Whitehead, L. (eds) *Transitions from Authoritarian Rule: Comparative Perspectives*, Baltimore & London: Johns Hopkins University Press, pp. 47–66.

Ramesh, S. (2011) 'Laws to be Reviewed to Deal With Harmful Online Conduct',

Channel NewsAsia; www.channelnewsasia.com/stories/singaporelocalnews/view/ 1159646/1/.html#.TpnCg5XQxI4.facebook accessed 15 October 2011.

Reilly, B. (2007) Political Engineering in the Asia-Pacific, *Journal of Democracy*, 18(1), 58.

Reporters Without Borders (2013) 'Reporters Without Borders – Singapore', *Reporters Without Borders for Freedom of Information*; http://en.rsf.org/press-freedom-index-2013,1054.html accessed 17 April 2013.

Saad, I. (2011) 'Younger S'poreans "More Likely to Back Opposition"', *Channel News-Asia*; www.channelnewsasia.com/stories/singaporelocalnews/view/1157219/1/.html#. Tor-wXR99B0.facebook accessed 4 October 2011.

Saad, I. (2012) 'Workers' Party Expels Yaw Shin Leong', *ChannelNewsAsia*, 15 February; www.channelnewsasia.com/stories/singaporelocalnews/view/1183169/1/.html accessed 15 February 2012.

Salimat, S. (2013) 'Ntu Clarifies Tenure Process After Outcry', *Yahoo! News Singapore*; http://sg.news.yahoo.com/denial-of-tenure-to-ntu-associate-professor-sparks-outcry-125052804.html accessed 1 April 2013.

Sartori, G. (2005) *Parties and Party Systems: a Framework for Analysis*, Colchester, UK: ECPR Press.

Schedler, A. (2010) 'Authoritarianism's last line of defense', *Journal of Democracy*, 21(1), 69–80.

Schlesinger, J. (1984) 'On the theory of party organization', *Journal of Politics*, 46(2), 369–400.

Seah, C.M. (1985) 'The civil service', in Quah, J.S.T., Chan, H.C. and Seah, C.M. (eds) *Government and Politics of Singapore*, USA: Oxford University Press, pp. 92–119.

Seah, C.M. (1987) 'Parapolitical institutions', in Quah, J.S.T., Chan, H.C. and Seah, C.M. (eds) *Government and Politics of Singapore*, USA: Oxford University Press, pp. 173–194.

Singapore Statistics (2011) 'Yearbook of Statistics Singapore', Department of Statistics, Singapore; www.singstat.gov.sg/Publications/publications.html accessed 25 July 2013.

Singh, P. (2011) 'Time to Reform the People's Association?' *Singapore 2025*; http://singapore2025.wordpress.com/2011/07/02/time-to-reform-the-peoples-association/ accessed 2 January 2012.

Slater, D. (2012) 'Southeast Asia: strong-state democratization in Malaysia and Singapore', *Journal of Democracy*, 23(2), 19–33.

Szep, J. (2005) 'Family Deaths Stir Casino Debate in Singapore', *Reuters*; www.singapore-window.org/sw05/050320re.htm accessed 28 December 2011.

Tan, K.P. and Lam, P.E. (1997) *Managing Political Change in Singapore: the Elected Presidency*, London & New York: Routledge.

Tan, K.P. and Tan, A. (2003) 'Democracy and the grassroots sector in Singapore', *Space and Polity*, 7(1), 3–20.

Tan, N. (2013) 'Institutional sources of hegemonic party stability in Singapore' in *Stability and Performance of Political Parties in Southeast Asia*, Singapore: ISEAS.

Tan, N. (in press) 'Manipulating Electoral Laws in One-Party Hegemonic States: The Case of Singapore', *Electoral Studies*; www.sciencedirect.com/science/article/pii/ S0261379413001145, http://dx.doi.org/10.1016/j.electstud.2013.07.014.

Teo, X.W. (2011) 'It is a Surprise For Us that the Resentment is So Deep', *Today Online*, 12 May; previously available at www.todayonline.com/Hotnews/EDC110512–0000330/ It-is-a-surprise-for-us-that-the-resentment-is-so-deep accessed 13 May 2011.

Thio, L.-A. and Tan, K. (2009) *Evolution of a Revolution: Forty Years of the Singapore Constitution*, NY: Routledge.

TOC (2012) 'TOC dismayed by Apparent Reversal of "Light Touch" Approach to Internet Regulation', *The Online Citizen*; previously available at http://theonlinecitizen. com/2012/02/toc-dismayed-by-apparent-reversal-of-light-touch-approach-to-internet-regulation/ accessed 21 February 2012.

US Department Of State (2011) *2010 Human Rights Report: Singapore*, The Office of Electronic Information, US Bureau of Democracy, Human Rights, and Labor; www.state.gov/g/drl/rls/hrrpt/2010/eap/154401.htm accessed 23 December 2011.

Van de Walle, N. (2006) 'Tipping games: when do opposition parties coalesce?' In *Electoral Authoritarianism: The Dynamics of Unfree Competition*, Boulder, CO: Lynne Rienner, pp. 77–94.

Wong, T. (2011) 'Efficient Government Still Top Concern of Voters: IPS Survey', *Straits Times*; www.straitstimes.com/PrimeNews/Story/STIStory_688665.html accessed 9 July 2011.

Wong, T. (2012) 'Psychiatrist Declares M. Ravi Fit to Practise Law', *Straits Times*, 11 October; www.straitstimes.com/breaking-news/singapore/story/psychiatrist-declares-m-ravi-fit-practise-law-20121011 accessed 3 April 2013.

Zakaria, F. (1994) 'A conversation with Lee Kuan Yew, *Foreign Affairs*, 73(2), 109–126.

Part IV

Uncertain transitions to democracy

10 The democratic transition in Myanmar

Will the reforms be sustained?

Helen James

Introduction

The question which forms the core of this chapter, 'Will Myanmar's stunning transition from a military state to a multiparty pluralistic democratic state be sustained?', is of course that at the heart of every Myanmar scholar, citizen and activist, as well as the international community. On the one hand, there are those close to the centre of the political changes who observe the new air of confidence in Myanmar. They can point to the commitment to reform of its President Thein Sein, a former general and former prime minister who served in the military government of Senior General Than Shwe, and the significant steps towards national reconciliation subsequent to the 1 April 2012 by-elections. The latter led to the country's most prominent political dissident, leader of the opposition National League for Democracy (NLD), Daw Aung San Suu Kyi, taking her seat in the 440 member Lower House (Pyithu Hluttaw) of Parliament along with 42 other opposition politicians from her party. On the other hand, there are many, particularly among the expatriate community based in Western countries, and even among scholars of democratic transitions, who take a more sceptical view of the reforms and the transition processes. They are yet to be convinced that the reform processes will continue and that Myanmar will proceed to develop along a democratic trajectory, until it eventually becomes a recognizably consolidated democracy like Japan. Myanmar's chequered political history since independence from the colonial power, Britain, on 4 January 1948, does not give them confidence that this new beginning will be sustained. They look at Myanmar's entrenched authoritarian political culture, wherein the military establishment has been raised on the philosophy that they are best placed to ensure the continued security, unity and development of the country. The many miss-steps along the way to a democratic transition also suggest caution, including the world's longest running civil war, of over five decades, and the country's unsavoury history of repression and egregious human rights abuses perpetrated against Myanmar's ethnic minority people as well as dissidents within its majority Burman population, as tabled annually at the United Nations (UN), and catalogued by international human rights organizations such as Human Rights Watch. There is no doubt of the urgent need for wide-ranging 'root and branch' reform of all aspects of Myanmar's socio-political governance and institutions, if the visions of a thoroughly democratic Myanmar led by a civilian government which receives the loyalty of a subordinated military sector are to be eventually realized. In practical terms, given the extent of the required transformation processes, the movement from the democratic transition phase to a more consolidated democracy, wherein democratic principles are deeply distilled in the general electorate, will take some time.

At this point, although it is possible to refer to many issues which might support either the optimistic or the sceptical perspective on the long-term viability of Myanmar's democratic transition, it is not possible to say definitively which viewpoint will be proven correct; however, the preponderance of views both from Myanmar citizens and elder statesmen in the country, as well as key figures in the international community, suggest that this newest member of the democracy club may be able to gradually make the necessary governance changes to ensure that it will not resile from the reformist programme it has set itself. Drawing on its own internal resources as well as those now made available to the country through the encouraging stance of the international community, Myanmar may be able to sustain this transitional process and emerge into a more mature phase of civilian rule, as Indonesia appears to have accomplished. In examining these key issues, this chapter will discuss some significant political and socio-economic aspects of this transition.

The political framework

Since elections in 2010 pursuant to a national constitution on which a referendum was controversially held in May 2008 whilst the country was reeling from the devastation of Cyclone Nargis, Myanmar has apparently embraced the conventions of civilian government.[1] The NLD had declined to participate in the slow evolution of the constitution drafting process, first commenced in 1993, in protest at what it perceived to be undemocratic practices in the formulation of the constituent assembly. The subsequent almost 20 years of hostilities between the NLD as the main opposition party and the military gave few indications that by 2012 the impasse would be broken and the NLD seated in an elected parliament.

The pace of the reform process has surprised many, raising the hopes of the majority of citizens that Myanmar will at last give priority to improving the standard of living of its entire people. It has also opened the doors to much-needed foreign investment, now in the order of US$800 million over the past nine months (*Mizzima News* 12 February 2013). In 2012, the Asian Development Bank (ADB) estimated that total foreign direct investment since 2007 has been in the order of US$3.8 billion, with some US$2.9 billion being in the oil and gas sectors. Mining (US$450 million) and power (US$390 million) have also attracted significant foreign investment (Asian Development Bank 2012: 31) leading the ADB to proffer an expected 6.3 per cent growth in GDP for the financial year 2012/2013, which is considerably more conservative than that of the notoriously unreliable government estimates of 12.2 per cent, but in advance of the 4.7 per cent estimated by the International Monetary Fund (IMF) in 2012 (Asian Development Bank 2012: 1). In tacit recognition of the importance of economic investment in sustaining the reform process, the World Bank in 2012 re-engaged with Myanmar. It sent experts to assist the elected government with modernizing its economic infrastructure, banking and finance sectors. It also joined an IMF team advising on reforming the country's outdated currency exchange rate (*The Irrawaddy Magazine* 20 February 2012), which until recently was set at six kyats to the US dollar. The Myanmar kyat currently achieves a market rate of around 820 kyats to the US dollar; it is predicted by the Economist Intelligence Unit (EIU) to rise to around 790 kyats to the US dollar in 2013 on the back of strong export growth particularly in the oil and gas sectors, and agricultural products. In this context, the EIU in mid-2012 felt comfortable in predicting a rapid expansion in the Myanmar economy in tandem with ongoing political reforms (Economist Intelligence Unit 2012).

The international community has thus responded positively to the sweeping reform agenda of the new President Thein Sein, and his apparent sincerity in taking steps towards inclusive governance based on multiparty democratic principles. The by-elections of 1 April 2012 which finessed the seating in the Parliament of Daw Aung San Suu Kyi were a critical, symbolic aspect of this series of change processes. They signalled to the outside world that the new Myanmar government formally recognized the necessity to adhere to the changing mores governing state relations with their own citizens as well as with the larger international community. Having 43 representatives in the 440 member Lower House may seem a small proportion (ten per cent), but in terms of Myanmar's political evolution these numbers encapsulate a giant leap forward, as the NLD has now not only officially come out of the cold, but also has assumed an important status as part of a formally functioning opposition bloc which can legally contest the next national elections due in 2015. Until these by-elections, the NLD had been deregistered in 2010 as a consequence of not meeting the electoral laws. Its re-registration and electoral success has been the culmination of a political reform process which has been years in the making, and is an essential step in the much-vaunted national reconciliation agenda, itself a consequence of non-recognition by the then military junta of the electoral victory of the NLD in the previous 1990 elections. Nevertheless, the difficulties in overcoming what Ian Holliday (2011: 192) calls the 'legacy of dictatorship' are substantial, as the electorate seeks to take on the attributes of critical thinking, independent decision-making, and support for capacity building in the civil society sector. Not the least of these difficulties is the fact that the NLD is perceived by its own adherents, as well as those looking on from the outside, to be dysfunctional and in search of relevant policies which will appeal to the electorate ahead of the 2015 elections (*New York Times* 10 March 2013). The re-election of Daw Aung San Suu Kyi as Secretary-General of the NLD at their March 2013 congress will not necessarily alleviate these concerns as many of her supporters have reservations about her recent alleged support for the military, and her siding with the Chinese company

Wanbao against the farmer protesters near Monywa at the site of the Letpadaung copper mine (*New York Times* 14 March 2013; *The Irrawaddy Magazine* 20 February 2012, 15 March 2013). Becoming a politician may prove to be far more complex for Daw Aung San Suu Kyi than was being the country's most prominent dissident.

This almost seamless transformation of Daw Aung San Suu Kyi from political prisoner who has borne long periods of house arrest, to member of the nation's Parliament, should not obscure the important associated reforms of the President and the new government, all of which are almost as significant in terms of restoring the civil and political rights of citizens as is the new status of the NLD leader. Since early 2011, major political initiatives have included release of political prisoners, establishment of an active Human Rights Commission under the venerable Karen scholar, U Tun Aung Chain, commitment to the principle of a free press, repeal of censorship laws and institution of a Myanmar Press Council, and commitment to the principle of freedom of association. Previously, government permission had to be sought for any gathering greater than five persons. The hugely successful Myanmar Writers' Festival, held on 1–3 February 2013 at the Inya Lake Hotel, Yangon, is tangible evidence of the implementation of the reforms respecting freedom of association and the press. Daw Aung San Suu Kyi addressed an assembled throng at the Writers' Festival, which included numerous international guests, many of whom watched her speech broadcast on large screens in the hotel grounds, as the number of participants was too large to fit into the hotel conference hall. Arriving later in the evening of 3 February 2013, I witnessed the excitement pervading the crowd as this symbol of the end of censorship came to a successful conclusion.

Whilst much remains to be done to give real impact to both the political and the socio-economic reforms, and sceptics consider these to be merely superficial moves to win the support of the USA and key Western countries, there is no doubt that the Myanmar people themselves, ordinary citizens, welcome the new approach to governing their country. There is a new air of optimism and hope for the future as Myanmar people travel more, access more news and information, and see more opportunities for participation in the governance structures of their country. A poor fisherwoman from the Delta now has plans to run for national office when the next elections are held in 2015, a formerly unheard of vision.[2] A senior official with a major non-governmental organization (NGO) confidently expects to see Daw Aung San Suu Kyi as the newly elected President when the 2015 elections are held, and he is not afraid to express his views publicly.[3] Clearly, civil society is vibrant and expanding, no longer 'nascent' (James 2004: 66; 2005) or 'fledgling' (Smith 2005: 72), and no longer limiting itself to the provision of social welfare services (Kyaw Yin Hlaing 2007: 167). This development has gathered pace since the 2008 Cyclone Nargis gave the impetus to expansion of the civil society sector (Centre for Peace and Conflict Studies 2009). Expectations of the peaceful transfer of power pursuant to the next national elections in 2015 seem to be permeating the consciousness of many citizens, a significant development in a country which has long witnessed major episodes of political violence (1962, 1974, 1988, 1996 and 2007) along with the repression of democratic aspirations.[4]

Indeed, looking back to the violence and repression manifest in 2007 as a consequence of the 'monks' uprising', itself economic in origin rather than political, it is difficult to recognize the same country. The question is often asked, what precipitated such a profound change? Whilst it is possible to trace the evolution of the democratic transition in the rhetoric of the successive military governments across a number of decades, and particularly since the mid-1990s, this of itself may not fully account for the rapidity of the change. Surely the answer lies partly in the devastation wrought by Cyclone Nargis which opened space for domestic civil society to flourish and come into the open after May 2008 in tandem with the recovery and reconstruction phases. Also this disaster went a long way towards convincing the then military leadership that international assistance was necessary to cope with the magnitude of the losses. The disaster in effect helped to bring about a rapprochement between the then military leadership and the international community.

However, these series of events, which included the visit to the country by UN Secretary-General Ban Ki Moon in 2008, should not obscure the fact that the change processes were set in train and brought to fruition by Myanmar people themselves. They were effected by the then military leadership, which tenaciously (and to the surprise of many observers) held to their outlined plan of action for finalization of a new constitution, a referendum on the constitution, and then national elections. They were also effected by the Myanmar citizens who turned out to vote despite calls from some sections of the international community for them to boycott the elections, and by some of the domestic political parties which worked through the election laws to take their seats in the Parliament. In 2010 when these change processes were in train, the presence of the international community was still relatively absent, only returning in force once the elections had been held and the new civilian government ensconced. In effect, this has been a socio-political change initiated from the 'top', by 'top-down' processes, not one derived from grassroots forces acting in a 'bottom-up' approach. Myanmar's democratic transition has come about and is evolving more along the lines of South Korea's in the early 1990s, and Chile's in a similar time frame, rather than by revolution from below, or invasion from without, a fact that may ultimately contribute significantly to the prospects for future democratic consolidation in the country.

By mid-2012, after some 18 months in office, the new government had ticked some of the most important boxes of political reform, including a new constitution, a bicameral parliament (albeit with 25 per cent of seats reserved for appointed military personnel) and the holding of national elections. Whilst these elections were not free from blemish they did provide Myanmar's citizens with a greatly welcomed opportunity to participate in a process long withheld from them. Other achievements include the NLD seated in the parliament, and freedom of the press and freedom of association now included in the public policy processes of governance. In return, and in recognition of the importance of these changes, in 2012 the USA, EU and Australia moved to lift or 'suspend' most of the sanctions in place against the country. This policy change was long overdue. It implicitly acknowledged that a range of issues unique to Myanmar, which included 'its geopolitical relationships, its comparative de-linking from the global international trade regime ... [and] its firm support in the Security Council by China and Russia' (James 2010: 443) meant that sanctions alone would not achieve their stated objective of restoring democracy to Myanmar. Some sanctions remain which restrict the visa and travel arrangements of those most associated with egregious human rights abuses during the era of military dictatorship. In March 2013, the USA removed the financial sanctions affecting four of Myanmar's banks, implicit recognition of the importance of supporting the political economy of the new governance arrangements (*The Irrawaddy Magazine* 15 March 2013). Lifting or suspension of the sanctions in itself has been controversial, as opponents among the exile and activist communities outside the country continue to caution against what they see as too rapid a scaling back of the international sanctions regime lest there be a regression from the reform programme. However, under the administration of President Obama, the USA and major Western countries have considered that it is timely to take these steps as part of a concerted programme to encourage Myanmar to continue with its democratic transition. There is also recognition that the suspension of sanctions is part of the essential mix of measures required to address the dire poverty that afflicts the majority of Myanmar's citizens, some 25–35 per cent of whom live below the internationally recognized poverty line of less than US$2 per day (Asian Development Bank 2012). In 2002, the agriculture sector (including livestock, fisheries and forestry) was reported to employ 64 per cent of the labour force and provide 48 per cent of GDP (World Bank 2002). However, in 2012, the ADB stated that agriculture now provides 36 per cent of GDP, but still accounts for the majority of the labour force (Asian Development Bank 2012: 18), reportedly the 70 per cent who are small-scale farmers (*The Irrawaddy Magazine* 20 February 2012). The change over the last few years derives from the much larger proportion of GDP now provided by the oil and gas sectors, said to be in the realm of around 43 per cent (Asian Development Bank 2012: 29). Widespread industrialization has not yet come to Myanmar, despite the vast wealth beginning to flow into the country from its oil and gas reserves, and from increasing foreign direct investment.[5]

A series of international visits by President Thein Sein to the USA in 2012 and to Norway in March 2013, and by Daw Aung San Suu Kyi to the USA and Europe in mid-2012, was accompanied by a highly successful visit to Myanmar by President Obama on 19 November 2012. The first ever visit to Myanmar by a US President, Obama met with President Thein Sein at the new capital at Naypyidaw and visited the famous Shwe Dagon Pagoda in Yangon. Citizens of Myanmar streamed into the streets of Yangon to catch a glimpse of his motorcade as he drove to Yangon University where he addressed the assembled academic community, students and carefully selected invited guests. On that day, Daw Aung San Suu Kyi also was welcomed at Yangon University and addressed the assembly, a very important mark of the reconciliation processes being implemented. These series of visits, greatly welcomed by the people of Myanmar, were widely interpreted as restoring international recognition to Myanmar for its progress in implementing civil and political rights. Further recognition was accorded by the Association of Southeast Asian Nations (ASEAN) when Myanmar was placed in line to assume the chair of the association in 2014, a far cry from the earlier attempt some years previously which was blocked by the USA and major Western nations.

Many commentators use the overworked term 'fragile' to describe the democratic transition in Myanmar (*Guardian* 22 March 2012; *Democratic Voice of Burma* 8 August 2012; *New York Times* 21 September 2012), and from one perspective, it could hardly be otherwise given the country's decades (1962–2010) of repressive authoritarian military rule since Ne Win's coup of March 1962, and the difficulties in negotiating the transition among the many vested interests both civilian and military, which hold significant economic power through the Union of Myanmar Economic Holdings (UMEH), as well as military power. Indeed, it has often been said that the Myanmar military represent a 'state within a state' who have 'amassed enormous wealth and power' (Callahan 2004: 212–214) through their control of state resources and state-building activities during their decades in power. In addition to the wide-ranging civilian business and bureaucracy-based interests whose activities spun off the military institutions, these vested interests represent a very significant bloc which the new government needs to navigate and negotiate with, as it seeks to embed a reformist culture based on the rule of law and respect for human rights.

A stark reminder of how skin-deep the implementation of civil and political rights is was provided in November 2012 when police resorted to violence against protesters at the Letpadaung copper mine in Upper Myanmar outside the town of Monywa, who were exercising their newly restored rights of association and protest (*The Irrawaddy Magazine* 29 November 2012; BBC News 24 January 2013). The amazing backflip by police who were prevailed on to apologize to protesters, formerly an unheard of outcome, was perhaps an indicator of Myanmar's recent concerted attempts to uphold the restored civil and political rights. A formal investigation into the events was set in train under the aegis of Daw Aung San Suu Kyi, and a report was presented on 13 March 2013 (*Agence-France Presse* 13 March 2013; *Mizzima News* 13 March 2013). This disappointed the protesters, however, as she recommended that they cease their protests and recognize that the mining operations would be beneficial to the economy. Another parallel investigation has been launched by the country's Human Rights Commission in recognition of the implications of the appalling actions of police against the demonstrators.[6] From another perspective, government reactions to the incident could be interpreted as an indicator of the importance of current President Thein Sein in guiding the transition, an issue which will be discussed further in this chapter.

Nevertheless, the government is not without its own domestic critics. Many consider that the reforms are superficial, are being implemented too slowly, and do not sufficiently go to the heart of changing Myanmar's authoritarian governance cultures and structures. Nor, it is felt, do they address the necessary socio-economic structural changes which will bring better quality of life to the majority of citizens. While much needs to be done, citizen expectations in the new socio-political environment are high, but frustrated by the slow pace of delivery, in itself an inherent part of the democratic processes requiring negotiation and consultation, as well as legislation. Moreover, there is a perception among some of the more educated citizenry that the government is too slow in delivering the benefits of democracy.[7] However, while Freedom House (2013: 8) continues to cite abuses of power arising from corruption and lack of an independent judiciary, it also concedes that political rights and civil liberties in Myanmar have improved. Significantly, in a comparative context, the Freedom House report compares Myanmar favourably with the People's Republic of China: 'For all its lingering problems, Burma (*sic*) has now surpassed China on both political rights and civil liberties.' This aspect of the changing governance in Myanmar has been made apparent in the numerous protests by Myanmar farmers who are anxious about the new draft Land Act, and the widespread land-grabs in Ayeyarwaddy and Yangon divisions as well as other parts of the country. As priority is being given to turn agriculture into an export-oriented business, instead of a sector based on small farms (*The Irrawaddy Magazine* 20 February 2012), the 70 per cent of the country's work force who are small farmers fear that their livelihoods will be eroded.

Conscious of the 'great expectations' among the citizenry, in August 2012 President Thein Sein launched into the second tranche of his political reforms. He announced a cabinet reshuffle which was widely welcomed both inside Myanmar and in the international press as long overdue. It was seen as a necessary step towards regaining momentum for the reform processes through strengthening the democratic and civilian characteristics of his government. Interpreted as a move to bring capable technocrats from non-military backgrounds into the inner policymaking circles of his government, the cabinet reshuffle seemed intended to give the President more scope for limiting the influence of the conservatives among the military representatives in the Parliament. Approved by Parliament on the final day of the session,[8] the reorganization emphasized two key aspects of Myanmar's continuing evolution to full democratic governance: (1) socio-economic reform and (2) inclusive peace with the ethnic minority peoples, perhaps the most important and difficult issue facing the new government. The changes enabled the President to draw on ministers and deputy ministers with sound economic credentials who are expected to support his reformist programme. They entail streamlining the two Ministries of electric power into one, and abolishing the Myanmar Industrial Development Ministry, leaving the government operating around 31 Ministries, but with an overall increase in the number of ministers and deputy ministers to 36, including 15 new deputy ministers.

Thus the ministers attached to the Prime Minister's Office were increased to six, a change expected to expedite decision-making (*Myanmar Times* 3–9

September 2012). These include U Aung Min (former Minister for Rail Transportation) who is recognized as contributing to the ceasefire talks with the ethnic minority armies, and U Hla Tun (former Minister for Finance) and U Soe Thein (former Minister for Industry), both considered key contributors to ongoing economic reforms. Amongst those elevated to the Ministry were former Deputy Minister for National Planning and Economic Development, Professor Kan Zaw, a former rector of the Agricultural University in Upper Myanmar who did his doctorate in Japan and has published widely on development economics, and the former Acting Rector of the Institute of Economics, Professor Khin San Yee, who did her doctorate in Germany, and is recognized as a committed reformer and lateral thinker who is not afraid to take the initiative. Professor Khin San Yee was appointed as the new Deputy Minister for National Planning and Economic Development. In another 'first', Dr Myat Myat Ohn Khin, a medical doctor and former Deputy Minister for Health, was appointed Minister for Social Welfare, Relief and Resettlement, the 'first and only' female Minister in the Cabinet. (*The Irrawaddy Magazine* 7 September 2012). Other former deputy ministers promoted to the full Ministry are: U Htay Aung, Minister for Tourism; Dr Ko Ko Oo, Minister for Science and Technology; U Win Shein, Minister for Finance and Revenue; U Kyaw Lwin, Minister for Construction; U Maung Myint, Minister for Labour (formerly Deputy Minister for Foreign Affairs); and U Aye Myint Kyu, Minister for Culture (and formerly Deputy Minister for Sport). New Auditor-General Thein Htike, the former Mining Minister, replaces Lun Maung, one of those who resigned or, in Myanmar parlance, were 'permitted to retire', while Civil Service Board member, Dr Myint Aung, was appointed to succeed Thein Htike as Minister of Mining. Joining the cabinet also is key economic adviser, U Set Aung, a move interpreted as a sign of 'growing political openness' (*Myanmar Times* 3–9 September 2012).

A change considered very significant for those monitoring Myanmar's democratic progress was the removal of the powerful former Minister for Information, U Kyaw Hsan, to become the Minister for Cooperatives, and his replacement by former Labour Minister, U Aung Kyi. As Minister for Information, U Kyaw Hsan had presided over the pre-publication censorship of the press, no longer appropriate in view of the President's initiatives towards removing restrictions on media freedom. Another change seen as strengthening the hand of the reformers is the replacement of arch-conservative Thiha Thura U Tin Aung Myint Oo (resigned for 'health' reasons) by the new chief Admiral Nyan Tun as one of Myanmar's vice-presidents. Admiral Nyan Tun is seen as a moderate, believed to be committed to the reform process and not to have been involved in human rights violations (*Wall Street Journal* 15 August 2012). The other significant change was the replacement of former Defence Minister, Lt General Hla Min by Lt Gen Wai Lwin. Overall, President Thein Sein was perceived to be drawing on the strengths of moderate elements in the military bloc and capable technocrats and civilians on whom he could rely to carry forward his reform agenda. In making these changes, the President seems to have given considerable care to being perceived to be 'inclusive', and not making changes which could be interpreted as seeking to exclude the military from office. In this, his approach is reminiscent of that of Nelson Mandela after the end of apartheid in South Africa when President Mandela in 1994 was concerned to follow policies which specifically included the key institutions among the military and airforce of the former regime, a conciliatory move intended to demonstrate that all had a place in the new society.

Whilst the changes were welcomed by a wide variety of representatives including those from some of the key ethnic minority groups, notably silent among commentators was direct mention of the Education portfolio, in late 2012 the centre of controversy over proposed legislation regarding greater autonomy for the universities. This is a key issue in view of the need for far-reaching educational reform which will lay the groundwork for the human resource development not only critical to Myanmar's economic development, but also to its continued evolution towards democratic consolidation. Shortly before the August 2012 cabinet reshuffle, Dr Myo Myint was moved from the Foreign Affairs portfolio to become one of the new Deputy Ministers in the Education Ministry, responsible for International Relations, an indicator of expected increasing collaboration with foreign universities and academics. Given that a key critic of the draft legislation put forward by the Minister for Education, Dr Mya Aye, is the powerful speaker of the Lower House and member of the military bloc in the Parliament, former general Shwe Mann, this piece of legislation could be one of the litmus tests of the new cabinet line up. This is because universities have always been considered sources of dissent and potential mobilization for democratic voices urging further reform (*Mizzima News* 7 August 2012). Many serving academics, however, are not enthusiastic about decentralization of responsibility to the universities and prefer the current hierarchical arrangements whereby all approvals need to be sought from Ministerial level. These are still unresolved issues. They go to the heart of developing a citizenry which can participate in, and benefit from, the democratic processes now underway in Myanmar. Discussions in Yangon in February 2013, however, confirm the government's intentions to reintroduce a revised Education Bill which will provide the basis for far-reaching educational reforms.[9]

Concurrent with approval of the new Ministerial line up, Parliament also approved the new Foreign Direct Investment Law, designed to offer greater incentives to foreign companies to invest (*New York Times* 29 August 2012). This not only signals that economic reform is at the top of the President's agenda, but that also its inherently political nature and the political difficulties involved in delivering and implementing economic reform are not simple. Vested domestic economic interests long entwined with UMEH and considerable government involvement in the economy may need to be accommodated, reformed or phased out as foreign direct investment proceeds. There is already considerable citizen hostility to wide-ranging Chinese investment in the resources sector (BBC News 24 January 2013). Whilst citizen expectations for democratic governance are high, they also want to see the benefits of democracy flow to all the people, not just the few, as in the days of military dictatorship.

In a country where poverty alleviation measures on a national scale are urgent, the consequences of the government failing to deliver on socio-economic reform could be dire. It is well to note that, historically, periods of civil unrest in Burma/ Myanmar have frequently been associated with economic difficulties. The government therefore needs to examine the institutional structures which guide the distribution of the nation's wealth to the citizenry, including taxation reform, a very sensitive issue. Citing the need to increase government revenues in order to fund the necessary socio-economic reforms, the Asian Development Bank (2012: 5–6) reported that of all regional countries, Myanmar has the lowest government income from taxation, a mere 3.6 per cent of GDP during the period 2004–2010.

Socio-economic reforms

There is widespread recognition among the electorate that while the reforms affecting the civil and political fabric are important, they are still quite superficial. Major steps need to be taken to bring about meaningful improvement in the quality of life of the majority of citizens. There is an urgent need to undertake a thoroughgoing reform of the legal system, much of which has been inherited from the colonial era, and to improve and strengthen the independence of the judiciary. Similarly pressing are measures to root out corruption and to modernize and streamline the regulations governing the bureaucracy to make it more efficient, if the citizenry is to be able to benefit from improved economic, social and cultural rights, which are the other side of the coin from civil and political rights. The infrastructure in Yangon has improved, potholes have been filled in, old buildings renovated and painted, luxury cars and new taxis abound, and coffee shops, Internet cafes, and new businesses are springing up everywhere. Nevertheless, the restrictive legislation governing the bureaucracy and everyday life of the citizenry is still in place. Outside Yangon and Mandalay, the second city, infrastructure is desperately in need of repair and development.

While the conversion to electoral politics after the decades of authoritarian military rule is greatly welcomed and celebrated in the country both in urban and rural areas, there is also a strong sense that electoral politics is only part of the picture. Meaningful reforms of the institutional structures affecting the distribution of the nation's wealth are now not only anxiously awaited, but expected. As in other countries across Asia, the people of Myanmar want the benefits of democratic governance to flow to them in real, measurable ways which produce an improved quality of life, better education, better health services, housing, transport, employment opportunities, and capacity to participate fully in the nation's life and future. If the civil and political reforms are not followed by meaningful socio-economic improvements, but result in the benefits of democratic governance staying in the hands of an elite few, then it is highly likely that a sense of disillusionment will set in. As Morten Pedersen (2008: 104–105) reminds us, civilian politicians and civilian political parties have historically not been held in high esteem in Myanmar. Many have been seen as venal and self-seeking. If the civilian government falters or fails to deliver an improved quality of life for the Myanmar people, the resulting discontent could prove fertile ground for any ambitious individual seeking to reverse the democratic changes.

An important aspect of the socio-economic reform programme will be reskilling the younger generation to facilitate access to quality education which will support the country's economic development. The parlous state of the country's human resource development (James 2003, 2004, 2005, 2006, 2010; Tin Maung Maung Than 2007; Asian Development Bank 2012) is sometimes cited as an impediment to its economic recovery and to its capacity to participate fully in the market economy which increased foreign direct investment is bringing. In recognition of this nexus between education and economic development, the Australian Foreign Minister, Bob Carr, during his brief visit to Myanmar in June 2012, announced a major upgrade in Australia's aid programme targeted at assisting the improvement in Myanmar's primary education. This, however, is but one aspect; similar major contributions need to be made to improve all other aspects of Myanmar's education system – middle school, high school, tertiary and technical education – to support its fledgling democracy. At present, children in many rural areas often cannot even complete primary school education unless there is a teacher who can teach both of the final two years of the primary school curriculum. If they are fortunate enough to have such a teacher in the school, they may then be unable to travel the significant distances required to a middle or high school or they may be unable to travel there safely often because of the dangerous rivers that must be crossed. For many children therefore, education stops before the end of primary school, between the ages of nine and ten years old.[10] In recognition of this need, the USA and key American universities have embarked on major technical assistance programmes in strategic areas of education and health.[11] These are long-term investments; it will take several decades for Myanmar to address all the socio-economic aspects of its reform programme, and the patience of both its citizenry and the international community will be often tested. Yet it is imperative to remember that democracy in the West has also had a long gestation, and while Myanmar is in a position to benefit from the examples and missteps of other countries, it is not unreasonable to expect that, like neighbouring Thailand, there will be some temporary backward steps along its path to democratic consolidation.

One of the major expected benefits of Myanmar's move towards democratic governance of course is an anticipated heightened respect for human rights, which have been violated by successive governments in Burma/Myanmar since independence in 1948. While there is not necessarily a direct correlation between economic prosperity, democratic governance, upholding the rule of law, and respect for human rights, it is certain that poverty breeds the conditions in which repression, dictatorship and corruption flourish – and that all of these are precursors of human rights abuse. As economic reforms and more equitable distribution of the nation's wealth deliver more widespread enjoyment of prosperity among the majority of Myanmar's people, the resources to redress the causes of human rights abuses should become available at the institutional levels of government. Redressing the widespread human rights abuses for which Myanmar has been infamous requires a concerted economic reform programme, including major investment from abroad, further liberalization of investment and reformed taxation laws, and a revamped education system that rewards merit.

As mentioned above, the socio-economic reforms will need to include a total renovation of the judiciary and the legal system, both the system of criminal justice, and property rights and common law more broadly. If the rule of law is a major cornerstone of democratic governance and respect for human rights, instituting an independent and incorruptible judiciary must be a high priority. High on the reformers' agenda are measures to address corruption throughout society, from the criminal justice system to the routine of 'buying' employment and examination results. Widespread corruption may not seem to be in the same category of human rights abuses as those carried out against ethnic minority peoples, but they impugn the socio-economic rights of citizens to a similar degree, preventing them from achieving their full capacity and enjoying the freedom to build their lives as they might wish. Steps towards dealing with this problem were taken on 7 February 2013, when the Myanmar government announced anti-corruption measures against 17,000 civil servants, a sign of the government's policy to achieve 'clean' government.

Threats to the sustainability of the transition

The current optimism and indeed euphoria of the transition depends largely on the continuing guidance of current President Thein Sein, who is seen as a peacemaker. Yet paradoxically, one of the major threats to the transition could also reside with him, specifically his health. While one would not wish to overplay this element, there is no doubt that he has a huge responsibility to deliver on the expectations which the transition has aroused, and any serious impediment to his health or his being able to continue in office until the next elections may set in train a series of adverse events. He is reported to have said that he will be happy to see Daw Aung San Suu Kyi become president if the people elect her at the 2015 elections; he is also reported to be considering stepping aside from office at the 2015 elections (*Mizzima News* 12 February 2013) as part of a strategy to assist the peaceful transfer of power, a critical element in the transition processes and Myanmar's continuing progress towards becoming a consolidated democracy. Clearly the President does not wish to be seen as an elected leader who then is unable to leave the office when his term expires.

A second threat could arise after the 2015 elections if, as is supposed, Daw Aung San Suu Kyi wins the elections, becomes President and uses her new office to set in train another series of political reforms aimed at changing the constitution to eliminate or reduce the military bloc in the parliament as she foreshadowed following the 1 April 2012 by-elections. This could provoke a coup by the military bloc who are not yet acculturated to serving under a civilian government, and continue to view civilian politicians with disdain. An ominous move in this direction became apparent in late February 2013 when Air Force General Myat Hein was appointed as Union Minister for Communications and

Information Technology. This appointment has been interpreted as the military bloc flexing its muscles to ensure that any perception that it was being reduced in importance following the earlier cabinet reshuffle was misconceived (*The Irrawaddy Magazine* 27 February 2013). Simultaneous confirmation of a US$1.15 billion budget for the military, equal to about 21 per cent of the national budget, seemed intended to reassure the military of the continuing support of the civilian government and the priority being accorded to national security. The majority of MPs, some 445, approved the budget allocation, with only 60 against and seven abstaining.

It is not yet sure, of course, that Daw Aung San Suu Kyi will be victorious in the 2015 elections, although many in civil society confidently expect her to become President. At present, her support in the Parliament is quite small in numerical terms, and although there could well be divergent views among both the military bloc inside and outside the Parliament, it is not impossible that another 'civilianized' former general could emerge to contest the 2015 elections. In some quarters, the name of the powerful Speaker of the House, former general Shwe Mann, is touted as a successor to President Thein Sein. Whoever contests the elections, it would appear certain that it is too early for Myanmar to seek to eliminate the military bloc in the Parliament through changing the constitution which guarantees them 25 per cent of the seats. Regardless of whoever wins the 2015 elections, a critical element in the sustainability of Myanmar's transition will be changing the culture of the Myanmar military to acculturate them to serving loyally under a civilian government, as in the consolidated democracies of the West. This will take some time, astute handling, and the willingness of key regional players like Australia to provide training opportunities for middle level Myanmar military personnel in the policies and institutional culture required of the military in a civilian government. It will be necessary for the Myanmar military to realize that their vested interests and socio-economic advantages are not threatened under a democratically elected civilian government, otherwise the propensity for the Myanmar military to resort to coups to protect their status and privileged position in society could become a frequent occurrence, as has happened in neighbouring Thailand. However, the Myanmar military is not monolithic, and diverse political views abound (Taylor 2009: 476–485; Pedersen 2008: 150–168), a feature made overtly public during the 2007 'monks' uprising' in the aftermath of which a number of senior military figures reportedly absconded and fled to Thailand in protest at the violence exacted against the Buddhist monks.

A third potential threat to the democratic transition could arise from within the international community itself through the USA overplaying its hand, and perhaps seeking more political, economic and strategic advantages than the Myanmar government is presently willing to grant. The US encirclement of China policy may have encouraged it to change its approach to Myanmar and to seek to make the country an ally for the future, given its key geopolitical position, but there will be many in Myanmar government circles who do not forget that China has been a good and trusted friend to the country when there were few others. This role for China was recently on display when it sent representatives to take part in the peace negotiations with the Kachin Independence Organization in February 2013 (*Straits Times* 9 February 2013). Given extensive Chinese investment in the country, and the strategic importance of Myanmar to both the USA and China, and the long-term contracts placed with China for Myanmar's oil and gas resources, it is too early to count China out of the equation. Myanmar is likely to keep old friends while welcoming new ones, and if new friends prove difficult, Myanmar could possibly return to its traditional 'balancing' policies.

A fourth threat to the stability of the new government is perhaps the most difficult for it to deal with. This is the continuing violence in the ethnic minority areas, specifically in the north in Kachin state, and in the southwest in Rakhine state with respect to the Rohingya people. The concerted peacemaking efforts of the civil society leader, Reverend Saboi Joi, head of the Shalom Foundation, at last appear to be bearing fruit to bring about a ceasefire and negotiations in Kachin state, but the communal violence in Rakhine state appears almost insoluble. The Office of the United Nations High Commissioner for Refugees (UNHCR) and the Myanmar Human Rights Commission have both exerted serious efforts to achieve a settlement which will satisfy both the international community and the Myanmar citizenry, many of whom have extremely negative views of the disenfranchised, stateless Muslim Rohingya. Since the latest eruption of communal violence in June 2012 between the Muslim Rohingya and the Buddhist Rakhine following the rape and murder of a Buddhist woman by three Muslim men, emotions and tensions have run very high on both sides, leading to atrocities, burning of villages, and mass exodus of Muslim Rohingya by boat to seek refuge in neighbouring Bangladesh, which closed its border against them, and to Malaysia. Even rational Myanmar citizens hold very negative views of Rohingya, who must be among the most deprived people on earth. If the issue of ethnic violence cannot be satisfactorily resolved in accordance with international norms, the new democratically elected government may find that its credentials are not as well recognized as they perhaps should be. In late February 2013, Daw Aung San Suu Kyi, responding to international criticism of Myanmar over its treatment of Rohingya, reportedly stated that citizenship for the Rohingya (of which they were deprived under the 1982 Citizenship Law) is an internal matter for Myanmar to resolve (*The Irrawaddy Magazine* 27 February 2013), a stance which disconcerted many of her international supporters. If one of the hallmarks of a consolidated democracy is that it is inclusive in its public policy and governance structures towards all those who live within its boundaries, another is its capacity to build a successful multicultural society around diverse groups and cultures. The case of the Rohingya will be a critical test for the new democratic government. Myanmar will need to find ways to achieve these characteristics if its transition is to prove both credible and sustainable.

It is also possible to exaggerate the 'threats' to the continuation of the transition and to its capacity to give rise to a consolidated democracy. Political analysis tends to be dichotomous, framed around Western perceptions of how it is envisaged 'ideal' democracies should work, while overlooking that most democracies operative today are far from 'ideal' in the way they distribute power throughout their societies. Distancing oneself from the usual military/civilian categorization of governance, it is possible to see that government in Burma/Myanmar typically draws on the strengths of both sectors in a context where the political classes and Myanmar people more generally give high priority to stability, national unity and national security and this perception crosses the alleged military/civilian divide. The NLD itself is stocked with ex-military personnel, just as successive 'civilian' governments in the country have at times drawn on the military sector for the required skilled personnel. It might be timely to adjust our thinking on Myanmar governance and cease dichotomous categorizations. Along these lines, Aung-Thwin and Aung-Thwin correctly point to the 'hybrid' (2012: 283) character of government in Myanmar, arguing that the 'oscillation between the two forms of government' (i.e. civilian and military) tends to obscure the 'symbiotic relationship' between the two sectors 'whereby members of one invariably participated in the other' (Aung-Thwin and Aung-Thwin 2012: 283). This approach allows resource sharing across the sectors, which may be beneficial in the present situation. It may assist the country to overcome the deep historically-based schisms and be able to move towards a more unified society. Certainly, Myanmar's turbulent modern history has generated distaste for chaos and instability among large sectors of the population, so that this 'oscillation', as Aung-Thwin and Aung-Thwin identify, the major military/civilian synergies, tends to see government gravitate to stable institutions and eschew unstable ones. This natural, perhaps uniquely Myanmar, tendency in the approach to government could provide the country with the resources to navigate the shoals of the democratic transition without resiling from its socio-economic and political reform programme. Perhaps in recognition of the fact that she may need the support of the military to both achieve and stay in power, Daw Aung San Suu Kyi in early 2013 reportedly stated that she is 'very fond' of the military (*New York Times* 10 March 2013), a position which her domestic supporters found as disconcerting as her stance on the Rohingya for her international supporters.

Conclusion

While it is early in the democratic transition for Myanmar, indications at present are that there is significant goodwill in the international community towards the country and that this is resulting in the provision of the assistance and resources Myanmar needs to enable it to progress from transitional state to consolidated democracy. Reforms embracing freedom of the press, multiparty elections, freedom of association, establishment of a Human Rights Commission, and a new foreign direct investment law, have all been received with plaudits in both the international community and among Myanmar citizens. They give hope that Myanmar will be able to progress towards becoming a consolidated democracy. Achieving successful elections in 2015 and a peaceful passage of power will be critically important; achieving far-reaching socio-economic reforms which improve the quality of life of the majority of citizens will take longer, but will be no less important to the long-term sustainability of the democratic transition. As the twenty-first century proceeds, and the possibility of major power competition between the USA and China intensifies, the geopolitics inherent in Myanmar's future democratic governance could be of paramount importance for the future security of the Asian region. Current US investments in the democratic transition in Myanmar are doubtless designed within this regional security context. This set of circumstances also has major implications for the Myanmar military, which could well take a central role in future regional security policy, a fact not lost on US international policy strategists. As in the Cold War era, the Myanmar military could once again become the recipients of substantial US military aid. Thus perhaps President Thein Sein's conciliatory policies towards the military bloc in the Parliament are not just driven by short-term domestic considerations. Perhaps they should be viewed in the wider and longer-term context of a necessary, ongoing and central role for the Myanmar military both in sustaining the democratic transition, and in moving with the country towards democratic consolidation.

Notes

1 Cyclone Nargis swept up the eastern side of the Burmese Delta, leaving over 140,000 dead or missing on the night of 2–3 May 2008. The exact number of mortalities may never be known.
2 Fieldwork in the Burmese Delta, November 2012.
3 Personal communication, November 2012.
4 Interview with NGO leader, November 2012.
5 Myanmar is reported to have natural gas reserves of between 7.8 and 10 trillion cubic feet. It exports over 1.16 billion cubic feet per day from the Yetagun and Yadana fields to Thailand. Although national income from these sales is not transparent, in 2007 it was estimated at US$2.7 billion. See *World Security Network* (2007). It also has reported proven oil reserves of 2.1 billion barrels. See Asian Development Bank (2012: 16).
6 Personal discussion with chairman of Human Rights Commission February 2013.
7 Discussions with NGO leaders, Yangon, November 2012 and February 2013.
8 Parliament approved the President's nominees for the Ministries of Defence; Railways; Construction; Social Welfare, Relief and Resettlement; Culture; Finance and Revenue; Labour; Tourism; National Planning and Economic Development; Mining; Science and Technology; and a new Auditor-General.
9 Discussion with Deputy Education Minister, Dr U Ba Shwe, 4–5 February 2013.
10 To get to a middle school, many children living in the Burmese Delta would need to travel for several hours and cross a wide dangerous river if they were to go to the next level of education, as there are no roads from their villages to the schools. This means that they stop education at primary level.
11 The Integrated Household and Living Conditions Survey (UNDP 2010) shows that many Sub Rural Health Centres, which are closest to farming villages, in the four most densely populated southern divisions, have no trained medical staff, few medicines, and are only open for a few days per month.

References

Agence-France Presse, 13 March 2013.

Asian Development Bank (2012) *Myanmar in Transition: Opportunities and Challenges*, Manila: Asian Development Bank.

Aung-Thwin, Michael and Maitri Aung-Thwin (2012) *A History of Myanmar since Ancient Times: Traditions and Transformations*, London: Reaktion Books.

BBC News, 24 January 2013.

Callahan, M. (2004) *Making Enemies: War and State Building in Burma*, Singapore: Singapore University Press, NUS.

Centre for Peace and Conflict Studies (2009) *Listening to Voices from Inside: Myanmar Civil Society's Response to Cyclone Nargis*, Pnom Penh: CPCS.

Democratic Voice of Burma, 8 August 2012.

Economist Intelligence Unit (2012) *Myanmar Country Report*, February.

Freedom House (2013) 'Freedom in the World: Annual Report on Political Rights and Civil Liberties'; www.freedomhouse.org accessed 15 March 2013.

Guardian, 22 March 2012.

Holliday, I. (2011) *Burma Redux: Global Justice and the Quest for Political Reform in Myanmar*, New York: Columbia University Press.

James, H. (2003) 'Cooperation and community empowerment in Myanmar', *Journal of Asian-Pacific Economic Literature*, 17(1), 1–21.

James, H. (2004) 'King Solomon's Judgment', in John H. Badgley (ed.) *Reconciling Burma/Myanmar: Essays on U.S. Relations with Burma, NBR Analysis*, 15(1): 55–66.

James, H. (2005) *Governance and Civil Society in Myanmar: Education, Health and Environment*, London and New York: RoutledgeCurzon.

James, H. (2006) *Security and Sustainable Development in Myanmar*, Contemporary Southeast Asia Series, London and New York: RoutledgeCurzon.

James, H. (2010) 'Resources, rent-seeking and reform in Thailand and Myanmar (Burma): the economics-politics nexus,' *Asian Survey*, 50(2), 426–448.

Kyaw Yin Hlaing (2007) 'Associational life in Myanmar', in N. Ganesan and Kyaw Yin Hlaing (eds) *Myanmar: State, Society and Ethnicity*, Singapore: ISEAS, pp. 143–171.

Mizzima News, 7 August 2012.

Mizzima News, 12 February 2013.

Mizzima News, 13 March 2013.

Myanmar Times, 3–9 September 2012.

New York Times, 29 August 2012.

New York Times, 21 September 2012.

New York Times, 10 March 2013.

New York Times, 14 March 2013.

Pedersen, M. (2008) *Promoting Human Rights in Burma: A Critique of Western Sanctions Policy*, New York: Rowman and Littlefield Publishers.

Smith, M. (2005) 'Ethnic politics and regional development in Myanmar: the need for new approaches', in Kyaw Yin Hlaing, R.H. Taylor and Tin Maung Maung Than (eds) *Myanmar: Beyond Politics to Societal Imperatives*, Singapore: ISEAS, pp. 56–85.

Straits Times, 9 February 2013.

Taylor, R. (2009) *The State in Myanmar*, London: Hurst and Company.

The Irrawaddy Magazine, 20 February 2012.

The Irrawaddy Magazine, 7 September 2012.

The Irrawaddy Magazine, 29 November 2012.

The Irrawaddy Magazine, 27 February 2013.
The Irrawaddy Magazine, 15 March 2013.
Tin Maung Maung Than (2007) 'Mapping the contours of human security challenges in Myanmar', in N. Ganesan and Kyaw Yin Hlaing (eds) *Myanmar: State, Society and Ethnicity*, Singapore: ISEAS, pp. 172–218.
UNDP/Ministry of National Planning and Economic Development (2010) *Integrated Household and Living Conditions Survey*, Yangon: Quebec; IDEA International Institute.
Wall Street Journal, 15 August 2012.
World Bank (2002) *World Development Report 2000/2001: Attacking Poverty*, New York: Oxford University Press.
World Security Network (2007) 'Pipeline Politics: India and Myanmar', 10 September; www.worldsecuritynetwork.com/India-Asia/Lundholm-Gideon/Pipeline-Politics-India-and-Myanmar accessed 10 October 2007.

11 Democratization in Hong Kong

A theoretical exception

Joseph Y.S. Cheng

Introduction

Hong Kong is a rather unique case in the discussion of democracy/democratization in East Asia. In the first place, it is not a sovereign state, but a special administrative region under the sovereignty of the People's Republic of China (Hong Kong Special Administrative Region of the PRC, HKSAR), which has pledged to maintain a high degree of autonomy in the territory in the Sino-British Joint Declaration of 1984. It has an 'executive-led' system of government meaning that power is highly concentrated in the Chief Executive, and the selection process is tightly controlled by the Chinese leadership, as well demonstrated in the election in 2012. The legislature, to a certain extent, plays an effective checks and balances role, as new legislation and financial appropriations must be approved by the Legislative Council. However, the electoral system was designed so that the pro-democracy camp cannot secure a majority of seats, despite the fact that it often manages to secure about 60 per cent of the votes in the direct elections to the legislature.

Most academics categorize Hong Kong's political system as a hybrid regime with varying levels of democracy in various political institutions. At the same time, there is a common understanding inside and outside the territory that unless there is genuine democracy in China, there can be no real democracy in Hong Kong. Theoretically, Hong Kong therefore offers an interesting example of how soft authoritarianism works, and what are the general challenges ahead.

This chapter traces the political development in Hong Kong and, in the next section, identifies its salient features. The third section attempts to explain the apparent theoretical contradictions, and the last section considers the challenges ahead in the context of the demands for change.

Political development in Hong Kong after 1997

The first Tung administration was seen to be willing to sacrifice Hong Kong people's freedoms to please Beijing. Democratization came into the picture because people were dissatisfied that they had no part in selecting C.H. Tung as the Chief Executive, and when he performed poorly, there was no way to get rid of him. Various arguments against the premature introduction of full democracy, i.e. universal suffrage, as articulated by the pro-Beijing united front fell flat because in the final years of the Tung administration the community believed that any candidate would be better than he was.

The Chinese leadership was acutely aware of this and anxious to help to maintain the territory's political and social stability. Chinese leaders understood that they had to soften the opposition to Tung at least within the pro-Beijing united front and the business community. They therefore chose to help Hong Kong solve its economic problems. Assistance included a sharp increase in the number of tourists allowed to visit Hong Kong (the Individual Travel Scheme), the Closer Economic Partnership Arrangement (CEPA), which gives Hong Kong better access to the China market, and political pressure on Guangdong to improve cooperation with the territory. People in Hong Kong appreciated the economic support from the central government, and in general had a very good impression of the new leaders in China, namely, Hu Jintao and Wen Jiabao.

The victory of the pro-democracy camp in the District Council elections in November 2003 and the general perception that it might have a small chance of securing half of the seats in the Legislative Council elections in September 2004 symbolized the revival of the pro-democracy movement as well as the extent of public dissatisfaction with the Tung administration. The Chinese authorities therefore felt compelled to be more involved to ensure that the pro-establishment candidates would be able to retain a solid majority in the Legislative Council elections in 2004. Support from Beijing included some shadowy activities too, such as cadres in the Pearl River Delta mobilizing Hong Kong residents to vote for pro-Beijing candidates, the Central Liaison Office in Hong Kong coordinating among pro-Beijing candidates to minimize counterproductive competition, and so on. In general, the public perception in the territory was that the Chinese authorities were much more involved, both openly and clandestinely, in Hong Kong affairs because they were worried about the territory's social and political stability. In early December 2011, many media reports on the Central Liaison Office's (the central government's agency in Hong Kong) alleged involvement in the District Council elections the previous month.

The heavy involvement of Chinese leaders in Hong Kong affairs further weakened the legitimacy and effectiveness of the HKSAR government. Business leaders probably felt that if they needed anything, they should lobby Beijing. Soon after the 1 July 2003 protest rally, Vice-President Zeng Qinghong received delegations from the three pro-Beijing parties, namely, the Democratic Alliance for the Betterment of Hong Kong, the Hong Kong Progressive Alliance and the Liberal Party, in a high-profile manner and praised them for their contributions to Hong Kong. This was unprecedented and may be interpreted as political intervention in support of the pro-Beijing political parties, as the Chinese authorities had been refusing any contact with the territory's pro-democracy camp since the Tiananmen Incident.

The Chinese leadership still considers that economic growth remains the key to the territory's social and political stability. Since the status quo is still satisfactory to the community, which has no intention to challenge the Chinese authorities, moderate economic growth is adequate to dampen grievances, to maintain stability. However, the government lacks the legitimacy to redefine the priorities even in the economic and social services field. In view of Beijing's perception of threats from the pro-democracy movement, it is unlikely that it will release a timetable and a roadmap to democracy based on universal suffrage.

Fifteen years after the territory's return to China, there has been no significant progress in democracy. In fact, interference from Beijing increased after July 2003 compared with the first three years after 1997. The Chinese authorities' dogmatic insistence on an 'executive-led' system of government means that the systemic difficulties in the executive-legislature relationship have not been tackled. Meanwhile, the absence of serious civil service reforms has resulted in declining performance of the system, as well as accumulating frustration.

Explaining the theoretical contradictions

Dankwart Rustow (1970) argues that democratization is a long process which may take several generations. Samuel Huntington (1984), however, considers that a linear model 'does not necessarily represent the matter in democratic transition'. Huntington proposes that there may be another 'cyclical model of alternating despotism and democracy' in which regular elections cannot lead to the defeat of the government in power. In developing countries, there may be a third model which is the oscillation between authoritarian regimes and democratic ones. According to Huntington, the expansion of middle-class participation in politics may eventually bring about the collapse of authoritarian regimes and the installation of democratic ones.

The general literature of comparative democratization assumes that the role of the middle class is a key variable linking economic development and democracy. Modernization theory considers that economic development promotes political democracy because it transforms a traditional society into a modern society that constitutes a necessary and sufficient condition for democratic politics (Huntington 1991; Lipset 1960). The societal transformations include the spread of education, urbanization, increase in upward social mobility opportunities, and so on. In line with economic growth, a modern society becomes more diversified and sophisticated and cannot be easily controlled by an authoritarian regime. Some scholars argue that economic development destabilizes an authoritarian regime by cultivating a politically autonomous and empowered middle class (Dahl 1971; Fukuyama 1993; Glassman 1995; Huntington 1993; Lipset 1959; Moore 1966). It is generally expected therefore that the middle class would not accept authoritarianism and instead would demand political participation. Modernization theory considers that the expansion and strengthening of the middle class would enhance the pro-democracy forces. According to the structural functional school of the modernization theorists, the middle class is the agent needed for bringing about the changes leading to a democratic polity. In sum, economic development transforms the social environment, giving rise to the middle class, who in turn promotes democratization, which establishes a political arrangement serving its interests (Boix 2003; Xiao 2003).

Hong Kong contradicts these tenets of the modernization theory, and it is not the only exception (Robison and Goodman 1996; Rodan 1996). When the core values and basic rights of the people of Hong Kong were seen to be threatened, as in the cases of the Tiananmen Square Incident in June 1989 and the 'anti-Article 23 legislation' protests in 2003, the community showed a strong demand for democracy, with political participation reaching extremely high levels. This forced the British colonial administration, the UK government, and in fact the international community to respond in 1989–1990 and the Chinese leadership to seriously adjust its Hong Kong policy in 2003–2004. Subsequently, when the political situation calmed down, Hong Kong people's political passion also declined.

Cost–benefit analysis

One explanation is a cost–benefit analysis. In view of the maintenance of the rule of law, the protection of basic human freedoms and the impressive economic growth during the British administration era from the 1950s to the 1980s, the people of Hong Kong were generally satisfied with the status quo. At the same time, the risks of confronting the colonial authorities were substantial. There were also opportunities for emigration to Western countries. Pursuit of democracy might have led to intervention by Beijing or the recovery of the territory by China, which the bulk of the population feared. On balance, the demand for political participation and democracy was dampened because the costs and risks were considerable, while the benefits were neither obvious nor significant.

Similar analysis and conclusion probably exist today in Hong Kong. The status quo is still acceptable. The rule of law and the protection of basic human freedoms have been basically maintained, though there have been criticisms of increasing self-censorship and censorship as well as certain erosion of the independence of the judiciary. Economic growth in the past decade has not been very impressive in the eyes of Hong Kong people, but still respectable (see Table 11.1). At the same time, the community understands that the local economy has been increasingly dependent on that of China (see Table 11.2), and it lacks the political will to confront the Chinese authorities over the issue of democratization. Nationalism has become a more important factor in the values of the people of Hong Kong, who appreciate the rising status of the Chinese nation and China's achievements in the economic, scientific and technological, sports and other arenas.

They realize that the Chinese leadership is reluctant to grant genuine democracy to the territory, i.e. accepting the outcomes of democratic elections without exerting any influence in the electoral processes. Although a significant majority of them is in support of democracy, as reflected by opinion surveys, in view of Beijing's hard-line position on political reforms, the community tends to return

Table 11.1 Gross Domestic Product (GDP) of Hong Kong, 1997–2012

| Year | GDP | | | | Implicit price deflator of GDP | | Per capita GDP | | | |
| | At current market prices | | At chained (2010) dollars | | (2007=100) | % change | At current market prices | | At chained (2007) dollars | |
	HK$ million	% change	HK$ million	% change			HK$	% change	HK$	% change
1997	1,373,083	11.2	1,147,418	5.1	119.7	5.8	211,592	10.2	176,817	4.2
1998	1,308,074	-4.7	1,079,919	-5.9	121.1	1.2	199,898	-5.5	165,032	-6.7
1999	1,285,946	-1.7	1,106,989	2.5	116.2	-4.1	194,649	-2.6	167,561	1.5
2000	1,337,501	4.8	1,191,821	7.7	112.2	-3.4	200,675	3.1	178,818	6.7
2001	1,321,142	-1.2	1,198,506	0.6	110.2	-1.8	196,765	-1.9	178,501	-0.2
2002	1,297,341	-1.8	1,218,361	1.7	106.5	-3.4	192,367	-2.2	180,656	1.2
2003	1,256,669	-3.1	1,255,597	3.1	100.1	-6.0	186,704	-2.9	186,545	3.3
2004	1,316,949	4.8	1,364,835	8.7	96.5	-3.6	194,140	4.0	201,199	7.9
2005	1,412,125	7.2	1,465,672	7.4	96.3	-0.2	207,263	6.8	215,122	6.9
2006	1,503,351	6.5	1,568,747	7.0	95.8	-0.5	219,240	5.8	228,777	6.3
2007#	1,650,756	9.8	1,670,163	6.5	98.8.	3.1	238,676	8.9	241,482	5.6
2008#	1,707,487	3.4	1,705,703	2.1	100.1	1.3	245,406	2.8	238,607	1.5
2009	1,659,245	-2.8	1,663,158	-2.5	99.7	-0.4	237,960	-3.0	238607	-2.7
2010*	1,776,783	7.1	1,776,783	6.8	100.0*	0.3	252,952	6.3	252,952	6.0
2011	1,936,058	9.0	1,862,957	4.9	103.9	3.9	273,779	8.2	263,442	4.1
2012	2,040,104	5.4	1,889,830	1.4	108.0	3.9	285,146	4.2	264,142	0.3

Source: Census and Statistics Department, The Government of the Hong Kong Special Administrative Region, 'Hong Kong Statistics – Statistical Tables'. Retrieved from www.censtatd.gov.hk/hong_kong_statistics/statistical_tables/index.jsp?charsetID=1&subjectID=12&tableID=030 on 22 January 2010 and 22 August 2010.

Notes

1 Figures in this table are the latest data released on 13 November 2009.

2 # indicates that the figures will be finalised when data from all regular sources are incorporated.

3 * Figures in this table are the latest data released on 11 November 2011; the implicit price deflator is calculated with reference to 2009, i.e. 2009+100.

to its traditional political apathy as it is reluctant to sacrifice stability and prosperity in the pursuit of democracy. Since 2003, the pro-democracy movement has been organizing a protest rally on 1 July every year, with the main theme of realizing democracy in the form of direct election of the Chief Executive and the entire legislature on the basis of universal suffrage. There are other themes depending on the political issues of the times, and the turnout depends on the general level of dissatisfaction with the HKSAR government. Apparently this cost-benefit calculus exists among the middle class in China today too (Tang 2011).

Somewhat in contrast to Taiwan, the development of civil society remains relatively limited in Hong Kong in the sense that the proportion of citizens taking part in civil groups of various kinds and engaging in voluntary work is still comparatively low. S.K. Lau (1982) argues that in the 1960s and 1970s Hong Kong people realized that they could solve their problems through their own efforts without having to exert pressure on the government by political participation; he describes this culture as 'utilitarian familism'. The community's values have undergone some changes, which will be discussed below, but the 'utilitarian' aspect certainly remains strong.

In general, political parties in Hong Kong are cadre parties, not mass parties. The pro-Beijing Democratic Alliance for the Betterment and Progress of Hong Kong is now the largest political party in Hong Kong, and it has a membership of over 10,000, with a large number of professionals, including lawyers. As the flagship pro-Beijing party in the territory, it offers a good platform to build networks with government officials and businessmen. In a way, it serves the same purpose as the Rotary Clubs or the Lions Club. Card-carrying members believe they have a certain advantage working in China; as more and more professionals have to engage in business activities in the Mainland – they consider that the benefits of joining the party far outweigh the small costs. For the more ambitious, dedicated service for the party is often rewarded by senior government appointments, such as appointments to prestigious official advisory committees, and official honours. Appointments as deputies to the National People's Congress and their local counterparts, as well as delegates to the National Committee of the Chinese People's Political Consultative Conference and their local organs, are also possible rewards for party services and donations. These are significant honours with high political and social status; for example, deputies to the National People's Congress can ask to meet provincial governors and central ministers, and one can easily imagine what the privilege means for those doing business in Mainland China.

On the other hand, the pro-democracy parties are much less attractive to those who consider political participation from a cost-benefit analysis point of view. It is significant that the Civic Party, which is a pro-democracy party with considerable appeal to the middle class, does not even have one middle-level or senior executive of a major business corporation among its members. The pro-democracy parties often manage to secure as a group 60 per cent of the votes in the direct elections to the legislature; hence obviously they manage to attract

Table 11.2 Trade, investment and tourism between mainland China and Hong Kong, 1978–2010

Year	Trade (US$ billion)			Entrepôt trade			Investment (US$ billion)		Tourism (1,000 persons)	
	Mainland exports to HK	Mainland imports from HK	Total	Mainland exports to HK	Mainland imports from HK	Total	Mainland investment in HK	HK investment in mainland	No. of mainland visitors to HK	No. of HK visitors to mainland***
1978	1.35 (–)	0.04 (–)	1.39 (–)	–	0.03	–	–	–	–	1,562
1981	3.78 (8.99)	1.41 (2.12)	5.19 (11.11)	–	1.03	–	–	–	15	7,053
1986	10.47 (9.78)	7.55 (5.61)	18.02 (15.39)	–	5.24	–	–	– (1.33)	44	21,269
1991	37.61 (32.14)	26.63 (17.46)	64.24 (49.60)	51.77*	19.66	71.43	2.59 (–)**	– (2.58)	112	30,506
1996	73.13 (32.91)	61.46 (7.83)	134.59 (40.73)	87.63	53.56	141.19	4.94 (–)	6.94 (20.87)**	2,311	44,229
2001	87.43 (46.54)	70.02 (9.42)	157.45 (55.96)	103.64	63.66	167.30	4.06 (–)	8.50 (16.72)	4,449	74,345
2002	91.93 (58.46)	78.62 (10.73)	170.55 (69.19)	110.77	73.32	184.09	4.87 (1.15)	15.94 (17.86)	6,825	80,808
2003	100.72 (76.27)	95.20 (11.12)	195.92 (87.39)	123.99	90.49	214.48	7.95 (2.63)	7.68 (17.70)	8,467	77,527
2004	117.73 (100.87)	113.92 (11.80)	231.64 (112.67)	145.57	109.06	254.63	9.35 (3.42)	18.56 (19.00)	12,246	88,421
2005	134.53 (124.47)	129.82 (12.23)	264.35 (136.70)	168.36	124.09	292.45	13.94 (6.93)	16.71 (17.95)	12,541	95,928
2006	152.94 (155.31)	148.23 (10.78)	301.17 (166.09)	187.35	143.07	330.42	13.36 (13.73)	21.36 (20.23)	13,591	98,318
2007	170.47 (184.44)	167.74 (12.80)	338.20 (197.24)	204.84	162.53	367.37	23.04 (38.64)	36.40 (27.70)	15,486	101,136
2008	180.86 (190.73)	175.70 (12.92)	356.56 (203.64)	218.94	171.24	390.18	–	27.59 (41.04)	16,862	101,317
2009	160.83 (166.23)	3.44 (8.71)	164.27 (174.95)	–	–	159.18	37.0 (38.51)	– (46.08)	17,957	100,054
2010	196.62 (218.30)	4.01 (12.26)	200.63 (230.56)	234.06	201.41	435.47	– (35.65)	37.21 (60.57)	22,684	102,495
2011	218.10 (267.98)	3.95 (15.49)	222.05 (283.48)	259.00	220.57	479.57		– (70.50)	28,100	103,048

Sources: Census and Statistics Department, The Government of the Hong Kong Special Administrative Region, 'Hong Kong Statistics', www.censtatd.gov.hk/hong_kong_statistics/index.jsp; *A Statistical Review of Tourism* (1981, 1986, 1991 and 1996 issues), Hong Kong, Research Department, Hong Kong Tourism Association, 1982, 1987, 1992 and 1997; Hong Kong Tourism Board, *Visitor Arrival Statistics* (published monthly), http://partnernet.hktourismboard.com; State Statistical Bureau, People's Republic of China (comp.), *China Statistical Yearbook* (1983, 1987, 1992, 1997, 2003, 2004, 2006, 2008 and 2009 issues), China Statistics Press, Beijing, 1983, 1987, 1992, 1997, 2003, 2004, 2006, 2008 and 2009; and Ministry of Commerce, National Bureau of Statistics, and State Administration of Foreign Exchange, People's Republic of China, *2008 Niandu Zhongguo duiwai zhijie touzi tongji gongbao (2008 statistical bulletin of China's outward foreign direct investment)*, September 2009, http://hzs.mofcom.gov.cn/accessory/200909/1253868856016.pdf.

Notes
1 Figures may not add up to the totals due to rounding.
2 '–' indicates that statistical data are unavailable, unknown, or negligible.
3 Statistics from mainland Chinese sources are given in brackets.
4 Figures for mainland imports from HK exclude HK's re-exports to China.
5 * Figure for 1992.
6 ** Figures for 1998.
7 *** No. of Hong Kong visitors to the mainland includes visitors from Macau.

many middle-class voters who offer them donations, also as reflected by the successful street fundraising efforts during the annual 4 June candlelight vigils and 1 July protest rallies. Admittedly, employees of major business groups do not want to be seen belonging to the pro-democracy parties, though some of them vote for these parties and offer them small donations.

In the 2011 elections of the Election Committee, which has the power to nominate and elect the Chief Executive, the pro-democracy movement did very well in the social welfare, legal, higher education and education sectors. The design of the electoral system is such that the pro-democracy groups can only hope to secure seats in the professional functional constituencies, as the business groups are expected to support the pro-Beijing, pro-establishment candidates. The pro-democracy groups remain competitive in those sectors which do not have many ties with the establishment and the major business groups, and they do very well in those sectors which do not accord a high priority to their respective sectoral interests and instead consider the core values of the community most important.

Satisfaction with the status quo on the part of the Hong Kong people is related to their comparing Hong Kong with its neighbours. Though the community found the two Chief Executives, C.H. Tung and Donald Tsang, far from satisfactory, it is in general happy with the performance of the civil service, which is highly efficient and free from corruption. This satisfaction also helps to tilt the balance of the cost-benefit analysis towards the acceptance of the status quo.

The refugee mentality and utilitarianism

In the immediate post-war years, many people in Hong Kong who came from Mainland China shared a refugee mentality. Some also perceived emigration to Western countries as a way to improve their opportunities. This wave of emigration gradually increased when in the 1980s Hong Kong people became concerned about the future of the territory. According to the figures given by the Security Branch of the British administration, the outward emigration flow stayed at a level of about 20,000 people per annum between 1981 and 1986, and then rose to 30,000 in 1987, 45,000 in 1988 and 42,000 in 1989. The Sino-British negotiations were an obvious cause of more people leaving Hong Kong. The delay in the statistics is because families needed at least two or three years to deliberate, decide, apply and then finally move. The Tiananmen Incident in 1989 prompted more people to depart, and the figures further rose to 61,700 in 1990, 59,700 in 1991, 66,200 in 1992, 53,400 in 1993, 61,600 in 1994, 43,100 in 1995 and 40,300 in 1996 (*South China Morning Post* 1997). The return flow of former emigrants also expanded as Hong Kong approached 1997. It was reported that for every 100 emigrants leaving Hong Kong in 1995, 60 former emigrants returned to the territory from overseas. The corresponding proportions in previous years were 27.9 per cent in 1994, 29.1 per cent in 1993, 16.2 per cent in 1992, 7.7 per cent in 1991 and 7.2 per cent in 1990 (*Ming Pao* 1996). Many Hong Kong families found it difficult to settle in the West. Those in their mid-careers encountered considerable difficulties starting second careers in other countries; adjustments required for beginning from the bottom ranks were often too hard to swallow. Hence when political stability was restored in the territory, many returned after securing their insurance policies (their new passports). Attempts to secure insurance policies have not ceased after 1997, hence a substantial segment of the middle class in Hong Kong possesses foreign citizenships. A senior Canadian consular official informed the author at the end of 2011 that she believed that up to half a million Hong Kong residents held Canadian passports.

This phenomenon also helps to explain why most people in Hong Kong support democracy in principle but are unwilling to fight or sacrifice for it. Their cost-benefit calculus is that they have the exit option, but Hong Kong is the place where they can best develop their careers. The same element of utilitarianism applies here. Arguably a segment of the middle class in Taiwan has also secured foreign passports, and there are many scandals concerning politicians' foreign passports and rights of permanent residence abroad. In contrast to Hong Kong, the pro-democracy movement in Taiwan during the era of authoritarian rule until the late 1980s had strong emotions of being suppressed, which was absent from Hong Kong. The territory's pro-democracy movement also lacked the passion of its counterpart in South Korea in the 1960s–1980s.

The people of Hong Kong work very long hours. This applies to those in the lower socio-economic strata who are under pressure to make ends meet as well as to the middle and upper-middle classes who are keen to advance their careers. The community often complains that there is insufficient time to spend with family. This fatigue adversely affects political participation and reinforces the utilitarian attitude. An interesting observation is that while Hong Kong parents are very serious about their children's education, they are reluctant to attend parent-teacher meetings and take part in their children's school functions.

Perceptions of China and the sense of political impotence

During the colonial era, people in Hong Kong did not have any strong incentive to fight for independence, partly because they valued the refuge and were largely satisfied with the conditions of the colony relative to those in Mainland China, and partly because they realized that independence was not a realistic option. This explained the absence of a strong emotion of being suppressed and a sense of political impotence on the part of the community.

Today Hong Kong people are acutely aware that the territory still enjoys better conditions than those on the Mainland and that the Chinese authorities would not allow independence, which has never been considered an option. During the panic in the wake of the Tiananmen Incident, there were suggestions of buying an island for the resettlement of the population, but the proposal was soon abandoned for obvious reasons. As the community understands at this stage that decisions on democratization in Hong Kong are made in Beijing, and that there is unlikely to be genuine democracy in Hong Kong until there are serious political reforms in China, the feeling of political impotence is natural.

In the long term, Hong Kong people realize that the territory's economy is increasingly dependent on that of the Mainland (see Table 11.2). This rising dependence has been accompanied by a relative decline in Hong Kong's international economic competitiveness. Over the past decade, the leaders of Shanghai no longer looked to the territory as a model for emulation; they have turned their eyes to New York and London. At the time of Hong Kong's return to China in 1997, the Guangdong authorities were keen to establish closer economic ties with the HKSAR, but Hong Kong's top civil servants wanted to avoid a high degree of economic integration with the Mainland and were cool to Guangdong's overtures. In recent years, Guangdong has been following the footsteps of Shanghai, trying to attract investment from multinational corporations listed in the Fortune 500. The value of Hong Kong as an economic partner has thus been falling. In sum, dependence on the Mainland and the decline in relative bargaining power have exacerbated Hong Kong people's willingness to accept Beijing's position on the territory's electoral reforms.

At the same time, their confidence in China's future continues to strengthen. Apparently this is related to their increasingly positive perception of China's international standing. A public opinion survey conducted by the New Youth Forum in March 2009, for example, revealed that 86 per cent of the respondents thought that China had considerable international influence; about 77 per cent believed that China would definitely or possibly overtake the USA as a world superpower within 50 years; 80 per cent felt that China was a peace-loving country; and 60 per cent believed that China's development would not threaten the Asia-Pacific region (*South China Morning Post* 2009). The successful Beijing Olympics certainly helped, and various space and military technology achievements also impressed Hong Kong people. The community believed that China, in contrast to the USA, emerged from the global financial tsunami in 2008–2009 with its international status improved.

Apparently the local economic difficulties and political controversies in recent years have weakened the Hong Kong community's trust in the central government and its confidence in 'one country, two systems' (see Table 11.3). Given that the territory's economy is heavily dependent on the Mainland economy and the central government's policy support, and that the HKSAR government was chosen by China's leaders, Hong Kong people might have held the central government responsible for the performance of their economy and government. The power of the electoral machinery of the pro-Beijing united front as demonstrated in the District Council elections in November 2011, and the competition between the two pro-establishment candidates in the Chief Executive election campaign in late 2011 and early 2012, also revealed Beijing's heavy-handed intervention in the territory's politics. Partly as a result, while Hong Kong people's trust in the central government and their confidence in 'one country, two systems' had been strengthening from 1997 to 2008 or so, since then, both trends have reversed.

In 2008, Hong Kong people's trust in the central government was at its peak. It was considerably higher than its trust in the Hong Kong government, in contrast to the situation in the 1990s before the return of the territory to China. In a survey conducted in December 2008 (one of the series recorded in Tables 11.3 and 11.4), 53 per cent of respondents said they trusted the central government. By comparison, 43 per cent indicated that they trusted the HKSAR government, and 19 per cent indicated that they distrusted it. The 14 per cent gap between those who trusted the central government and those who trusted the HKSAR government was the greatest since the end of 2003 (*South China Morning Post* 2009).

In contrast, an earlier 1996 opinion poll conducted by the Chinese University of Hong Kong revealed that 42 per cent of respondents trusted the British administration; those who trusted the British government amounted to less than 20 per cent, while only 12 per cent trusted the Chinese government (*Sing Tao Evening Post* 1996). A similar pattern emerged in various polls on the same subject in the 1990s. Hence, the Chinese authorities should be satisfied with the achievements of its united front charm offensive in the territory. This trust in the central government and confidence in 'one country, two systems' implies that Hong Kong people are less inclined to demand democracy as a mechanism of checks and balances against Beijing, in contrast to the mentality of 'the exploitation of democracy as a bulwark against communism', which hit its peak in the wake of the Tiananmen Incident in June 1989 (Cheng 1990).

Previous studies of Hong Kong people's political attitudes reveal that the middle class shares a stronger democratic orientation in terms of its appreciation of the Western liberal democracy model and its support for due process and democratic political procedures. This is especially so when a high level of education is considered an important attribute of the middle class. At the same time, people of the grassroots socio-economic strata have a stronger sense of patriotism and identification with China. However, the middle class's stronger democratic orientation has not been an adequate motivating force prompting it to fight for democracy. Instead, a majority of the middle class today has jobs related to China business, and this business connection has probably weakened its intention to challenge the Chinese authorities' position on the progress of democratization in Hong Kong.

Democracy is premised on the ideal that life is meaningful through political participation in the community to which one belongs. An individual realizes his or her full potential only through this participation in running the community's affairs. In the political calculus of most Hong Kong people, this is too demanding an ideal for them and they instead opt for economic power at the micro-level to secure an optimal measure of control over the socio-economic aspects of their own lives. Even in democracies, for the less politically active, political participation remains a demanding ideal. The voter turnout rates at various levels of elections in the USA are good evidence of the less than enthusiastic response to the demands of political participation. In view of Hong Kong people's hectic lives, political participation is perceived to be even more demanding and less appealing.

While every individual would like to have a good measure of control over his or her own life, this objective has been proven extremely difficult to fulfil

Table 11.3 Hong Kong people's confidence in China and trust for the Chinese leadership as reflected by public opinion surveys, 1997–2011 (half-yearly average)

Date of survey	Confidence in China's future (A)		Trust in the Central Government (B)		Confidence in 'one country, two systems' (C)	
	Confident (%)	Not confident (%)	Very trust/quite trust (%)	Quite distrust/very distrust (%)	Confident (%)	Not confident (%)
7–12/2012	68.7	22.2	29.2	37.4	50.2	40.9
1–6/2012	72.7	18.9	35.2	35.7	53.1	37.6
7–12/2011	73.0	19.2	34.0	32.5	55.0	36.6
1–6/2011	78.7	12.2	37.3	27.6	60.5	32.8
7–12/2010	79.2	14.3	39.4	26.9	61.6	30.8
1–6/2010	84.4	11.6	44.7	30.4	60.6	35.0
7–12/2009	87.2	8.5	49.6	18.8	68.1	26.0
1–6/2009	88.2	8.2	52.6	15.4	72.5	21.7
7–12/2008	88.1	7.9	53.1	14.4	71.8	21.6
1–6/2008	87.9	7.9	54.9	13.4	74.6	18.7
7–12/2007	87.6	7.8	54.4	15.6	74.9	18.8
1–6/2007	87.5	8.1	49.9	15.5	72.9	20.8
7–12/2006	85.7	9.3	44.6	19.7	70.4	23.6
1–6/2006	85.0	9.3	48.5	18.7	69.4	22.6
7–12/2005	82.0	11.0	46.8	24.4	65.1	25.3
1–6/2005	79.0	11.4	43.2	24.7	57.2	28.2
7–12/2004	83.4	9.2	47.0	20.9	59.3	28.4

Period						
1–6/2004	82.6	8.8	40.0	25.6	51.7	33.1
7–12/2003	82.7	8.3	45.7	20.6	53.7	30.9
1–6/2003	79.1	11.0	37.6	29.4	49.2	38.4
7–12/2002	81.7	9.6	41.0	26.2	52.7	34.3
1–6/2002	81.1	8.6	48.6	20.6	58.7	28.3
7–12/2001	79.9	10.0	43.9	22.1	59.2	27.3
1–6/2001	–	–	33.8	31.1	56.7	30.4
7–12/2000	–	–	31.6	31.0	58.2	27.5
1–6/2000	–	–	31.9	27.3	62.0	22.5
7–12/1999	–	–	29.3	29.7	56.3	29.6
1–6/1999	78.6	10.5	27.3	27.4	57.7	28.3
7–12/1998	–	–	30.5	30.7	66.6	21.9
1–6/1998	71.0	15.0	28.7	30.1	64.5	20.8
7–12/1997	73.1	11.8	32.4	29.9	64.0	18.7

Source: Public Opinion Programme, The University of Hong Kong, http://hkupop.hku.hk/, retrieved on 24 February 2012.

Notes

1 Question asked for (A) – Do you have confidence in China's future? The other option was 'don't know/hard to say', which is not included in this table.

2 Question asked for (B) – On the whole, do you trust the Beijing Central Government? The other options were 'half-half' and 'don't know/hard to say', which are not included in this table.

3 Question asked for (C) – On the whole, do you have confidence in 'One Country, Two Systems'? The other option was 'don't know/hard to say', which is not included in this table.

Table 11.4 Hong Kong people's trust in the HKSAR government as reflected by public opinion surveys, 1992–2011 (half-yearly average)

Question: On the whole, do you trust the Hong Kong Government?

Collapsed data

Date of survey	Total sample (half-yearly)	Subsample (half-yearly)	Trust (%)	Half-half (%)	Distrust (%)	DK/HS (%)	合計 total (%)
7–12/2012	2,066	1,206	39.4	27.2	31.0	2.4	100.0
1–6/2012	2,025	1,150	35.5	27.8	34.0	2.7	100.0
7–12/2011	2,043	1,046	39.4	28.1	29.7	2.8	100.0
1–6/2011	2,037	1,073	38.3	31.7	28.2	1.9	100.0
7–12/2010	2,024	2,024	48.7	31.1	18.7	1.5	100.0
1–6/2010	2,009	2,009	43.8	26.4	28.7	1.1	100.0
7–12/2009	3,033	3,033	46.6	31.2	20.8	1.4	100.0
1–6/2009	3,046	3,046	48.2	33.8	17.0	1.0	100.0
7–12/2008	3,102	3,102	42.8	36.9	18.7	1.6	100.0
1–6/2008	3,039	3,039	62.6	27.4	8.3	1.8	100.0
7–12/2007	3,035	3,035	59.7	28.2	9.8	2.3	100.0
1–6/2007	3,040	3,040	57.3	33.4	7.2	2.1	100.0
7–12/2006	3,036	3,036	52.5	34.0	11.9	1.6	100.0
1–6/2006	3,045	3,045	62.4	28.0	7.6	2.0	100.0
7–12/2005	3,029	3,029	59.3	25.1	13.1	2.6	100.0
1–6/2005	3,061	3,061	47.1	29.4	18.6	4.9	100.0
7–12/2004	3,063	3,063	38.7	28.4	28.8	4.0	100.0
1–6/2004	3,090	3,090	32.5	30.3	31.7	5.5	100.0
7–12/2003	3,058	3,058	29.9	29.8	34.9	5.3	100.0
1–6/2003	3,109	3,109	29.9	21.3	42.8	6.0	100.0
7–12/2002	3,072	3,072	34.4	24.1	35.2	6.2	100.0
1–6/2002	3,182	3,182	47.4	25.0	22.1	5.5	100.0
7–12/2001	3,169	3,169	40.3	26.5	27.8	5.4	100.0
1–6/2001	3,126	3,126	44.2	27.4	25.1	3.3	100.0
7–12/2000	3,145	3,145	39.3	26.1	28.3	6.4	100.0
1–6/2000	2,152	2,152	41.5	30.8	20.2	7.4	100.0
7–12/1999	1,627	1,627	39.1	31.0	22.8	7.1	100.0
1–6/1999	2,110	2,110	38.7	36.1	18.0	7.3	100.0
7–12/1998	1,624	1,624	38.2	34.9	21.0	5.8	100.0
1–6/1998	1,600	1,600	37.1	37.6	16.5	8.8	100.0
7–12/1997	2,602	2,602	52.1	27.9	9.5	10.4	100.0
1–6/1997	3,276	3,276	63.2	18.8	13.5	4.5	100.0
7–12/1996	3,177	3,177	60.6	22.2	12.7	4.5	100.0
1–6/1996	3,380	3,380	54.5	24.1	16.0	5.5	100.0
7–12/1995	3,395	3,395	48.4	22.0	22.1	7.5	100.0
1–6/1995	3,505	3,505	48.4	22.4	23.3	6.0	100.0
7–12/1994	3,165	3,165	46.6	22.8	24.0	6.6	100.0
1–6/1994	3,160	3,160	47.7	23.7	21.5	7.0	100.0
7–12/1993	3,607	3,607	54.8	16.8	21.8	6.6	100.0
1–6/1993	3,965	3,965	53.9	17.5	20.7	7.9	100.0
7–12/1992	640	640	56.9	14.7	23.8	4.6	100.0

Source: Public Opinion Programme, The University of Hong Kong, http://hkupop.hku.hk/, retrieved on 24 February 2012.

Notes

DK means 'don't know'. HS means 'hard to say'.

because of the asymmetry in power between the individual on one hand, and authoritarian regimes, big businesses, organized interest groups, and so on, on the other. This asymmetry in power is often reflected in the asymmetry in information held, which in turn is a result of the lack of transparency on the part of the powerful. Hong Kong people are acutely aware of this asymmetry when they complain about the 'hegemony' of real-estate developers and when they felt cheated by the financial institutions' various derivative products during the global financial crisis in 2008–2009.

In recent years, Hong Kong people have gradually come to realize the extremely limited control they enjoy over their own life. This realization has not prompted them to emigrate, as they understand that the situations in democracies are not significantly better (Hirschman 1970). They may be more inclined to take part in the increasingly frequent protest activities to vent their anger and frustration. This is one type of response found under authoritarian regimes and in democracies. Some will raise their level of political participation and seek to redress the asymmetries in power through collective action. This is in line with the general theory of democratization. But obviously only a small number of people choose this option.

The HKSAR government's legitimacy deficit and the demands for change

The British administration secured its legitimacy by performance. The HKSAR government's unsatisfactory performance means that it suffers from a legitimacy deficit. Hong Kong people are worried about the widening of the gap between rich and poor, the reduction in opportunities for upward social mobility and the decline in the territory's international competitiveness. They do not believe that the C.H. Tung and Donald Tsang administrations have offered any effective policy programmes, in fact they doubt whether they have made any serious efforts to come up with relevant policy programmes.

In 2001, the Gini coefficient in Hong Kong had already reached 0.525; it was expected to be even higher at this stage (Legislative Council Secretariat 2004). In fact, Hong Kong now has the largest gap between rich and poor among the major cities in the world. In September 2010, Oxfam of Hong Kong published its report on poverty in the territory, which showed that the number of working poor families[1] had been increasing, from around 172,600 more than five years ago to about 192,500, a rise of 12 per cent. The report also indicated that the incomes of the poorest one-fifth of the families had no improvement in the past five and a half years, and the median monthly incomes of the poorest one-tenth and one-fifth of the families were HK$3,000 and HK$6,000, respectively. In comparison, the median monthly income of the richest one-tenth of the families had risen by 16 per cent to HK$80,900, about 27 times that of the poorest one-tenth of the families, reflecting that the gap between the rich and the poor had been widening in the past five and a half years (*Ming Pao* 13 September 2010).

Earlier, in August 2009, the Life Quality Research Centre of the Chinese University of Hong Kong released a set of statistical and survey data which demonstrated that the overall quality of life of Hong Kong people in the previous year had deteriorated to approximately the level in 2003 when the territory suffered from the Severe Acute Respiratory Syndrome (SARS) epidemic; the overall index declined by 3.5 per cent when compared with that in 2007. The community's evaluation of the economy and its ability to purchase an accommodation through mortgage had dropped most sharply, falling by 30 per cent and 33 per cent, respectively; the index on satisfaction with the government's performance also dropped by 29 per cent (*Ming Pao* 2009).

In September 2010, a survey revealed that among the fourth-generation Hong Kong people (born between 1976 and 1990) interviewed,[2] 20 per cent had experienced downward social mobility in the past five years, i.e. moving down the occupational ladder. This downward movement was more conspicuous among the low-skilled and unskilled workers' strata, which constituted 44 per cent of the affected interviewees group. Over half of the respondents admitted that they had no opportunities for upward social mobility because of low educational qualifications (*Ming Pao* 20 September 2010).

In this connection, the group which is just above the social security net has been attracting the most attention. The number of workers earning a monthly income of between HK$10,000 and HK$20,000 each had increased from 1.02 million in 2007 to 1.17 million at the end of 2011 (*Ming Pao* 2011). For a two-person family, if its monthly income exceeded HK$12,000, its members would not qualify for transport subsidy, and if its monthly income was over HK$14,100, it would not qualify for public housing. Recently, a professor of sociology told the author that a recent university graduate expressed doubt whether he could be considered a member of the middle class. Given his educational background, by traditional standards he would definitely be considered as such, but in view of his income and low expectation of future improvement, he realized that he would not be able to buy private housing and would indeed have difficulty raising a family.

In view of the above, it is natural that people should lament (or deplore) the widening socio-economic gap. An opinion survey report released in early December 2011[3] showed that 76 per cent of respondents considered that the gap between the rich and the poor in Hong Kong was 'serious or very serious', and only 5 per cent believed that the problem was 'not serious or not very serious'. Moreover, 56 per cent of respondents were dissatisfied with the government's performance in handling the issue, and 59 per cent thought that the government 'comparatively took care of the rich' (*Ming Pao* 2011).

In the last year or two, the local media have observed much resentment against the rich among Hong Kong people, which may have an impact on political participation in the territory. Normally there is much envy of the rich, with newspapers and magazines full of reports of the lifestyle of the rich, which apparently make popular reading. This 'resentment against the rich' probably reflects dissatisfaction with the widening socio-economic gap and the government's policies favouring the major business groups and real-estate tycoons. The government feels the pressure, hence the gesture of the establishment of a Community Care Fund.

Dissatisfaction in the society is accumulating, but most people's response has been a sense of helplessness, not anger. Radical political actions symbolized by the protests of the League of Social Democrats, though far from radical by Western European standards, can only attract the support of a minority, normally estimated to be around 10 per cent of the public. Most Hong Kong people resent its protest activities, and it (together with its splinter group, People Power) lost badly in the District Council elections on 6 November 2011. The community's value orientations tend to be conservative, and it favours the maintenance of the status quo. It selectively supports gradual reforms, and is worried that radical political campaigns may destabilize the society. The most popular political leaders attract the public's support by moderate images, and are perceived to have been articulating the voices of the silent majority. They are definitely not revolutionary leaders (Cheng 2007).

The Chief Executive election of 2012 helped to illustrate some of the issues raised above. In contrast to 1997, when Hong Kong people were anxious to avoid major changes, now they seemed to welcome a new Chief Executive who was ready to introduce reforms. C.Y. Leung fully exploited this demand for change to establish a solid lead in popular support over Henry Tang, who was broadly perceived to be status quo oriented. Tang was the candidate favoured by Beijing initially.

The scandals and 'dirty tricks' in the campaign prompted the Chinese authorities to intervene and assume almost full control of the electoral process. Beijing was suspicious that the two candidates had been collecting information against each other, and it considered that such exposures and adverse publicity would discredit the entire establishment. Hong Kong people had vivid experiences of a 'small circle election' as they acutely felt that they had no part in the election of their leader. In contrast, the business community wielded considerable influence, and worse still, it was ready to defy public opinion when almost all the local tycoons openly nominated Henry Tang at the peak of his scandals.

The support from Beijing proved costly for the popularity of C.Y. Leung, and the legitimacy of his electoral victory was considerably compromised. There is substantial worry regarding the increasingly blatant influence of Beijing in local politics, but people in Hong Kong avoid open confrontation with the Chinese authorities. The latter will continue to support the territory economically to contain the community's grievances.

The challenges facing Hong Kong at this stage require a paradigm shift in policymaking. Beijing hopes to see a more visionary Chief Executive leading a pro-active administration. But the absence of democracy and the exacerbating social and political polarization deprive the administration of the legitimacy to push for reforms. This legitimacy deficit on the part of the Donald Tsang administration led to a mentality of avoiding major issues and focusing on gestures to win popularity. The C.Y. Leung administration from its very beginning has also suffered from many scandals as well as from the community's deep suspicions of it. It has considerable difficulties establishing a consensus and generating sufficient support. The withdrawal of the national education programme in September 2012 is a good example. Meanwhile, it is obvious that the Chinese leadership is not satisfied with the governance of Hong Kong, and Chinese officials no longer try hard to avoid any public comments on the Hong Kong situation which may generate a perception of compromising the territory's high degree of autonomy.

The rising discontent among the voters as reflected in the Legislative Council elections in September 2012 again demonstrate the demand for a new approach and innovative policies. The performance of the radical pro-democracy movement was impressive. People Power and the League of Social Democrats collected a 14.6 per cent share of the votes in the direct elections. In terms of seats, they improved from three to four. The rise of the radical wing of the pro-democracy movement reflects a gradual change in the political culture and also the exacerbation of grievances and dissatisfaction at the grassroots level and among young people. They support strong protest acts to air their grievances, and have no intention of pursuing policy changes through compromises. This certainly makes coordination among the pro-democracy groups increasingly difficult.

The political orientation of the new leadership in China is a significant variable. If it intends to pursue political reforms in China, it will likely allow Hong Kong to experiment with genuine democracy. If not, the Chinese authorities' present frustrations with the Hong Kong situation may continue to encourage them to intervene to ensure political stability and economic prosperity.

In 2013, political reforms emerge as the dominant issue in democratization in the coming years. The Chinese authorities have promised that Hong Kong may elect its Chief Executive in 2017 and all seats in the legislative in 2020 by universal suffrage. The pro-democracy movement has been mobilized to demand that this promise be implemented, and threatens to mobilize massive protests if its demands are not met. Whether genuine democracy will be granted in Hong Kong depends on many factors including the political reform orientations of the Chinese leadership, the resistance of the local business community, and the appeal and mobilization power of the pro-democracy camp in Hong Kong. The outcome will be another significant test of the political wisdom of all parties concerned.

Conclusion

The democratization or the lack of it in Hong Kong presents an interesting case study posing challenges to modernization theory. There are unique features in the Hong Kong case, mainly in the context of its special relationship with the Mainland. But the behaviour patterns and value orientations of its middle class are not unique. The first major question is whether political participation is part of a meaningful life. Under a soft authoritarian regime like the British colonial administration, the HKSAR government, the Singaporean government and perhaps even the Chinese government today, a considerable segment of the respective populations probably does not believe that political participation is a significant source of satisfaction in life. In recent years in Taiwan, there is a sense of disillusionment regarding democracy among a part of the concerned public; the people affected avoid political participation through established parties and instead opt for voluntary work in civil society. Similar disillusionment exists among minorities in established democracies too. In the hectic life of modern society, political participation has to compete with many other demands even for those who cherish democracy.

Hong Kong people have tended to derive their satisfaction from family life and career development because of their political alienation and also, historically, a refugee mentality in a colonial setting. A stable government providing the rule of law and a basic level of services would satisfy them. If they do not have to fight for it, they would be happy to support the status quo. If they have to struggle for it, they would have to consider the cost. There is the option of emigration, and there is also the choice of providing essential services like housing, children's education, pension, and so on through one's own efforts. There is no intention to strive for democracy at all costs.

There is also an element of utilitarianism and cynicism regarding democracy on the part of Hong Kong people. About 60 per cent of the electorate vote for the pro-democracy political groups in direct elections to the legislature in Hong Kong; most of these voters perceive the pro-democracy groups as checks and balances against the soft authoritarianism of the HKSAR government. They do not, however, believe that the pro-democracy movement would provide a credible alternative government, and they are doubtful whether a democratic government would offer a more effective and efficient administration. Moreover, Hong Kong's pro-democracy political parties do not succeed in attracting many voluntary workers and substantial donations. Even in established democracies, more and more voters see their votes as a means to punish governments that have not performed, while they have low expectations of all political parties and politicians.

In Hong Kong, the cynicism is perhaps stronger because even in the 1960s, the community was critical of the 'British disease', i.e. strong trade unionism and the over-generous welfare society. Today, it has little sympathy for the European welfare states suffering from excessive national debts. Hong Kong people typically prefer to keep money in their own pockets and do not trust income redistribution and the welfare state. Their values have been changing in recent decades, but the change is still inadequate to persuade them to fight for democracy in a costly way. There is an increasing sense of helplessness especially in confronting the Chinese authorities and big business groups. But this feeling of political incompetence is also spreading to some extent in established democracies, as symbolized by the 'Occupy Wall Street' campaign.

Notes

1 A working poor family is one which has at least one employed member, and its monthly income is less than half of the median monthly income of families in Hong Kong with the same number of members.
2 The survey was conducted by a consultancy firm commissioned by the Hong Kong Association of Professionals and Senior Executives in May–July 2010.
3 The poll was conducted by the Chinese University of Hong Kong and the Hong Kong Association of Professionals and Senior Executives between 26 September and 7 October 2011.

References

Boix, C. (2003) *Democracy and Redistribution*, Cambridge University Press: Cambridge.

Cheng, J.Y.S. (1990) 'Prospects for democracy in Hong Kong', in G. Hicks (ed.) *The Broken Mirror: China After Tiananmen*, Essex: Longman, pp. 278–295.

Cheng, J.Y.S. (2007) 'Hong Kong since its return to China: a lost decade?', in J.Y.S. Cheng (ed.) *The Hong Kong Special Administrative Region in Its first Decade*, City University of Hong Kong Press: Hong Kong, pp. 35–47.

Dahl, R. (1971) *Polyarchy: Participation and Opposition*, New Haven, Connecticut: Yale University Press.

Fukuyama, F. (1993) 'Capitalism and democracy: the missing link', in L. Diamond and M.F. Plattner (eds), *Capitalism, Socialism and Democracy Revisited*, Baltimore: The Johns Hopkins University Press, pp. 94–105.

Glassman, R. (1995) *The Middle Class and Democracy in Socio-Historical Perspective*, Leiden: E.J. Brill.

Hirschman, A.O. (1970) *Exit, Voice and Loyalty: Responses to Decline in Firms, Organizations and States*, Cambridge, MA: Harvard University Press.

Huntington, S.P. (1984) 'Will more countries become democratic?', *Political Science Quarterly*, 99(2), 193–218.

Huntington, S.P. (1991) *The Third Wave: Democratization in the Late Twentieth Century*, Norman, Oklahoma: University of Oklahoma Press.

Huntington, Samuel (1993) The clash of civilizations?, *Foreign Affairs*, 72(3), 22–49.

Lau, S.K. (1982) *Society and Politics in Hong Kong*, Hong Kong: The Chinese University Press.

Legislative Council Secretariat (2004) *Fact Sheet: Gini Coefficient (FS07/04–05)*, Hong Kong: Legislative Council Secretariat.

Lipset, S.M. (1959) 'Some social requisites of democracy: economic development and political legitimacy', *American Political Science Review*, 53(1), 69–105.

Lipset, S.M. (1960) *Political Man: the Social Basis of Politics*, New York: Doubleday.

Ming Pao, 11 September 1996.

Ming Pao, 14 August 2009.

Ming Pao, 13 September 2010.

Ming Pao, 20 September 2010.

Ming Pao, 2 December 2011.

Moore, B. (1966) *Social Origins of Dictatorship and Democracy: Lord and Peasant in the Making of the Modern World*, Boston: Beacon.

Robison, R. and Goodman, D.S.G. (1996) *The New Rich in Asia: Mobile Phones, McDonald's and Middle-class Revolution*, London: Routledge.

Rodan, G. (ed.) (1996) *Political Oppositions in Industrializing Asia*, London: Routledge.

Rustow, D.A. (1970) 'Transition to democracy: toward a dynamic model', *Comparative Politics*, 2(3), 337–363.

Tang, M. (2011) 'The Political Behavior of the Chinese Middle Class', *Journal of Chinese Political Science*, 16(4), 373–387.

Sing Tao Evening Post, 5 February 1996.

South China Morning Post, 15 February 1997.

South China Morning Post, 30 March 2009.

Xiao, G. (2003) 'The rise of the technocrats', *Journal of Democracy*, 14(1), 60–65.

12 The quest for constitutional democracy in contemporary China

Chongyi Feng

Introduction

Unlike the developing and consolidated democracies in the region, China has become the leading authoritarian regime after the collapse of most communist party-states in 1989–1991. China's political future may be projected in the following direction: collapse, democratization or stagnation. Few think that China will collapse, even fewer believe that China will democratize in the near future (Gilley 2004). Apparently, the majority of analysts believe that China will be stagnant but remain resilient as an authoritarian regime (Nathan 2003; Pei 2006; Shambaugh 2008). This chapter presents a cautious optimism about China's prospects for democratic transition triggered by the crises of governance and legitimacy.

The chapter begins with a brief account of the post-totalitarian regime as a social condition and major obstacle for democratic transition in contemporary China. It then explores the rights defence movement as a new and more effective form of Chinese democracy movement, and finally assesses the prospects for democratic transition in China in the perceivable future. The chapter argues that politics in China is tilting in favour of a democratic breakthrough as aspiration for constitutional democracy is running unprecedentedly high among the thinking public and a consensus is emerging within the new leadership of the Chinese Communist Party (CCP) to break the status quo and take the risk of democratic political reform.

Frustrated practice of socialist democracy in a post-totalitarian society

The theoretical framework of post-totalitarianism is particularly useful for understanding politics in China today (Feng 2008). Using the element of pluralism as the key criterion, Linz and Stepan classify political systems in the contemporary world into five regime types: democracy, authoritarianism, totalitarianism, post-totalitarianism and sultanism (Linz and Stepan 1996: 44–45). Based on their research on the former communist states in Eastern Europe, they defined post-totalitarianism as a continuum varying from 'early post-totalitarianism' to 'frozen post-totalitarianism' to 'mature post-totalitarianism'. According to them, early post-totalitarianism is close to the totalitarian ideal type but differs from it on at least one key dimension, namely some constraints on the supreme leader. The defining feature of 'frozen post-totalitarianism' is a mix of the persistent tolerance of some civil society critics of the regime and the maintenance of almost all the other control mechanisms of the party-state. In 'mature post-totalitarianism' there has been significant change in all the dimensions of the post-totalitarian regime, except that politically the leading role of the party is still sacrosanct (Linz and Stepan 1996: 42).

By the end of the 1970s the totalitarian order in China had eventually lost its vitality, not only because of the death of Mao and the erosion of political and ideological fanaticism, but also because of the measures taken by the ruling elite to protect themselves from the abuses engendered by the personal cult and law-lessness of the Cultural Revolution. However, rather than being replaced by con-ventional authoritarianism, not to mention constitutional democracy, the totalitarian order in China has evolved into a post-totalitarian rule, which allows economic, social and cultural pluralism but not political pluralism. The power structure of one-party autocracy remains intact, with the CCP legally accorded the leading role in the polity. The political leadership, though more technocratic in character, is still exclusively recruited from the structure created by the regime, with an emphasis on political loyalty. Despite growing disjunction between official ideological claims and realities, the party-state in China still maintains a highly articulated ideology justifying the leading role of the party and defining most aspects of society.

In the meantime, socialist democracy in China under the post-totalitarian con-ditions has made a positive turn towards constitutional democracy, making both ideological and institutional changes to accommodate to a certain extent demo-cratic procedures, human rights and the rule of law. Several waves of 'mind emancipation' in China since the 1980s have fundamentally altered the land-scape of the official ideology (Nathan 1985; Ding 1994; Mok 1998; Qiu 1998; Goldman and Lee 2002). While Marxism-Leninism-Mao Zedong Thought is still maintained as the official ideology, the agenda and policies of 'reform and opening to the outside world' have been largely informed and guided by prag-matic strategies known as Deng Xiaoping Theory, Thought of Three Represents and the Scientific Concept of Development. Cult of personality, over-concentration of power, lawlessness, obscurantism and other aspects of despot-ism have been labelled 'remnants of feudalism' and attacked in a systematic way. The previously alien concepts of human rights and the rule of law and even constitutionalism (*xianzheng*) have now become parts of the official vocabulary or principles. Also, democrats within the CCP have spearheaded the political reforms, underpinned by the universal values of human rights, democracy and the rule of law (Feng 2008). These ideological and political changes have served well the dual purposes of easing the legitimacy crisis of the CCP rule and improving economic efficiency.

In terms of institutional change to generate the building blocks for constitu-tional democracy, major progress has also been made in all of the economic, social and political spheres. Property rights and private ownership have been firmly established through abandonment of the people's commune system for family farming and the legalization of private economy and free enterprises. Social space has been created for individual autonomy and independent citizens thanks to the relaxation of *danwei* (work unit) system, the *hukou* (household registration) system and other social control mechanisms. Through numerous measures, such as the official embrace of human rights, the legalization of non-governmental organizations (NGOs) and improvements in the People's Congress System, the legal framework and political process have been reformed to partially accommodate the popular demand for genuine political participation and a nascent civil society. As a result, the three components of constitutional democracy, namely protection of human rights, the rule of law and fulfilment of popular sovereignty through democratic procedures and institutions have all appeared on the horizon and at least rhetorically have been endorsed by the CCP regime.

Since the 1980s, efforts have been made by the regime to carry out legal reforms and come to terms with human rights norms as embodied in international treaties. By the 2000s, for the first time in Chinese thinking, a clear distinction has been made between the rule of law (*fazhi* 法治, rulers subject to and limited by the law for protection of human rights and justice) and rule by law (*fazhi* 法制, law as a tool for the rulers to control the population). In the meantime, the CCP leadership has created and allowed space for the growth of the legal profession, with more than 200,000 lawyers employed at 19,000 law firms in China today. The 1989 Administrative Litigation Law authorized the judicial review of government decisions and lawsuits against government agencies. The government signed The International Covenant on Economic, Social and Cultural Rights in 1997 (ratified in 2001) and The International Covenant on Civil and Political Rights in 1998 (ICCPR, pending ratification). More broadly, legal reform and development in China have been characterized by massive transplantation of Western laws into the Chinese legal system, and many of these new laws grant further rights to Chinese citizens (Zou 2006).

The CCP's response to the pressure for the rule of law is a mix of reluctant accommodation and profound fear. The party-state continues to routinely violate basic human rights of citizens, legally or otherwise. The Criminal Law of the PRC maintains the clauses of loosely-defined political crimes, such as 'subversion of state power' or 'inciting subversion of state power', similar to the 'crime of counter-revolution' during the Mao years. The party-state also maintains its notorious system of 're-education through labour', which is a system of administrative detentions carried out arbitrarily by the police rather than through the judicial system. Detainees are subject to forced political education and varying forms of torture. The internal security apparatus, armed with the world's largest paramilitary, of over one million, continues to take political and religious dissidents rather than conventional criminals as primary targets. By the same token, the propaganda apparatus continues to control the circulation of information through strict censorship. Despite media commercialization in China, the mass media are owned and run by the state, and the Internet is brought under strict state control, with politically sensitive websites blocked, politically sensitive words filtered, and disobedient cyber writers banned. Journalists who do not exercise sufficient self-censorship and who overstep the boundaries are met with such ruthless punishments as dismissal and imprisonment. The crackdown on democracy movement leaders, human rights activists and other dissidents has been so intensive and extensive in recent years that legal scholars at home and abroad have pointed out a retrogression of Chinese official legal reform towards the rule of law (Cohen 2009; Jiang 2009). Media reports in China showed that at least 150 political criminals have been imprisoned under the Hu–Wen leadership over the past ten years (Bei 2012). Currently China is as bad as Iran in jailing dissident journalists. Reporters Without Borders ranked China 174 out of 179 countries in its 2011/2012 worldwide index of press freedom (Reporters Without Borders 2012).

In the area of democratic institution building, the reform of the People's Congress system, the village democracy, and the intra-party democracy have been widely highlighted by the CCP and the academic community as the three most salient items of progress (Wong 2005). However, the progress falls far short of a real breakthrough towards 'institutionalized democracy', let alone constitutional democracy. In China today, no government official with significant power of decision-making is publicly elected through open and fair competition. The CCP only wants to pursue democracy under one party autocracy, which by definition rules out democratic elections, just as the rule of law under one party dictatorship means that the legal system serves the interests of the party-state.

The Chinese authorities claim that 'the people's congress system is the fundamental political system by which the Chinese people act as masters of the state' and that the National People's Congress (NPC) is 'the highest organ of state power' (The State Council Information Office of the PRC 2005). However, the CCP stands above this 'highest organ of state power'. The reform and institutionalization to increase the institutional power and autonomy of the NPC since the 1980s has been firmly kept within the limit of maintaining the supremacy of the Party. Together with the power to legislate both the constitution and other national laws, the NPC appears to be equivalent to the parliament in the West, but the analogy is misleading in view of the absence of an opposition party. Over the last three decades, more than 200 laws have been passed by the NPC and thousands of regulations by the local peoples' congresses, with some of them going through lengthy discussions and repeated revisions, such as the cases of the enactment of the Property Law in 2007 and the Labour Contract Law in 2009. The NPC and the local people's congresses also occasionally turned down the work reports presented by the government departments and the candidates nominated for the government posts as high as vice governor of a province. But the fact remains that all of those laws and regulations, as well as major decisions on personnel and other issues, were ultimately made by the Party. The Party also strictly controls the selection of deputies to the people's congress, rather than allowing free and fair elections. In 2011 when the Chinese authorities encountered the upsurge of campaign announcements by 'independent candidates', who run for deputies to the people's congresses in accordance with the provision in the Electoral Law that accepted nomination by ten or more citizen voters in one constituency, these candidates were rejected on the grounds that their campaign activities had not been approved and organized by the official electoral committees (People's Daily 2011). These candidates are not only prevented from getting on official ballots, but also persecuted by local officials and security apparatus, with physical assaults, surveillance, extralegal detention, intimidation of their families and supporters, and even arrest (Liu 2011).

The much praised 'village democracy' has helped to train the peasantry for democratic elections as a massive educational process but failed to deliver the 'grassroots democracy'. The provisional Organic Law on the Village Committees was passed in November 1987, providing political autonomy for the villagers from direct governmental control and making each Village Committee accountable to a Village Assembly consisting of residents 18 years of age or older. Measures such as anonymous ballots, secret voting booths and multiple candidacies were used to ensure that elections for officials of Village Committees are 'free, fair and competitive', with some localities even introducing the mechanism of *haixuan* (sea election) in which candidates are directly and freely nominated by villagers alone. However, after the initial experiments, the rural grassroots units of the CCP have been authorized to 'control the correct orientation' of the elections and to 'provide leadership for the Village Committee' since 1998 (Guo and Bernstein 2004). Worse still, after more than 20 years of experiments, the grassroots democratic elections have been limited to the village level, which does not count as a level of government, although dozens of pilot projects have been allowed at the township level.

The high profile 'intra-party democracy' operates within the framework of 'democratic centralism'. The concept of 'intra-party democracy' was coined by Ye Jianying, then a powerful Vice-Chairman of the CCP Central Committee, in his concluding remarks at the Central Work Conference on 13 December 1978, to refer to relatively free debates and discussions (Ye 2009). The achievements of the 'intra-party democracy' to date include a collective decision-making process at party committees and a level of institutionalization in the sensitive areas of leadership politics. In particular, a collective decision-making process at the all-powerful Politburo and its Standing Committee has been established to restrain the ability of the Party boss to acquire dictatorial powers, as Mao Zedong did (Miller 2011). In order to make power succession more stable and predictable, the system of compulsory retirement according to age limit was introduced in the 1980s and, after the retirement of Deng Xiaoping in 1989, the top Party and State positions were limited to two five-year terms. However, the process of institutionalization remains far from complete, not least because open competition and formal democratic election for senior positions has not been adopted. As one step of the promotion process, the mechanism of 'democratic assessment' does involve votes by a selective constituency, but the number of votes is not disclosed, nor does it determine the outcome of winners. Rather the number of votes can be used as a criterion to eliminate the least popular candidates.

As a matter of fact, maintaining stability at all costs has been the dominant Party line since 1989, leading to the establishment and consolidation of the 'system of stability preservation' (维稳体制 *weiwen tizhi*). It was Deng Xiaoping who first put forward the thesis 'stability overrides everything' (Deng 1993: 285). The 'system of stability preservation' emerged in the aftermath of the 4 June 1989 Tiananmen crackdown. In March 1990, the CCP Central Committee of Political and Legal Affairs, which had been abolished in 1988 as part of the political reform to 'separate the Party from the government' and promote judiciary autonomy, was re-established to oversee the work of law enforcement. In February 1991, the Central Comprehensive Controlling Committee for Public Security, with counterparts down to the county level and personnel drawn mainly from the security apparatus and the propaganda apparatus, was set up to formulate policies and coordinate the measures for internal security. In April, the CCP Central Committee issued a 'Circular on Strengthening Law Enforcement Work for Preserving Social Stability', making clear that preserving stability is a political task of utmost importance to the Party and to the entire nation.

The 'system of stability preservation' took shape in 1998–1999, following the death of Deng Xiaoping in 1997. The Central Leading Group for Stability Preservation Work as well as its Office was established in 1998. The personnel and functions of the Office for Stability Preservation at all levels largely overlapped with those of the Office of the Comprehensive Controlling Committee for Public Security. In 1998, former student leaders of the 1989 demonstrations were joined by the veteran dissidents of the Democracy Wall Movement of the late 1970s to organize the China Democracy Party. The party was crushed, with all of its leaders jailed for up to 14 years (Wright 2004). In his comments on the report by the Ministry of Public Security about the re-emergence of the underground Autonomous Union of University Students at Beijing University and Qinghua University in April 1999, the General Secretary of the Party, Jiang Zemin, issued the call to 'nip every element of instability in the bud' (Xiaocankao 1999). Beginning in June 1999, this new strategy was put into practice on a spectacular scale in the campaign to crackdown on the Falun Gong (Chan 1999). According to the insightful observations of the deposed Party chief, Zhao Ziyang, in 2000, there were five major measures taken by the Jiang Zemin leadership to preserve stability: suppression of dissent by the military and police forces; control and manipulation of the media; elimination of social unrest in the embryonic stage; strict ban on the oppositional organizations; and delivery of economic benefits for settlement in some cases (Du 2010: 230).

The 'system of stability preservation' has been consolidated by the Hu Jintao leadership since 2002, when the first smooth succession of power was achieved at the 16th National Congress of the CCP. Zhou Yongkang and Li Shangchun, two protégé of Jiang Zemin, were appointed as Politburo Standing Committee members in charge of internal security and propaganda, respectively, to ensure the maintenance of domestic stability. The Hu Jintao leadership has expanded the personnel and budget for stability preservation and resumed the Mao-style 'mass line' in carrying out the stability preservation work to the effect of rolling back the rule of law. Since 2009 there has been a nationwide drive to establish the 'Grassroots Centre for Petition, Comprehensive Control and Stability Preservation' down to the level of street and township or even village. These centres have the responsibility to keep close surveillance on several categories of 'instability suspects' such as Falun Gong adherents, the floating population and petitioners, so that any small rumblings of unrest can be nipped in the bud. (Hu 2010) It was in 2009 that the formal budget for internal public security started to surpass the huge budget for defence, hitting the level of ¥487 billion, compared to the ¥480 billion of the defence budget (The PRC Ministry of Finance 2010; Xu, Chen and Li 2011).

However, these efforts have not resulted in a more stable society. Instead, more seeds of social instability, known in China as the vicious cycle of 'stability preservation leading to more instability' have been sown (Social Development Research Group 2010). Obviously, the CCP leadership is seeking a special kind of stability in which the priority is no regime change, rather than stability based on social justice, the rule of law and the protection of civil liberties and human rights. In contrast, the Chinese public have a different definition of stability, which seeks genuine social stability, as demonstrated by the increasingly vigorous rights defence movement. In the view of a leading Chinese sociologist, the artificial 'stability' imposed by the party-state at the expense of social justice, reform and progress, has led to more dangerous instability and what some term 'social decay' with serious symptoms, such as runaway state power, structural corruption and a 'situation beyond governance' (Sun 2009). Viewed from this perspective, the transition to constitutional democracy in China is likely to unfold as the process of asserting the rights of citizens and as a way out of the stalemate engendered by the 'system of stability preservation'.

The rights defence movement as a winding path to constitutional democracy

It has been argued that the rights defence movement (*weiquan yundong*) emerging in China in the first decade of this century foreshadows a new, more optimistic political scenario in which smooth transition to constitutional democracy through constructive interactions between state and society may occur (Feng 2009; Benny 2012). This broadly-based social movement involves all social strata throughout the country and covers every aspect of human rights, taking individual litigations, Internet campaigns and public protests as the main forms. 'Mass incident' is the term coined by the security apparatus to describe those protests, including unapproved strikes, assemblies, demonstrations, petitions, blockages and collective sit-ins. They numbered 60,000 in 2003, 74,000 in 2004 and 87,000 in 2005, an average of more than 200 protests a day, according to official figures (Yu 2007). Leading scholars in the field found that the number reached as high as 180,000 in 2010 (Sun 2011), and the actual number for 2011 could be more than 200,000. Some of them involved thousands of people and resulted in police and paramilitary intervention, leading to loss of lives. The steady increase of social unrest indicates that while the population do appreciate the economic achievements and improvement in living standards under the current regime, as shown by the opinion polls carried out by international surveys agencies such as the Pew Research Center, which found in the spring 2010 survey of the Global Attitudes Project that 87 per cent of Chinese said they were satisfied with the way things were going in their country (Bell 2011), a large proportion of the population have at the same time become increasingly less tolerant of social injustice and rights violations.

Two major events kick-started the rights defence movement in 2003: the Sun Zhigang case, which resulted in the abolition of State regulations on the detention of migrants and the entire custody and repatriation system targeting migrant workers, and the case of the Severe Acute Respiratory Syndrome (SARS) epidemic, which led to a new wave of openness in the media (Wang 2003; Fan 2005; Teng 2006). The year 2003 was also named 'the first year of rights (*quanli yuannian*)' in China (Qiu 2003; Hu 2003; Xian 2004). Most cases of this rights defence movement aim to defend economic and social rights, including protests by peasants against excessive taxes, levies and forced seizures of farmland; strikes of workers against low pay, arrears of pay and poor working conditions; protests by laid-off urban workers against unfair dismissal by their employers; protests by home owners against forced eviction by government and developers; protests of residents against forced relocations; campaigns by citizens against unpaid social entitlements; campaigns for the rights of women and children; and protests of affected residents against environmental pollution. However, the cases of defending civil and political rights are also on the rise, including campaigns by lawyers, journalists and writers for the freedom of speech and press; campaigns by practitioners of the Christian house churches and Falun Gong practitioners for the freedom of religions, beliefs, assembly and association; campaigns against arbitrary detention, 're-education through labour', torture and the death penalty; protests by peasants against the irregularities and manipulations in village elections; campaigns by victims of the party-state agents against injustice and abuses of public power, particularly by thousands of petitioners who flocked to Beijing or provincial capitals from all over the country to seek redress from perceived injustice. The rights defence movement is greatly enhanced by the rapid development of the Internet with roughly 500 million netizens and the incipient civil society with about four million NGOs and semi-NGOs.

It can be argued that the rights defence movement is a new form of democracy movement. After the Tiananmen Massacre in 1989, the Chinese democracy movement sank to its low ebb. 'Farewell to revolution' became the mainstream thinking among students and intellectuals who shifted their focus from politics to material and professional pursuits due to fear or despair. At the outset, either in the form of individual litigations or in the form of collective demonstrations, the rights defence movement sought compromise with the government, confining its main scope to social and economic demands. The movement seeks protection of legal rights within the existing legal-political framework, in contrast to the regime change sought by the pro-democracy activists. Rights defence lawyers have fought in the frontline and provided leadership to the emerging rights defence movement (Carnes 2006). These lawyers have been hailed as the 'heroes of our times' or 'men of the hour', and have enjoyed an increasingly high profile in the Chinese and international media (Ji and Wang 2005; Hu 2006; Mosher and Poon 2009). They have political aspirations for democracy, although initially they tried to attain a democratic breakthrough by first of all strengthening the rule of law with an independent judiciary.

As it unfolds, the rights defence movement shows itself to be inherently a pro-democracy movement, with the protection of rights as an immediate demand and democratic change as an implicit goal. It is true that such demands as freedoms of speech and association fall within the parameter of liberalization rather than democratization (O'Donnell and Schmitter 1986: 7; Huntington 1991: 9). However, Chinese liberal elements consider comprehensive realization of human rights an intrinsic part of the democratization process. In this regard, Charter 08, a manifesto initially signed by 303 Chinese citizens and published on 10 December 2008 to coincide with the 60th anniversary of the Universal Declaration of Human Rights, can be seen to be a result of the rights defence movement, as well as a guide for the future development of the movement, combining demands for concrete rights and benefits with a political blueprint for constitutional democracy (Feng 2010). It pools together the major demands raised in the movement, ranging from the demand by the peasants for land ownership, to the demand by the migrant peasant workers for equal national treatment as urban residents; from the demand by the rich for the freedom of establishing enterprises, to the demand by the poor for basic social security; and from the specific demand for abolishing the re-education through labour system, to the general demand for the protection of human rights and the environment. It also provides the movement with a political goal and direction by spreading the democratic ideas advocated by Chinese liberal intellectuals in recent years. The relative isolation of students and intellectuals is identified as a major setback of the 1989 Chinese Democracy Movement (Cherrington 1991; Goldman 1994; Zhao 2000). In contrast, the main force of the rights defence movement represents the mainstream of the society, including workers, peasants, business people and professionals of all trades. By providing political and intellectual guidance and articulating social, economic and political demands across all social strata, and by nurturing the spirit of justice, peace, rationality and the rule of law, Charter 08 heralds a coalition between intellectuals and the 'broad masses of the people' and the convergence of social movement and political democratization.

There are many reasons why the CCP leadership has chosen to suppress the rights defence movement. After all, the movement, either in the softer form of court room litigations and petitions to the authorities or in the harder form of street demonstrations, challenges the vested interests of the ruling elite. Rapid predatory economic development since the 1980s has also made financial and other resources abundantly available for the party-state to take strong measures against political opposition. China is the only major country in the contemporary world to create a new administrative institution for 'stability preservation' along-side other regular institutions and branches of the government, which is already exceptionally large. Besides the world's largest 2.3 million-strong People's Liberation Army, which also has a domestic stability mandate on top of its national defence duty, and the world's largest 1.8 million-strong police force, China has created the world's largest and most advanced special paramilitary force of 880,000-strong People's Armed Police to ensure domestic security. Facing the challenge from the population with a growing rights consciousness, the hardliners within the CCP leadership are still locked in a mentality that drives them to suppress the legitimate demands of the people by force.

However, there is a liberal and democratic force within the CCP working on an accommodation with the rights defence movement in order to bring about a democratic transition (Feng 2009). There are several high profile rights defence cases solved through an accommodative approach. The protests by residents of the coastal city of Xiamen in the second half of 2007 forced a giant petrochemical plant (investment of US$1.41 billion) with strong political connections and government support to be relocated elsewhere, probably the first direct concession made by the Chinese government to public demands through demonstrations. In November 2008, starting from Chongqing, one of China's four provincial-level municipalities, and extending later to Jingzhou, Lanzhou, Sanya, Dali, Shantou and other cities, thousands of taxi drivers went on strike over high operating costs, high traffic fines, shortages of natural gas and the government's lack of efforts in reining in unlicensed taxi operators who were stealing fares away. Local governments in these cities negotiated with strikers and took emergency measures to address their demands. In a similar manner, sustained protests for three months by local residents against the placement of a large garbage incinerator in Panyu district, Guangzhou, successfully halted plans for its construction in December 2009. Early in July 2012, violent protests for three days by residents forced the local government of Shifang City, Sichuan Province, to abandon a major copper refinery project. And at the end of July, within hours of popular protests, the local government of Qidong City, Jiangsu Province, cancelled an industrial waste pipeline project of a Japanese-invested paper mill. It is worth mentioning that all of these popular protests have been greatly assisted by Internet campaigning, which provides an alternative to an organization at the national level in communication and in mobilizing nationwide or even world-wide support.

More significantly, the Chinese authorities have also yielded to the pressure in dealing with some political rights defence cases. In September 2011, 20,000 peasants in Wukan Village, Guangdong Province, launched a protest to dismiss a corrupt party official who had sold 660 hectares of communal village land to developers at nominal prices to enrich the developers and officials. The local government sent in the police force to arrest many of the protesters and a village representative died in police custody. In December 2011, the villagers went a step further, barricading roads leading into Wukan, confronting security forces and setting up their own administration. The Guangdong provincial government backed down with rare concessions to give some compensation for the land sale, punished several responsible officials and allowed villagers an open and fair election. In January 2012, such an election was held in due course, with 'rebel leaders' elected to the new village management.

The case of Chen Guangcheng is equally significant. A blind legal advocate for women's rights and the rural poor, Chen is also known as a 'barefoot' lawyer' who practices law without a formal licence. Due to his assistance to lawsuits to expose the abuses of forced abortions and forced sterilization, he was sentenced in August 2006 to four years and three months for a dubious crime of 'damaging property and organizing a mob to disturb traffic'. Chen was released from prison on September 2010 after serving a full sentence, but remained under house arrest and constantly guarded. He and his family members were repeatedly beaten. Any visitors, including journalists and lawyers, were harassed and turned away. On 22 April 2012, with the help of human rights activists, Chen escaped his house arrest and fled to the US Embassy in Beijing. The Chinese government negotiated with the American government to get Chen out of the embassy and went through a speedy process in arranging for Chen to study law in New York, accompanied by his family.

These examples are significant because the Chinese government, with its tradition of top-down decision-making, secretive deliberations and little tolerance for political dissent, usually sees popular protests as an act of subversion. The positive responses from the government were precisely what had been expected by the activists and other participants of the rights defence movement. The soft approach has also been named as the 'middle way model of rights defence' (Fan 2005, 2010a, 2010b). Apart from striking a balance in the middle way between violent revolution and obedience to autocracy, the success of the 'middle way model of rights defence' is also predicated on the positive interactions between the government and society. The cases of Wukan Village and Chen Guangcheng indicate that attempts have been made by at least a section of the CCP leadership to change the depressing hard line in stability preservation and to find a viable way to achieve stability maintenance through institutional accommodation of conflicting social groups, and by establishing rules and mechanisms for safeguarding the citizens' rights and legitimate popular interests.

The tipping point of democratic breakthrough

In accounting for democratic transition, four schools of theoretical approach are identified in the literature (Guo 1999). The structuralist approach believes that the outcomes of democratic transition are determined by economic, social and cultural structures (Lipset 1959; Moore 1966; O'Donnell 1979); the political economy approach lays emphasis on the interplay of politics and economy, particularly the correlation between economic and political reforms (Haggard and Kaufman 1995; Encarnacion 1996); the institutionalist approach emphasizes the constraints of preexisting institutions as a key variable in the inauguration and process of democratic transition (March and Olsen 1984; Powell and DiMaggio 1991; Karl and Schmitter 1991); and the strategic choice approach focuses on the strategic choices made by both ruling and opposition elites as the most important factor in democratic transition (Linz and Stepan 1978; O'Donnell and Schmitter 1986).

Viewed from these differing theoretical frameworks, all of the social and economic conditions are ripe for democratization in China. But it is the institutional context and the preference of the ruling elite that hold China back. The post-totalitarian regime has made absence of organized opposition, disorganization of society and atomization of individuals as the preconditions for the survival of the party-state. Based on the calculation that communist one-party rule will survive as long as isolated popular protests are not organized as a nationwide campaign and can be suppressed one by one, the ruling elite have strictly banned political opposition and restricted the development of civil society. A dual management system has been devised to set the scope and limit for the development of civil society, which is welcome to provide needed service to the party-state but not allowed to function beyond state control. The Regulations on the Registration and Management of Social Organisations issued by the State Council in 1989 (revised in 1998) require social organizations to seek prior approval by and affiliations to a government or Party body as the 'professional management unit' (业务主管部门) responsible for their operations. After approval is granted, they must register with the Ministry of Civil Affairs or its local bureaus, which acts as the 'registration management unit' (登记管理机关) responsible for their annual review. The regulations also stipulate that in a given sector of a given administrative jurisdiction only one social organization can be approved (The State Council of the PRC 1989). As a result, there is no space for the incipient civil society to reach its full potential. NGOs are either GONGOs[1] run by the government with rich financial and human resources, or grassroots NGOs, which are independent from the government but not properly registered and which do not enjoy legal protection or official financial support.

There are some indications that the ruling elite in China are approaching the critical point of changing their attitudes towards democratization due to both new challenges and new opportunities. First of all, the predicament of the 'China model' of development means that among the three choices facing the CCP leadership democratization has emerged as a more feasible option than stagnation and retrogression. China's spectacular economic success over the past three decades highlights the experience and superiority of combining unlimited political power of one-party rule with rapid state-led economic growth (Lewis and Teets 2009; Zou and Ouyang 2009). This hybridity has been described by some Western commentators as 'market Leninism', in which the Leninist party-state is sustained by the combination of relatively free-market economics and autocratic one-party rule (Kristof 1993). It is also known among Chinese scholars as 'power elite capitalism' (权贵资本主义), which benefits a small minority of power holders and their associates at the expense of the public and environment

(Wu 2011). The 'China model' has served the interests of the power elites and produced the effect of rendering further economic or political reform redundant. However, as many scholars have argued, the economic growth based on the combination of high investment, high pollution, high energy consumption and high export with low salary, low domestic consumption and low efficiency is not sustainable in the long run, not to mention the suppression of human rights and the neglect of social welfare, which is immoral (Wu 2005; Chen 2010).

Added to this is the economic slowdown beginning in early 2012, which calls for a change in direction (Richburg 2012). Given that economic boom is the principal factor legitimizing CCP rule, a sharp economic slowdown is of particular significance for the leadership to break free from the existing 'path dependency'. The social, political and economic troubles serve as a warning that maintaining the status quo is no longer a viable option. These troubles have actually engendered renewed calls within the government and among the populace for profound economic, social and political transformations, offering a variety of blueprints for future development of China, including Constitutional Democracy, New Democracy, Socialism of Constitutionalism, Social Democracy, and Confucian Socialism (Zhang 2011; Ma 2012; Wu 2012).

The demise of Bo Xilai and the 'Chongqing model' also demonstrated that neo-Maoism is not the answer to China's social injustice. Bo represents a return to the cynical Maoist approach for political solution to social tensions by channelling the desire of participation into a chorus of revolutionary songs in praise of the Party, the desire of redistribution into housing provision, and the resentment against corruption and disparity into extralegal attacks on the selected targets. The Bo Xilai scandal has once again discredited Maoism, which confronts corruption and social disparity with a reign of terror and other totalitarian measures. It has exposed in the most paradoxical sense the profound flaws in China's political system, including the danger of the almost unstoppable rise of a demagogue and corruption within the core of the system. Furthermore, after 30 years of legal reform and the 'institutionalisation of Chinese politics', there is still no basic legal protection of life for even high-ranking officials, and there are no enforceable rules, nor independent arbiters, to decide who governs the world's most populous nation.

On the brighter side, the turnover of leadership at the 18th Party Congress in November 2012 and the 12th National People's Congress in March 2013 provided a rare opportunity for major political change, as the new generation of leadership who are more entrepreneurial and more open to Western influence may respond to the legitimacy crisis by seizing the opportunity for democratization with an open mind (Feng 2013). At the press conference on 14 March 2012, Premier Wen advised his colleagues that there is an urgent task to change 'the leadership system of the party and the state', warning that

> Without successful political reforms, it's impossible for China to fully institute economic reform, and the gains we have made in these areas may be lost, and new problems that popped up in the Chinese society will not be

fundamentally resolved, and such historical tragedies as the Cultural Revolution may happen again in China.

(Wen 2012)

The new leadership headed by General Party Secretary, State President and Commander in Chief Xi Jinping and Premier Li Keqiang does bring political reform as well as economic reform back on the agenda. Xi Jinping chose Guang-dong Province as the destination of his first inspection tour, a highly symbolic imitation of Deng Xiaoping's 1992 Southern Tour to demonstrate his determina-tion in forging ahead with reform. Addressing the 30th anniversary of China's revised Constitution on 4 December 2012, Xi pledged to pursue the rule of law and stressed that 'the Constitution is a legal weapon that guarantees rights' and 'any violators of the constitution and law will be held responsible' (Xi 2012). Following his speech, an announcement has been made to phase out the uncon-stitutional re-education through labour system, a notorious extrajudicial mech-anism adopted in 1957 as a convenient tool by the police to imprison political dissidents and petty offenders for up to four years without going through legal process. At the inaugural press conference on 17 March 2013, Premier Li also vowed to make a painful 'self-imposed revolution' in reducing government power for further development of market economy and fairer distribution of wealth and benefits (Li 2013). It is hopeful the new leadership will demonstrate a greater commitment to human rights, democracy and the rule of law, although it remains to be seen whether they have the political will to rise above huge vested interests of the party and push the reform beyond the framework of the party-state.

Conclusion

In the reform era since the 1980s, the crisis of political legitimacy of communist rule in China due to the worldwide collapse of communist ideology has been eased by the performance legitimacy based on economic achievements, a signi-ficant rise in living standards and the rise of nationalism. In the meantime, the party-state has made some positive changes in response to the numerous chal-lenges posed by the Chinese people and by the international community, as described earlier. However, the CCP leadership dominated by the hardliners has rejected the option of democratization and instead taken social and political lib-eralization as measures to 'strengthen party leadership'. The pitfall of 'socialist democracy' in China, as in other communist societies, is that it is based on Len-inist class theory with a vanguard party, denying the principle of the universal political equality of autonomous individuals, which is the very foundation of modern democracy. As elsewhere, when the CCP rules China in Leninist fashion without allowing free, fair and open competitive elections, it usurps the authority and power from the people for the self-interest of the communist bureaucracy as the New Class (Djilas 1957), no matter how beautiful its promises and claims are. In the final analysis, a communist party-state is not compatible with the rule of law, less with constitutional democracy, as the party-state is based on the Leninist theory that 'the state is a machine for maintaining the rule of one class over another' (Lenin 1970: 11).

Under the social conditions of 'market Leninism' and post-totalitarianism, which allow some extent of economic and social pluralism but strictly ban political opposition, the Chinese democracy movement has taken a special form of the 'rights defence movement' by exploiting the official discourse on property right and human rights and by combining aspirations for constitutional democracy with assertion of entitlement and rights written in the Chinese Constitution and other laws. This powerful 'rights defence movement' and the beginning of economic slowdown is forcing the party-state to review its 'system of stability preservation', which has become the root cause of serious 'social decay' and social tensions. The recent talk of political reform by the top leaders such as Wen Jiabao and Wang Yang and the dramatic demise of Bo Xilai should be understood in the light of the latest changing fortunes of the CCP regime. Chinese society is ready for profound political transformation, while the ruling elites are facing immense challenges at home and abroad. In a recent high profile commentary by the Commentary Department of *People's Daily*, usually representing the Party line, a strong warning is issued to the entire Party and the nation that 'reform is risky but the Party is in a greater danger not to reform' (Commentary Department of *People's Daily* 2012). There is now a possibility that bold political reforms may be initiated by the moderates within the Party to accommodate the 'rights defence movement', and to bring about a breakthrough towards constitutional democracy.

Note

1 A GONGO is an NGO established and sponsored by the government. GONGO is an abbreviation of 'Government NGO', a self-contradictory term. GONGOs in China include the official Trade Unions, Women's Federation and other 'mass organizations' established by the party-state.

References

Bei, Feng (2012) 'Hu-Wen zhuzheng shinian lai ruyu zhengzhifan' (Imprisoned Political Criminals during the Past Ten Years under the Hu-Wen Leadership); https://docs. google.com/spreadsheet/pub?key=0AsKDF8_HXe4IdHZLZE1VSzdnZTR4dGk5dTZ MNzFzWFE&output=html accessed 25 July 2013.

Bell, James (2011) 'Upbeat Chinese Public May Not Be Primed for a Jasmine Revolution'; http://pewresearch.org/pubs/1945/chinese-may-not-be-ready-for-revolution accessed 24 July 2013.

Benny, Jonathan (2012) *Defending Rights in Contemporary China*, London: Routledge.

Carnes, Tony (2006) 'China's new legal eagles: evangelical lawyers spur civil rights movement forward', *Christianity Today*, September.

Chan, Cheris Shun-ching (1999) 'The Falun Gong in China: a sociological. perspective', *The China Quarterly*, 179, 665–683.

Chen, Zhiwu (2010) *Meiyou zhongguo moshi zhehuishi* (China Model Never Exists), Taipei: Sino Books.

Cherrington, Ruth (1991) *China's Students: The Struggle for Democracy*, London: Routledge.

Cohen, Jerome A. (2009) 'China's hollow "rule of law"'; http://edition.cnn.com/2009/OPINION/12/31/cohen.china.dissidents/index.html accessed 25 July 2013.

Commentary Department of *People's Daily* (2012) 'Ningyao weici, buyao weixian' (Better to Receive Criticism than Sink into Crisis), *People's Daily*, 23 February; http://opinion.people.com.cn/GB/40604/17192845.html accessed 24 July 2013.

Deng, Xiaoping (1993) 'Yadao yiqie de shi wending' [stability overrides everything], in *Deng Xiaoping Wenxuan* (Selected Works of Deng Xiaoping), vol. 3, Being: Renmin Chubanshe.

Ding, Xue Liang (1994) *The Decline of Communism in China: Legitimacy Crisis, 1977–1989*, Cambridge: Cambridge University Press.

Djilas, Milovan (1957) *The New Class: An Analysis of the Communist System*, New York: Praeger.

Du, Daozheng (2010) *Du Daozheng Riji: Zhao Ziyang Hai Shuodu Shenmo* (Diary of Du Daozheng: What Else Did Zhao Ziyang Say), Hong Kong: Tiandi Tushu Gongsi.

Encarnacion, Omar G. (1996) 'The Politics of Dual Transitions', *Comparative Politics*, 28, 482–483.

Fan, Yafeng (2005) 'Weiquan zhengzhi lun' (The Politics of Rights Defence); http://blog.yam.com/philosopher100/article/5334697 accessed 25 July 2013.

Fan, Yafeng (2010a) 'Hexie wending moshi he feichang zhengzhi de weiji, lun weiquan yundong yu xianzheng zhuanxing de zhongdao moshi' (Harmonious Stability and Crisis of Emergency Politics: on the Middle Way Model in the Rights Defence Movement and Transition to Constitutional Democracy); http://21ccom.net/articles/zgyj/xzmj/article_201001204485.html accessed 24 July 2013.

Fan, Yafeng (2010b) 'cong jiaohui weiquan dao zhongdao weiquan moshi' (From Church Rights Defence to the Middle Way Model in the Rights Defence); http://biweekly.hrichina.org/article/360 accessed 25 July 2013.

Feng, Chongyi (2008) 'Democrats within the Chinese Communist Party since 1989', *Journal of Contemporary China*, 17(57), 673–688.

Feng, Chongyi (2009) 'The rights defence movement, right defence lawyers and prospects for constitutional democracy in China', *Cosmopolitan Civil Societies: An Interdisciplinary Journal*, 1(3); http://epress.lib.uts.edu.au/research/handle/10453/10578 accessed 24 July 2013.

Feng, Chongyi (2010) 'Charter 08, the troubled history and future of Chinese liberalism', *The Asia-Pacific Journal*, 2 (January); http://japanfocus.org/-Feng-Chongyi/3285 accessed 24 July 2013.

Feng, Chongyi (2013) 'China's New Dawn', *Australian Financial Review*, (18 January).

Gilley, Bruce (2004) *China's Democratic Future: How It Will Happen and Where It Will Lead*, New York: Columbia University Press.

Goldman, Merle (1994) *Sowing the Seeds of Democracy in China: Political Reform in the Deng Xiaoping Era*, Cambridge, MA: Harvard University Press.

Goldman, Merle and Leo Ou-Fan Lee (eds) (2002) *An Intellectual History of Modern China*, Cambridge: Cambridge University Press.

Guo, Sujian (1999) 'Democratic transition: a critical overview', *Issues & Studies*, 35(4), 133–148.

Guo, Zhenglin and Thomas P. Bernstein (2004) 'The impact of elections on the village structure of power: the relations between the village committees and the party branches', *Journal of Contemporary China*, 13 (39), 257–327.

Haggard, Stephan and Robert R. Kaufman (1995) *The Political Economy of Democratic Transitions*, Princeton: Princeton University Press.

Hu, Ben (2010) 'Linshigong chengqi de weiwen tixi (The System of Stability Shored Up by Casual Staff), *Southern Weekend*, 20 August.

Hu, Ping (2003) 'Huigu 2003 nian gongmin weiquan yundong' (Reflections on Rights Defence Movement in 2003); www.epochtimes.com/b5/4/2/3/n459600.htm accessed 25 July 2013.

Hu, Ping (2006) 'Weiquan lüshi: women shidai de yingxiong' (Rights Defence Lawyers: Heroes of our Times); www.rfa.org/mandarin/pinglun/huping/hp-20060210.html accessed 25 July 2013.

Huntington, Samuel (1991) *The Third Wave: Democratization in the Late Twentieth Century*, Norman, OK: University of Oklahoma Press.

Ji, Shuoming and Wang Jianmin (2005) 'Zhongguo weiquan lüshi: fazhi xianfeng (Rights defence lawyers in China: the vanguard of the rule of law), *Yazhou Zhoukan (Asia Weekly)*, 19(52), 12–20.

Jiang, Ping (2009) 'Zhongguo de fazhi chuzai yige da daotui shiqi' (The Rule of Law in China is in the Stage of Major Retrogression'; www.gongfa.org/bbs/redirect. php?tid=4037&goto=lastpost accessed 24 July 2013.

Karl, Terry Lynn and Philippe C. Schmitter (1991) 'Modes of Transition in Latin America, Southern and Eastern Europe', *International Social Science Journal*, 43(2), 272–274.

Kristof, Nicholas D. (1993) 'China Sees 'Market-Leninism' as Way to Future', *The New York Times*, 6 September.

Lenin, Vladmir (1970) *The State*, Beijing: Foreign Languages Press.

Lewis, Orion and Jessica Teets (2009) 'A China Model? Understanding the Evolution of a Socialist Market Economy', *Glasshouse Forum*, August, 4–25.

Li, Keqiang (2013) 'Guowuyuan zongli da zhongwai jizhe wen' (Premier's Replies at Press Conference); http://lianghui.people.com.cn/2013npc/GB/357321/359033/ accessed 24 July 2013.

Linz, Juan J. and Alfred Stepan (eds) (1978) *The Breakdown of Democratic Regimes*, Baltimore: Johns Hopkins University Press.

Linz, Juan J. and Alfred Stepan (1996) Problems of Democratic Transition and Consolidation: Southern Europe, South America, and Post-Communist Europe, Baltimore and London: The Johns Hopkins University Press.

Lipset, Seymour Martin (1959) 'Some Social Requisites of Democracy', *American Political Science Review*, March, 69–105.

Liu, Chang (2011) 'Why Liu Ping's Candidacy Failed', *Caixin Online*, 7 June; http://english.caixin.com/2011–06–07/100266830.html accessed 24 July 2013.

Ma, Licheng (2012) *Dangdai zhongguo bazhong shehui sichao* (Eight Schools of Thoughts in Contemporary China), Beijing: Sheke Wenxian Chubanshe.

March, James G. and Johan P. Olsen (1984) 'The new institutionalism: organizational factors in political life', *American Political Science Review*, 78(3), 734–748.

Miller, Alice L (2011) 'The Politburo Standing Committee under Hu Jintao', *China Leadership Monitor*, 35 (21 September); www.hoover.org/publications/china-leadership-monitor/article/93646 accessed 25 July 2013.

Mok, Ka-ho (1998) *Intelletuals and the State in Post-Mao China*, New York: St. Martin's Press.

Moore, Barrington (1966) *Social Origins of Dictatorship and Democracy*, Boston: Beacon Press.

Mosher, Stacy and Patrick Poon (eds) (2009) *A Sword and a Shield: China's Human Rights Lawyers*, Hong Kong: China Human Rights Lawyers Concern Group.

Nathan, Andrew (1985) *Chinese Democracy*, Berkeley: University of California Press.

Nathan, Andrew (2003). 'Authoritarian resilience', *Journal of Democracy*, 14(1), 6–17.

O'Donnell, Guillermo A. (1979) *Modernization and Bureaucratic Authoritarianism: Studies in Southern American Politics*, Berkeley: Institute of International Studies, University of California.

O'Donnell, Guillermo A. and Philippe C. Schmitter (eds) (1986) *Transitions from Authoritarian Rule: Tentative Conclusions about Uncertain Democracies*, Baltimore and London: The Johns Hopkins University Press.

Pei, Minxin (2006) *China's Trapped Transition: The Limits of Developmental Autocracy*, Cambridge, MA: Harvard University Press.

People's Daily (2011) 'China Rejects "Independent Candidate" 9 June; http://english. people.com.cn/90001/90776/90882/7404449.html 25 July 2013.

Powell, Walter W. and Paul J. DiMaggio (eds) (1991) *The New Institutionalism in Organisational Analysis*, Chicago: Chicago University Press.

Qiu, Feng (2003) 'Xin minquan xingdong nian' (The year of new rights movement), *News Weekly*, 161, 2–5.

Qiu, Shi (ed.) (1998) *Jiefang wenxuan: zhongguo dangdai jiefang sixiang de licheng* (Selected Papers: the Process of Thought Liberation in Contemporary China, 1978–1998), Beijing: Jingji Ribao Chubanshe.

Reporters Without Borders (2012) 'Press Freedom Index 2011–2012'; http://en.rsf.org/ press-freedom-index-2011–2012,1043.html accessed 24 July 2013.

Richburg, Keith B. (2012) 'As China's Economy Slows, its Leaders Face an Impasse on which Levers to Pull'; www.washingtonpost.com/world/2012/06/05/gJQA7KaEGV_ story.html accessed 24 July 2013.

Shambaugh, David (2008) *China's Communist Party, Atrophy and Adaptation*, Washington, DC: Woodrow Wilson Center Press.

Social Development Research Group, Tsinghua University Department of Sociology (2010) '*Weiwen* xin silu: yi liyi biaoda zhiduhua shixian shehui de chang zhi jiu an' (New thinking on *weiwen*: long-term social stability via institutionalized expression of interests), *Southern Weekend*, 14 April; www.infzm.com/content/43853 accessed 24 July 2013.

Sun, Liping (2009) 'Zhongguo de zuida weixian bus hi shehui dongdang ershi shehui kuibai' (The Biggest Threat to China is not Social Turmoil but Social Decay); www. chinadigitaltimes.net/2009/03 accessed 24 July 2013.

Sun, Liping (2011) 'Shehui shixu zui hexin de shi quanli shikong' (Runaway Power is the Core of Social Disorder); http://big5.ycwb.com/sp/2011-09/06/content_3555777.htm accessed 25 July 2013.

Teng, Biao (2006) 'Zhongguo weiquan yundong xiang hechu qu?' (Whither the Rights Defence Movement in China); http://hzaze.wordpress.com/2011/05/17/zgwqydwhcq/ 25 July 2013.

The PRC Ministry of Finance (2010) '2009 nian quanguo caizheng zhichu juesuan biao' (Table of the Final National Expenditure Accounts in 2009); http://yss.mof.gov.cn/200 9nianquanguojuesuan/201007/t20100709_327128.html accessed 24 July 2013.

The State Council Information Office of the PRC (2005) 'Building of Political Democracy in China'; www.china.org.cn/english/2005/Oct/145718.htm accessed 25 July 2013.

The State Council of the PRC (1989) 'Shehui tuanti Dengji Guanli Tiaoli' (Regulations on Registration and Management of Social Organisations); www.xuebao.tyut.edu.cn/webpage/zcyfg5.htm accessed 24 July 2013.

Wang, Yi (2003) '2003: "Xin minquan yundong" de faren he caolian' (2003: The origins and practices of the 'new civil rights movement'), *Guangcha* (Observation), 19 December.

Wen, Jiabao (2012) 'Wen Says China Needs Political Reform, Warns of Another Cultural Revolution if Without'; http://news.xinhuanet.com/english/china/2012-03/14/c_1314 66552.htm accessed 25 July 2013.

Wong, Yiu-Chung (2005) *From Deng Xiaoping to Jiang Zemin: Two Decades of Political Reform in the People's Republic of China*, Lanham, Maryland: University Press of America.

Wright, Teresa (2004) 'Intellectuals and the politics of protest: the case of the China Democracy Party', in Edward Gu and Merle Goldman (eds) *Chinese Intellectuals Between State and Market*, London & New York: RoutledgeCurzon, pp. 158–180.

Wu, Jinglian (2005) *Zhongguo zengzhang moshi jueze* (The Choice of the Mode of Economic Growth in China), Shanghai: Yuandong Chubanshe.

Wu, Jinglian (2011) 'Dangqian zhongguo zui yanzhong weixian shi quangui ziben zhuyi' (Power Elite Capitalism is the Most Serious Danger for China); http://finance.sina.com.cn/review/hgds/20111222/083411039346.shtml accessed 24 July 2013.

Wu, Jinglian (2012) 'Zhongguo zhanzai xin de shizhi lukou (China Standing at a New Historical Crossroads)'; http://finance.jrj.com.cn/opinion/2012/02/17090312272409.shtml accessed 24 July 2013.

Xi, Jinping (2012) 'Zai shoudu gejie jinian xianxing xianfa gongbu shixing sanshi zhou-nian dahui shang de jianghua' (A Speech at the Congress in Beijing Marking the 30th Anniversary of the Implementation of Current Constitution); http://news.xinhuanet.com/politics/2012-12/04/c_113907206.htm accessed 25 July 2013.

Xian, Jianglin (2004) 'Quanli yuannian yu zhidu weiquan' (The First Year of Rights and Institutional Rights Defence); http://article.chinalawinfo.com/Article_Detail.asp?ArticleId=24672 accessed 26 July 2013.

Xiaocankao (1999) 'Chuan gaozilian you chengli, gongchandang geng jinzhang (The CCP Nervous About the News that the Autonomous Union of University Students has been Established Again)', *Xiaocankao Daily News*, 418 (9 May 1999); www.bignews.org/990509.txt accessed 24 July 2013.

Xu, Kai, Chen Xiaoshu, and Li Wei-ao (2011) 'Gonggong anquan zhangdan' (The accounts of public security), *Caijing*, 11; http://magazine.caijing.com.cn/2011–05–08/110712639.html accessed 24 July 2013.

Ye, Xiangzhen (2009) 'Ye Jianying zhongyang gongzuo huiyi jianghua qicao ji' (Notes on Drafting Ye Jianying's Speech at the Central Work Conference); www.360doc.com/content/09/0410/01/90591_3078319.shtml accessed 25 July 2013.

Yu, Jianrong (2007) *Dangdai nongmin de weiquan douzheng: Hunan Hengyang kaocha* (Rights Defence Struggles of Contemporary Peasants: an Investigation into Hunan's Hengyang), Beijing: Zhongguo wenhua chubanshe.

Zhang, Musheng (2011) 'Zai da biange shidai xunzhao gongshi' (Seeking Consensus in the Age of Grand Change); www.21ccom.net/articles/zgyj/gqmq/2011/0514/35451_4.html accessed 24 July 2013.

Zhao, Suisheng (ed.) (2000) *China and Democracy: Reconsidering the Prospects for a Democratic China*, New York & London: Routledge.

Zou, Dongtao and Ouyang Rihui (eds) (2009) *Zhongguo daolu yu zhongguo model, 1949–2009* (China Path and China Model, 1949–2009), Beijing: Shehui Kexue Wenxian Chubanshe.

Zou, Keyuan (2006) *China's Legal Reform Towards the Rule of Law*, Boston: Martinus Nijhoff Publishers.

Conclusion

Edmund S.K. Fung and Steven Drakeley

This book began with two basic propositions: first, democracies in Eastern Asia, as elsewhere, are under stress facing an array of issues and challenges, and second, democratization is a continuing process without a definite end. There is no single political theory that can fully explain the continuing wave of democratization in the Eastern Asia region, let alone all of its rips and eddies. The general aim of this book, through an examination of the major issues and challenges facing the governments of the region, is to show how complex the actual experience of Eastern Asian democracy and the politics surrounding it has been and no doubt will continue to be. Each of the contributors has drawn on political theories that best serve their purposes as they attempted to answer a number of similar empirical questions and shed light on the challenges that have done much to shape democracy and democratization in the selected countries. These countries have been placed in different categories and in different parts of the book either because they have reached a more or less similar stage of democratization or because they are confronting similar problems. Yet even in each category there are circumstances peculiar to each of the countries with their own political and cultural traditions. Although democracy may be the best system of government, there are many democratic forms, different paths to democracy and different strategies of democratic consolidation and improvement. The process by which transition to democracy is accomplished is a complicated one, no less so than where democracy is consolidated, or fails to be consolidated, or relapses, or resurrects. Perhaps we should say processes because while we can point to some similarities (not commonalities) there are clearly a great many variables and much nuance. As the contributors have shown collectively, country-specific circumstances are paramount.

Nonetheless it is possible to identify a number of themes that emerge from the most recent Eastern Asian experience described in this book. The first is the need for liberal democracies, stable as they may be like Japan, South Korea and Taiwan, to continue a process of nurturing and more strongly institutionalizing their democracies. There is always a proportion of citizens who feel discontent, disenfranchised or feel that 'it is simply not good enough'. There is no room for complacency even in an established democracy which, like new democracies, must constantly seek to adjust to social change, and become more responsive to popular demands and diverse interests in society. Nor are liberal democracies immune to corruption, crony capitalism and social injustice. As a matter of fact, official corruption in one form or another exists in Japan, South Korea and Taiwan to varying degrees, just as it is rife in the flawed and low-level democracies of the region. In any case, citizen pressures for more open and accountable governance are strong.

Another theme is the importance of political leadership and strong institutions, as Robert Scalapino (1998) has long maintained. The end of the state, wrote Harold Laski, is 'the satisfaction, at the highest possible level, of its subjects' demands' (Laski 1935: 160). A democratic state is best placed to satisfy popular demands. But it takes much more than a democratic form of government to provide good governance and to meet the end of the state. It requires stable, strong leadership with well-conceived policies designed to tackle real problems. This is particularly important for electoral democracies that are not strongly institutionalized, are flawed or malfunctioning; they have a long way to go towards deepening and consolidation. Even in Japan and Korea, strong leadership is no less important. The recent return of LDP leader Shinzo Abe, prime minister from 2006 to 2007, to the top job as the seventh prime minister since Junichiro Koizumi stepped down in 2006 raises the question of whether he can re-energize the economy and restore longer-term stability to Japanese politics with a rerun of his right-wing politics and nationalistic credentials. It remains to be seen what South Korea's newly elected first female president, Park Guen-hye of the conservative Grand National Party and daughter of the former military strongman, President Park Chung-hee (1963–1979), can do about tackling the issues described by Chong-Min Park in Chapter 2. Other issues confronting her government include generational inequality, boosting employment, increasing female participation in the workforce and ending crony capitalism.

Strong leadership should not be equated with autocratic policy- and decision-making. The required form of strong leadership is one that provides effective and efficient government. One where the leaders have visions, an ability to lead and shape public opinion rather than be led by the media, and a political will to meet the multiple challenges that confront them and to make necessary changes that are responsive to popular demands and in the general interest of the population. Electoral democracies are not enough to wrestle with problems such as official corruption, entrenched elite power and socio-economic inequalities, as the cases of the Philippines, Indonesia and Thailand demonstrate. Of course, the dearth of such leadership is not confined to Eastern Asia.

A third theme is the relationship between economic development (prosperity generated by market capitalism) and transition to democracy resulting from the rise of a well-educated middle class with liberal democratic aspirations. It is generally true that over the long term, economic progress will undermine authoritarian rule and promote democratization. However, it is clear that economic growth per se does not necessarily produce democratization. The case of Hong Kong shows that the territory's wealth does little to strengthen the people's resolve to confront the government in Beijing in pursuit of democracy, despite popular dissatisfaction with the past and current HKSAR Chief Executives. Here, as elsewhere, the affluent middle class is not an undifferentiated class; many of its members, politically conservative and busy making money, actually support the government of the day that protects their interests and elite positions in society.

Paradoxically, it is the slowdown in the economy after a long period of spectacular growth, not continued growth itself, which could bring about democratic change. To date China's new wealth has not produced a democratic breakthrough. While it remains to be seen whether China will democratize and in what fashion under the new Xi Jinping-Li Keqiang leadership, Beijing's efforts to keep the economic engine going at high speed after a year of modest growth in 2012 are likely to be accompanied by some political reforms that could help to curb official corruption and to strengthen the rule of law.

Indonesia is another case in point. It was the sudden shock of the Asian economic crisis in the second half of 1997 after decades of double digit growth which provided the spark for Indonesia's unexpected democratic transformation the following year. The growth and economic development of the preceding decades prepared the path and arguably have made democracy's survival in Indonesia more tenable, but it took a crisis to propel the taking of that path and its attendant risks. Those who confronted the regime at this critical juncture seeking democratization, including many from the middle class, took the associated risks to their lives and liberty. But the existing elite, including many intimately tied to the regime, also took a risk when they decided to embrace and seek to manage change rather than to continue resisting it.

A fourth theme is the way in which authoritarian regimes have responded to growing societal pressures for democratization. Some have opted for a more proactive response. South Korea and Taiwan, having experienced profound levels of economic and social development under the discipline of authoritarian regimes made successful transitions to democracy. These ambitious, steadily implemented transitions were consciously embarked upon by ruling parties that were all but synonymous with the states they controlled. In the process these ruling parties deliberately metamorphosed into democratic parties able to compete on a level democratic playing field. Singapore and Malaysia could follow Taiwan and South Korea in this regard. The economic progress prerequisite is already in place. Moreover, no new constitutional arrangements would be necessary, as were the cases in South Korea and Taiwan. All that would be required would be for PAP and UMNO to cease distorting the existing democratic processes. But will they make such a decision before it is forced upon them or even before it is too late to manage the process of change? We are back to the role of leadership again as well as to the unpredictable pressures from below.

The tensions between elite-led or elite-captured democracy and societal pressures from below are significant. In countries like Thailand, Indonesia, the Philippines, Malaysia and even Singapore, oligarchic distortions of basic democratic processes such as elections and the operations of parliaments and the like obstruct democratic consolidation and produce a low quality democracy. In such cases, there is also a heightened risk of mass disenchantment with democracy or perhaps some prospect of a renewed push for democratic change. Either of these reactions could have unpredictable consequences, including a high likelihood of serious levels of civil strife and attendant economic disruption as part of the process of change. Conceivably, quite different regimes could come to power as a result, and not necessarily more democratic ones. Military intervention would be a distinct possibility in each of these countries for example, and a Hugo Chavez-style of populist authoritarianism or an Islamist regime is not totally inconceivable for the Philippines and Indonesia, respectively.

This brings us to a fifth theme: the dynamics and critical role of internal demands for democratic change. To be sure, external influences and support (overt or covert, moral or material) are important, and the demonstration effects of one society on another could also be significant. We have witnessed the influence and role of the USA in the spread of democratic ideas around the world over the decades and sometimes also in effecting regime changes. We are also aware of the ramifications of recent developments in the Middle East and North Africa for other societies seeking democratic change. However, foreign influences and support are never enough to bring about democratic change where the ruling elites choose not to implement it and the people are unable to actively and persistently press for it. Accordingly, this book has focused on domestic issues because the contributors all see the societal pressures for change to which governments need to respond in a way that is more local than global.

In countries where changes are slow in coming, domestic politics, local issues and cultural peculiarities are important variables. In Myanmar, while a great deal of foreign goodwill and support for the Thein Sein government augurs well for the current changes, the sustenance of those changes is contingent on the strategic choice of the political leadership[1] in response to growing popular demands and opposition forces rather than to pressures from foreign governments. In China, the absence of a political 'Chinese Spring', much wished for by Western governments, demonstrates with rare clarity that endogenous factors are crucial. No amount of foreign aid and abetting could bring about a regime change in Beijing as long as the majority of Chinese still accept CCP rule. Any democratization would be the result of a strategic choice of the political leadership responding to societal pressures and to problems within the Party itself. Democracy cannot be imposed from without. Fundamentally it has to come from within, embraced by the elites (unless they are removed or replaced in the process) as well as ordinary citizens, as the American experience in Afghanistan and Iraq demonstrates. Of course, because exporting US-style democracy is driven largely by self-interest rather than by altruism, it is not surprising that such efforts often lead to nationalistic responses in countries like China.

Now what are the prospects for democracy in the region? Seeing a new wave of global democratization, Diamond (2012: 5) writes with optimism: 'If there is going to be a big new lift to global democratic prospects in this decade, the region from which it will emanate is most likely to be East Asia [his term for

Eastern Asia].' As global power shifts from the West to the East in the Asian Century, the aspirations of the vast majority of Asians for more democratic and accountable government run deep. Even in China, Diamond notes, the CCP regime faces a looming crisis of political legitimacy, which provides a new opportunity for a transition to democracy.

We are cautiously optimistic as democracies in the region remain under stress. One reason for optimism is that the peoples of the region where democracy exists have shown a high level of public support for the democratic *system* as opposed to the democratic *process*; they evince no desire to see a return to authoritarian rule of any form. Another is that developments in information technology and the Internet promote democracy, because they enhance citizen participation in a new form of 'public sphere', forcing governments to improve their responsiveness and accountability. The Internet has revolutionized the way people respond to political and social issues, giving rise to a concept of 'cyber democracy' or 'e-democracy' (Bryan, Tambini and Tsagarousianou 1998). Even in China, censorship, intimidation and political controls have failed to stop netizens from expressing views critical of the authorities. *Weibo* (the Chinese equivalent of Twitter) writers exposing official corruption, abuse of power and other wrongdoings have become a force to contend with.

There are also grounds for caution because of the persistence of some unresolved problems in many of the societies examined in this book. Despite a vibrant civil society and a dynamic opposition party, Taiwan's liberal and robust democracy is characterized by political and social polarizations and complicated by cross-Straits relations. Currently, with President Ma Ying-jeou's approval rating at a dismal 17.9 per cent at the time of writing (News ifeng [Taiwan] 2013), the need for strong leadership and for a less polarized society cannot be greater. Apparently Taiwan's democracy, which often gets a better rating in US-style democracy assessments, will take more time to mature and become more institutionalized.

In Hong Kong, the roadmap to democracy remains unclear. The Chief Executive, C.Y. Leung, seen by critics as being too close to Beijing, has been under siege since he took office in July 2012. In addition to a credibility crisis resulting from alleged illegal extensions to his residence, Leung, trying to be populist, has been struggling to tackle the housing problem in the territory where land is in short supply and vested interests are too many. For Leung as well as for the very many 'have-nots', resolving pressing socio-economic issues is a far more important thing than a fast track to democracy. In the meantime, the people of Hong Kong are free to demonstrate against the Chief Executive and his administration over policies they disapprove of.

The Philippines remains a low-level democracy with the current government appearing unable to resolve the chronic problems described by Quimpo in Chapter 6. Indonesia's democracy, too, remains stuck at a low-quality level, and its resilience will be tested during the 2014 presidential and parliamentary elections. At the same time, Singapore and Malaysia are unlikely to become liberal democracies like Japan in the near future. There could even be backsliding, setbacks or democratic recessions in the years ahead. We are also circumspect about the political reforms being implemented in Myanmar. To be sure, there is significant goodwill from the international community, but Myanmar's road towards a consolidated democracy is likely to be a long one. Much will depend on the outcome of the 2015 elections, the quality and strengths of the opposition parties, the achievement of far-reaching socio-economic reforms, the resolution of ethnic and religious conflicts as well as the role of the powerful military. And in Cambodia, the slide from the rule of law to rule *by* law, coupled with the entrenchment of the CPP in power and in the state apparatus, does not augur well for Cambodia's embattled democracy, offering further proof for the hazards of largely externally driven democratization projects.

Finally on the Chinese mainland, where the movement for constitutional democracy is continuing, a democratic breakthrough is still far from view. The CCP's fragility and the extent of popular discontent with the regime may have been exaggerated by critics like Minxin Pei (2012), but one thing seems certain – any democratic transition will have to await a vibrant, autonomous civil society and, more importantly, the emergence of a new generation of more liberal-minded and more accountable leaders, not only at the top of the echelon but also at local government levels. Chinese democracy, should it be realized one day, is likely to be elite-led and with minimalist electoral politics, while policies designed to improve the living standard of the population continue to be implemented to bring about a fairer distribution of the country's growing wealth. We can expect to see an amalgam of intra-party democracy, democratic socialism, a more liberal press and a semblance of political opposition rather than a liberal democracy. For now, not only has 'Western-style politics' been categorically rejected by the new leadership at the 12th National People's Congress (March 2013), but the populace on the whole is enjoying the fruits of economic growth and the delights of a consumer society, despite political controls, social injustice and environmental degradation.

All things considered, the weight of evidence leans towards the positive side. It is fair to conclude that the region's experience with democracy over the last decade or two must put to rest any further claims for Asian exceptionalism with respect to democracy. The region's diverse peoples have repeatedly demonstrated powerful aspirations for democracy and the capacity, as much as anywhere, to implement what is a difficult and delicate political system. In this lies our strongest grounds for cautious optimism that democracy in Eastern Asia will make additional progress and consolidate further.

Note

1 Edward Friedman (1995) has long maintained that democratic breakthrough is contingent on the choice of the political leadership.

References

Bryan, Cathy, Tambini, Damian and Tsagarousianou, Roza (eds) (1998) *Cyberdemocracy, Technology, Cities and Civic Networks*, London: Routledge.

Diamond, Larry (2012) 'The coming wave', *Journal of Democracy*, 23(1), 5–13.

Friedman, Edward (1995) *National Identity and Democratic Prospects in Socialist China*, Armonk, NY: M.E. Sharpe.

Laski, Joseph Harold (1935) *The State in Theory and Practice*, New York: The Viking Press.

News ifeng (Taiwan), 29 July 2013; http://news.ifeng.com/taiwan/1/detail_2013_07/29/28017760_0.shtml accessed 31 July 2013.

Pei Minxin (2012) 'Is CCP rule fragile or resilient?' *Journal of Democracy*, 23(1), 27–41.

Scalapino, Robert A. (1998) 'A Tale of Three Systems', in Larry Diamond and Marc F. Platter (eds) *Democracy in East Asia*, Baltimore: The Johns Hopkins University, pp. 3–16.

Index

Page numbers in **bold** denote figures.

For Product Safety Concerns and Information please contact our EU
representative GPSR@taylorandfrancis.com
Taylor & Francis Verlag GmbH, Kaufingerstraße 24, 80331 München, Germany

www.ingramcontent.com/pod-product-compliance
Lightning Source LLC
Chambersburg PA
CBHW060153280326
41932CB00012B/1743